# Theories of Infant Development

# Theories of Infant Development

Edited by

Gavin Bremner and Alan Slater

Blackwell
Publishing

350 Main Street, Malden, MA 02148-5020, USA
108 Cowley Road, Oxford OX4 1JF, UK
550 Swanston Street, Carlton, Victoria 3053, Australia





First published 2004 by Blackwell Publishing Ltd

*Library of Congress Cataloging-in-Publication Data*

Theories of infant development / edited by Gavin Bremner and Alan Slater.
p. cm.
Includes bibliographical references and index.
ISBN 0–631–23337–7 (hc : alk. paper) — ISBN 0–631–23338–5 (pbk. : alk. paper)
1. Infants—Development. 2. Child development. I. Bremner, J. Gavin, 1949– II. Slater, Alan.

RJ134.T48 2003
305.232—dc21 2003045328

A catalogue record for this title is available from the British Library.

Set in 10/12 pt Palatino
by Graphicraft Limited, Hong Kong
Printed and bound in the United Kingdom
by TJ International, Padstow, Cornwall.

For further information on
Blackwell Publishing, visit our website:
http://www.blackwellpublishing.com

In memory of George Esmond Butterworth,
November 8, 1946–February 12, 2000

# Contents

# Contributors

**David I. Anderson**, San Francisco State University and University of California, Berkeley, USA.
**Lorraine E. Bahrick**, Florida International University, USA.
**Marian J. Bakermans-Kranenburg**, Leiden University, The Netherlands.
**Marianne A. Barbu-Roth**, Laboratoire de PsychoBiologie du Développement, CNRS, EPHE, Paris, France.
**Gavin Bremner**, Lancaster University, UK.
**Peter E. Bryant**, University of Oxford, UK.
**George Butterworth**, deceased.
**Joseph J. Campos**, University of California, Berkeley, USA.
**Alan Costall**, University of Portsmouth, UK.
**Alan Fogel**, University of Utah, USA.
**Eugene C. Goldfield**, Children's Hospital, Carnegie 2, 300 Longwood Avenue, Boston, USA.
**Mark H. Johnson**, Birkbeck College, University of London, UK.
**Scott P. Johnson**, Cornell University, USA.
**Annette Karmiloff-Smith**, Neurocognitive Development Unit, Institute of Child Health, London, UK.
**Andrew N. Meltzoff**, University of Washington, USA.
**David Messer**, South Bank University, London, UK.
**Philippe Rochat**, Emory University, USA.
**Alan Slater**, University of Exeter, UK.
**Marinus H. van IJzendoorn**, Leiden University, The Netherlands.
**Peter H. Wolff**, Children's Hospital, Carnegie 2, 300 Longwood Avenue, Boston, USA.

# Preface

Following George Butterworth's tragic and untimely death in February 2000, there was a widespread feeling that something should be done to commemorate his life and contribution to developmental psychology. This is one attempt to do so. Given George's strong interest in the development of theory, our first thought was of a book on theories of infant development. We are most grateful to Blackwell Publishing for supporting us in this endeavor, and we hope that the result is a fitting tribute to George Butterworth's work.

The volume and diversity of research on human infancy has grown enormously over the past 40 years. Back in the 1960s a small group known as Correspondents on Research in Infancy began meeting, and from this grew the International Society for Infant Studies, whose biennial conference attracts 1,000 or more participants from all over the world making over 750 research presentations. As a consequence, what we know about the infant's perceptual, cognitive, social, and emotional development has advanced significantly. Additionally, new theoretical accounts have emerged and old accounts have been modified and reevaluated.

Recently in particular, and in a number of areas, vigorous debate has arisen concerning the appropriate theoretical frameworks through which to explain infant development, and it appeared to us that this was a particularly good time to put together a book that focused specifically on theory. Thus we asked prominent individuals in a variety of areas across the breadth of the discipline to write chapters that concentrated on specific theoretical accounts or particular theoretical controversies within their area of expertise. Given the constraints on length, we had to be relatively selective in our coverage, and so we aimed to identify authors who would address theoretical issues that are currently at the heart of debate.

The book is in three parts. Part I covers the development of perception and action. The first chapter in this section is by Goldfield and Wolff, who explore the contribution of dynamical systems theory to our understanding of infant development. Dynamical systems theory is now being applied to a wide range of developmental issues in infancy, and here we see it applied to the development of infant action, the topic that it has probably been most successful in clarifying. In the second chapter, Anderson, Campos, and Barbu-Roth tackle the relationship between perception and action from a rather different perspective. The term "visual proprioception" stems from Gibson's theory of direct perception, and in this chapter the authors look at the development of perception–action coupling, considering both how visual information is used to control posture and locomotion and how the development of locomotion leads to changes in visual proprioception. Following this chapter, there are two chapters that focus specifically on the ecological theory of J. J. Gibson. Costall provides a scholarly analysis of this theoretical approach, while Bahrick explores the development of multimodal perception which has its theoretical underpinnings firmly in Gibsonian theory. In the final chapter in Part I, Johnson and Karmiloff-Smith provide a neuroscience perspective, indicating how this approach can help to elucidate issues regarding both typical and atypical development in infancy.

The first two chapters of Part II offer contrasting perspectives on the Piagetian account of cognitive development and the more recent theories, such as neo-nativism, that have followed in its wake. Meltzoff makes the case for a developmental cognitive science that suggests how initial innate representations are modified by learning processes during development. This differs from strong nativist accounts in attributing less to innate factors, and also differs from Piagetian and dynamical systems accounts by arguing that representations can be developed through observation as well as action. Johnson presents a rather different account that stresses the importance of early perceptual and memory skills as underpinnings for cognitive development. Thus, emergence of the object concept depends on the development of earlier perceptual skills as well as on experience and learning about objects at a cognitive level. The final chapter in this section shifts the focus to infant memory. In addition to the distinction between implicit and explicit memory, Fogel identifies the need to recognize a third form of memory in infancy, participatory memory, which involves reliving past experiences in the present. Participatory memories are fundamentally emotionally based and are often cued by a similar context in the present as accompanied the original experience. The focus on emotion makes this a good link chapter to the final part of the book.

Part III concerns social and communicative development. In the first chapter of this section Van IJzendoorn and Bakermans-Kranenburg consider attachment theory. Here they review the causal factors in attachment formation, focusing specifically on maternal sensitivity and infant temperament and concluding that the former is more important as a cause in attachment formation than the latter. The focus on emotion continues in Rochat's chapter on the emergence of co-awareness. Contrary to other accounts of the development of self-awareness, he proposes that from the beginning infants develop a primarily subjective view of the social world. In contrast to the objective physical world, this is an unpredictable world of emotion and passion, and Rochat argues that it is against this that infants come eventually to recognize themselves. The final two chapters focus on the development of communication. Messer considers two topics: joint attention and language acquisition. His argument is that to understand development in these domains, we must look beyond the behaviors themselves to ask questions about the forms of knowledge necessary to support these communicative abilities. With this in mind, he develops an account that distinguishes between *procedures* (the communicative activities themselves) and *assumptions* (the infant's knowledge or perspective on the world), arguing that the form of the latter influences the form of the former. Appropriately, the final work in this section comes from George Butterworth. In a reprinted chapter, he provides a comparative analysis of joint visual attention, looking in particular at how gaze direction and pointing are both used and interpreted by humans and other species. His conclusion is that although nonhuman primates use gestures similar to pointing, unlike human infants they do not appear to interpret these gestures as referential. In humans, it appears that pointing relates in unique ways to both tool use and the acquisition of language. This chapter is followed by a short piece by Peter Bryant in appreciation of George Butterworth's contribution to developmental psychology.

When we planned this book, we felt it inappropriate to profit from its sales. We were delighted to find that the authors of the chapters readily shared our view. Given George's commitment to the European Society for Developmental Psychology and the vigor with which he pursued means of facilitating postgraduate attendance at meetings of the society, it seems appropriate that all editorial and authors' royalties will be paid into a fund, administered by the European Society, to provide support for postgraduate attendance at its meetings.

Gavin Bremner
Alan Slater

# Part I
# Development of Perception and Action

Contents

# 1

# A Dynamical Systems Perspective on Infant Action and its Development

*Eugene C. Goldfield and Peter H. Wolff*

## Introduction

The study of motor development has again become one of the most active areas of infancy research, in part because a dynamical systems perspective has introduced new ways to address longstanding questions about the organization of motor skills and how these skills develop (see, e.g., the introduction by Lockman & Thelen, 1993, and other papers in a special issue of *Child Development* devoted to "Developmental Biodynamics"). The task for any general theory of motor development in infancy is to disentangle the complex causal and functional relationships between the motor repertoire of the newborn and the differentiated motor skills of the 2-year-old infant. Such a theory must address important questions like the following: Do primitive motor patterns (reflexes) prepare for the acquisitions of complex and apparently voluntary motor skills? If yes, how do they? If not, what happens to them after they "disappear"? How do qualitatively new forms and functions of coordinated motor action emerge from antecedent motor patterns with which they share neither form nor function? In other words, what do we mean when we speak about emergence, spontaneous pattern formation, and self-organization?

This chapter presents a dynamical systems perspective on motor development. We focus on the question, what are the sources of order by which new complex forms and functions emerge? This question has been of great interest for developmental scientists in several fields (see, e.g., Gilbert, 2000). The Darwinian view of the emergence of new forms is that selective processes act on a population of variant forms that express themselves in different ways given particular environmental opportunities (Mayr, 1982). Some developmental biologists (Kauffman, 1993, 1995) and neuroscientists (Gottlieb, 1992) have recently challenged the view that Darwinian selection is the sole source of emergent order in learning, ontogeny, and evolution. Kauffman, for example, proposes that self-organization arises in systems with very large numbers of interconnected elements (e.g., the genome, immune system, nervous system). Such systems can achieve organizational states ranging from ordered (highly resistant to change) to chaotic (i.e., subject to an avalanche of changes, or "damage"). Selection acts on this range of organizational possibilities to produce "complexity," a state that is ordered, yet poised near the edge of chaos. We propose that motor development is a process by which the infant's earliest behaviors (e.g., sucking, kicking, babbling) are self-organizing, and that the selective processes of active exploratory behavior transform these self-organizing systems so that they become useful for performing the "complex" adaptive behaviors that we call eating, walking, and speaking.

Self-organization and selection are heuristically powerful processes because they can account for both the small and the dramatic changes observed in motor behavior during infancy. Periods of relative stability in acquisition of a skill such as crawling allow the infant to introduce variations in performance (e.g., trying out a new way to shift weight onto the arms) without dramatic consequences, such as falling. By contrast, during periods of rapid organismic changes that are not under the infant's direct control, such as weight gain, similar modifications in behavior may result in a sudden loss of balance. Despite their best efforts, infants may suddenly find that former ways of successful locomotion are no longer effective. These changing organismic constraints on self-organizing processes open new opportunities for exploring how the body can be used to achieve particular goals.

## The Dynamical Systems Perspective

The dynamical systems perspective on motor development stands apart from other developmental approaches in at least three ways:

1 It specifies how interactions among the parts of a system induce organizational changes in the whole (i.e., self-organization), without direction by an external agent (see, e.g., Wolff, 1987, 1991). For example, we show that there are lawful ways by which interacting behavioral rhythms (e.g., sucking, breathing, kicking, arm waving, babbling) influence each other to establish coordinated wholes, or synergies.
2 It specifies how selective processes work in conjunction with self-organization to induce new patterns of motor coordination. We view the selective process as the outcome of exploratory activity by the infant's interrelated perceptual systems (Gibson & Pick, 2000). So, for example, as infants kick, there is visual, proprioceptive-kinesthetic, and haptic information from contact between the foot and ground surface during vertical displacement of the body against the force of gravity. The exploratory process may be guided by caregivers, and the spatiotemporal regularities in feeding routines, games, speech intonation, and other "fields of promoted action" may play a significant role in motor development (see, e.g., Reed & Bril, 1996).
3 A dynamical systems perspective treats the nervous system as part of an embodied system (Thelen, 2000), in that: (a) the brain is considered a medium for imposing general laws that yield patterns of coordination, but the brain is not the sole source of coordination and control (Kay & Warren, 2001), and (b) the brain is "informationally coupled" to a structured environment (Gibson, 1966, 1979; Warren, 1998). So, rather than simply correlating changes in limb configurations with myelination patterns in order to explain developmental progress in locomotion, as in classic treatments by McGraw (1945) and others, we address how infants may use visual information to coordinate posture and gait as they negotiate inclines and avoid barriers (e.g., Adolph, Vereijken, & Denny, 1998; Kay & Warren, 1998, 2001). Similarly, when considering the development of reaching, we discuss how muscle activation (measured by EMG) capitalizes on the forces acting on the body (Spencer & Thelen, 2000), rather than identifying EMG correlates of behavioral change (Forssberg, Stokes, & Hirschfeld, 1992).

These three distinctive characteristics of a dynamical systems perspective originate from an attempt to show how biological systems exploit physical laws to achieve complex organizational patterns. The physical laws include not only the fundamental laws of Newtonian mechanics that guide the field of biomechanics (see, e.g., Winter, 1990), but also the laws governing far-from-equilibrium systems (see, e.g., Prigogine, 1980; Winfree, 1980). The methodologies and mathematical tools adopted from these disciplines, such as topological analysis (Beek & Beek, 1988), mathematical modeling (e.g., Haken, Kelso, & Bunz, 1985; Kelso, Ding, & Schöner, 1992), and computer simulation (e.g., Saltzman & Munhall, 1989), are only now becoming part of the methodological tools of developmental scientists, so in the sections below, we take the opportunity to briefly describe how these methods can be used to address questions about infant motor development.

## *The goal of the chapter*

The major goal of this chapter is to outline a dynamical systems perspective to the study of motor development by examining the core question of the sources of order by which new complex forms and functions emerge. Because this is a difficult and many-faceted question, we unpack it to take the form of four related ones, used to organize the chapter:

1 What are the origins of order and flexibility in far-from-equilibrium systems that are characterized by fluid part–whole relationships among their component parts?
2 How do changes in the interactions between the parts of a complex system induce organizational change in the whole?
3 What is the relation between early forms of a behavior and later ones, e.g., between kicking and walking, or between pacifier sucking and breast- or bottle-feeding?
4 How do infants discover when to produce muscular activity in order to maintain an ongoing oscillatory behavior?

Our general strategy for each of the questions is to highlight a developmental phenomenon, introduce theory and methodology from a dynamical systems perspective appropriate to that phenomenon, and illustrate how some recent developmental research from the dynamical systems perspective has addressed it.

# Four Questions Concerning Infant Motor Development

## QUESTION 1
## *The origins of order and flexibility in complex systems*

### SELF-ORGANIZING SYSTEMS

A fundamental question about motor development concerns the ordering, or assembly, of component systems, during both ontogeny and performance, that makes possible the planning and control of stable, yet flexible, action (Saltzman & Kelso, 1987). The challenge in addressing this question was concisely articulated in a paper by George Butterworth (1993) on the causes of development:

> The forms of the organism and its constituent subsystems (formal cause) distinguish the same organism at different points in development. Developmental theories, however, must not only explain the succession of static forms that can be observed, but also how forms change in a continuous progression. (*p. 173*)

We begin to address this challenge here by considering two sources of order (and flexibility) in complex nonequilibrium systems: self-organization and selection. The former refers to the integrated behavior of systems coordinating the actions of many elements. When systems are both complex and open to energy flux with the environment (i.e., far from equilibrium), this integration is due to the mutual interactions of the elements themselves rather than to any outside agent. Self-organizing systems are capable of forming patterns that have remarkable regularity, such as stripes in animal fur, and other aspects of morphology that have fascinated naturalists for centuries (see, e.g., Winfree, 1987). The question of interest for the study of infant motor behavior is whether self-organization, the emergence of patterns that are induced by the components themselves rather than by some outside agency, provides a parsimonious explanation of observed organizational changes.

### NEWBORN SLEEP AND WAKEFULNESS

Observations of newborn sleep and wakefulness illustrate that even the earliest postnatal motor behaviors are stable self-recalibrating ensembles, what Wolff (1987) has called behavioral states. During "regular" (non-REM) sleep, the breathing rhythm is stable, the eyelids are firmly closed, and there is an absence of general body movements and vocalizations. By contrast, during "irregular" or REM sleep, breathing is irregular, and there are intermittent limb, trunk, head, and mouth movements. The awake infant may be in a state of quiet alertness: the eyes are open and make intermittent conjugate movements, the limbs and trunk are mostly at rest, and breathing is more stable than during irregular sleep.

Behavioral states are not merely different states of arousal. The temporary formation of each of these ensembles provides a distinctive organismic context for responding to environmental stimulation, and this has been experimentally verified in two ways. First, attempts to elicit "reflexive" behaviors yield different outcomes in each of the states. For example, during regular sleep and wakefulness, the Moro[1] and tendon reflexes are readily elicited, but during irregular sleep they are markedly diminished (Lenard, von Bernuth, & Prechtl, 1968). Second, the behaviors that define a state have different degrees of resistance against external perturbation, i.e., context dependence of behavior. Wolff (1966) found, for example, that a continuous monotonous sound converted irregular to regular breathing during irregular sleep, but the same "white noise" had little effect in modifying breathing during regular sleep.

We argue here that (1) the basis for the emergence of these ordered spatial and temporal patterns of sleep and wakefulness is self-organization, the tendency of the elements to "settle" into a small number of preferred configurations or states, called *attractors*, and (2) that the ensemble affects all of its parts just as each part contributes to the ensemble. To elaborate these points, the next section develops some of the concepts and techniques for studying attractor dynamics.

## ATTRACTORS

One of the tools of dynamicists is the state space, a graphical means for displaying all the states that may be reached by a system, together with the trajectories for doing so. An attractor is a region of state space where trajectories come to rest. It can be a

[1] The Moro reflex occurs in response to a sudden loud sound or "dropping" the baby. The baby suddenly startles, throws its head back, and the arms and legs stretch out, and these quickly return to a central position.

point, cycle, or area of state space. For example, the behavior of a mechanical system, such as a clock pendulum, can be described completely by a two-dimensional state space, with axes of position and velocity. A distinctive property of attractors is their return to stability following an external perturbation: despite different initial conditions, trajectories will trace distinctive shapes as they settle, or come to equilibrium. With a point attractor, for example, the system is attracted to one point, and spontaneously returns to it after perturbation. The above example of the Moro reflex illustrates a system that exhibits point attractor dynamic: the elicited arm posture comes to rest at approximately the same endpoints. A limit-cycle attractor is a closed oscillation maintained by a competition between forces. Limit-cycle behavior is exhibited by a pendulum whose oscillation is sustained against the gravitational pull on the pendulum bob by the potential energy stored in a spring and released in "squirts" by an escapement. In later sections, we explore the possibility that behaviors such as sucking and walking exhibit limit-cycle attractor dynamics.

There is a range of techniques for identifying attractors. As an initial verification, one can construct a state space, where the coordinate axes are the state variables of position and velocity. By measuring position and velocity of a marker on a limb segment, for example, it is possible to examine the convergence of a family of trajectories on a stable cycle (e.g., when a supine infant kicks a leg). For rhythmic kicking, a closed orbit of trajectories, with a certain confidence band, is suggestive of a limit-cycle attractor. Stronger inferences can be made about the identity of the attractor by examining whether its phase can be shifted in time by applying a mechanical perturbation, called phase resetting (Kay, Saltzman, & Kelso, 1991), and by measuring its dimensionality (e.g., Robertson, Cohen, & Mayer-Kress, 1993). It should be noted that the methodology for phase-resetting experiments and the mathematics for determining dimensionality are each nontrivial exercises, and this may account for the paucity of infant studies that have used these techniques.

## BABBLING: AN ILLUSTRATION OF THE SELF-ORGANIZATION OF AN ATTRACTOR

One of the stunning features of motor development is the abrupt appearance of a new form of behavior: infants may suddenly stand up by themselves and take a first step, or begin to produce the repetitive vocalizations that we call babbling. For example, babbling begins at about 7 months of age. It is characterized by relatively rhythmic cycles of alternation between a closed and open mouth accompanied by phonation, or vocal fold vibration (Oller, 2000). A series of studies by MacNeilage and colleagues (e.g., Davis & MacNeilage, 1995; MacNeilage, Davis, Kinney, & Matyear, 2000) shows that across different languages there are only three particular couplings of vowels (V) and consonants (C) that emerge from all possible combinations during babbling and early speech: coronal consonants co-occur with frontal vowels (e.g., /da/), dorsal consonants with back vowels (e.g., /go/), and labial consonants with central vowels (e.g., /ba/). They argue that the cyclical CV alternation underlying a syllable reflects a tendency to organize speech according to basic biomechanical constraints of the mandible.

From a dynamical systems perspective, babbling is a consequence of changing patterns of interaction or "coupling" of components. Kent, Mitchell, and Sancier (1991), for example, argue that babbling emerges from the coupling of new capabilities in respiratory/laryngeal and supraglottal functioning. In respiratory/laryngeal functioning, infants become able to sustain phonation with possible interruption for phonetic segments, and in supraglottal functioning, infants are able to produce trains of repeated closant-vocant syllables. Thus, because the segments are produced in regular rhythmic fashion, and phonation is not disrupted by production of phonetic segments, the novel form of behavior that we call babbling may emerge from the coupling of systems with their own attractor dynamics. We next turn to concepts and techniques from the study of adult motor control for studying such attractor coupling.

## SYNERGIES AS SELF-ORGANIZING SYSTEMS

Coordinated motion involves the cooperation of the following approximate numbers of degrees of freedom of motor subsystems: $10^2$ in joint space, $10^3$ in muscle space, and $10^{14}$ in neuronal space (Newell, 1996). Moreover, the components of these subsystems are of different sizes (neurons and muscles), interacting in many different ways (e.g., muscles acting as agonists or antagonists, and contracting by different amounts in equal time), and at different time scales. How, then, does cooperativity arise in such a complex system? One insight into this problem came from Bernstein (1967, 1996), who proposed that a system's degrees of freedom do not act independently, but rather are linked in such a way that they preserve a functional relationship to each other during performance. So, for example, when a skilled marksman sights a target, the wrist and shoulder joints are constrained to act as a single unit, such that any horizontal oscillation in the wrist is matched by an equal and opposite oscillation in the shoulder. The term "synergy" has been used to describe a functional system in which there is a cooperativity of degrees of freedom and a damping out of faster variables by those with a slower time scale (Turvey, 1990). The concept of synergy may provide a basis for explaining how the earliest observable motor behaviors of infants become organized into coordinated patterns.

## HOW ARE SYNERGIES FORMED?

The premier example of the formation of synergies at the time scale of observable motor behavior is rhythmical oscillation, apparent in behavior as diverse as fin oscillations in the fish *Labrus* (von Holst, 1939/1973) to the sucking behavior of human neonates (Wolff, 1991). Von Holst proposed that the oscillation of each fin of *Labrus* had a preferred frequency, and that there were three fundamental processes by which any two fins became coordinated: they could compete with each other, e.g., by continuing their preferred frequency (a maintenance tendency), they could combine in additive fashion (superimposition), or they could cooperate by achieving a common frequency with constant relative phase (magnet effect). The significance of the maintenance tendency is that it demonstrates the independent, autonomous nature of each oscillation. However, when the fins are active together, their mutual influences (maintenance tendency and superimposition) become apparent.

## COORDINATION OF RHYTHMS IN EARLY INFANT BEHAVIOR

Respiratory and sucking rhythms are among the earliest organized behaviors of human infants. Decades of study have revealed that these rhythms have an endogenous origin (see, e.g., Wolff, 1991). However, the principles by which these temporal patterns influence each other are only now being elucidated. Goldfield, Wolff, and Schmidt (1999a,b) examined the dynamics of pacifier sucking and breathing among healthy and high-risk low-birthweight infants who reached their term date, and in healthy newborns. We compared these three groups in order to determine whether measures of coordination could be used to identify how prematurity affected the developing nervous system. Our hypotheses were that in a high-risk premature group compared with healthy full-term or premature infants, (1) the integer frequency ratios of sucking and breathing would be lower (1/1 or 2/1, rather than 3/1 or 3/2) and (2) sucking frequency would have less influence on respiratory frequency (i.e., von Holst's magnet effect), as measured by differences in breathing during sucking bursts and pauses. The group of high-risk low-birthweight preterm infants produced simpler patterns of sucking and breathing (as measured by the ratio of their sucking and breathing frequencies) and sucking and breathing frequencies had less of an effect on each other than they did in the other two groups. Thus, all of the infants produced only a small number of different coordination patterns, and birth status was distinguished by simpler and less stable patterns.

In summary, a dynamical systems approach provides a unique perspective on the fundamental developmental question of the emergence of new behaviors. Rhythmic behaviors such as sucking and breathing are self-organizing systems capable of influencing each other so that they become coupled together in new ways. Most importantly, the coupling is induced by the components themselves, rather than from the outside. Ongoing research in our laboratory is beginning to address whether similar analyses can be applied to the respiratory and vocal components of babbling and speech.

## *Question 2*
## *Transitions between stable states*

### DEVELOPMENTAL TRANSITIONS

We have just seen that stable coordinative patterns may arise from the self-organizing dynamics of interacting oscillations, and next turn to the question of how transitions between stable patterns may arise from these same dynamics. Self-organization implies that particular patterns emerge from whatever components are available, and so the prediction for developing motor systems from a dynamical systems perspective is that infants should take multiple paths toward a developing skill. Consider locomotion. Classic studies of infant locomotion by Gesell (1946) and McGraw (1945) highlight the apparent stage-like sequence of prone progression in which crawling follows creeping. During creeping, both arms are extended, and both legs flex symmetrically. During crawling, by contrast, both arms are extended so that the hands are directly below the shoulders, and then each hand extends forward, alternately. At the same time the legs push the body forward, so that the arm and leg on opposite sides of the body move simultaneously. However, Adolph et al. (1998) and Goldfield (1989, 1993) have found that not all infants follow the same sequence: some creep before they crawl, others skip creeping all together and go directly to crawling.

Another illustration of multiple paths comes from the densely detailed longitudinal study of infant reaching, first reported by Thelen, Corbetta, Kamm, Spencer, Schneider, and Zernicke (1993). A remarkable finding in this work is that some infants begin the process of learning to reach by wildly flailing the arms, and only gradually achieve smooth trajectories; while others hardly move at all prior to reaching. The task of learning to reach is, thus, different depending upon the context of the limb's initial motion. In the former case, the infant must damp out energetic movements by stiffening the limbs, while in the latter, the infant must scale up the velocity and force of reaching. We see, then, that there are apparently multiple paths to crawling and reaching. Nevertheless, self-organization is still apparent, since for both reaching and crawling, all of the different paths do eventually lead to a common goal. But what, precisely, is the mechanism for change?

## STABILIZING AND DESTABILIZING ATTRACTORS IN DEVELOPMENT

Thelen and her colleagues propose that locomotion (e.g., Jensen, Thelen, Ulrich, Schneider, & Zernicke, 1995; Thelen & Ulrich, 1991) and reaching (Spencer, Vereijken, Diedrich, & Thelen, 2000) are governed by a set of subsystem attractors. Consider, for example, a series of studies on the intrinsic dynamics of spontaneous limb movements (Jensen et al., 1995; Spencer & Thelen, 2000; Thelen et al., 1993) whose starting premise follows from Bernstein (1967): acquiring a motor skill (or, in dynamical terms, locating an attractor within a potential landscape and reducing instability) requires solving the problems of moving limbs in an environment of forces. Jensen et al. (1995) take a critical step in modeling the forces (kinetics) influencing muscular control by considering more closely the body's actual biomechanical properties, namely, the elastic quality of the muscles. Their developmental question was the nature of the transition from early, stereotypic leg flexions and extensions to the complex and differentiated control of the joints required for walking (e.g., flexion at the hip while extension occurs at the knee as the leg is oriented for the next footstrike).

They found that this transition, roughly between ages 3 and 7 months, was made possible when the force of kicking relied less on simultaneously stiffening the leg at all of the joints, and instead began to modulate the spring-like stiffness of the leg (evidenced by increasingly differentiated slopes of lines depicting the relationship of peak velocity and amplitude). Thus, it is the combined influences of muscular forces and gravitational and other forces acting on the body that attract leg flexions and extensions into a stable attractor well.

Thelen's work captures the way that motor development follows multiple paths, and that there are multiple influences that push the developing motor system toward certain paths and not others. However, a difficult challenge in using a "landscape" of attractors to model developmental processes is that it requires specification of an attractor and its control parameter for many interacting subsystems (see, e.g., Muchisky, Gershkoff-Stowe, Cole, & Thelen, 1996). Another difficulty is capturing specific relations between musculoskeletal and neural subsystems. Can we, for example, identify specific influences of the brain on the organization of the body's intrinsic dynamics?

## BREAKING SYMMETRY

A striking feature of vertebrate morphology is its bilateral musculoskeletal symmetry. Nevertheless, most humans use a preferred hand to perform certain skilled motor behaviors, such as writing. Hand preferences appear to be related to the functional organization of the brain: in right-handers, there is functional asymmetry of the motor cortex between the dominant and nondominant hand (Civardi, Cavalli, Naldi, Varrasi, & Cantello, 2000). Left-handers do not show this organization, but the epigenetic developmental process by which handedness becomes established may include a complex set of asymmetrical influences on the eye-head system that can account for both right- and left-handed individuals (see, e.g., Michel, 1987). As we confront the question of transitions in motor development, the body's musculoskeletal symmetry and central nervous system asymmetrical biases may point to complementary roles played by the body and brain in maintaining a balance between stability and change. One possibility, for example, is that the self-organizing tendency of bilaterally symmetric pendula, masses, and springy tendons (like a suspended puppet being oscillated by a single spring) is to fall into stable synchronous patterns. Functional asymmetries of the nervous system may introduce biases in the temporal recruitment of muscle groups on one side of the body that modify these synchronous patterns in order to introduce change in behavior. Is there evidence that synchrony is a strong attractor for intrinsic oscillation of symmetric systems, and that lateral asymmetries are involved in breaking symmetry?

To address this question, we turn to the mathematical modeling used by Turvey (e.g., Turvey & Carello, 1996) and others to study the dynamics of synergies, i.e., the nature of coordination between oscillations. The starting point is a limit-cycle attractor, described by a variable, relative phase. Relative phase is an example of an order parameter, a macroscopic quantity chosen because it captures the spatiotemporal details of a system and changes more slowly than the variables characterizing the states (e.g., velocity, amplitude) of the component subsystems. The mathematical model of interest (see Turvey & Carello, 1996, for details) expresses the opposing tendencies between coupling and competition among interacting effectors. The phase relation observed varies as a function of both the strength of coupling of the two oscillations and the size of their competition.

When competition between the two oscillations does not equal zero (such as when the preferred frequency of one oscillation is different from the other), the symmetry of the dynamics is broken. Broken symmetry results from the fact that the various components do not play an identical role in the coordination pattern. Consider, for example, the task of holding a pendulum in each hand and swinging them parallel to the sagittal plane about an axis in the wrist (Kugler & Turvey, 1987). Frequency competition is brought about when the lengths of the pendula are unequal, so that the swinging motion of each occurs at a different frequency. Kugler and Turvey (1987) find, for example, that frequency competition has different effects on deviations from a required phase during antiphase and in-phase oscillations. The critical point, here, is that *when symmetry is broken, changes in coupling can bring about richly varied changes in the behavior of the synergy*.

The analysis of pendular motion frequencies provides a natural extension to the oscillation of the body segments. Broken symmetry of pendular body motions, e.g., the way that the two hands contribute to bimanual tasks in different ways, may play a fundamental role in the development of skills. One possibility, for example, is that the left and right sides of the brain are characterized by coupling differences, such that there are lateral differences in the relative stability of attractors among limb segments (Byblow, Chua, & Goodman, 1995; Carson, 1993). Treffner and

Turvey (1995) provide some support for this claim in a pendulum-swinging experiment during which right- or left-handed adults oscillated pendula of the same length. Even when there were no differences in the oscillation frequencies of the two pendula, there was a small but reliable right-hand lead for right-handed participants, and the opposite was true for the left-handers. Handedness, in other words, broke the symmetry of pendular oscillation.

## POSTURAL ASYMMETRIES AND ORGANIZATIONAL TRANSITIONS: CRAWLING

Goldfield (1989, 1993) examined the possibility that lateral asymmetries in hand preference might play a role in the developmental transition to crawling. Prior to crawling, infants use both hands to support the body as the legs propel it forward (Adolph et al., 1998; Freedland & Bertenthal, 1994). However, in order to change position along a support surface, one hand must be free to reach ahead to something that affords approach. These two functional capabilities of the hands, stance and transport, may compete with each other as the infant attempts to perform both at the same time: an attempt to reach promotes falling and using both hands for support does not change the body's progress toward the goal. Lateral asymmetry of hand use may resolve this competition by providing a division of labor: instead of performing stance and transport *at the same time*, stronger spatiotemporal coupling of synergies on the preferred side for reaching may allow the infant to use that hand for extending forward toward the goal, while the other hand maintains support (with the legs, an adequate tripod stance). The temporal sequencing of stance and support that we call crawling may, thus, result from broken symmetry.

A study by Goldfield (1989) provides some evidence for symmetry-breaking in the development of crawling. Goldfield (1989) observed infants in a condition during which they were encouraged by the mother to approach an object while seated independently on the floor. The infant's hand preference for reaching, scored during a separate task, was used to classify each infant as either predominantly right- or left-handed. A coder blinded to this classification scored the hand upon which the infant first landed when he or she fell forward to begin to crawl. There was a strongly significant association between the infant's hand preference and the hand that first contacted the floor: right-handed infants landed significantly more often on their left hand, and reached out to begin crawling with their preferred right hand. The converse was true for the left-handed infants. Thus, in falling from upright into a crawl posture, infants appear to be landing in a way that leaves their preferred hand free to reach ahead of them as they begin to crawl.

To summarize, a dynamical systems perspective emphasizes that novel behavior emerges from unique combinations of interacting capabilities, each with its own rate of development. The particular functional system that emerges depends on competition and cooperation among its components. We next turn to the question of how newly emergent behaviors are related to their antecedents.

## *Question 3*
## *The relation between early and later forms of behavior: Selective processes acting on self-organizing systems*

### TRANSITIONS BETWEEN FORMS

Prechtl (1981) has highlighted the transient nature of many newborn motor behaviors, including rooting, sucking, palmar and plantar, and stepping "reflexes," and suggests that each appears to be "replaced" by more mature forms. For example, in the early form of orienting the head to receptor stimulation of the cheek, there is a somewhat frantic-looking rhythmic side-to-side headturning. Gradually, though, infants seeking the nipple will orient the mouth toward a source of milk, using multiple sources of information about its location (Prechtl, 1981). A fundamental question in development is how to characterize this relation between early and later forms. Here, we consider this question in the context of the relationship between self-organization of early oral motor behaviors and selective processes that are at work in eliminating certain patterns in favor of others.

### TWO TYPES OF SUCKING BEHAVIOR

From a perspective that distinguishes "reflexive" and "rhythmic" behaviors (see, e.g., Gallistel, 1980), the non-nutritive sucking (NNS) behavior described earlier is an oddity. On the one hand, like the classic Sherringtonian reflex, it can be elicited by a particular means of stimulation, such as gently placing a finger inside the baby's mouth. However, once elicited, the infant continues to produce a 2 Hz rhythmic oscillation, pausing briefly every few seconds, and continuing until the finger is removed or sleep ensues. Moreover, the careful observer can detect the same 2 Hz jaw oscillation during some periods of sleep, even with no oral stimulation. An additional feature that further blurs the classic distinction between sucking reflex and rhythm is the effect of milk flow on the sucking pattern. In experiments that control milk flow to an artificial nipple, when milk does not flow, infants produce the 2 Hz NNS pattern (positive pressure). When milk flow is initiated, the sucking frequency decreases to 1 Hz and there appears a negative pressure component coupled 1 : 1 with positive pressure. When milk flow is again interrupted, the negative pressure component dramatically decreases or drops out, and positive pressure returns to a 2 Hz burst–pause pattern. The implication of such experiments is that the motor system is organized in such a way that it is both capable of generating intrinsic dynamics and can be modified by the flow of milk from a nipple.

## PHASE RESETTING

One way to conceptualize a motor control system that makes possible both earlier behaviors with intrinsic "reflexive" organization and later behavior that is modifiable by sensory information is with reference to a central "clocking" mechanism that can be adjusted by peripheral events. With such a mechanism as a foundation for motor control, the developmental phenomena of progress, regressions, and apparent disappearances might all indicate the relative degree to which central clocking can be influenced by feedback information about the current state of body articulators.

Experiments that have attempted to identify a central timing network that both drives the articulatory periphery and is influenced by feedback from the periphery have used a phase-resetting paradigm. During phase-resetting experiments, a sudden perturbation is applied to an effector participating in the rhythmic oscillation. The goal of phase-resetting analyses is to determine whether perturbations delivered during an ongoing rhythm have a permanent effect (i.e., a phase shift) on the underlying temporal organization of the rhythm. The presence of a phase shift indicates that coordination is not rigidly specified over the sequence, but rather evolves fluidly and flexibly. The methodology involves measurement of the amount of temporal shift introduced into a sequence, relative to the sequence's timing prior to the perturbation.

For example, Kay et al. (1991) found that transient mechanical perturbations delivered to a finger altered the underlying temporal structure of oscillation by means of a phase advance, relative to where the perturbation occurred in the sequence. More recently, Saltzman, Lofqvist, Kay, Kinsella-Shaw, and Rubin (1998) have used phase resetting to examine the temporal control of successive opening and closing movements of the lips and the larynx in voiceless consonant production. They applied downward-directed mechanical perturbations to the lower lip during both repetitive and nonrepetitive utterances, and found that the lips and larynx were phase advanced as a relatively coherent unit. Both of these studies, then, support the claim that temporal control of both manual and oral sequences involves central clocking that both drives and is sensitive to peripheral dynamics.

## CENTRAL CLOCKING AND PERIPHERAL TUNING IN ORAL-MOTOR BEHAVIOR

Finan and Barlow (1998) have examined whether infant non-nutritive sucking can be characterized by central clocking that both drives and is sensitive to peripheral dynamics. For this purpose, they developed an "actifier," a device for cyclic mechanical stimulation of oral peripheral mechanoreceptors in a way that mimicked the effects of natural movement. However, rather than using a strict phase-resetting paradigm, they instead examined whether they could modify the oscillation frequency of ongoing sucking so that it matched that of the mechanical stimulation. Some of the infants either increased or decreased cycle period so that it established 1 : 1 synchronization with the rhythmic mechanical stimulation. It should be noted that at the onset of stimulation, one infant simply stopped sucking, and three others raised or lowered the jaw while continuing to suck. At this point, then, while there is some evidence that the temporal organization of non-nutritive sucking can be modulated by rhythmic oral stimulation, further work needs to be done to firmly establish whether there is bidirectional coupling.

In summary, a dynamical systems perspective on the relationship between early and later forms of behavior emphasizes two roles for early forms of behavior. First, early-appearing behaviors serve an immediate adaptive role that ensures that the infant is motorically active. Second, these behaviors move the receptor surfaces of different body organs so that they reveal patterns of sensory input.

## QUESTION 4
## *How do infants discover when to produce muscular activity in order to maintain an ongoing oscillatory behavior?*

### DYNAMICS AND THE ENVIRONMENT

Given the critical importance of receptor input in modifying dynamical systems so that they can adapt to a changing environment without losing their intrinsic stability, Butterworth (1993) and others (e.g., Goldfield, 1995) have turned to the work of James J. Gibson (1966, 1979) for insights into the nature of information. Gibson envisioned the actor/perceiver as being enveloped by fields that are patterned by the substances and surfaces of the environment. As animals and humans move through these fields, successive points of observation (in the case of vision) identify a trajectory of motion. On the one hand, this trajectory specifies the actor/perceiver's displacement during locomotion through the environment and, on the other, provides successive samples of the field that may be detected by the various perceptual systems (visual, auditory, haptic, taste-smell) during the displacement. By virtue of the evolution of nervous systems that vary in complexity, and of bodies that attain different sizes and forms, some animals are able to select information inherent to these patterns in a way that others cannot. For humans, the increasing selectivity from patterned fields during ontogeny is not only a function of development of the brain's receptor fields, but also due to increasing control of the means by which receptor organs are moved (Bertenthal & Bai, 1989; Bertenthal, & von Hofsten, 1998; Breniere, Bril, & Fontaine, 1989; Bril & Ledebt, 1998).

### INFANT EXPLORATORY BEHAVIOR

In her influential theoretical and empirical work, Eleanor Gibson (e.g., Gibson, 1988; Gibson & Pick, 2000) has proposed that exploratory behavior is the primary means by which infants learn the relationships between their actions and the properties of the environment. Moreover, the selectivity of infant exploratory activity changes with the increasing postural control of the eye-head system and with mobility. So, due to limited eye-head and trunk control up until the age of about 4 months, infants explore only their immediate surroundings. They orient to sights and to the sounds that accompany visual events, and use haptic mouthing to discover object properties. For example, Butterworth and Hopkins (1988) demonstrate the importance of the mouth as an exploratory organ in their observations of newborns bringing their hands to their mouths. Newborns will bring the hand to another part of the face, open the mouth in anticipation of the hand's arrival, and bring the hand to the mouth. When the hand is in the mouth, sucking has an exploratory function, as is evident in the types of active mouthing that are observed (Rochat, Blass, & Hoffmeyer, 1988).

Infants progressively explore more distal parts of the body, including the hands and the legs. We saw above that the reaching–grasping–handling system develops as the head and trunk are controlled more independently. Exploratory activity of the legs seems to be related to the body's axial (left–right) organization. For example, Rochat and Morgan (1995) used an experimental presentation of televised images of an infant's own legs to show that by 5 months, the infants detect the spatial discrepancy between an image that corresponds to what they experience while looking at their own moving legs and a spatially reversed image. Spencer and Thelen (2000) used kinematic and EMG data to examine the particular muscle combinations that were active within demarcations of a spherical region surrounding the infant's body. The study found a clear developmental relationship between movement within particular spatial regions and EMG activity: (1) early in the first year, infants moved through many spatial regions, including the one where the toy was located, but many of these early movements involved only biceps or triceps muscle activation, useful for moving the hand toward or away from the mouth; (2) after infants first learned to reach for toys at midline, the early muscle-activity patterns were replaced by deltoid-related ones, which served to move the hand toward the toy; and (3) infants increased muscle coactivity when near spatial regions in which the toy was located. Thus, over longitudinal observations of reaching, infants seemed to have learned which muscles moved their hand toward the toy, and which served to keep the hand near the toy's location. The variable being controlled appears to be end-effector position in body space.

As infants become more independently mobile during the first year, they begin to explore the relationship between their body orientations and the spatial layout of the environment. One way they do this is by using the arms and hands during crawling. According to a detailed longitudinal study by Adolph (1997), as infants move forward across the floor, they pause, pat the floor, and rock back and forth over their wrists. What does such exploration reveal to the infant that may be useful for guiding locomotion? Using the hand to pat the floor is probably a means for testing the suitability of a surface ahead for locomotion. Indeed, studies on the visual cliff show that some crawling infants will reorient the body to extend forward the longest appendage, a leg, rather than the arm, to test a surface to be crossed (Campos, Bertenthal, & Kermoian, 1992). The use of the hands for exploratory purposes in the development of postural control has also been demonstrated in a paradigm developed by Barela, Jeka, and Clark (1999). During longitudinal measurements of independent upright stance (e.g., pulling to stand, standing alone, and walking), Barela et al. measured the force of infant hand contact with the surface of a small, suspended cube. They found that prior to walking, infants used greater force in touching the cube, indicating that they were using it for support (i.e., body sway occurred in advance of hand contact). However, once infants began to walk, hand contact preceded body sway, and was used prospectively to modulate sway before it occurred. Do infants use other types of exploratory activity to learn to walk?

## LOCOMOTION WITH REFERENCE TO AN INVERTED MASS-SPRING PENDULAR SYSTEM

The human body under the influences of a gravitational field behaves like an inverted pendulum: any displacement away from the vertical (e.g., with the foot on a flat surface) causes an angular acceleration that must be compensated for by applying torque (i.e., force along a joint angle of rotation) at a joint (e.g., the ankle) (Woollacott & Jensen, 1996). The muscles and tendinous elements exhibit the additional properties of elasticity and damping. Based upon consideration of these constraints, Holt (1998) has developed a force-driven hybrid pendulum-spring model of the preferred gait patterns of adults. The model includes a periodic forcing function by which the muscles overcome dissipative (damping) losses across gait cycles, and two conservative forces, one due to the body's inertia in a gravitational field, and the other due to the spring energy return from the muscles and soft tissue. Whereas the Kay and Warren model probed the nature of the coupling of posture and gait, this model questions how each observed organization of the body's biomechanical properties – its segment lengths and masses, elasticity, and damping – reflects an optimal transmission of energy from the force-producing muscles of the leg to the body center of mass of an inverted pendulum. Understanding how force production is related to the dynamics of walking is crucial not only for healthy adults but also for adults and children with cerebral palsy.

The model addresses two well-documented findings for walking: (1) there is a preferred combination of stride frequency and length (a speed) at which energy expenditure per unit distance is minimized at approximately 0.79 cal/kg/m; and (2) any change in stride frequency or length away from this preferred combination results in increases in energy expenditure (Holt, Jeng, Ratcliffe, & Hamill, 1995). An account based on self-organization is that these findings reflect an actor's discovery of a particular frequency of limb oscillation at which a fixed force produces maximal amplitude (or, at which a minimal force produces a fixed amplitude). This frequency is called the resonant frequency of a system. A dynamical systems perspective predicts that the nervous system does not choose frequency or stride length; they are emergent properties of a linear oscillator operating in its resonant mode. To test this prediction, Holt, Hamill, and Andres (1990) experimentally increased inertial load by adding ankle weights during walking. If frequency is driven by the dynamics, then it should change according to the resonant period for the new inertial condition. The predictions were confirmed for adults and 9-year-olds.

## DO INFANTS DETECT RESONANCE PEAKS IN THE FREQUENCIES OF THEIR OSCILLATORY BEHAVIORS?

We just saw that the fundamental property of a nonlinear oscillator, such as a mass attached to a spring, is that it requires a minimal amount of force to sustain oscillation of a mass when driven at its natural frequency. When a driver forces a mass-spring system, a peak occurs in the amplitude response near its natural frequency. At this peak, the system is said to "resonate" to the driver, and so this is called a resonance peak. On the basis of this work with adults, Goldfield, Kay, and Warren (1993) conducted longitudinal observations of infants learning the dynamics of a mass-spring system: their own body suspended in a harness with feet touching the floor from a spring of known stiffness and damping. Videotape recordings were made in the home once each week over a period of several weeks, as the infants learned to bounce.

Using a mass-spring model, Goldfield et al. tested the hypothesis that the infants we observed were controlling how much force to apply and how fast to apply the force of kicking. As in Holt's study, our model captures the optimality property of resonance. That is, the amplitude of the mass's oscillations is maximal at a specific frequency. It was further hypothesized that over longitudinal observations, infants were searching frequency-stiffness space to find the resonant frequency. The resonant frequency depends upon the stiffness of both the spring and the legs, so in order to achieve maximum amplitude, the infant should match leg stiffness to spring stiffness. This was indeed the case. There was also an increase in amplitude over sessions, consistent with the hypothesis of exploration of a resonance peak, observed when a system is driven at its resonant frequency. More recently, Foo, Goldfield, Kay, and Warren (2001) examined what infants learned during this task by experimentally manipulating the system parameters of mass and spring stiffness once infants had already achieved their peak bout length while bouncing in the jumper. The major question was whether infants learned particular parameter settings *per se*, or learned the dynamics of the task, which would allow them to quickly adapt their leg stiffness and kicking frequency to new conditions. Both the mass and spring manipulations were effective in changing the bouncing frequency. One infant, for example, bounced at a frequency of 1.63 Hz at the session of the peak bout length; when an additional 2.30 kg mass was added to the bouncer, the infant bounced at 1.71 Hz; and when an additional spring was added in parallel, the observed mean bouncing frequency increased to 1.84 Hz. Moreover, at their first opportunity under each of the experimental conditions, infants began to bounce, indicating that they were exploring the dynamics of their actions rather than learning a particular parameter setting. Thus, as in the original Goldfield et al. (1993) study, after a period of exploring the stiffness by force parameter space, the infant is able to discover and exploit the stability of the attractor.

## Conclusion

The foregoing account of a dynamical systems approach to infant motor development highlights the processes of self-organization and selection by which new behaviors emerge. Its promise as a unique approach lies in the methods by which new questions about motor development can be addressed. By developing mathematical models and computer simulations that attempt to capture neural, biomechanical, and environmental contributions to the emergence of new behaviors, the approach will continue to be useful for addressing the complexities of motor behavior. Its greatest challenge remains in providing ways to understand the relation between action and the domains that have traditionally been treated as separate human capabilities, namely, cognition, language, and social discourse.

## REFERENCES

Adolph, K. E. (1997). Learning in the development of infant locomotion. *Monographs of the Society for Research in Child Development*, 62 (Serial No. 251).

Adolph, K. E., Vereijken, B., & Denny, M. A. (1998). Learning to crawl. *Child Development*, 69, 1299–1312.

Barela, J. A., Jeka, J. J., & Clark, J. E. (1999). The use of somatosensory information during the acquisition of independent upright stance. *Infant Behavior and Development*, 22, 87–102.

Beek, P. J., & Beek, W. J. (1988). Tools for constructing dynamical models of rhythmic movement. *Human Movement Science*, 7, 301–42.

Bernstein, N. A. (1967). *The coordination and regulation of movements*. London: Pergamon.

Bernstein, N. A. (1996). Levels of construction of movements. In M. Latash & M. Turvey (Eds.), *Dexterity and its development* (pp. 115–70). Mahwah, NJ: Erlbaum.

Bertenthal, B., & Bai, D. (1989). Infants' sensitivity to optical flow for controlling posture. *Developmental Psychology*, 25, 936–45.

Bertenthal, B., & von Hofsten, C. (1998). Eye, head and trunk control: The foundation for manual development. *Neuroscience and Biobehavioral Review*, 22, 515–20.

Breniere, Y., & Bril, B. (1998). Development of postural control of gravity forces in children during the first 5 years of walking. *Experimental Brain Research*, 121, 255–62.

Breniere, Y., Bril, B., & Fontaine, R. (1989). Analysis of the transition from upright stance to steady state locomotion in children with under 200 days of autonomous walking. *Journal of Motor Behavior*, 21, 20–37.

Bril, B., & Ledebt, A. (1998). Head coordination as a means to assist sensory integration in learning to walk. *Neuroscience and Biobehavioral Reviews*, 22, 555–63.

Butterworth, G. (1993). Dynamic approaches to infant perception and action: Old and new theories about the origins of knowledge. In L. B. Smith & E. Thelen (Eds.), *A dynamic systems approach to development: Applications* (pp. 171–87). Cambridge, MA: MIT Press.

Butterworth, G., & Hicks, L. (1977). Visual proprioception and postural stability in infancy: A developmental study. *Perception*, 5, 255–63.

Butterworth, G., & Hopkins, B. (1988). Hand–mouth coordination in the new-born baby. *British Journal of Developmental Psychology*, 6, 303–14.

Byblow, W. D., Chua, R., & Goodman, D. (1995). Asymmetries in coupling dynamics of perception and action. *Journal of Motor Behavior*, 27, 123–37.

Campos, J. J., Bertenthal, B. I., & Kermoian, R. (1992). Early experience and emotional development: The emergence of wariness of heights. *Psychological Science*, 3, 61–4.

Carson, R. G. (1993). Manual asymmetries: Old problems and new directions. *Human Movement Science*, 12, 479–506.

Civardi, C., Cavalli, A., Naldi, P., Varrasi, C., & Cantello, R. (2000). Hemispheric asymmetries of cortico-cortical connections in human hand motor areas. *Clinical Neurophysiology*, 111, 624–9.

Davis, B. L., & MacNeilage, P. F. (1995). The articulatory basis of babbling. *Journal of Speech and Hearing Research*, 38, 1199–1211.

Finan, D. S., & Barlow, S. M. (1998). Intrinsic dynamics and mechanosensory modulation of non-nutritive sucking in human infants. *Early Human Development*, 52, 181–97.

Foo, P., Goldfield, E. C., Kay, B. A., & Warren, W. H., Jr. (2001, November). Infant bouncing: The assembly, tuning, and transfer of action systems. Paper presented at the 9th International Congress on Research in Physical Activity and Sport, Valence, France.

Forssberg, H., Stokes, V., & Hirschfeld, H. (1992). Basic mechanisms of human locomotor development. In M. Gunnar & C. Nelson (Eds.), *Developmental behavioral neuroscience. Minnesota symposia on child psychology* (Vol. 24, pp. 37–73). Hillsdale, NJ: Erlbaum.

Freedland, R. L., & Bertenthal, B. I. (1994). Developmental changes in interlimb coordination: Transition to hands-and-knees crawling. *Psychological Science*, 5, 26–32.

Gallistel, C. R. (1980). *The organization of action: A new synthesis*. Hillsdale, NJ: Erlbaum.

Gesell, A. (1946). The ontogenesis of infant behavior. In L. Carmichael (Ed.), *Manual of child psychology* (pp. 295–331). New York: Wiley.

Gibson, E. J. (1988). Exploratory behavior in the development of perceiving, acting, and acquiring knowledge. *Annual Review of Psychology*, 39, 1–41.

Gibson, E. J., & Pick, A. D. (2000). *An ecological approach to perceptual learning and development*. New York: Oxford University Press.

Gibson, J. J. (1966). *The senses considered as perceptual systems*. Boston: Houghton-Mifflin.

Gibson, J. J. (1979). *The ecological approach to visual perception*. Boston: Houghton-Mifflin; reprinted (1986), Hillsdale, NJ: Erlbaum.

Gilbert, S. F. (2000). *Developmental biology* (5th ed.). Sunderland, MA: Sinauer.

Goldfield, E. C. (1989). Transition from rocking to crawling: Postural constraints on infant movement. *Developmental Psychology*, 25, 913–19.

Goldfield, E. C. (1993). Dynamic systems in development: Action systems. In L. B. Smith & E. Thelen (Eds.), *A dynamic systems approach to development: Applications* (pp. 51–70). Cambridge, MA: MIT Press.

Goldfield, E. C. (1995). *Emergent forms: Origins and early development of infant acting and perceiving*. New York: Oxford University Press.

Goldfield, E. C., Kay, B. A., & Warren, W. H., Jr. (1993). Infant bouncing: The assembly and tuning of action systems. *Child Development*, 64, 1128–42.

Goldfield, E. C., & Wolff, P. H. (2002). Motor development in infancy. In A. Slater & M. Lewis (Eds.), *Introduction to infant development* (pp. 61–82). New York: Oxford University Press.

Goldfield, E. C., Wolff, P. H., & Schmidt, R. C. (1999a). Dynamics of oral-respiratory coordination in full-term and preterm infants. I. Comparison at 38–40 weeks postconceptional age. *Developmental Science*, 2, 363–73.

Goldfield, E. C., Wolff, P. H., & Schmidt, R. C. (1999b). Dynamics of oral-respiratory coordination in full-term and preterm infants. II. Continuing effects at 3 months post-term. *Developmental Science*, 2, 374–84.

Gottlieb, G. (1992). *Individual development and evolution*. New York: Oxford University Press.

Haken, H., Kelso, J. A. S., & Bunz, H. (1985). A theoretical model of phase transition in human hand movements. *Biological Cybernetics*, 51, 347–56.

Holt, K. G. (1998). Constraints in the emergence of preferred locomotory patterns. In D. A. Rosenbaum & C. A. Collyer (Eds.), *Timing of behavior: Neural, psychological, and computational perspectives* (pp. 261–91). Cambridge, MA: MIT Press.

Holt, K. G., Hamill, J., & Andres, R. O. (1990). The force-driven harmonic oscillator as a model for human locomotion. *Human Movement Science*, 9, 55–68.

Holt, K. G., Jeng, S. F., Ratcliffe, R., & Hamill, J. (1995). Energetic cost and stability in preferred human walking. *Journal of Motor Behavior*, 27, 164–79.

Jensen, J. L., Thelen, E., Ulrich, B. D., Schneider, K., & Zernicke, R. F. (1995). Adaptive dynamics of the leg movement patterns of human infants: III. Age-related differences in limb control. *Journal of Motor Behavior*, 27, 366–74.

Kauffman, S. A. (1993). *The origins of order: Self-organization and selection in evolution*. New York: Oxford University Press.

Kauffman, S. (1995). *At home in the universe: The search for laws of self-organization and complexity*. New York: Oxford University Press.

Kay, B. A., Saltzman, E., & Kelso, J. A. S. (1991). Steady-state and perturbed rhythmical movements: A dynamical analysis. *Journal of Experimental Psychology: Human Perception and Performance*, 17, 183–97.

Kay, B. A., & Warren, W. H., Jr. (1998). A dynamical model of the coupling between posture and gait. In D. A. Rosenbaum & C. A. Collyer (Eds.), *Timing of behavior: Neural, psychological, and computational perspectives* (pp. 293–322). Cambridge, MA: MIT Press.

Kay, B. A., & Warren, W. H., Jr. (2001). Coupling of posture and gait: Mode locking and parametric excitation. *Biological Cybernetics*, 85, 89–106.

Kelso, J. A. S., Ding, M., & Schöner, G. (1992). Dynamic pattern formation: A primer. In J. Mittenthal & A. Baskin (Eds.), *Principles of organization in organisms* (pp. 397–439). New York: Addison-Wesley.

Kent, R. D., Mitchell, P. R., & Sancier, M. (1991). Evidence and role of rhythmic organization in early vocal development in human infants. In J. Fagard & P. H. Wolff (Eds.), *The development of timing control and temporal organization in coordinated action* (pp. 135–49). Amsterdam: Elsevier.

Kugler, P. N., & Turvey, M. T. (1987). *Information, natural law, and the self-assembly of rhythmic movement*. Hillsdale, NJ: Erlbaum.

Lee, D. N., & Lishman, J. R. (1975). Visual proprioceptive control of stance. *Journal of Human Movement Studies*, 1, 87–95.

Lenard, H. G., von Bernuth, H., & Prechtl, H. F. R. (1968). Reflexes and their relationships to behavioral state in the newborn. *Acta Paediatrica Scandinavica*, 3, 177–85.

Lockman, J. J., & Thelen, E. (1993). Developmental biodynamics: Brain, body, behavior connections. *Child Development*, 64, 953–9.

McGraw, M. (1945). *Neuromuscular maturation of the human infant*. New York: Hafner.

MacNeilage, P. F., Davis, B. L., Kinney, A., & Matyear, C. L. (2000). The motor core of speech: A comparison of serial organization patterns in infants and languages. *Child Development*, 71, 153–63.

Mayr, E. (1982). *The growth of biological thought*. Cambridge, MA: Belknap/ Harvard University Press.

Michel, G. F. (1987). Self-generated experience and the development of lateralized neurobehavioral organization in infants. In J. S. Rosenblatt, C. G. Beer, M. C. Busnel, & P. C. Slater (Eds.), *Advances in the study of behavior* (Vol. 17, pp. 61–83). New York: Academic Press.

Muchisky, M., Gershkoff-Stowe, L., Cole, E., & Thelen, E. (1996). The epigenetic landscape revisited: A dynamic interpretation. In C. Rovee-Collier & L. P. Lipsitt (Eds.), *Advances in infancy research* (Vol. 10, pp. 121–59). Norwood, NJ: Ablex.

Newell, K. (1996). Learning, retention, and transfer. In M. Latash & M. Turvey (Eds.), *Dexterity and its development* (pp. 393–429). Mahwah, NJ: Erlbaum.

Oller, D. K. (2000). *The emergence of the speech capacity*. Mahwah, NJ: Erlbaum.

Prechtl, H. F. R. (1981). The study of neural development as a perspective of clinical problems. In K. Connolly & H. Prechtl (Eds.), Maturation and development: Biological and psychological perspectives. *Clinics in Developmental Medicine* (No. 77/78, pp. 198–215). Philadelphia: Lippincott.

Prigogine, I. (1980). *From being to becoming: Time and complexity in the physical sciences*. San Francisco: Freeman.

Reed, E. S., & Bril, B. (1996). The primacy of action in development. In M. Latash & M. Turvey (Eds.), *Dexterity and its development* (pp. 431–51). Mahwah, NJ: Erlbaum.

Robertson, S. S., Cohen, A. H., & Mayer-Kress, G. (1993). Behavioral chaos: Beyond the metaphor. In L. B. Smith & E. Thelen (Eds.), *A dynamic systems approach to development: Applications* (pp. 119–50). Cambridge, MA: MIT Press.

Rochat, P., Blass, E. M., & Hoffmeyer, L. B. (1988). Oropharyngeal Control of hand–mouth coordination in newborn infants. *Developmental Psychology*, 24, 459–63.

Rochat, P., & Morgan, R. (1995). Spatial determinants in the perception of self-produced leg movements by 3- to 5-month-old infants. *Developmental Psychology*, 31, 626–36.

Saltzman, E. L., & Kelso, J. A. S. (1987). Skilled actions: A task dynamic approach. *Psychological Review*, 94, 84–106.

Saltzman, E. L., Lofqvist, A., Kay, B., Kinsella-Shaw, J., & Rubin, P. (1998). Dynamics of intergestural timing: A perturbation study of lip–larynx coordination. *Experimental Brain Research*, 123, 412–24.

Saltzman, E. L., & Munhall, K. G. (1989). A dynamical approach to gestural patterning in speech production. *Ecological Psychology*, 1, 333–82.

Spencer, J. P., & Thelen, E. (2000). Spatially specific changes in infants' muscle coactivity as they learn to reach. *Infancy*, 1, 275–302.

Spencer, J. P., Vereijken, B., Diedrich, F. J., & Thelen, E. (2000). Posture and the emergence of manual skills. *Developmental Science*, 3, 216–33.

Thelen, E. (2000). Grounded in the world: Developmental origins of the embodied mind. *Infancy*, 1, 3–28.

Thelen, E., Corbetta, D., Kamm, K., Spencer, J. P., Schneider, K., & Zernicke, R. F. (1993). The transition to reaching: Mapping intention and intrinsic dynamics. *Child Development*, 64, 1058–98.

Thelen, E., & Spencer, J. P. (1998). Postural control during reaching in young infants: A dynamic systems approach. *Neuroscience and Biobehavioral Reviews*, 22, 507–14.

Thelen, E., & Ulrich, B. D. (1991). Hidden skills: A dynamic systems analysis of treadmill stepping during the first year. *Monographs of the Society for Research in Child Development*, 56 (Serial No. 223).

Treffner, P. J., & Turvey, M. T. (1995). Handedness and the asymmetric dynamics of bimanual rhythmic coordination. *Journal of Experimental Psychology: Human Perception and Performance*, 21, 318–33.

Turvey, M. T. (1990). Coordination. *American Psychologist*, 45, 938–53.

Turvey, M. T., & Carello, C. (1996). Dynamics of Bernstein's level of synergies. In M. Latash & M. Turvey (Eds.), *Dexterity and its development* (pp. 339–76). Mahwah, NJ: Erlbaum.

von Holst, E. (1973). *The collected papers of E. von Holst. Vol. 1. The behavioral physiology of animal and man* (Ed. & Trans. R. Martin). Coral Gables, FL: University of Miami Press. (Original work published 1939.)

Waddington, C. H. (1957). *The strategy of the genes*. London: Allen & Unwin.

Warren, W. H., Jr. (1998). Visually controlled locomotion: 40 years later. *Ecological Psychology*, 10, 177–219.

Winfree, A. (1980). *The geometry of biological time*. New York: Springer.

Winfree, A. (1987). *The timing of biological clocks*. New York: W. H. Freeman.

Winter, D. A. (1990). *Biomechanics of human movement*. (2nd ed.). New York: Wiley.

Wolff, P. H. (1966). The causes, controls, and organization of behavior in the neonate. *Psychological Issues*, 5, 1–99.

Wolff, P. H. (1987). *The development of behavioral states and the expression of emotions in early infancy*. Chicago: University of Chicago Press.

Wolff, P. H. (1991). Endogenous motor rhythms in young infants. In J. Fagard & P. H. Wolff (Eds.), *The development of timing control and temporal organization in coordinated action* (pp. 119–33). Amsterdam: Elsevier.

Woollacott, M. H., & Jensen, J. L. (1996). Posture and locomotion. In H. Heuer & S. Keele (Eds.), *Handbook of perception and action* (Vol. 2, pp. 333–403). San Diego: Academic Press.

# 2
# A Developmental Perspective on Visual Proprioception

*David I. Anderson, Joseph J. Campos, and Marianne A. Barbu-Roth*

## Introduction

Control over posture is a major factor in the young child's behavioral and psychological development because maintaining a stable relation with the environment is critical to learning about the world and one's place in it. The importance of accurately orienting the eyes, ears, and nose to information required for planning and executing actions highlights the special significance assigned initially to developing control of the head. Postural control itself is a prerequisite to the attainment of more sophisticated motor skills, such as reaching, grasping, and locomotion, that increase the complexity of interactions with the world, considerably expanding what can be explored and facilitating the acquisition of information critical to further perceptual, motor, cognitive, social, and emotional development (Campos, Anderson, Barbu-Roth, Hubbard, Hertenstein, & Witherington, 2000; Rochat & Bullinger, 1995).

Preparation of this chapter was supported by a Research Infrastructure in Minority Institutions award from the National Center for Research Resources with funding from the Office of Research on Minority Health, NIH grant #5 P20 RR11805 in addition to NICHD grants HD-36795 and HD-39925 and NSF grants SBR-9116151 and BCS-0002001.

The development of postural control is, not surprisingly, a topic that has received considerable attention in the research literature for well over 50 years (e.g., Bayley, 1969; Gesell & Thompson, 1934; Shirley, 1931). However, only recently has attention been focused on the processes that underlie developmental changes in postural control and, in particular, the specific role of perceptual development and motoric experience in these changes. The focus has coincided with recent interest in the coupling between perception and action during development, with paradigms designed to study the perceptual basis of postural control offering to provide rich insights into the growth of perception–action coupling (Anderson et al., 2001; Bertenthal, Rose, & Bai, 1997; Schmuckler, 1993), the nature of multisensory integration (Woollacott & Shumway-Cook, 1990), and the nature of intermodal perception and its role in the control of action (Stoffregen, Smart, Bardy, & Pagulayan, 1999).

Vision's role in postural control has attracted far more attention than the roles of the other perceptual systems. Despite this focus, however, our understanding of the nature of visual–postural coupling and the process by which it changes is currently in a state of flux, with many outstanding problems and questions. Is vision more important than the other perceptual systems in the control of posture? Are certain areas of the retina specialized to detect information for postural control? Are some types of visual information used more effectively than others for postural control? What contextual factors influence visual–postural coupling? What are the origins of visual–postural coupling and what factors lead to changes in this coupling? These are some of the more compelling questions that can be asked about vision's role in the development of postural control and, concomitantly, about the role of postural control and other actions on the development of vision and visual–postural coupling.

We will provide answers to the aforementioned questions in the subsequent sections, though our focus will be on the factors that contribute to the emergence and subsequent recalibration of visual–postural coupling. Specifically, we stress the reciprocity between perception and action and highlight the importance of experience in markedly changing and then fine-tuning the coupling between vision and postural control. The significance of self-produced locomotor experience for revealing (and facilitating the use of) increasingly specific patterns of visual information for postural control is a central tenet of this chapter. Our aim is to organize prior work on the development of visual–postural coupling into a coherent set of findings to set the stage for the next round of research and theorizing on this important issue. Given the centrality of postural control in all behavioral development (Reed, 1989) and the insights that research on visual–postural coupling can provide on the growth of perception–action coupling, not to mention the clinical implications of this type of work (e.g., Paulus, Straube, & Brandt, 1984, 1987; Wade & Jones, 1997; Wann, Mon-Williams, & Rushton, 1998), our aim is very timely.

## What is Visual Proprioception?

At least three broad sources of information are required to maintain or change one's orientation to the environment. The first is information about the layout of the environment – where are objects, surfaces, people, and events relative to each other? The second is information about the positions and movements of the body parts relative to each other, and the third is information specifying the relation between the two former sources of information, that is, information about the positions and movements of the body and body parts relative to the environment. Drawing on the seminal work of James Gibson (1958, 1966), David Lee (1978) suggested that the term *exteroception* be used to refer to the first source of information about the relations among environmental features, that *proprioception* be used to refer to the second source of information about the position and movements of the body parts relative to each other, and that the term *exproprioception* be used to refer to the relation between the two.

From the distinctions made among the three sources of information, it is apparent that there is not a one-to-one match between each perceptual system and the information that it provides. Rather, there is redundancy across perceptual systems in the information available for movement control (for an alternative viewpoint see Stoffregen & Bardy, 2001). However, Lee and his colleagues (e.g., Lee & Lishman, 1975, 1977) have argued that vision provides by far the richest source of exteroceptive and exproprioceptive information, perhaps accounting for why many argue that it dominates the other perceptual systems in perceptual judgments, motor control, and motor learning (e.g., Posner, Nissen, & Klein, 1976; Rock & Harris, 1967).

Gibson (1966) originally coined the term "visual proprioception" to draw attention to vision's ability to provide information about self-movement above and beyond that traditionally associated with the kinesthetic (somatosensory) and vestibular systems. It is relevant to note here that visual proprioception would be referred to as visual exproprioception using Lee's terminology, though to maintain consistency with much of the research in this area, we will adopt Gibson's terminology in this chapter. The point is relevant because it highlights a fundamental distinction between vision and the somatosensory and vestibular systems – vision always provides information about self-motion that is relative to the physical features of the environment (exproprioceptive information), whereas the other systems can provide information that exclusively reflects self-motion (proprioceptive information). This notion is easier to understand if one considers that the visual system provides an external frame of reference for movement detection and control.

The importance of the visual frame of reference for general orientation in space is supported by the strong bias that a tilted frame or mirror can exert on an observer's perception of upright (see Rock, 1992, for a brief review of much of this work), as well as the increase in postural sway seen when a frame is oscillated from side to side in front of an observer (e.g., Wapner & Witkin, 1950; Witkin & Wapner, 1950). Thus, the visual scene provides a coordinate system within which the positions of the self and environmental features are referenced. The notion of a frame of reference is useful to distinguish visual proprioception from one's ability to detect that something in the environment has moved, both of which can be understood relative to Gibson's concept of optical flow (e.g., Gibson, 1979). When a feature of the environment moves, there is a local change in the optical pattern of light rays registered by the eye. In other words, only a portion of the optical array sampled by the eye flows across the retina. In contrast, when the head moves, either during turning or postural sway or body transport, the entire visual frame of reference flows across the retina. The direction and velocity of the flow specifies an observer's direction and velocity of motion.

These global patterns of optical flow have a distinct structure to them during locomotion – a structure that is not uniform across the visual field (see figure 2.1). For example, they assume a radial (or expanding) structure in the central visual field, much like a starburst pattern, and a lamellar (or parallel) structure in the visual periphery (Cutting, 1986; Koenderink & van Doorn, 1981), like the lines of longitude on a globe (Stoffregen, 1986), when the observer's line of sight spatially coincides with the direction of motion, what Gibson (1966) referred to as the "focus of expansion." However, different patterns of optical flow will be experienced if the direction of gaze changes during locomotion (Bardy, Warren, & Kay, 1999). Furthermore, the velocity of

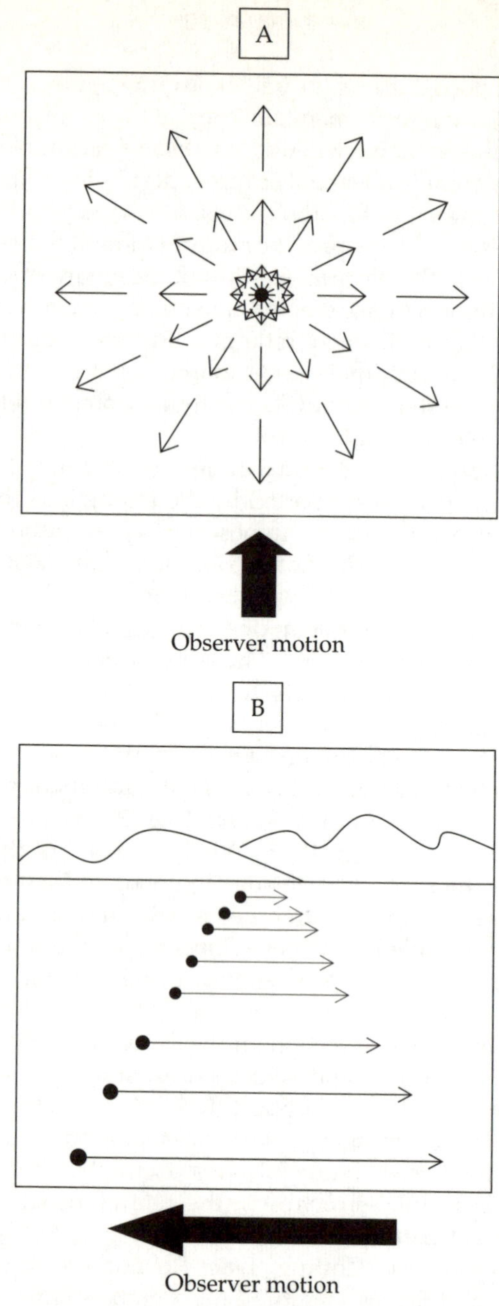


**Figure 2.1** Radial optical flow (A) presented to the central visual field and lamellar optical flow (B) presented to the peripheral visual field when the head is aligned with the direction of locomotion (from Campos et al., 2000. Copyright © 2000 by Lawrence Erlbaum Associates, Inc. Reprinted with permission).

optical flow is not uniform across the visual field. It increases with increasing eccentricity from the focus of expansion. The slowest points are in the radially structured flow and the fastest points are in the lamellar structure, peaking at 90 degrees from the direction of gaze.

Thus, as an observer sways or moves through the environment, changes in the optical array give rise to patterns of optical flow that can be picked up by the visual system. Such patterns provide a visual complement to the internally generated information about locomotion provided by the somatosensory and vestibular systems (Gibson, 1966, 1979).

## Assessing Perceptual Contributions to Postural Control

Two basic paradigms have been used to assess how the various sensory inputs contribute to postural control – *intersensory conflict* and *sensory restriction*. A conflict between visual, vestibular, and somatosensory information is created in the former paradigm to determine if one source of information can override the others. Two subparadigms can be identified within this general paradigm – the *moving-platform paradigm* (e.g., Nashner & McCollum, 1985) and the *optical flow paradigm* (e.g., Bardy, Marin, Stoffregen, & Bootsma, 1999) (see figures 2.2 and 2.3 for cartoons of these two paradigms). The moving-platform paradigm is typically used to observe how posture is controlled with respect to a sudden displacement of the support surface. The participant stands on a platform that is rotated or shifted forward and backward. A conflict can be created between the somatosensory inputs from the ankle joints and the inputs from the visual and vestibular systems by rotating the platform in the direction of body sway.

This conflict can be understood if one considers that the primary somatosensory contribution to upright postural control comes from the ankle joints (Nashner & Berthoz, 1978). When we sway forward the muscles at the back of the ankle are stretched, and when we sway backwards the muscles at the front of the ankle are stretched. However, if the platform rotates in the direction of body sway, the angle between the foot and the shank does not change and the stretch receptors in the muscles surrounding the ankle joint are not activated. In such a circumstance, the inputs from the ankle are discordant with inputs from the visual and vestibular systems and the individual is forced to use the latter systems to maintain an upright position. It should be noted that

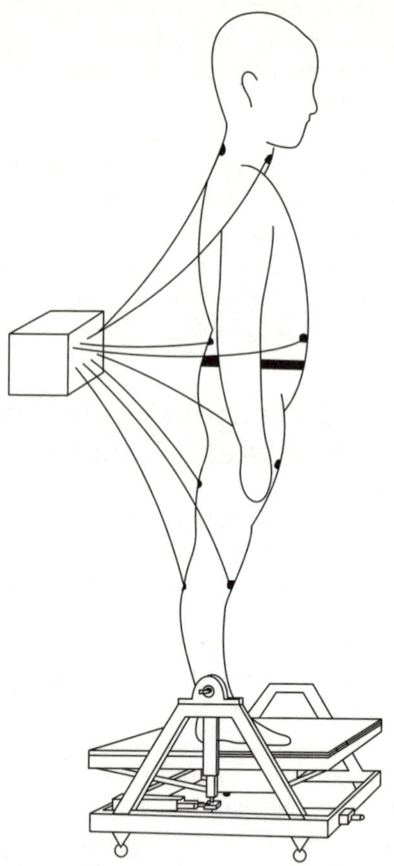

**Figure 2.2** Depiction of the moving-platform paradigm. Postural control is studied with respect to sudden translations (forward–backward) and rotations (up–down) of the support surface (from Woollacott, Shumway-Cook, & Williams, 1989. Copyright © 1989 by University of South Carolina Press. Reprinted with permission).

postural control in the seated position could also be tested in this paradigm, though the location of the relevant somatosensory inputs is different from standing.

The optical flow paradigm also uses a perturbation to assess postural control. However, unlike the mechanical perturbation in the moving-platform paradigm, the perturbation is induced by moving a visual framework around a stationary observer such that information about self-motion from the visual system is placed in conflict with information from the other perceptual systems.

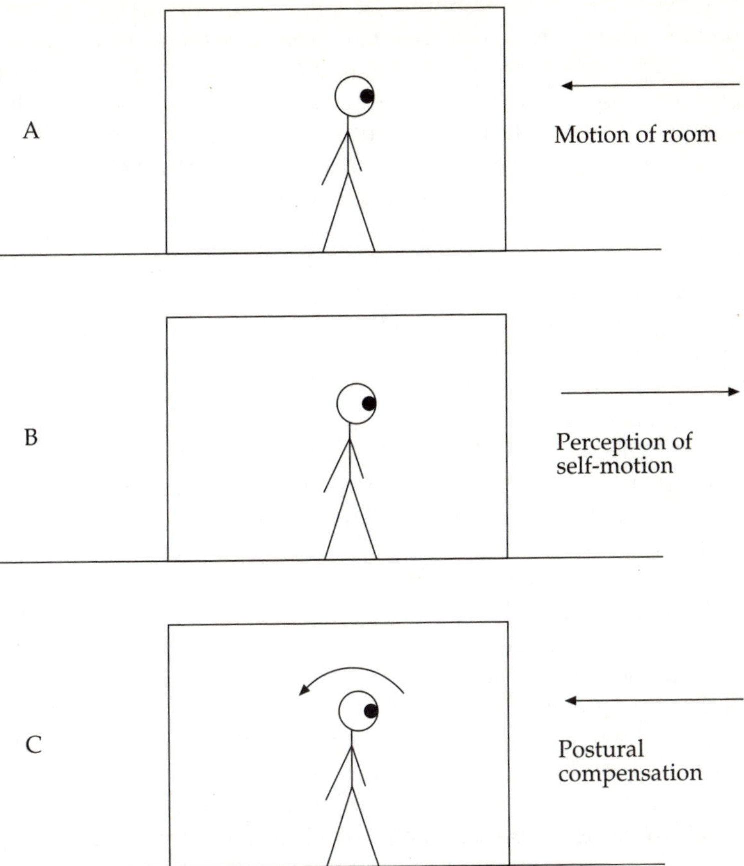


**Figure 2.3** The moving room is commonly used to assess postural compensation to a moving visual scene in the optical flow paradigm. When the room moves toward the observer (A), self-motion in the opposite direction is perceived (B) and the observer compensates by moving the body in the same direction as the room (from Campos et al., 2000. Copyright © 2000 by Lawrence Erlbaum Associates, Inc. Reprinted with permission).

The visual system receives information specifying self-motion whereas the vestibular and somatosensory systems provide information specifying stasis. Typically, the visual framework consists of a drum or a rectangular box (room), although computer-generated displays that are projected onto screens or monitors have been used recently to simulate optical flow in this paradigm (Andersen & Dyre, 1989; Dijkstra, Schöner, & Gielen, 1994; Jouen,

Lepecq, Gapenne, & Bertenthal, 2000). It is important to note that one can also use this paradigm to create a discrepancy within the visual system by moving one part of the optical array but not another. We will return to this point in the discussion of the contribution of central and peripheral vision to postural control.

The sensory restriction paradigm is quite different from the intersensory conflict paradigm in that it requires the participant to stand quietly for a period of time while the inputs available for postural control are systematically eliminated until only vestibular inputs remain (Woollacott & Shumway-Cook, 1990). Not surprisingly, it is the availability of visual information that is usually manipulated in this paradigm.

The two major paradigms can also be combined so that two perceptual systems receive discordant information while the third is eliminated. However, regardless of the variations of the basic paradigms, it is important to note that they provide only limited insights into how the various inputs are weighted and used when all these inputs are available and concordant. Moreover, the implicit premise of these paradigms is that the perceptual systems work antagonistically to provide veridical information for the control of action, with the system offering the "best" information for a particular task and context tending to dominate the others. Stoffregen and Bardy (2001) have argued strongly against this notion, suggesting instead that the perceptual systems operate cooperatively by tuning into higher-order patterns of information across stimulus energies. It will be interesting to see whether this idea gains support in the research community.

Ultimately, it is necessary to assimilate findings from a number of convergent research operations to determine with confidence the separate contributions made by the perceptual systems to postural control (e.g., Ashmead & McCarty, 1991). We would also do well to remember that it is the nature of the integration among these various systems that likely holds the key to understanding the perceptual regulation of posture (Stoffregen & Bardy, 2001; Wade & Jones, 1997).

## Vision's Role in Adult Postural Control

### *Vision vs. the other systems*

According to Lee and his colleagues (e.g., Lee & Lishman, 1975, Lishman & Lee, 1973), when all sensory inputs are available, vision typically dominates the other perceptual systems in adult postural control (and motor control in general). The primacy of vision likely stems from the richness of the expproprioceptive information it provides for motor control and its ability to provide a global frame of reference for orientation in space. In addition, the somatosensory system has some important limitations. For example, it can only sample limited parts of the environment at an instant in time and it is subject to drift in the absence of vision (Craske, 1967; Harris, 1965; Paillard & Brouchon, 1968) – the felt position of the whole body or body parts can shift over time when vision is not available. Moreover, the somatosensory system undergoes considerable change during growth and maturation rendering the inputs from the system unfamiliar and in need of continual calibration. The vestibular system is also limited because it appears to be more sensitive to movements that are higher in frequency than those associated with standing normally (Birren, 1945; Howard, 1986) and less sensitive overall than the visual or somatosensory systems. Hence, vision is thought to take the leading role in the development of a new posture or skill. Presumably, it plays the role of calibrating or tuning the somatosensory (and possibly vestibular) system so that control can ultimately be exercised independently of vision. Though Lee and his colleagues have recently championed this notion, the idea can be traced back as far as Stratton (1896).

## Central and peripheral vision in postural control

There is considerable controversy about the role of central and peripheral vision in postural control. There are at least two reasons for this controversy. First, researchers have tended to confuse experiments on *vection* (the perception of self-motion assessed by verbal report) with experiments on postural compensation to imposed optical flow. At first blush, one might assume that postural compensation to imposed optical flow is logically dependent on vection; however, this assumption has been questioned recently (Paulus et al., 1984; Straube, Krafczyk, Paulus, & Brandt, 1994). The second problem is the widely disparate procedures that have been used by researchers interested in central and peripheral vision. One of the most troubling differences is in the sizes of the central and peripheral visual field that have been stimulated, which have varied in the case of central vision from 1 degree of visual angle (approximately the size of the fovea) to over 60 degrees of visual angle, with the peripheral visual field varying concomitantly. Many other parameters vary among experiments.

## VECTION FROM IMPOSED OPTICAL FLOW

It is beyond the scope of this chapter to cover the work on vection in detail and an excellent review of much of the early work in this area can be found in Dichgans and Brandt (1978). However, it must be noted before proceeding further that the majority of research on vection has not assessed postural compensation to imposed optical flow. Nevertheless, many researchers have assumed that vection experiments are informative about the role of vision in postural control.

The typical experiment on vection assesses the subjective perception of self-motion when an observer is stationary within a continuously moving visual field. A variety of different moving visual fields have been used, including rotating drums (e.g., Dichgans & Brandt, 1978), rooms in which optical flow is projected onto the walls (e.g., Berthoz, Pavard, & Young, 1975), and video monitors that display optical flow (Johansson, 1977). The overwhelming majority of this research has shown that stimulation of the peripheral visual field leads to a much more compelling sense of self-motion than stimulation of the central visual field.

Brandt and colleagues (e.g., Paulus et al., 1984; Paulus, Straube, Krafczyk, & Brandt, 1989) have identified a number of parameters that can influence the visual perception of self-motion, including the overall structure of the three-dimensional environment, the size and contrast of objects, the density (spatial frequency) of moving texture, the distance between the observer and features of the environment, whether the moving texture is in the foreground or background of the moving field, the velocity with which optical texture moves across the retina, the density (spatial frequency) of optical texture, the size of the visual field stimulated, motion parallax, thresholds for the detection of self and object motion, illumination, accommodation, visual acuity, and general oculomotor performance. Failure to control for many of these factors has contributed to the uncertainty surrounding the role of central and peripheral vision in the subjective perception of self-motion.

## POSTURAL COMPENSATION TO IMPOSED OPTICAL FLOW

Postural compensation is actually measured in a variation of the optical flow paradigm used to assess vection. This is typically done by noting the degree of body lean associated with a particular pattern and velocity of optical flow. Using this paradigm, Lestienne, Soechting, and Berthoz (1977) have shown that the amplitude of the postural displacement to a continuous, linearly moving optical texture presented to the visual periphery increases as the density of the moving texture, the size of the moving texture, and the velocity of the moving texture increase. Flückiger and Baumberger (1988) have reported that the latency of the postural reaction to a continuously moving optical flow is much shorter when the flow is projected onto the ground than in other locations of the environment – a finding that is perhaps not surprising given that most of the optical flow one encounters when moving through a terrestrial environment comes from the ground.

Another way to assess postural compensation to imposed optical flow is to measure the degree of entrainment or coupling between the visual simulation and postural sway. This is usually done in the moving-room paradigm where the cross-correlation between the room movement and postural sway often serves as a measure of such entrainment. The major difference between research on visual–postural coupling vs. research on vection or postural compensation to continuous, unidirectional optical flows is that the optical flows are made to oscillate over a period of time and the amplitude and velocity of the optical flows are typically below thresholds required to reach conscious awareness. Reference was made earlier to Lee and Lishman's (1975) experiment, which was one of the first to show a high degree of coupling between postural sway and room movement. However, Stoffregen (1985, 1986) has provided by far the best insights into the extent to which oscillations presented to the central and peripheral visual field lead to visual–postural coupling.

Stoffregen (1985) presented radial and lamellar optical flow to the central and peripheral visual fields of his participants. This was accomplished by independently oscillating either the front or side walls or the whole room while the participant stood in front of either the front wall or a side wall and the head was oriented toward that wall or turned 90 degrees to face the other wall. In addition, a frame inside the room allowed portions of the walls to be occluded. As mentioned earlier, this particular technique creates a conflict between the visual information specifying postural sway and the somatosensory and vestibular information, which specify no sway. However, it also creates a discrepancy between the information specifying postural sway in the central and peripheral visual fields.

The results were quite clear in showing that global optical flow from the whole-room movement led to the highest degree of coupling between postural sway and room movement. The cross-correlation between the postural sway time series (measured by a potentiometer attached to the participant) and the moving-room times series was 0.49. The interesting finding was that flow structure interacted with the part of the visual field exposed such that the lamellar flow resulted in the greatest degree of coupling, although the coupling was higher when lamellar flow was presented to the peripheral (cross-correlation = 0.45) than to the central visual field (cross-correlation = 0.24). Radial optical flow produced a small degree of coupling when presented to the central visual field (cross-correlation = 0.25), but led to no coupling when presented to the periphery (see figure 2.1 for a reminder of the distinction between radial and lamellar optical flow). Furthermore, the coupling generally increased as the size of the visual field stimulated increased.

Because the velocities of the radial and lamellar flows were necessarily different in the first series of experiments, Stoffregen (1986) subsequently tested whether the failure of radial optical flow to produce postural compensation when presented to the periphery of the visual field resulted from the elements of the flow being below the thresholds for motion detection in the retinal periphery. Contrary to prediction, visual–postural coupling decreased in all of the central and peripheral conditions when the optical flow velocity was above the conscious threshold for motion detection and participants reported a perception of room movement as opposed to self-movement. This finding contrasts sharply with the linear relation between one's perception of self-motion velocity and the velocity of a unidirectional, peripheral optical flow that has been reported in the vection literature (Dichgans & Brandt, 1978; Lestienne et al., 1977).

## SELF-GENERATED SWAY WITH STATIC CENTRAL AND PERIPHERAL OPTICAL TEXTURE

The final set of findings relevant to understanding the contribution of the central and peripheral visual field to postural control comes from research that has used the sensory restriction paradigm. The basic paradigm measures spontaneous postural sway when static optical texture is available in a part of the central or peripheral visual field, in contrast to the previous methods where optical flow is imposed on the individual. For example, Paulus et al. (1984) reported that spontaneous sway when viewing a textured wall was lower when 30 degrees of the central visual field was available than when 30 degrees of the peripheral visual field was available, suggesting that the central visual field was better suited to regulating postural sway. The findings were particularly evident for lateral (side-to-side) sway compared to fore–aft sway though, interestingly, they were contrary to previous research using a strobe-light technique, which had shown the superiority for peripheral vision for postural control (Amblard & Carblanc, 1978, 1980).

However, subsequent experiments confirmed the superiority of central vision for postural stabilization (Paulus et al., 1989; Straube et al., 1994), though there is some evidence that when somatosensory information is made less reliable by having participants stand on a foam pad, peripheral vision can be more effective than central vision for regulating fore–aft sway (Nougier, Bard, Fleury, & Teasdale, 1997). While this issue remains to be resolved, the weight of evidence suggests that central vision is effective for the control of lateral and fore–aft sway, whereas peripheral vision is effective only for the control of fore–aft sway and less so than central vision. The general superiority of central vision noted in these experiments is thought to reflect the lower thresholds for motion detection found near the fovea relative to the retinal periphery.

## *What can we conclude so far?*

Vision plays a very important and perhaps dominant role in postural control. Adults appear able to use both the central and peripheral visual field to maintain stability. Moving visual scenes create the most efficacious conscious perception of self-motion when they result in the continuous projection of lamellar optical flow to the visual periphery. Similarly, continuous linear flow presented to the periphery of the visual field (either to the lower half or the sides) can induce a sustained body tilt, with the magnitude of tilt increasing as the velocity of flow increases. The highest degree of entrainment between optical flow and postural sway occurs when lamellar optical flows that are of low amplitude and low frequency are oscillated in the periphery of the visual field.

Though central vision might be able to provide greater stabilization of stationary upright posture, the flexibility to use information from either central or peripheral vision is likely to be what provides us with our remarkable capacity for adaptability and resourcefulness. For example, the ability to rely on peripheral optical flow for postural control during locomotion frees central vision to engage in other tasks required to effectively control locomotion, such as steering around obstacles and detecting whether surfaces afford support (E. J. Gibson & Schmuckler, 1989; J. J. Gibson, 1966, 1979), or in other tasks that can be done in parallel with locomotion, like reading a book or inspecting an object in the hand. Similarly, the latter two tasks can be done while stationary if postural stability is maintained on the basis of information in peripheral optical flow.

The ability to differentiate and make use of the specificity of flow information for controlling different tasks concurrently is a hallmark of efficiency in motor performance (Schmuckler & Gibson, 1989) and efficiency is assumed by many to be a consistent goal of all behavior (Diedrich & Warren, 1995; Hoyt & Taylor, 1981; Riccio & Stoffregen, 1988; Sparrow & Newell, 1998; Stoffregen et al., 1999). Though efficiency is typically not discussed with respect to perceptual processes, many would argue that becoming skillful is critically dependent on searching for the minimum information necessary to support effective performance so that attentional resources can be deployed in a flexible manner during the control of action (e.g., Abernethy, 1993; Gibson & Pick, 2000). The concepts of specificity and efficiency will be very relevant to the second half of this chapter where we describe research on the development of visual proprioception and propose an explanation for infants' ability to differentiate central-radial and peripheral-lamellar optical flow for postural control. We will argue that infants must learn to use peripheral-lamellar optical flow for postural control and that such learning is facilitated by the onset of self-produced locomotion.

## The Development of Visual Proprioception

### *Historical and theoretical context*

Gibson did not discuss the origins of visual proprioception when he first proposed that it provided an important source of information for the perception and control of self-motion. Yet, an assumption in the Gibsonian perspective is that perceptual competence is observable quite early in life, even though such competence is subject to considerable improvement as the child or adult learns to differentiate those aspects of the stimulus array that are most relevant to the control of action. It is perhaps not surprising, then, that much of the early work on visual proprioception aimed to determine the earliest age at which the phenomenon could be demonstrated.

The role of experience in the origins and subsequent development of visual proprioception has been of central importance in both earlier and later studies, though, surprisingly, few of these studies have actually manipulated experience. Rather, when age-related differences were found, they were simply attributed to variations in experience. One of the notable exceptions to this general tendency was a study by Higgins, Campos, and Kermoian (1996) that examined the role of locomotor experience in infants' ability to use central-radial and peripheral-lamellar optical flow for postural control. As this study is integral to our interpretation of the processes underlying developmental changes in visual proprioception, we will show in this section of the chapter how it stands out from other studies in the area and discuss its implications at length in the final section of the chapter.

## A THEORETICAL CAVEAT

In the previous section it was noted that vision often takes a lead role in the control of action, particularly during the early stages of skill acquisition when information from the somatosensory system is presumed to be unfamiliar and therefore less reliable to the learner. Based on this conclusion, it is generally well accepted that young children (under the age of 6 or 7 years) are reliant on visual information for postural control (Assaiante & Amblard, 1992; Lee & Aronson, 1974; Woollacott, Debû, & Mowatt, 1987; Woollacott & Shumway-Cook, 1990), with reliance decreasing as the visual system calibrates the other perceptual systems for postural control. However, it is prudent to note that some research has shown that children, unlike adults, do not sway appreciably more with their eyes closed than with their eyes open (Ashmead & McCarty, 1991; Odenrick & Sandstedt, 1984; Riach & Hayes, 1987).

At first blush, the latter findings appear to undermine the notion that young children are reliant on visual information for postural control. However, it is likely that the larger sway amplitudes seen in children compared to adults at least partially explain the finding. In other words, children already sway closer to their functional limit than adults, such that if they increased their sway to the same relative extent as adults, they might fall or have to take a step (Odenrick & Sandstedt, 1984; Nougier, Bard, Fleury, &

Teasdale, 1998). Moreover, even if children are capable of controlling posture effectively on the basis of somatosensory and vestibular information, it is likely that vision dominates the other perceptual systems when it is available (Woollacott et al., 1987). We will review several studies in this section that claim to support such a conclusion. Nevertheless, we should keep in mind that the ability to regulate posture on the basis of visual proprioception is not an all-or-none phenomenon, but instead is a skill that shows continual developmental change across the childhood years (Higgins et al., 1996; Nougier et al., 1998; Woollacott & Shumway-Cook, 1990; Zernicke, Gregor, & Cratty, 1982). Accounting for such change is an important theoretical undertaking.

#### A METHODOLOGICAL CAVEAT

Though the overwhelming majority of research with infants and young children has used the optical flow paradigm to assess vision's role in the control of posture, comparisons across experiments are often quite difficult to make because of differences in the parameters that have been used in each experiment. In the moving-room paradigm, for example, there are differences in the size of the room, the optical texture on the walls (e.g., polka dots, vertical stripes, marble patterns), the amplitude and velocity of room movement, and the way in which postural compensation is assessed. Unfortunately, while the effects of some of these variations have been examined in the adult vection literature, no attempt has been made to systematically examine their effects in the moving-room paradigm, especially with children. It is important to keep this caveat in mind as we describe developmental research on visual proprioception because procedural differences among experiments might lead to spurious conclusions about the developmental course of this important skill. However, where appropriate, we will highlight the relevant methods in the to-be-described experiments to facilitate the comparison process.

### *The origins of responsiveness to global optical flow*

#### POSTURAL SWAY MAGNITUDE AS A FUNCTION OF GLOBAL OPTICAL FLOW

Lee and Aronson (1974) were the first to examine visual proprioception in young children. Their study is one of the most widely cited as showing that visual information overrides vestibular and somatosensory information in the early stages of acquiring postural control, and its basic procedure has been replicated many times in developmental research on visual proprioception. In the study, 13- to 16-month-old infants, who had between 1 and 22 weeks of walking experience, were tested in a room that swung either toward or away from them over a distance of 94 cm and at a maximum velocity of 40 cm/sec. It is relevant to note here that the amplitude and velocity of room movement did not simulate the global optical flow that an infant would experience while standing and swaying but, instead, simulated the optical flow that would be experienced when falling or moving rapidly. The results clearly showed that this type of perturbation had a pronounced effect on the infant's ability to maintain balance. They showed postural compensation on 82 percent of trials – 26 percent of responses were classified as sways, 23 percent as staggers, and 33 percent as falls.

Researchers were quick to follow up on the original work by Lee and Aronson (1974). Using a smaller room that moved a smaller amplitude but with approximately the same velocity, Butterworth and Hicks (1977) replicated Lee and Aronson's findings with infants who ranged in age between 12.5 and 17 months and had between 0.5 and 6.5 months of walking experience. Moreover, postural compensation was also found when infants stood facing the side wall so that lamellar optical flow was presented to the central visual field, although the infants were less perturbed in this condition than when facing the front wall. (Stoffregen, 1985, 1986, used a similar procedure with adults except that his participants faced the front wall and turned their heads to face the side wall.)

The second experiment reported by Butterworth and Hicks (1977) was particularly interesting because it showed that standing experience was not a prerequisite to demonstrating postural compensation in the moving room. Both younger infants (mean age = 10.9 months), who had no standing experience, and older infants (mean age = 15.8 months), who did have standing experience, showed postural compensation when sitting facing the front and side wall, though the magnitude of sway was attenuated in sitting compared to standing, as one might expect. The likelihood of observing a postural compensation was higher in the younger group, suggesting to Butterworth and Hicks that the ability to resist the visual perturbation from the moving room increased with age and experience.

Pope (1981, as cited by Butterworth & Pope, 1981) also provided evidence to suggest that vision has a proprioceptive function prior to the onset of standing. Using procedures almost identical to those of Butterworth and Hicks, he reported that even 2- and 3-month-old infants (who were seated in a chair that provided support for the trunk, but not the head) made directionally appropriate head movements in response to whole-room movement on 63 percent of trials. Furthermore, Pope also reported that the amount of sway in response to room movement decreased with age.

Despite the aforementioned findings, the conclusion that vision has a proprioceptive function prior to the onset of standing appears to be somewhat specific to the nature of the optical flow presented to the infants and the posture in which they are tested (and perhaps other procedural variables). For example, Brandt, Wenzel, and Dichgans (1976, as cited in Dichgans & Brandt, 1978) reported that postural sway to simulated roll motions (the visual field in front of the observer was rotated) was not observed in sitting children between the ages of 6 and 12 months. In contrast, children between 2 and 5 years of age were markedly influenced by simulated roll motion, while the postural sway was increasingly moderated between 5 and 15 years of age and into adulthood. Thus, certain types of visual proprioception seem to be functional prior to the onset of standing, but not others.

Butterworth and Cicchetti (1978) also reported findings suggesting that visual proprioception is posture specific and dependent on experience. They found that differently aged groups of infants with Down's syndrome (DS) were as responsive to whole-room movement as typically developing infants (who were matched with the DS infants in terms of standing experience) when tested while standing. Moreover, the degree of postural sway declined as a function of standing experience in both the DS and typically developing infants. As both the typically developing and DS groups were comprised of subgroups with different amounts of standing experience, these data provide some of the best evidence that experience leads to improvements in the ability to resist the perturbing effects of imposed optical flow. However, younger groups of DS infants, who were matched with typically developing infants in terms of sitting experience, showed much less postural sway than the typically developing infants when tested in the sitting posture. Again, experience was related to a decrease in postural sway in the typically developing infants – the less proficient sitters in the typically developing group were literally bowled over by the simulated optical flow. Surprisingly, though, the same DS infants who had been tested in the sitting posture swayed as much as the typically developing infants when both groups were tested while standing with support. Thus, the detection or use of optical flow was highly dependent upon the posture in which the DS infants were tested. They were responsive when tested while standing with support but not when tested while sitting.

## THE COUPLING BETWEEN POSTURAL SWAY AND GLOBAL OPTICAL FLOW

A more recent study by Delorme, Frigon, and Lagacé (1989) used an oscillating room to test the coupling between whole-room movement and postural sway. Over a 60 sec period, the room oscillated sinusoidally with an amplitude of 12.5 cm (each direction) and an average velocity of 12.5 cm/sec (i.e., at 0.5 Hz). Five groups of children, whose average ages were 7.5, 9.9, 13, 27.7, and 48.6 months, were tested while standing with support from a T-bar. The mean amplitude and standard deviation of sway (as indexed by strain gauges mounted at the base of the T-bar), as well as the coupling between the time series of room movement and postural sway, revealed that all infants swayed in response to the room movement.

Frequency analysis indicated that most infants showed a peak sway frequency that matched the room movement frequency on at least one of two trials. The cross-correlation between postural sway and room movement increased from 7.5 months of age to 9.9 months of age (where it peaked), and then declined to an intermediate level from 13 to 27.7 to 48.6 months of age. The cross-correlations were 0.46, 0.75, 0.54, 0.68, and 0.65 for the five age groups, respectively. Thus, the least coupling was found in the infants who could only stand with support, suggesting that the ability to use visual proprioception for postural control while standing with support is less well developed in these infants. This conclusion must be accepted cautiously, however, because the lower cross-correlation in the youngest group might simply have reflected a higher degree of distractibility in this group during the 60 sec trials.

Bertenthal, Rose, and Bai (1997) have also used an oscillating room to assess changes in the coupling between postural sway (when the baby was seated in a small plastic chair that rested on a force plate) and global optical flow. Five-, 7-, 9-, and 13-month-old infants were tested with two room movement frequencies (0.3 and 0.6 Hz) and two movement amplitudes (9 cm and 19 cm), resulting in velocities that varied from 5.4 to 21.6 cm/sec. Their data revealed systematic coupling between postural sway and room movement as early as 5 months of age, though the degree of coupling increased as a function of age, frequency of room movement, and amplitude of room movement. The coupling between room movement and postural sway peaked at 9 months of age (where the cross-correlation was 0.3), and then tended to level off between 9 and 13 months of age.

However, the temporal lag between the onset of wall motion and the onset of postural sway showed a sudden drop from 5 months of age to 7 months of age in a constant-frequency condition and from 7 months of age to 9 months of age in a variable-frequency condition. In addition, the magnitude of postural sway (as measured by the root-mean-square) showed a nonlinear developmental trajectory, decreasing from 5 to 7 months of age and then increasing from 7 to 9 to 13 months of age. Finally, the degree of coupling was higher when the room moved at 0.6 Hz compared to 0.3 Hz and when it moved 18 cm compared to 9 cm.

## A SUMMARY AND INTERPRETATION OF THE FINDINGS

Taken together, the findings suggest that infants show greater sway in response to global optical flow in the early acquisition of a new posture, but that their ability to resist the perturbing effects of optical flow increases as experience with the new posture increases. In other words, with experience, infants are better able to resolve the discrepancy between information from the visual system that is discordant with that from the vestibular and somatosensory systems. Recently, Foster, Sveistrup, and Woollacott (1996) have lent support to this suggestion by reporting that postural sway in response to a 48 cm/sec forward-and-then-backward room movement increased as infants progressed from an ability to sit independently to an ability to pull to stand, only to decrease thereafter as the children accrued walking experience. However, similar to Lee and Aronson's (1974) findings, the newly walking infants had the largest number of balance losses. Unfortunately, the younger infants were tested while standing with support, so it cannot be concluded with certainty that the newly walking infants were more responsive to the optical flow than the infants who could only sit or pull to stand and were tested while standing with support. However, Schmuckler and Gibson (1989) have also reported that the magnitude of the postural disturbance caused by imposed global optical flow decreases as a function of standing and walking experience.

When the degree of coupling between room movement and postural sway is quantified over an extended period of time (as is the case with most of the adult research), and infants are tested standing with support or sitting in a small chair, the coupling appears to systematically increase up to about 9 months of age; at 13 months of age it stayed at approximately the same level in the case of Bertenthal et al. (1997), whereas for Delorme et al. (1989) it declined to an intermediate level. It is intriguing to note that the coupling between global optical flow and postural sway peaks at approximately 9 months of age, as at this age infants are typically proficient (or at least are becoming proficient) at moving themselves through the environment. As such, they have had the opportunity to pair their own movement with patterns of optical flow that are similar in velocity and amplitude to the optical flows that have been simulated in developmental research. Shortly, we will discuss the role of crawling experience in helping infants to notice and use lamellar optical flow in the visual periphery for postural control; however, crawling experience may also play a role in infants' ability to use global optical flow for postural control. While we have no direct evidence to support this suggestion, we feel that it deserves mention given the consistencies between the two infant studies that have addressed the coupling between global optical flow and postural sway.

## A CAUTIONARY NOTE

At this point, it is appropriate to raise a cautionary note about the developmental research described thus far and the conclusions we have drawn. We alluded to this caution earlier in the section when we noted that much of the research on the origins of visual proprioception has stressed the importance of experience in accounting for infants' ability to resist the perturbing effects of imposed optical flow, yet few studies have appropriately manipulated experience to assess its role in the development of visual proprioception. In most studies, age and experience are confounded, leaving open the possibility that maturational factors account for some, and perhaps all, of the changes that have been noted.

Second, while it does appear that infants and young children are most vulnerable to the perturbing effects of large and fast optical flows during the early acquisition of a new posture, we also know that the organization of behavior is much less stable and prone to any perturbation during the formative period of skill acquisition (Anderson, 2002; Thelen & Smith, 1994). Whether the ability to resist the perturbing effects of imposed optical flow represents a developmental change in the way in which visual proprioception is used for postural control, or whether it simply provides an index of the ever-increasing stability of behavior, is at this point unknown. It also remains to be determined whether the coupling between global optical flow (within the range of amplitudes and velocities normally experienced during sitting and standing) and postural sway increases or decreases as a function of age and experience. Clearly, there is considerable scope for additional research in this area.

## *Responsiveness to central-radial and peripheral-lamellar optical flow*

### RESEARCH WITH OLDER INFANTS

Given the interest that has been devoted to the role of central and peripheral vision in adult postural control, it is not surprising that researchers have been interested in determining how infants respond to central and peripheral optical flow. Bertenthal and Bai (1989) were the first to show that standing infants (mean age = 13.9 months) showed a higher number of sways, staggers, and falls in response to global and peripheral-lamellar optical flow than to central-radial optical flow. They used the same room as Bertenthal et al. (1997), but moved the front and side walls independently to simulate central and peripheral optical flow. The front wall subtended a visual angle of 48 × 48 degrees at its farthest location from the infant and 62 × 62 degrees at its nearest location, and the walls moved 41 cm in a single direction each trial at an average velocity of 10.16 or 20.32 cm/sec.

In a subsequent experiment, Bertenthal and Bai (1989) used a force transducer system to gather more accurate estimates of the magnitude of postural sway in 5-, 7-, and 9-month-old infants as they were exposed to global, central-radial, and peripheral-lamellar optical flow while seated in a sling. The results showed clear effects of age and condition. The largest magnitude of sway was found in the global condition, followed by the peripheral, and then the central condition. These conditions were significantly different from each other. There was a linear increase in the magnitude of sway to global and peripheral flow as a function of age, with 9-month-olds showing greater sway than 7-month-olds and 7-month-olds showing greater sway than 5-month-olds. The 5-month-olds were essentially unresponsive in this experiment, contrary to what was found in later studies using slightly different methodologies (e.g., Bertenthal et al., 1997;

Foster et al., 1996). Most notable in Bertenthal and Bai's (1989) study was the clear developmental shift between 7 and 9 months of age in the infants' responsiveness to peripheral-lamellar optical flow – a shift that the authors suggested might have been linked to the onset of crawling.

Following the lead of Bertenthal and Bai (1989), Higgins et al. (1996) more precisely specified that the shift in responsiveness to peripheral-lamellar optical flow occurred between 7 and 8 months of age. Using a room that had the same dimensions and approximately the same visual angles as the one used by Bertenthal and Bai (1989), but that moved a distance of 36 cm in 2 sec, Higgins et al. computed the cross-correlation between the seated infants' postural sway (as measured by force transducers under the infants' chair) and wall movement. The cross-correlation between side-wall movement and postural sway was significantly higher in the 9- and 8-month-olds than in the 7-month-olds.

The more interesting results were found in the second experiment, where 8-month-old infants who were proficient at crawling on hands and knees or moving about in wheeled walkers showed significantly higher cross-correlations between side-wall movement and postural sway than 8-month-old infants without locomotor experience (see figure 2.4). The groups showed equal responsiveness to global optical flow and equal, though slight, responsiveness to front-wall motion, suggesting that the ability to

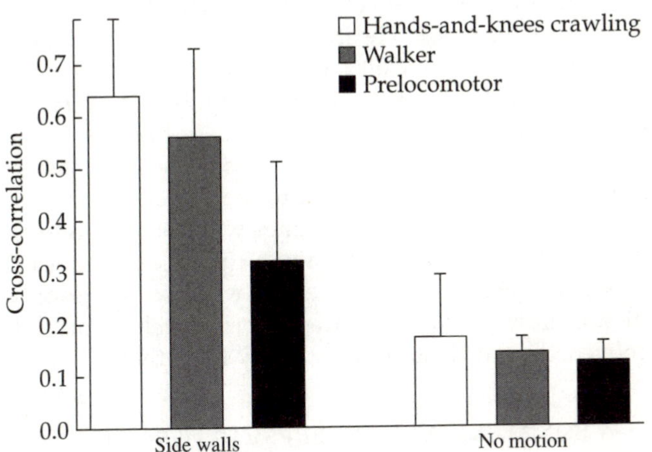


**Figure 2.4** Responsiveness to side-wall motion and no motion in the moving room as a function of locomotor status (from Campos et al., 2000. Copyright © 2000 by Lawrence Erlbaum Associates, Inc. Reprinted with permission).

discriminate peripheral-lamellar optical flow for postural control was the primary factor differentiating the locomotor from the prelocomotor infants. These findings have recently been replicated (Uchiyama, 2000). Thus, locomotor experience is associated with a transition from the use of large global optical flow patterns for postural control to smaller peripheral-lamellar optical flows.

## RESEARCH WITH YOUNGER INFANTS

The research described thus far suggests that locomotor experience markedly facilitates infants' ability to use peripheral-lamellar optical flow for postural control. However, this suggestion does not imply that infants are unresponsive to peripheral optical flow prior to the onset of locomotion. Quite to the contrary, Jouen and his colleagues (e.g., Jouen, 1988, 1990; Jouen et al., 2000) have documented very precocious responsiveness to peripheral optical flow under highly controlled conditions. For example, Jouen et al. (2000) exposed neonates (3-day-olds), who were reclined in a specially designed infant seat, with a continuously moving optical pattern to test responsiveness to peripheral optical flow. Identical pseudorandom dot patterns (23 cm wide × 18 cm high), whose angular size covered 56 degrees of each peripheral visual field, were displayed on each of two 14-inch monitors that were placed 31 cm apart and on either side of the infant's head. On each trial, the pattern was continuously displayed for 8 sec in a direction toward the infant and at one of seven physical velocities ranging from 10 cm/sec to 120 cm/sec. The infants were tested in a dark chamber and pressure-sensitive air bags (sampled at 60 Hz) measured any shift in their head position. The findings were very clear in showing that mean head pressure was greater in all experimental conditions than in motionless baseline trials. Moreover, head pressure was linearly related to the velocity of the moving patterns, a result that parallels findings with standing adults who are exposed to a continuously moving peripheral optical flow. However, the infants' responsiveness was specific to only one direction of flow – they responded appropriately to optical flow that moved toward them, but not away from them.

## A SUMMARY AND INTERPRETATION OF THE FINDINGS

Research examining whole-body postural sway has revealed a clear developmental shift in infants' compensation to peripheral-lamellar optical flow: a shift that is strongly linked to experience with self-produced locomotion. However, research examining only head movement has shown that even neonates show some type of postural compensation to peripheral optical flow under appropriately controlled conditions. Thus, as noted by Bertenthal et al. (1997), the visuomotor coordination necessary for controlling posture is functional prior to the emergence of postural control. However, the coordination between vision and posture becomes more finely tuned or reorganized as experience with self-produced movement permits specific, functional mapping of perception and action (Bertenthal et al., 1997). Jouen himself predicts that, despite his findings on neonatal responsiveness to optical flow, further developmental changes will be observed. He notes that "learning is not necessary for the emergence of optic flow sensitivity, although experience, and particularly self-produced mobility, may play a role in the subsequent development of visual postural coupling" (Jouen et al., 2000, p. 281).

Though Jouen et al. (2000) have recently reiterated the importance of self-produced motor activity in the development of visual–postural coupling, further examination of the differences between Jouen's paradigm and the moving-room paradigm can provide additional insights into the ontogeny of visual proprioception. As such, we will elaborate on these differences in the next section.

## What Leads to Improvements in Visual–Postural Coupling?

In discussing the significance of visual proprioception during infancy, George Butterworth (1992) posed a question that is as relevant to the current chapter as it is to the study of any developmental phenomena. He wondered how each new level of organization developed from the previous one. Indeed, this is perhaps the most fundamental question in the field of development. Answering it might even be viewed as the field's *raison d'être*. The question presupposes that development is a series of reorganizations of component systems and processes, with each reorganization reflecting the organism's current state as well as its prior history. But, why do things change? Why don't they simply stay the same?

There is no shortage of proposed answers to the above questions, and a trite response would posit that any one or combination of a multitude of factors could contribute to changes in physical appearance and behavior. However, some factors must be more important than others at different points during the life cycle. Our approach to the question, while acknowledging the importance of transactions between genes and environment, stresses the role played by self-produced motor activity, particularly locomotor activity, in the reorganization and refinement of behavior (e.g., Campos et al., 2000). We will outline our view on the role of self-generated experience in the development of visual proprioception in this section.

## *The reciprocity between perception and action*

Consistent with the views espoused by James Gibson and his colleagues (e.g., E. J. Gibson & Pick, 2000; J. J. Gibson, 1966, 1979), our view stresses the importance of action and movement in revealing information in the world that contributes both to control of the action or movement and to the development of perceptual, and ultimately psychological, competence. Indeed, much of the information that is essential for perceptual development cannot be obtained until appropriate action systems are functional (E. J. Gibson & Pick, 2000). With respect to the development of visual–postural coupling, there are changes in the visual system, such as improvements in accommodation, convergence, thresholds for motion detection, and general oculomotor coordination as well as systematic widening of the field of view, that must contribute to the increasing effectiveness with which information can be picked up to control motor acts like posture and locomotion.

As the visual system's ability to pick up information improves, the minimal information for inducing a postural compensation will also change (Bertenthal et al., 1997). At the same time, however, changes in motor control must also contribute to more effective pick-up of information, information which could be used to further refine control of the action system that originally allowed it to be picked up or which could be used for another purpose. Thus, perception and action are dynamically coupled in the regulation of coordinated movement. The complexity of the coupling is exacerbated by virtue of the changes in the perceptual systems and the motor system that are associated with growth and maturation. Where to begin an examination of this coupling is truly a challenge for a developmentalist, though obvious points of entry would be at periods of transition in either perceptual development, postural control, or the coupling between the two.

## *How does locomotion facilitate visual proprioceptive development?*

Transitions in the coupling between vision and posture occur in the newborn with the development of head control, in the 5-month-old with the development of trunk control, in the 7-month-old with the acquisition of hands-and-knees crawling, in the 1-year-old with the development of independent walking, and between the ages of 4 and 6 years when the child apparently learns to integrate and effectively switch attention among the various sources of information available for postural control (e.g., Higgins et al., 1996; Sveistrup & Woollacott, 1996). These transitions suggest that as the components of the perceptual and motor systems change, there is need for continual updating and reorganization of the mappings between perceptual information and motor synergies. Experience appears to be crucial in orchestrating this process. The transition in responsiveness to peripheral optical flow that Higgins et al. (1996) have linked to the onset of prone locomotion has been documented more extensively than any of the other just-mentioned transitions and it appears to be particularly robust (Bertenthal & Bai, 1989; Higgins et al., 1996; Uchiyama, 2000). But, how might locomotor experience help to reorganize visual–postural coupling? After all, posture and locomotion appear to be fairly encapsulated and independent actions.

The preliminary answer to this question is related to the much earlier-mentioned demands placed on the visual system by the act of locomotion. According to Gibson (1979), vision has three major roles during locomotion to a destination. (See Goldfield, 1995, for a specific treatment of these roles with respect to hands-and-knees crawling.) First, it allows an animal to steer an appropriate course through the clutter that is encountered in the environment. Second, it provides information that specifies whether a surface can be traversed, and, perhaps not surprisingly, there is evidence that children with various amounts of locomotor experience differ in the properties of surfaces to which they attend (Schmuckler, 1993). Finally, vision provides an essential source of information for the maintenance of postural stability during locomotion. Thus, posture and locomotion are not independent actions. In stark contrast, postural control is integral to the control of locomotion and maintaining balance has been described as the immediate challenge and focus of attention of the nascent crawler (Adolph, 1997).

The second part of the answer to the original question relates to the patterns of optical flow to which infants are exposed during prone locomotion. Because of their heavy heads and their tendency to stiffly couple motions of the limbs, trunk, and neck during independent propulsion, newly crawling infants tend to look both at the floor and at their destination (which is often a target located on the floor). If distracted by an event in the periphery, infants stop crawling and assume a side-sitting posture to examine the distraction (Higgins, 1993). As such, the newly crawling infant is consistently exposed to the continuous visible texture associated with the surface of support and to the optical flow patterns described earlier – i.e., radial optical flow in the center of the visual field and lamellar optical flow in the visual periphery when the line of sight spatially coincides with the direction of locomotion.

Consistent exposure to these patterns of optical flow may be sufficient to allow infants to differentiate radial from lamellar flow, relate lamellar optical flow in the periphery to voluntary and involuntary forward and backward movement, and functionalize peripheral-lamellar optical flow for postural control during locomotion. In addition, given the demands on the visual system during locomotion (Gibson, 1979), the locomotor infant is likely to be pressed to differentiate spatially delimited patterns of optical flow so that the various locomotor subtasks – steering, attending to characteristics of the surface, and maintaining postural control – can be accomplished successfully and efficiently. In other words, more information for steering and attending to surface characteristics can be picked up if the infant can rely on less information (i.e., information that does not fill the entire visual field, e.g., E. J. Gibson & Schmuckler, 1989) to maintain postural control.

Again, as noted earlier, the ability to differentiate and make use of the specificity of flow information for controlling different tasks concurrently is a hallmark of efficiency in motor skill development (Schmuckler & Gibson, 1989), and efficiency is assumed by many to be a consistent goal of all behavior. Differentiation of perceptual information also draws upon the notions of "education of attention" proposed by J. J. Gibson (1966) and "optimization of attention" proposed by E. J. Gibson (1969), suggesting a mechanism by which locomotor development contributes to the development of responsiveness to peripheral optical flow.

In contrast to the locomotor infant, the prelocomotor infant is not compelled to look in the direction of travel when passively transported through the environment. As a result, the prelocomotor infant is exposed to a family of global optical flow patterns and freedom to look anywhere decreases the probability of experiencing significant amounts of peripheral-lamellar optical flow. In addition, the visual stimulation associated with locomotion is imposed on the passively moved infant and is likely to be less meaningful, relative to that "obtained" by an actively locomoting infant. Gibson (1966, 1979) argued for the value of stimulation obtained during action vs. that imposed on the organism by the environment.

Furthermore, the prelocomotor infant has no need to process information about the spatial layout and self-motion simultaneously, and so there is no need to differentiate the different types and locations of optical flow. In agreement with an argument made by Stoffregen, Schmuckler, and Gibson (1987), we believe it is likely that, prior to locomotion, children are sensitive and responsive to any large-field optical motion, regardless of its location, and that differentiation of spatially delimited regions of optical flow (e.g., central vs. peripheral) develops during the process of learning to locomote. Thus, the stimulus array provides all the information necessary for the perception of self-motion (Gibson, 1979), but factors like self-motion determine whether the information will be detected and used.

## *Precocious responsiveness to peripheral optical flow*

Given the above arguments, one might wonder how we would reconcile Jouen's reports of neonatal responsiveness to peripheral optical flow with the idea that motor experience plays an important role in the ontogenetic development of visual–postural coupling. Jouen's findings may represent a classic example of what Haith (1993) and Campos et al. (2000) have referred to as the "principle of partial accomplishments," where many skills are apparent in some rudimentary form before becoming fully functional or manifesting themselves in new contexts. This principle is similar in many ways to Gottlieb's (1983) notion of "forward reference," which suggests that many prenatal and early postnatal phenomena are preparatory or anticipatory of the emergence of later behavior. Both ideas reinforce the view that development is not an all-or-none phenomenon.

The idea that there are many precursors to the emergence of mature skills is also congruent with contemporary theories of development that view behavior at any point in the lifespan as a reflection of a number of component substrates assembled by a particular task and context (Thelen & Smith, 1994; Thelen & Ulrich, 1991; Turvey & Fitzpatrick, 1993). A major assumption in this perspective is that it is extremely difficult (if not impossible) to determine when infants and children truly have acquired a competence because behavioral expression is entirely context dependent (Thelen & Smith, 1994). An excellent example is the work on infant treadmill stepping, where it has been shown that infants who would not normally step demonstrate highly coordinated, alternating stepping movements when supported with their feet in contact with a slowly moving treadmill (Thelen & Ulrich, 1991). Moreover, treadmill steps were kinematically more mature than steps taken without the treadmill and intentional steps taken shortly before the onset of walking (Thelen & Cooke, 1987). Some infants even showed steps with characteristics typically seen in mature locomotion (Thelen, Bril, & Breniere, 1992). However, treadmill stepping is *not* mature locomotion. It is simply a reflection of a necessary subcomponent of a task that is eminently more challenging and one that is, itself, highly dependent on context for its expression.

The neonate's head compensation to optical texture in the visual periphery is similar in some ways to infant treadmill stepping because it is found when infants are given adequate postural support and when there is no need to differentiate static texture in the central visual field from distally moving texture in the periphery, as is the case when responsiveness to peripheral optical flow is tested in a fully illuminated moving room. In other words, the demands on the infant are much lower when he or she is tested with postural support in a dark room or a tunnel. Thus, the responsiveness to peripheral optical flow in this context seems to represent a necessary subcomponent of whole-body postural compensation to peripheral optical flow in a moving room, but it is *not* that skill – merely a component of that skill.

The interesting question for a developmentalist is not the earliest age at which a particular competence like this can be demonstrated, because these demonstrations will always be situation or context dependent, but how and when these competencies are integrated into more sophisticated skills. There are many fascinating puzzles to solve in disentangling the relation between later skills and their precursors, including why these precursors are seen in some contexts and not others, and why they can apparently disappear even when tested in the same context. Another question that is hardly ever addressed is how the functional experiences associated with integrating competencies into higher orders of behavior lead to changes in the competencies themselves. However, we must be mindful that there might be no "real" competencies (Thelen, 2000). Rather than dissuade us though, this thought should encourage us to focus on stability and change in the behaviors and contexts that are most meaningful to the infant or child.

## *The specificity of practice/experience*

An intriguing finding that is particularly relevant to a discussion of the importance of context in development is the high degree of specificity in skill acquisition. Karen Adolph has provided some excellent examples recently to support this notion. For example, she has shown that what infants learn about negotiating slopes in a crawling position shows no transfer whatsoever to the negotiation of slopes from a standing posture (e.g., Adolph, 1997). Infants must learn all over again which slopes are risky and which are not, and the learning is just as protracted as it was from the crawling posture. Similarly, Adolph (2000) has shown that infants will avoid reaching over a potentially dangerous gap in the substrate when tested in the sitting posture but not when tested in the crawling posture. In the latter case, infants plunge into the gap and must be rescued by an experimenter.

Based on the above-mentioned findings, Adolph (1997, 2000) concludes that the information for control of balance is learned from posture to posture with little to no transfer from one posture to another. Thus, the coupling between optical flow and postural control found in one posture is unlikely to generalize to other postures. As noted by Bertenthal et al. (1997), this finding is consistent with recent neuroanatomical speculations that visuomotor coordination involves the direct mapping of perceptual information onto specific motor response loci that do not show transfer to other actions (Goodale, 1988; Milner & Goodale, 1995). Thus, mappings between specific actions such as head stabilization and peripheral optical flow will have to be remapped during the learning of new actions.

How such mapping and remapping occur remains a mystery. However, if our analysis is correct, the amount of transfer from one action to another seems to depend on whether transfer is from an easier task to a more difficult task or from a more difficult task to an easier task. The very young infant's ability to respond with head movements to peripheral optical flow while reclining with support appears to show little evidence of transfer to the control of independent sitting when such control is tested in a moving room (e.g., Bertenthal & Bai, 1989). It is possible that whatever contribution sitting experience makes to the infant's ability to differentiate central and peripheral optical flow contributes minimally to the control of balance during hands-and-knees crawling. However, changes in the ability to use peripheral-lamellar optical flow during the control of prone locomotion appear to facilitate the ability to use such information in the seated posture. In other words, what is learned during prone locomotion can help to further tune or refine the visual-proprioceptive control of sitting. Though this conclusion has not been empirically validated, it seems reasonable given the data summarized in this chapter.

## Future Directions

In this chapter, we have attempted to detail what is currently known about the development of visual proprioception by highlighting research on visual–postural coupling in infants, children, and adults. It is readily apparent that much remains to be learned about the development of visual proprioception. Vision and posture appear to be coupled in the neonate, with infants showing responsiveness to peripheral optical flow; however, this ability is not found when infants are tested at later ages in different postural and environmental contexts, and only reemerges in a consistent fashion after the onset of self-produced locomotion. Why does this happen?

If our analysis is correct, the emergence of behavior at any point in the lifespan is a reflection of the multiple-component subsystems from which the behavior is assembled in concert with demands imposed on the organism by the task and context. Exactly what changes in the component subsystems and context lead to transitions in behavior is, at this time, unclear. However, what does appear to be clear is the important role of experience, particularly active, self-produced experience, in orchestrating reorganizations of component subsystems so that more sophisticated skills can emerge or so that existing skills can be maintained in the face of changing components and contexts. Thus, experience can act to tune or to reorganize behavior.

Exactly how factors like context and experience play a role in the development of visual proprioception remains to be determined. We have presented a possible scenario whereby locomotor experience allows the infant to notice and then functionalize peripheral-lamellar optical flow for postural control, but many questions remain. For example, is the acquisition of more sophisticated locomotor patterns such as skipping associated with reorganizations in visual–postural coupling, as suggested by Schmuckler (1997)? How is optical flow mapped onto postural control strategies? Is the coupling robust when the testing context is changed? What other experiences might facilitate visual–postural coupling? What changes in component subsystems contribute to changes in the visual control of posture? How specific is the learning that takes place in a particular postural and environmental context? How do changes in visual–postural coupling contribute to changes in other domains? Clearly, there is considerable scope for further research in this exciting and promising area of study.

## REFERENCES

Abernethy, B. (1993). Searching for the minimal essential information for skilled perception and action. *Psychological Research*, 55, 131–8.

Adolph, K. E. (1997). Learning in the development of infant locomotion. *Monographs of the Society for Research in Child Development*, 62 (Serial No. 251).

Adolph, K. E. (2000). Specificity of learning: Why infants fall over a veritable cliff. *Psychological Science*, 11, 290–5.

Amblard, B., & Carblanc, A. (1978). Rôle des informations fovéales et périphériques dans le maintien de l'équilibre postural chez l'homme. *Agressologie*, 19, 21–2.

Amblard, B., & Carblanc, A. (1980). Role of foveal and peripheral visual information in maintenance of postural equilibrium in man. *Perceptual and Motor Skills*, 51, 903–12.

Andersen, G. J., & Dyre, B. P. (1989). Spatial orientation from optic flow in the central visual field. *Perception and Psychophysics*, 45, 453–8.

Anderson, D. I. (2002). Do critical periods and readiness determine when to initiate sport skill learning? In F. L. Smoll & R. E. Smith (Eds.), *Children and youth in sport: A biopsychosocial perspective* (2nd ed., pp. 105–48). Dubuque, IO: Kendall/Hunt.

Anderson, D. I., Campos, J. J., Anderson, D. E., Thomas, T. D., Witherington, D., Uchiyama, I., & Barbu-Roth, M. A. (2001). The flip side of perception–action coupling: Locomotor experience and the ontogeny of visual–postural coupling. *Human Movement Science*, 20, 461–87.

Ashmead, D. H., & McCarty, M. E. (1991). Postural sway of human infants while standing in light and dark. *Child Development*, 62, 1276–87.

Assaiante, C., & Amblard, B. (1992). Peripheral vision and age-related differences in dynamic balance. *Human Movement Science*, 11, 533–48.

Bardy, B. G., Marin, L., Stoffregen, T. A., & Bootsma, R. J. (1999). Postural coordination modes considered as emergent phenomena. *Journal of Experimental Psychology: Human Perception and Performance*, 25, 1284–1301.

Bardy, B. G., Warren, W. H., & Kay, B. A. (1999). The role of central and peripheral vision in postural control during walking. *Perception and Psychophysics*, 61, 1356–68.

Bayley, N. (1969). *Manual for the Bayley scales of infant development*. New York: Psychological Corporation.

Bertenthal, B. I., & Bai, D. L. (1989). Infants' sensitivity to optic flow for controlling posture. *Developmental Psychology*, 25, 936–45.

Bertenthal, B. I., Rose, J. L., & Bai, D. L. (1997). Perception–action coupling in the development of visual control of posture. *Journal of Experimental Psychology: Human Perception and Performance*, 23, 1631–43.

Berthoz, A., Pavard, B., & Young, L. R. (1975). Perception of linear horizontal self-motion induced by peripheral vision (linearvection): Basic characteristics and visual–vestibular interactions. *Experimental Brain Research*, 23, 471–89.

Birren, J. E. (1945). Static equilibrium and vestibular function. *Journal of Experimental Psychology*, 35, 127–33.

Butterworth, G. (1992). Origins of self-perception in infancy. *Psychological Inquiry*, 3, 103–11.

Butterworth, G., & Cicchetti, D. (1978). Visual calibration of posture in normal and motor retarded Down's syndrome infants. *Perception*, 7, 513–25.

Butterworth, G., & Hicks, L. (1977). Visual proprioception and postural stability in infancy: A developmental study. *Perception*, 6, 255–62.

Butterworth, G., & Pope, M. (1981). Origine et fonction de la proprioception visuelle chez l'enfant. In S. de Schonen (Ed.), *Le Développement dans la première année* (pp. 107–28). Paris: Presses Universitaires de France.

Campos, J. J., Anderson, D. I., Barbu-Roth, M. A., Hubbard, E. M., Hertenstein, M. J., & Witherington, D. (2000). Travel broadens the mind. *Infancy*, 1, 149–219.

Craske, B. (1967). Adaptation to prisms: Change in internally registered eye-position. *British Journal of Psychology*, 58, 329–55.

Cutting, J. (1986). *Perception with an eye for motion*. Cambridge, MA: MIT Press.

Delorme, A., Frigon, J., & Lagacé, C. (1989). Infants' reactions to visual movement of the environment. *Perception*, 18, 667–73.

Dichgans, J., & Brandt, Th. (1978). Visual–vestibular interaction: Effects on self-motion perception and postural control. In R. Held, H. W. Leibowitz, & H. L. Teuber (Eds.), *Handbook of sensory physiology. Vol. 8. Perception* (pp. 755–804). Berlin: Springer.

Diedrich, F. J., & Warren, W. H. (1995). Why change gaits? Dynamics of the walk–run transition. *Journal of Experimental Psychology: Human Perception and Performance*, 21, 183–202.

Dijkstra, T. M. H., Schöner, G., & Gielen, C. C. A. M. (1994). Temporal stability of the action–perception cycle for postural control in a moving visual environment. *Experimental Brain Research*, 97, 477–86.

Flückiger, M., & Baumberger, B. (1988). The perception of an optical flow projected on the ground surface. *Perception*, 17, 633–45.

Foster, E. C., Sveistrup, H., & Woollacott, M. H. (1996). Transitions in visual proprioception: A cross-sectional developmental study of the effect of visual flow on postural control. *Journal of Motor Behavior*, 28, 101–12.

Gesell, A., & Thompson, H. (1934). *Infant behavior: Its genesis and growth.* New York: McGraw-Hill.

Gibson, E. J. (1969). *Principles of perceptual learning development*. Englewood Cliffs, NJ: Prentice-Hall.

Gibson, E. J., & Pick, A. D. (2000). *An ecological approach to perceptual learning and development*. Oxford: Oxford University Press.

Gibson, E. J., & Schmuckler, M. A. (1989). Going somewhere: An ecological and experimental approach to the development of mobility. *Ecological Psychology*, 1, 3–25.

Gibson, J. J. (1958). Visually controlled locomotion and visual orientation in animals. *British Journal of Psychology*, 49, 182–94.

Gibson, J. J. (1966). *The senses considered as perceptual systems*. Boston: Houghton-Mifflin.

Gibson, J. J. (1979). *The ecological approach to visual perception*. Boston: Houghton-Mifflin.

Goldfield, E. C. (1995). *Emergent forms: Origins and early development of human action and perception*. New York: Oxford University Press.

Goodale, M. A. (1988). Modularity in visuomotor control: From input to output. In Z. Pylyshyn (Ed.), *Computational processes in human vision: An interdisciplinary perspective* (pp. 262–85). Norwood, NJ: Ablex.

Gottlieb, G. (1983). The psychobiological approach to developmental issues. In M. Haith & J. Campos (Eds.), *Handbook of child psychology. Vol. 2. Infancy and developmental psychobiology* (4th ed., pp. 1–26). New York: Wiley.

Haith, M. M. (1993). Preparing for the 21st century: Some goals and challenges for studies of infant sensory and perceptual development. *Developmental Review*, 13, 354–71.

Harris, C. S. (1965). Perceptual adaptation to inverted, reversed, and displaced vision. *Psychological Review*, 72, 419–44.

Higgins, C. I. (1993). The origins of visual proprioception. Unpublished doctoral dissertation, University of California, Berkeley.

Higgins, C. I., Campos, J. J., & Kermoian, R. (1996). Effect of self-produced locomotion on infant postural compensation to optic flow. *Developmental Psychology*, 32, 836–41.

Howard, I. P. (1986). The perception of posture, self-motion, and the visual vertical. In K. R. Boff, L. Kaufman, & J. P. Thomas (Eds.), *Handbook of perception and human performance* (pp. 18.1–18.62). New York: Wiley.

Hoyt, D. F., & Taylor, C. R. (1981). Gait and the energetics of locomotion in horses. *Nature*, 292, 239–40.

Johansson, G. (1977). Studies on visual perception of locomotion. *Perception*, 6, 365–76.

Jouen, F. (1988). Visual-proprioceptive control of posture in newborn infants. In B. Amblard, A. Berthoz, & F. Clarac (Eds.), *Posture and gait: Development, adaptation and modulation* (pp. 59–65). Amsterdam: Elsevier.

Jouen, F. (1990). Early visual–vestibular interactions and postural development. In H. Bloch & B. I. Bertenthal (Eds.), *Sensory-motor organizations and development in infancy and early childhood* (pp. 199–215). Dordrecht: Martinus Nijhoff.

Jouen, F., Lepecq, J. C., Gapenne, O., & Bertenthal, B. I. (2000). Optic flow sensitivity in neonates. *Infant Behavior and Development*, 23, 271–84.

Koenderink, J., & van Doorn, A. (1981). Exterospecific component of the motion parallax field. *Journal of the Optical Society of America*, 71, 953–7.

Lee, D. N. (1978). The functions of vision. In H. L. Pick & E. Saltzman (Eds.), *Modes of perceiving and processing information*. New York: Erlbaum.

Lee, D. N., & Aronson, E. (1974). Visual proprioceptive control of standing in human infants. *Perception and Psychophysics*, 15, 529–32.

Lee, D. N., & Lishman, J. R. (1975). Visual proprioceptive control of stance. *Journal of Human Movement Studies*, 1, 87–95.

Lee, D. N., & Lishman, J. R. (1977). Visual control of locomotion. *Scandinavian Journal of Psychology*, 18, 224–30.

Lestienne, F., Soechting, J., & Berthoz, A. (1977). Postural readjustments induced by linear motion of visual scenes. *Experimental Brain Research*, 28, 363–84.

Lishman, J. R., & Lee, D. N. (1973). The autonomy of visual kinaesthesis. *Perception*, 2, 287–94.

Milner, A. D., & Goodale, M. A. (1995). *The visual brain in action*. New York: Oxford University Press.

Nashner, L. M. & Berthoz, A. (1978). Visual contribution to rapid motor responses during postural control. *Brain Research*, 150, 403–7.

Nashner, L. M., & McCollum, G. (1985). The organization of human postural movements: A formal basis and experimental synthesis. *Behavioral and Brain Sciences*, 9, 135–72.

Nougier, V., Bard, C., Fleury, M., & Teasdale, N. (1997). Contribution of central and peripheral vision to the regulation of stance. *Gait and Posture*, 5, 34–41.

Nougier, V., Bard, C., Fleury, M., & Teasdale, N. (1998). Contribution of central and peripheral vision to the regulation of stance: Developmental aspects. *Journal of Experimental Child Psychology*, 68, 202–15.

Odenrick, P., & Sandstedt, P. (1984). Development of postural sway in the normal child. *Human Neurobiology*, 3, 241–4.

Paillard, J., & Brouchon, M. (1968). Active and passive movements in the calibration of position sense. In S. J. Freedman (Ed.), *The neuropsychology of spatially oriented behavior* (pp. 37–56). Homewood, IL: Dorsey Press.

Paulus, W., Straube, A., & Brandt, Th. (1984). Visual stabilization of posture: Physiological stimulus characteristics and clinical aspects. *Brain*, 107, 1143–63.

Paulus, W., Straube, A., & Brandt, Th. (1987). Visual postural performance after loss of somatosensory and vestibular function. *Journal of Neurology, Neurosurgery, and Psychiatry*, 50, 1542–5.

Paulus, W., Straube, A., Krafczyk, S., & Brandt, Th. (1989). Differential effects of retinal target displacement, changing size and changing disparity in the control of anterior/posterior and lateral body sway. *Experimental Brain Research*, 78, 243–52.

Posner, M. I., Nissen, M. J., & Klein, R. M. (1976). Visual dominance: An information-processing account of its origins and significance. *Psychological Review*, 83, 157–71.

Reed, E. S. (1989). Changing theories of postural development. In M. H. Woollacott and A. Shumway-Cook (Eds.), *Development of posture and gait across the lifespan* (pp. 3–24). Columbia, SC: University of South Carolina Press.

Riach, C. L., & Hayes, K. C. (1987). Maturation of postural sway in young children. *Developmental Medicine and Child Neurology*, 29, 650–8.

Riccio, G. E., & Stoffregen, T. A. (1988). Affordances as constraints on the control of stance. *Human Movement Science*, 7, 265–300.

Rochat, P., & Bullinger, A. (1995). Posture and functional action in infancy. In A. Vyt, H. Bloch, & M. Bronstein (Eds.), *Early child development in the French tradition* (pp. 15–34). Hillsdale, NJ: Erlbaum.

Rock, I. (1992). Comment on Asch and Witkin's "Studies in space orientation II." *Journal of Experimental Psychology: General*, 121, 404–6.

Rock, I., & Harris, C. S. (1967). Vision and touch. *Scientific American*, 216, 96–104.

Schmuckler, M. A. (1993). Perception–action coupling in infancy. In G. J. P. Savelsbergh (Ed.), *The development of coordination in infancy* (pp. 137–73). Amsterdam: Elsevier.

Schmuckler, M. A. (1997). Children's postural sway in response to low- and high-frequency visual information for oscillation. *Journal of Experimental Psychology: Human Perception and Performance*, 23, 528–45.

Schmuckler, M. A., & Gibson, E. J. (1989). The effect of imposed optical flow on guided locomotion in young walkers. *British Journal of Developmental Psychology*, 7, 193–206.

Shirley, M. M. (1931). *The first two years: A study of twenty-five babies.* Minneapolis, MN: University of Minnesota Press.

Sparrow, W. A., & Newell, K. M. (1998). Metabolic energy expenditure and the regulation of movement economy. *Psychonomic Bulletin and Review*, 5, 173–96.

Stoffregen, T. A. (1985). Flow structure versus retinal location in the optical control of stance. *Journal of Experimental Psychology: Human Perception and Performance*, 11, 554–65.

Stoffregen, T. A. (1986). The role of optical velocity in the control of stance. *Perception and Psychophysics*, 39, 355–60.

Stoffregen, T. A., & Bardy, B. G. (2001). On specification and the senses. *Behavioral and Brain Sciences*, 24, 195–261.

Stoffregen, T. A., Schmuckler, M. A., & Gibson, E. J. (1987). Use of central and peripheral optic flow in stance and locomotion in young walkers. *Perception*, 16, 113–19.

Stoffregen, T. A., Smart, L. J., Bardy, B. G., & Pagulayan, R. J. (1999). Postural stabilization of looking. *Journal of Experimental Psychology: Human Perception and Performance*, 25, 1641–58.

Stratton, G. M. (1896). Some preliminary experiments on vision without inversion of the retinal image. *Psychological Review*, 3, 611–17.

Straube, A., Krafczyk, S., Paulus, W., & Brandt, Th. (1994). Dependence of visual stabilization of postural sway on the cortical magnification factor of restricted visual fields. *Experimental Brain Research*, 99, 501–6.

Sveistrup, H., & Woollacott, M. H. (1996). Longitudinal development of the automatic postural response in infants. *Journal of Motor Behavior*, 28, 58–70.

Thelen, E. (2000). Many roads lead to Rome: Locomotion and dynamics. *Infancy*, 1, 221–4.

Thelen, E., Bril, G., & Breniere, Y. (1992). The emergence of heel strike in newly walking infants: A dynamic interpretation. In M. Woollacott and F. Horak (Eds.), *Posture and gait control mechanisms* (pp. 334–7). Eugene, OR: University of Oregon Books.

Thelen, E., & Cooke, D. W. (1987). The relationship between newborn stepping and later locomotion: A new interpretation. *Developmental Medicine and Child Neurology*, 29, 380–93.

Thelen, E., & Smith, L. B. (1994). *A dynamic systems approach to the development of cognition and action*. Cambridge, MA: MIT Press.

Thelen, E., & Ulrich, B. D. (1991). Hidden skills: A dynamical systems analysis of treadmill stepping during the first year. *Monographs of the Society for Research in Child Development*, 56 (1, Serial No. 223).

Turvey, M. T., & Fitzpatrick, P. (1993). Commentary: Development of perception–action systems and general principles of pattern formation. *Child Development*, 64, 1175–90.

Uchiyama, I. (2000, July). Emotional responses in the moving room as a function of locomotor experience. Paper presented at the meetings of the International Society for the Study of Behavioral Development, Beijing, China.

Wade, M. G., & Jones, G. (1997). The role of vision and spatial orientation in the maintenance of posture. *Physical Therapy*, 77, 619–28.

Wann, J. P., Mon-Williams, M., & Rushton, K. (1998). Postural control and coordination disorders: The swinging room revisited. *Human Movement Science*, 17, 491–513.

Wapner, S., & Witkin, H. A. (1950). The role of visual factors in the maintenance of body-balance. *American Journal of Psychology*, 63, 385–408.

Witkin, H. A., & Wapner, S. (1950). Visual factors in the maintenance of upright posture. *American Journal of Psychology*, 63, 31–50.
Woollacott, M. H., Debû, B., & Mowatt, M. (1987). Neuromuscular control of posture in the infant and child: Is vision dominant? *Journal of Motor Behavior*, 19, 167–86.
Woollacott, M. H., & Shumway-Cook, A. (1990). Changes in postural control across the life span: A systems approach. *Physical Therapy*, 70, 799–807.
Woollacott, M. H., Shumway-Cook, A. & Williams, H. (1989). The development of posture and balance control in children. In M. H. Woollacott & A. Shumway-Cook (Eds.), *Development of posture and gait across the lifespan* (pp. 77–96). Columbia, SC: University of South Carolina Press.
Zernicke, R. F., Gregor, R. J., & Cratty, B. J. (1982). Balance and visual proprioception in children. *Journal of Human Movement Studies*, 8, 1–13.

# 3

# From Direct Perception to the Primacy of Action: A Closer Look at James Gibson's Ecological Approach to Psychology

*Alan Costall*

*I seem to be, to my surprise, a member of a large profession. There are some 20,000 psychologists in this country alone, nearly all of whom have become so in my adult lifetime. They are prosperous. Most of them seem to be busily applying psychology to problems of life and personality. They seem to feel, many of them, that all we need to do is consolidate our scientific gains. Their self-confidence astonishes me. For these gains seem to me puny, and scientific psychology seems to me ill-founded. At any time the whole psychological applecart might be upset. Let them beware!* **(Gibson, 1967, p. 142)**

## Introduction

James Gibson (1904–79) was convinced that the science of psychology was in deep trouble. His importance lies as much in his criticisms of traditional psychology as in his own attempts to develop an alternative, "ecological" approach to psychology (Gibson,

1979). Gibson quickly established an international reputation as an experimental psychologist, especially for his visual research relating to the training and testing of pilots in World War II (Gibson, 1947). As a critic, therefore, Gibson could hardly be dismissed as a mere armchair psychologist or an intrusive outsider. Nevertheless, his challenges to the assumptions of traditional psychology have been often willfully misunderstood, and his own theoretical proposals widely rejected by psychologists, sometimes in far from polite terms.

Gibson's ecological approach has, however, been frequently cited within developmental psychology, and in a generally sympathetic way. The fact that his wife, Eleanor Gibson, was a first-rate developmental researcher has certainly helped. For example, her research with Richard Walk on the "visual cliff" demonstrating that young children – and the young of many other species – can see that a deep "drop" affords falling was quickly incorporated into the introductory textbooks as a canonical study (E. J. Gibson & Walk, 1960). In addition, James Gibson's work has been regarded by developmental psychologists as presenting an important counterpart to Piaget's constructivist, action-based theory of knowledge.

James Gibson attempted, over the course of more than 30 years, to challenge the assumptions of traditional perceptual theory, and to develop an alternative theory of "direct perception." In the process, he came to place increasing emphasis within his theory upon the *activity* of humans and other animals, and also to address the problem of "meaning." He was attempting to deal with some very fundamental issues, and was continually changing his theoretical position. If he took unusual delight in "taking on" other psychologists, he was also remarkably disposed – *sometimes* unwittingly – to disagree with himself.

Gibson set out his final theoretical position in *The ecological approach to visual perception* (Gibson, 1979). In this chapter, I will trace the development of Gibson's theory and identify the variety of problems he sought either to address or subvert. Some problems (as the American philosopher John Dewey used to say) never get solved: we just get over them. And part of Gibson's genius was, more often than not, to *dissolve* rather than resolve troublesome puzzles.

The main point of my chapter may appear paradoxical in relation to a thinker who insisted upon the possibility of veridical perception – the "later Gibson" is not what he *seems*. I shall be arguing that his final work is better understood as a theory of *agency* rather than perception, and committed to the *mutuality* of animal and environment rather than a traditional kind of "realism" that would exclude *us*.

## The "Early Gibson"

When Gibson published his first main text, *The perception of the visual world*, in 1950, vision was widely regarded as an issue concerning *social* as much as *cognitive* psychology. There are many references in Gibson's first book to the influence of cultural schemas and "stereotypes" on our experience not only of other people but of the world more generally. There had been the recent rise of fascism and the persecution of Jews and many other minorities in Europe. And the references in Gibson's book to the early trials of witches within America were surely allusions to what was still going on – the witch-hunts in the 1940s and 1950s of communists and other "un-American" individuals, including Gibson himself (see Reed, 1988).

In his 1950 book, Gibson challenged the pessimism of social scientists about the possibility of escaping stereotypical or "schematic" perception. He argued that veridical or "literal" perception is also possible – even if restricted (and it is a serious restriction, given Gibson's purpose) to the physical properties of objects and surfaces rather than their *meanings*. Traditional perceptual theory has long maintained that a profound gulf exists between the perceiver and the world to be known. *One* of the main reasons for this assumption, and certainly the one most widely discussed in recent years, is that the stimulation available to the perceiver seems to be profoundly incomplete and ambiguous. After all, the same shape projected to the eye could in principle arise from an infinite (if constrained) set of possible objects in the world. We must therefore, it continues to be asserted, rely inevitably on a variety of "iffy" cues (e.g., familiar and relative size; height in the visual field; overlap, etc.), and supplement these inherently probabilistic cues by assumptions somehow based *on prior knowledge about the world* (see Cavanagh, 1999). Thus, the standard accounts of perception (empiricist, nativist, and rationalist) keep ending up by having to account for the possibility of perception in terms of prior knowledge, rather than the reverse. Our knowledge of the world is "explained" "by supposing that knowledge of the world already exists" (Gibson, 1979, p. 253).

Now, this is not to deny the importance of prior experience in perception. Both James and Eleanor Gibson placed great emphasis upon the issue of perceptual learning, although they did challenge the standard accounts of its role (see Gibson & Gibson, 1955). The real problem is that the traditional approaches to perception have never provided any coherent *naturalistic* account of where the *prior* knowledge that "explains" our *current* perception comes from. Descartes's early suggestion, that God implanted that knowledge into us, is certainly coherent, but hardly naturalistic. But to appeal to *past experience* (either of the individual or the species) will hardly do, given that traditional theory gives us no grounds for supposing that the gulf between perceiver and world could have been any less profound in the *past* than it is supposed to be *now*.

As a student at Princeton, Gibson was greatly influenced by Edwin B. Holt, who had, in turn, been taught and inspired by William James. Gibson was thus familiar with the Darwinian adaptationist orientation of American psychology. But during his early career at Smith College he was also in very close contact with two very eminent psychologists, Kurt Koffka and Fritz Heider, both of whom had emigrated from Europe. As a consequence, Gibson's approach brought together the functionalist emphasis upon the coordination of animal and environment with the Gestaltist reaction against atomistic analysis.

As Gibson put it in his 1950 text, the study of perception involves *two* tasks. First, there is the need to determine how what we perceive relates to the "proximal stimulation" (the structured energy impinging upon our receptors). This, of course, had been the almost exclusive concern of traditional sensory psychophysics. But, Gibson insisted, there is another equally essential task, of determining how the proximal stimulation relates, in turn, to the world in which the perceiver actually exists.

Gibson's first important point was that the world is itself structured or constrained in highly specific ways. We do not usually encounter ghostly outline "shapes" floating in a void but are surrounded by textured surfaces, including a textured ground surface that extends around us in all directions. He argued that perceptual researchers should take into account the constraints that exist in the actual environment, and abandon the traditional atomistic analysis of stimulation. We should attempt instead to identify "higher-order" structures within stimulation that might have a specific, one-to-one relation with objects and events in the world.[1]

Gibson's early perceptual theory was a deliberate attempt to provide a purely stimulus-response account of vision, and thereby establish what he called a "*perceptual* psychophysics." If proximal structures can be identified that are specific to properties of the environment, *and* if these proximal structures, in turn, can be shown to produce reliable and appropriate perceptual "effects," then, he argued, the traditional gulf between perceiver and world will have been bridged.

## The "Later Gibson"

### *Perceiving as an exploratory activity*

In his 1950 book, Gibson had discussed what he called "gradients of *deformation* of the retinal image," but these had been simply assimilated to his stimulus-response scheme, even though, as he himself acknowledged, many of these deformations are in fact "produced" by the perceiver:

> Heretofore we have been talking about visual perception for the most part as if the observer stood motionless in the environment and kept his head fixed in one position. The normal human being, however, is *active*. . . . If he is not walking or driving a car or looking from a train or airplane, his ordinary adjustments of posture will produce some change in the position of his eyes in space. Such changes will modify the retinal images in a quite specific way. (*Gibson, 1950, p. 117; emphasis added*)

It was only by the late 1950s, however, that Gibson came to realize that such *self-produced* change was hardly consistent with the central assumption of the stimulus-response scheme, that stimulation is *passively* received. He took up this issue in a study comparing passive and active touch (Gibson, 1962), where participants were required to recognize various objects either when these objects were simply placed into their motionless hands, or else when they were permitted to explore them in their hands. In passive touch, there is the dull sense of "something" sitting on the surface of the hand; in active touch, there is the vivid sense of a coherent object passing between the palm and fingers. Gibson's contrast between active vs. passive touch nicely encapsulates one of the radical shifts in his theoretical position. Having started from an explicit commitment to stimulus-response theory, he has, in fact, been one of very few psychologists to reject *entirely* the mechanistic framework of traditional perceptual theory. As Gibson came to realize, perceiving is an *embodied activity*, one involving skill and intelligence. Indeed, the very idea of perception as essentially disembodied is a largely unnoticed legacy of

Cartesian dualism: the assumption that the body (as part of the physical world) is entirely passive (see Ben-Zeev, 1984; Wilson, 1980).

Gibson's rejection of his early causal theory of perception marks a major break with traditional perceptual theory (and mechanistic psychology more generally), and yet many of his critics, who really should know better, persistently portray him as a mechanistic, stimulus-response theorist. Thus, Richard Gregory (1997, p. 9) continues to complain that Gibson provided "an essentially *passive* account of perception" because he "*failed*" to provide an account of the mediating processes intervening between the supposed "stimulus" and "response," or "input" and "output." But theories framed in terms of *intervening processes* are not alternatives to mechanistic thinking; they are merely an elaboration of that viewpoint. Indeed, insofar as theories about intervening processes are formulated in terms of computer models, they compound two different machine metaphors: a modern computer mechanism lodged within a traditional reflex mechanism. Cognitive psychologists make a big fuss about precisely which form the internal computer mechanism might take (e.g., symbolic or connectionist), but take the traditional stimulus-response model of the *body* simply for granted.

Gibson set out his new account of perceiving as an embodied exploratory activity in his second book, *The senses considered as perceptual systems* (1966).[2] In this book, Gibson defined the various senses, not anatomically (as has traditionally been the case), but *functionally*, as "active organs of attention." Considered this way, the visual system, for example, is not (as the title of a popular textbook might suggest) an "eye and brain" (Gregory, 1997). The eyes themselves are under muscular control, are part of a moving head, which, in turn, is set on top of a body that gets around in the world. Thus, as Gibson liked to put it, the visual system has legs. Indeed, when we bring an object to our eyes to inspect it more closely, our hands, from this functionalist perspective, should also be regarded as part of the visual system (Cowie, 1993).

In order to make "space" in his theory for an *active* perceiver, Gibson no longer came to define information in terms of stimulation actually impinging upon the receptors. He attempted, instead, to define information *without reference to a perceiver* (Gibson, 1961; see also Reed, 1996, p. 253). In his "ecological optics," Gibson set the perceiver to one side, as it were, and defined information in terms of the "optic array" – the light structured by reflection against the surrounding surfaces and converging upon a static or moving "point" in the environment. For Gibson, the purpose of this separation of information and the perceiver was to capture the idea that information is actively *obtained*, not imposed.

Perversely, the textbooks routinely force Gibson into the category of a "bottom-up" theorist. In "bottom-up" theories, the "processing" of the stimulation is supposed to be completely "data-driven," whereas in "top-down" theories, the input is assumed to be subject to active interpretation or hypothesis construction (Cavanagh, 1999).[3]

Now, if we really did spend all our lives *just waiting for things to happen to us* (as the participants in psychology experiments are typically required to do), then whatever "activity" is involved in perceiving would necessarily be confined to internal processing. But this was the very assumption Gibson was rejecting. Why, he argued, does activity, within psychological theory, have to be restricted to the subcutaneous? The distinction between "bottom-up" and "top-down" is irrelevant to Gibson's later theory precisely because he rejected the concept of the stimulus.

The sheer *awkwardness* of continuing to describe Gibson as a bottom-up theorist, once we concede this crucial point, is demonstrated in the following textbook account:

> Gibson's direct perception approach can be regarded as a bottom-up theory: he claimed there is much more information potentially available in sensory stimulation than is generally realised. However, he emphasised the role played in perception by movement of the individual within his or her environment, *so his is not a bottom-up theory in the sense of an observer passively receiving sensory stimulation.* (**Eysenck & Keane, 2000, p. 58; emphasis added**)

If we really *must* talk of Gibson in terms of "ups" and "downs," then the following slip of the pen from an examination paper at least sets out a refreshingly *new* option – "Gibson, the bottom-*down* theorist." And, when you think about it, it is not so wide of the mark. Gibson's example of active touch provides a good metaphor for understanding his wider theory – perceiving as a *reaching out* into the world.

## *The reality of meaning*

Although, in recent years, the psychology of perception has been primarily concerned with the issue of whether the information available to us is sufficient fully to specify the objects and events in our surroundings, there is another highly troublesome but less examined problem raised within the dualistic scheme of traditional physical science. This is the idea that some of the qualities we experience as existing in our environment do not really belong there at all, but are purely subjective. A case in point concerns our experience of color. The textbooks are wonderfully inconsistent on this. They routinely assert that color is, of course, entirely created within our own minds, and yet they also earnestly go on to attempt to convince us that color vision *evolved* for the good biological reason that it helps to keep us in touch with our surroundings.

Gibson's early theory itself largely went along with this basic division of objective vs. subjective properties of experience. As I have already noted, Gibson's initial concept of *literal* perception was meant to *complement* that of schematic perception. And literal perception concerned objective features of the world, whereas *meanings* were indeed subjectively imposed:

> The literal world is the background for the schematic world. It furnishes a kind of supporting medium of discriminative capacity and it also furnishes a basis for posture and locomotion. The schematic world is a shifting set of prominent *meanings* from which many of the literal qualities have dropped away. If there are two kinds of perception, two kinds of perceptual theory are needed. The two theories ought not to be contradictory, but supplementary. (*Gibson, 1951, p. 104; emphasis added*)

In his later work, however, Gibson attempted to include *meaning* within his theory of "direct perception"[4] through his concept of affordances (Gibson, 1979):

> The *affordances* of the environment are what it *offers* the animal, what it *provides* or *furnishes*, either for good or ill. . . . I mean by it something that refers to both the environment and the animal in a way that no existing term does. It implies the complementarity of the animal and the environment. (*Gibson, 1979, p. 127*)

Although grass does not *afford* eating for humans, it certainly does for cows. Its *meaning* as food is not something that cows mentally "project" upon a meaningless world. Grass itself actually affords eating *in relation to* a certain kind of animal, with appropriate dentition, digestive system, and so on. Indeed, many plants and animals have co-evolved because of what they afford one another, either positively or negatively. Needless to say, ecological and evolutionary biologists find it perfectly natural to talk in terms of *resources* (such as food) that sustain and provide the context of selection. But psychologists, who seem to regard unworldliness as a professional qualification (see Neisser, 1997), persistently treat meaning as entirely subjective, or exclusive to the realm of language. With the concept of affordances, Gibson challenged the deeply entrenched notion that meaning is purely internal, by questioning the dualism of the subjective and objective.

It has to be said that Gibson's account of affordances is both sketchy and confusing. To begin with, two different claims need to be properly distinguished. The first (which Gibson himself regarded as paramount) is that affordances can be "*directly* perceived." Now, in fact, it is very difficult to extract a clear definition of "direct perception" from Gibson's writings if we take into account *all* of the different kinds of contrast he sought to make with various kinds of "indirect" perception (Costall, 1989). The most obvious candidate is perception based upon information (in Gibson's strict sense). But, as it stands, this definition fails to delimit the *means* by which the information might be obtained or detected. Would, for example, the use of an artificial device to detect the information count as direct perception? Furthermore, although deeply inconsistent on this issue, Gibson did sometimes discount any kind of socially mediated perception as direct. Thus, *if* the question of direct perception is supposed to be definitive to the concept of affordances, and *if* directness entails absence of social mediation, then the concept of affordances really would have to be limited, for example, to "simple visually guided behaviour such as that of insects" (Bruce & Green, 1990, p. 390). Such a move, however, would not only be highly restrictive but largely undermine the point of Gibson's ecological project (Costall, 1995; Trettvik, 2001).

So let us turn to the second claim made by Gibson in his account of affordances: the claim that affordances are *real*. This is what I see as truly fundamental, since it challenges some of the most profound dualisms of modern western thought, most notably, the mental vs. the material, and the subjective vs. the objective. After all, how can we be said to perceive *anything* (either directly or indirectly) if what we experience is not really *there*? The standard scientific view has been that only that which can be described within the objectivist language of physical science truly exists, and that everything else must be "in our heads" (see Ingold, 1993, for an excellent discussion of this issue).

For me, the real importance of the concept of affordance is that it helps put meaning back into the world, not by "objectivizing" meaning but by recognizing the mutuality of animal and environment, and defining affordances *relationally*. And we need to be clear what that relation involves. The way Gibson himself put it was that "affordances are properties of things taken with reference to an *observer*" (Gibson, 1979, p. 137; emphasis added; see also Heft, 2001; Ingold, 2000). But the relation really concerns what animals can *do*. Affordances are relative to an animal as an *agent*. The simple yet very important ontological point of the affordance concept applies just as much to Gibson's notorious example of the mailbox, an eminently "cultural" object (Gibson, 1979, p. 139). There really have to be *things* like mailboxes around (plus systems of collection and delivery, etc.) if we are to do things like sending letters. And, even if the mailboxes in some countries do look disconcertingly like street litter bins, there must ultimately be *something* about those mailboxes that sets them apart for their mail systems to persist.

So far I have traced the development of Gibson's attempt to bridge the supposed gulf between perceiver and world, and, in particular, the ways in which activity increasingly entered into his theory of perception (see also, Costall, 2000). First of all, Gibson rejected his early stimulus-response formulation in place of an account of perception as an exploratory activity. Then, with the concept of affordances, the primary function of perception came to be redefined: to inform us not about a neutral world of shapes and objects but about the meanings of places, objects, and other animals for our activities. This emphasis on affordances challenges any ultimate division between perceiving and acting. Although much of the research on affordances has been restricted to studies of participants merely making judgments, perceiving affordances normally goes along with our acting in, and upon, our surroundings. *Doing* things with things is "part and parcel" of perceiving what they afford (Gibson, 1979, p. 235).

## Implications for Research and Theory in Infancy

For several centuries, western philosophy has not only been almost exclusively concerned with epistemology (the study of the nature and conditions of knowledge), but has been committed to a particular metaphor – the spectator theory of knowledge. In tracing the development of Gibson's theory, I have been trying to bring out the important ways in which activity and agency came to figure increasingly within his account of the coordination of animal and environment. In the remainder of this chapter, I want to look more closely at two ways James Gibson's ideas have been taken up within development psychology in light of this "pragmatic turn":

1 Gibson's supposed nativism.
2 The "opposition" between Gibson's "theory of direct perception" and Piaget's action-based account of mental development.

## *Gibson's nativism*

> *These voluminous discussions [about nativism/empiricism] are wholly futile, for there is no single phenomenon or problem of space.* **(Carr, 1935, p. 5)**

Gibson's radical approach has been assimilated not only to the standard opposition between top-down and bottom-up processing, but also to the long-standing nativism/empiricism controversy. Gibson, if the textbooks are to be believed, was a *nativist*: "three-dimensional space is not [for Gibson] constructed by the subject, but given from birth" (Nuallain, 2002, p. 67). Now we need to be clear that nativism is a *theoretical* position, not the mere acknowledgment of "neonatal competence" (Costall, 1994). According to traditional theory, the perception of "space" is *under*determined by the stimulation, and hence the stimulus must be supplemented by prior knowledge. Nativism is the claim that this prior knowledge is innately implanted.

Gibson, however, never even *tried* to solve the traditional problem of space perception, for the simple reason that he denied we ever perceive *space*. Space, he argued, is an abstraction – what we *see* are objects and surfaces in relation to one another and to ourselves, and the action possibilities they afford (see also Carr, 1935). Of course, the specific informative structures, based upon environmental constraints, claimed by Gibson to be available to the perceiver, would not require "filling in" or supplementation.

Furthermore, contrary to the common assertion that "Gibson assumed that most perceptual learning has occurred during the history of mankind, and so does not need to occur during the individual's lifetime" (Eysenck & Keane, 2000, p. 59), James and Eleanor Gibson placed great emphasis upon perceptual *learning*, though in terms not of supplementation but of the *differentiation* of informative structures (see Gibson & Gibson, 1955). They believed that the traditional nativism/empiricism dichotomy needed to be replaced by much more specific developmental questions relating to the particular ecology and "life-history strategies" of the animal in question (E. J. Gibson, 1991).

Clearly, by replacing the traditional assumptions that set up such a deep gulf between perceiver and world with such concepts as environmental constraints, information, affordances, and agency, James Gibson's approach does indeed lead us to expect "tremendously rich structure present at birth" (Bullock, 1987, p. 213). But the acknowledgment of such structure should be distinguished from *preformationalism*, the idea that development is preordained (cf. Bullock, 1987; de Gelder, 1985; Johnston, 1997; Oyama, 2000). Various mechanistic metaphors have been used in the textbooks to characterize Gibson's supposed "nativism": predispositions, hardwiring, blueprints, preprogramming, and inbuilt rules or "mechanisms." All of these metaphors are deeply *anti*developmental, because "they all presume what they are supposed to explain, namely the origin of order and organization" (Johnston, 1997, p. 88). In any case, they are metaphors that James Gibson, as far as I am aware, never used. Indeed, to Eleanor Gibson's chagrin, some of her own students have opted for such preformationist language. As she has complained:

> [The infant] must be equipped by nature with systems that make detection of the information possible, but to call such structures rules or logic or computing mechanisms sends one along the information processors' road of speculation, and not the road of biology. **(*E. J. Gibson, 1985, p. 75*)**

An important theme emerging in Gibson's later work concerned the *mutuality* of animal and environment. On this view, the animal and environment cannot be regarded as ultimately separate entities that (somehow) become coordinated. Our unit of analysis, therefore, has to be the developing *relation* between the animal and its world. As I shall now try to explain, such a mutualist perspective should help us avoid reifying the *process* of development (or, more generally, the coordination of animal and environment) in terms of frozen entities located either inside or outside the animal.[5]

## Beyond objectivism

> *The terms subjective and objective are not mutually exclusive concepts.* **(Carr, 1935, p. 5)**

Gibson often claimed that his theory supported the philosophical position known as "realism." Indeed, Edward Reed and Rebecca Jones named their edited collection of Gibson's papers *Reasons for realism* (1982). They characterized Gibson's realism as "his conviction that *we can directly perceive the world as it is*, if we only try, and his view that psychologists must seek to understand the world if they are to explain how we become aware of it and act upon it" (1982, p. 1; emphasis added). But there is a more fundamental, ontological sense of "realism" to which Gibson and also many of his followers have been committed, the very traditional idea that "the world as it is" not only exists independently of us, but *has to exclude us*, since we do not really belong within the natural order of things.

This, for me, is the tension at the heart of Gibson's final book. On the one hand, it can be read as an attempt to *objectify* information and meaning. Moreover, this is the way many commentators have taken this text:

> the information is all *there, objectively, in the light itself*
> (*Nuallain, 2002, p. 67*)

> Perception is not a matter of constructing a three-dimensional reality from the retinal image, either in development or in the perceptual acts of adults. The structure of the environment is *"out there"* to be picked up, and perception is a matter of picking up invariant properties of space and objects.
> (*Bremner, 1994, p. 118; emphasis added*)

Yet there is so much about Gibson's attempt to undermine the dualisms of traditional scientific psychology that implies a commitment to the reciprocity or mutuality of environment and organism, and invites a quite different understanding of his later project.

First of all, despite Gibson's attempt at reification, "information" is not an intrinsic property of structures in light, sound, and other forms of energy. "Information" is a *functional* concept – information in relation to a particular animal, in relation to a particular purpose, and "realized" within that relation. This is obviously the case for the information relating to affordances, since, surely, such information must relate to an agent. But the point, in fact, holds generally:

> Information has been an important concept in psychology, but it is also quite problematic. We often talk as if it were some influential substance located in specific parts of a system, so we ask

> whether information is *in* the organism or *in* the environment; we speak of information being *in* the genes and being *read out* of the genes during development; we ask what information is in the mother's voice and are thus led to ask how the infant extracts that information. In fact, information defines a kind of relationship, not a kind of substance. An informational relationship exists between two systems (such as a developing organism and its environment or between an infant and its mother) if one of them can influence the other in some systematic way.
>
> (***Johnston, 1997, p. 89***)

Second, despite Gibson's own attempt (in his ecological optics) to define information independently of any particular animal (Gibson, 1961; Reed, 1996, p. 253), one of his most important challenges to dualism concerned what he termed the proprioceptive or kinesthetic function of the senses – our "awareness of *being in the world*" (Gibson, 1979, p. 239; emphasis added):

> Vision picks up both movements of the whole body relative to the ground and movement of a member of the body relative to the whole. . . . The doctrine that vision is exteroceptive, that it obtains "external" information only is simply false. Vision obtains information about both the environment and the self. In fact all the senses do so when they are considered as perceptual systems.
>
> (***Gibson, 1979, p. 183***)

This point emerges clearly in Gibson's account of "optic flow," as the basis for our "awareness of movement or stasis, of starting and stopping, of approaching or retreating, of going in one direction or another, and of the imminence of an encounter" (Gibson, 1979, p. 236). But there is also his identification of the importance of the "visible horizon," which corresponds to our eye level and relates distant objects to our own bodies. For example, objects extending above the visible horizon are higher than eye level (and the horizon sections equally sized objects in equal proportions). As Gibson put it, the horizon "is neither subjective nor objective; it expresses the reciprocity of observer and environment" (Gibson, 1979, p. 164).

Most fundamentally, we can *see* not only our own bodies, our arms and legs, there *in* the world, but also our *selves* restricting our view:

> Ask yourself what it is that you see hiding the surroundings as you look out on the world – not darkness, surely, not air, not nothing, but the ego! (***Gibson, 1979, p. 112***)[6]

The perceptual specification of our selves-in-relation-to-the-world has been taken further, in important ways by George Butterworth (1995) and Ulric Neisser (1994). The simple point I wish to make here is that information *specifying* the self can hardly be "independent" of us. It cannot *exclude* the self!

Finally, there is the concept of affordances, which, as Gibson explained, he adopted precisely because it implied "the *complementarity* of the animal and the environment" (Gibson, 1979, p. 127; emphasis added). Nevertheless, Gibson himself and many of his followers have tried to maintain that affordances are not, in the end, *really* relational: "The organism depends on the environment for its life, but the environment does not depend on the organism for its existence" (Gibson, 1979, p. 129; see also Heft, 2001, pp. 123ff.; Reed, 1993). The point of the ecological approach is surely to move beyond the established dualistic options. Yet, as far as I can see, it is only on the traditional assumption that we are *not* part of nature that the dependence of affordances upon *agents* could render them unreal (Costall, 1995, 2001).

## *Coordinating James Gibson and Jean Piaget*

I had many wonderful discussions with George Butterworth, over the years, about the relations between the theoretical approach of Gibson and that of the developmental theorist Jean Piaget (e.g., Butterworth, 1994a,b; Costall, 1994). One of my first publications (Costall, 1981) appeared in a book edited by George, *Infancy and epistemology*, which was perhaps the first to bring together the perspectives of Gibson and Piaget. George was right to question Piaget's account of perception, and to see, in Gibson, an important alternative. But George would often insist upon a strong opposition between Piaget's constructivist account of knowledge (based upon the child's interactions with the environment) and Gibson's claim that structure does not need to be constructed *because it already exists in the world*. But I maintained, and still maintain, that we should not exaggerate the differences between the two approaches. Certainly, Gibson did not speak about neonatal activity in terms of "reflexes," and rejected Piaget's rationalist account of perceptual development (see Gibson, 1966, 1979). Yet there are interesting convergences of detail, such as the concept of invariant (Bohm, 1965), and the rejection of the notion of space as a container, but, instead, as constituted by objects and surfaces (Piaget, 1954, p. 98). More importantly, both Piaget and Gibson challenged the unworldliness of modern psychology by insisting upon the primacy of "being in the world" or "sensorimotor intelligence." Contrary to the dominant approaches within cognitive psychology and artificial intelligence, they did not take our capacities for representation and symbolism for granted, but saw clearly that representational activities need to be grounded in our interactions with our surroundings (see Butterworth, 1994a; Furth, 1969; Reed, 1991). As Rodney Brooks has nicely put it, our *being in the world* is not a "side issue":

> Typically, AI [artificial intelligence] "succeeds" by defining the parts of the problem that are unsolved as not AI. The principal mechanism for this partitioning is abstraction. Its application is usually considered part of good science, not, as it is in fact used in AI, as a mechanism for self-delusion. In AI, abstraction is usually used to factor out all aspects of perception and motor skills. . . . [Yet] these are the *hard* problems solved by intelligent systems.
>
> (***Brooks, 1991, p. 142; emphasis added***)

Finally, and most fundamentally, Piaget and Gibson were both drawing upon the evolutionary conception of adaptation or coordination as the dynamically changing, reciprocal relation between animal and environment. The problem is not (as psychologists usually formulate it) of how organism and environment "enter" into relationship, as though they could have existed outside of, and prior to, their relation. To explain the organization of the organism in terms of the information and affordances *in* the environment is all very well, but it needs to be done with a clear sense of historical process in which these structures came into existence through the co-evolution and co-development of organism and environment. As John Dewey, in lectures given in 1898, so lucidly put it:

> the increasing control [by the organism] over the environment is not as if the environment were something there fixed and the organism responded at this point and that, adapting itself by fitting itself in, in a plaster-like way. The organism reacts so as to bring the environment into use. . . . It would be just as true to speak of the adaptation of the environment to the organism, to the needs of the organism, making it more and more subservient to the life process all the time.
>
> The psychological or historical fallacy is likely to come in here [if] we conceive the environment, which is really the outcome of the process of development, which has gone on developing along

> with the organism, as if it was something which had been there from the start, and the whole problem has been for the organism to accommodate itself to that set of given surroundings.
>
> (*Dewey, 1898/1976, pp. 283–4*)

The fact that information and affordances exist "in" the environment is because we are there too. We are part of what nature has, and will, become.

## NOTES

1 As Koenderink (1998, p. 1073) has put it (ironically, of course): "using the scientifically respectable paradigm of stimulus reduction one easily shows that humans are quite unable to perceive depth relations. . . . We believe that the best scientific intentions have led to sterile and indeed largely irrelevant knowledge here."

2 This neglected text anticipated many of the ideas he set out later in the much more widely cited *Ecological approach to visual perception* (1979) and deserves to be more widely read. It is much more coherently presented and, unlike his other books, is not restricted to vision.

3 This modern-sounding distinction can, in fact, be found in Kepler's account, published in 1604, of the retinal image as the starting point of vision:

> In what manner this image or picture is brought together by the visual spirits which reside in the retina or in the nerves, and *whether it is made to appear before the soul or tribunal of the faculty of vision by a spirit within the cerebral chambers, or whether the faculty of vision, as a magistrate sent by the soul, goes out from the council chamber of the brain to meet this image in the optic nerves and retina descending to a lower court*, these things I leave to the natural philosophers . . . for disputing.
>
> (*Cited in Straker, 1976, p. 20; emphasis added*)

The underlying continuity between Kepler's account and most modern theories of vision concerns precisely the assumption that the body is a *passive recipient* of external stimulation.

4 It is important to note that Gibson's account of direct perception, like his earlier account of literal perception, does not deny the possibility (indeed predominance) of mediated or indirect perception. It is a theory *of* direct perception, not a *direct* theory of perception.

5 For some very thoughtful discussions of different ecological approaches to development, see Dent-Read and Zukow-Goldring (1997).

6 Ernst Mach made this same point as long ago as 1895: "*Problem*: To carry out the self-inspection of the Ego. *Solution*: It is carried out immediately" (Mach, 1959, p. 20).

## REFERENCES

Ben-Zeev, A. (1984). The passivity assumption of the sensation–perception distinction. *British Journal for the Philosophy of Science*, 35, 327–43.

Bohm, D. (1965). *The special theory of relativity*. New York: W. A. Benjamin.

Bremner, G. (1994). *Infancy*. Oxford: Blackwell.

Brooks, R. A. (1991). Intelligence without representation. *Artificial Intelligence*, 47, 139–59.

Bruce, V., & Green, P. (1990). *Visual perception: Physiology, psychology, and ecology* (2nd ed.). Hove: Erlbaum.

Bullock, D. (1987). Socializing the theory of intellectual development. In M. Chapman & R. A. Dixon (Eds.), *Meaning and the growth of understanding: Wittgenstein's significance for developmental psychology* (pp. 187–218). Berlin: Springer.

Butterworth, G. E. (1994a). Knowledge and representation: The acquisition of knowledge in infancy. In P. van Geert, L. P. Mos, & W. J. Baker (Eds.), *Annals of theoretical psychology* (Vol. 10, pp. 1–26). New York: Plenum.

Butterworth, G. E. (1994b). Reply to commentaries. In P. van Geert, L. P. Mos, & W. J. Baker (Eds.), *Annals of theoretical psychology* (Vol. 10, pp. 59–62). New York: Plenum.

Butterworth, G. E. (1995). An ecological perspective on the origins of self. In J. Bermudez, N. Eilan, & A. Marcel (Eds.), *The body and the self* (pp. 97–105). Cambridge: Cambridge University Press.

Carr, H. A. (1935). *An introduction to space perception*. New York: Longman, Green; reprinted (1966), New York: Hafner.

Cavanagh, P. (1999). Top-down processing in vision. In R. A. Wilson & F. C. Keil (Eds.), *The MIT encyclopedia of the cognitive sciences* (pp. 844–5). Cambridge, MA: MIT Press.

Costall, A. (1981). On how so much information controls so much behaviour. In G. Butterworth (Ed.), *Infancy and epistemology* (pp. 30–51). New York: St. Martin's/Brighton: Harvester.

Costall, A. (1989). A closer look at "direct perception." In A. Gellatly, D. Rogers, & J. A. Sloboda (Eds.), *Cognition and social worlds* (pp. 10–21). Oxford: Clarendon.

Costall, A. (1994). The competent neonate: Sleepless nights for representational theorists? In P. van Geert, L. P. Mos, & W. J. Baker (Eds.), *Annals of theoretical psychology* (Vol. 10, pp. 27–41). New York: Plenum.

Costall, A. (1995). Socializing affordances. *Theory and Psychology*, 5, 467–81.

Costall, A. (2000). James Gibson and the ecology of action. *Communication and Cognition*, 33, 23–33.

Costall, A. (2001). Darwin, ecological psychology, and the principle of animal–environment mutuality. *Psyke and Logos*, 22, 473–84.

Cowie, R. (1993, September). On acting in order to see things better. Paper presented at the Workshop on "The Primacy of Action,"

International Society for Ecological Psychology, University of Manchester, 1993.

de Gelder, B. (1985). The cognitivist conjuring trick or how development vanished. In C. J. Bailey & R. Harris (Eds.), *Developmental mechanisms of language* (pp. 149–66). London: Pergamon.

Dent-Read, C., & Zukow-Goldring, P. (Eds.). (1997). *Evolving explanations of development*. Washington, DC: American Psychological Association.

Dewey, J. (1976). *Lectures on psychological and political ethics: 1898* (Ed. with an introduction by D. L. Koch). New York: Hafner.

Eysenck, M. W., & Keane, M. (2000). *Cognitive psychology: A student's handbook* (4th. ed.). Hove: Psychology Press.

Furth, H. (1969). *Piaget and knowledge: Theoretical foundations*. Englewood Cliffs, NJ: Prentice-Hall.

Gibson, E. J. (1985). Whosoever hath, to him shall be given. *New Ideas in Psychology*, 3, 73–5.

Gibson, E. J. (1991). *An odyssey in learning and perception*. London: MIT Press.

Gibson, E. J., & Walk, R. D. (1960). The "visual cliff." *Scientific American*, 202, 64–71.

Gibson, J. J. (Ed.). (1947). Motion picture testing and research. Army Air Forces Aviation Psychology Program Research Reports. Washington, DC: US Government Printing Office.

Gibson, J. J. (1950). *The perception of the visual world*. Boston: Houghton-Mifflin.

Gibson, J. J. (1951). Theories of perception. In W. Dennis et al., *Current trends in psychological theory* (pp. 85–110). Pittsburgh: University of Pittsburgh Press.

Gibson, J. J. (1961). Ecological optics. *Vision Research*, 1, 253–62.

Gibson, J. J. (1962). Observations on active touch. *Psychological Review*, 69, 477–91.

Gibson, J. J. (1966). *The senses considered as perceptual systems*. Boston: Houghton-Mifflin.

Gibson, J. J. (1967). Autobiography. In E. G. Boring & G. Linzey (Eds.), *A history of psychology in autobiography* (Vol. 5, pp. 127–43). New York: Appleton-Century-Crofts.

Gibson, J. J. (1979). *The ecological approach to visual perception*. Boston: Houghton-Mifflin.

Gibson, J. J., & Gibson, E. J. (1955). Perceptual learning: Differentiation or enrichment? *Psychological Review*, 62, 32–41.

Gregory, R. L. (1997). *Eye and brain: The psychology of seeing* (5th ed.). Princeton, NJ: Princeton University Press.

Heft, H. (2001). *Ecological psychology in context: James Gibson, Roger Barker, and the legacy of William James's radical empiricism*. Mahwah, NJ: Erlbaum.

Ingold, T. (1993). The art of translation in a continuous world. In G. Palsson (Ed.), *Beyond boundaries: Understanding, translation and anthropological discourse* (pp. 210–30). Oxford: Berg.

Ingold, T. (2000). *The perception of the environment: Essays in livelihood, dwelling and skill*. London: Routledge.

Johnston, T. D. (1997). Comment on Cooper. In C. Dent-Read & P. Zukow-Goldring (Eds.), *Evolving explanations of development* (pp. 87–9). Washington, DC: American Psychological Association.

Koenderink, J. J. (1998). Pictorial relief. *Philosophical Transactions of the Royal Society of London, A*, 36, 1071–86.

Mach, E. (1959). *The analysis of sensations and the relation of the physical to the psychical* (Trans. from the first German edition by C. M. Williams, revised and supplemented from the fifth German edition by S. Waterlow, with a new introduction by T. S. Szasz). New York: Dover. (First German edition published 1885.)

Neisser, U. (1994). Self-perception and self-knowledge. *Psyke and Logos*, 15, 392–407.

Neisser, U. (1997). The future of cognitive science: An ecological analysis. In D. M. Johnson & C. E. Erneling (Eds.), *The future of the cognitive revolution* (pp. 247–60). New York: Oxford University Press.

Nuallain, S. O. (2002). *The search for mind: A new foundation for cognitive science*. Bristol: Intellect.

Oyama, S. (2000). *The ontogeny of information: Developmental systems and evolution* (2nd ed.). Durham, NC: Duke University Press.

Piaget, J. (1954). *The construction of reality in the child* (Trans. M. Cook). New York: Random House.

Reed, E. S. (1988). *James J. Gibson and the psychology of perception*. New Haven, CT: Yale University Press.

Reed, E. S. (1991). James Gibson's ecological approach to cognition. In A. Still & A. Costall (Eds.), *Against cognitivism* (pp. 171–97). Hemel Hempstead: Harvester.

Reed, E. S. (1993). The intention to use a specific affordance: A framework for psychology. In R. Wozniak & K. Fischer (Eds.), *Cognitive development in specific environments* (pp. 45–75). Hillsdale, NJ: Erlbaum.

Reed, E. S. (1996). James J. Gibson: Pioneer and iconoclast. In G. A. Kimble, C. A. Boneau, & M. Wertheimer (Eds.), *Portraits of pioneers in psychology* (pp. 247–61). Washington, DC: American Psychological Society/Mahwah, NJ: Erlbaum.

Reed, E. S., & Jones, R. (1982). *Reasons for realism: Selected essays of James J. Gibson*. Hillsdale, NJ: Erlbaum.

Straker, S. (1976). The eye made "other": Durer, Kepler, and the mechanisation of light and vision. In L. A. Knafla, M. S. Staum, & T. H. E. Travers (Eds.), *Science, technology, and culture in historical perspective* (pp. 7–25). University of Calgary Studies in History, No. 1.

Trettvik, J. (2001). En økologisk tilgang til perception og aktivitet. *Psyke og Logos*, 22, 485–513.

Wilson, M. D. (1980). Body and mind from the Cartesian point of view. In R. W. Rieber (Ed.), *Body and mind: Past, present, and future* (pp. 35–55). New York: Academic Press.

# 4
# The Development of Perception in a Multimodal Environment

*Lorraine E. Bahrick*

## Introduction

We live in a world of multimodal objects and events that present a constantly changing, richly structured flux of stimulation to all of our senses. Sounds typically come from visible, tangible objects. People provide an array of dynamic, concurrent, tactile, visual, auditory, and olfactory stimulation. The infant encounters this world of multimodal, dynamic objects and events and experiences it through a unified perceptual system (Gibson, 1969). Much early infant perception and learning emerges in the context of close face-to-face interactions with caretakers. This interaction scaffolds attention and provides a rich source of concurrent visual, vocal, tactile, vestibular, and kinetic stimulation. In these interactions, the adult's speech, facial movements, and gestures are typically temporally synchronous and coordinated, often accompanied by synchronous touch and movement of the infant ("multimodal motherese": see Gogate, Bahrick, & Watson, 2000; Zukow-Goldring, 1997), and intercoordinated with the temporal characteristics of the infant's behavior (e.g., Jaffee, Beebe, Feldstein, Crown, & Jasnow, 2001; Trevarthen, 1993). Infants also engage in active, self-directed, intermodal exploration of their own bodies

This research was supported by grants RO1 HD25669 from NICHD and RO1 MH 62226 from NIMH to the author.

(e.g., Butterworth & Hopkins, 1988; Rochat, 1993; van der Meer, van der Weel, & Lee, 1995) and the contingencies between their movements and those of the multimodal objects and events in their environment (e.g., Bahrick, 1995; Bahrick & Watson, 1985; Rochat & Morgan, 1995; Schmuckler, 1995). Exploration of the self provides the first and one of the most potent and reliable sources of multimodal stimulation, as proprioceptive feedback always accompanies self-generated visual, vocal, and tactile stimulation (see Rochat, 1995).

How and on what basis do infants begin to parse, perceive, and derive meaning from the flux of multimodal stimulation in a manner that lays a foundation for the perceptual world of the adult? How do infants determine which sights and sounds belong together and constitute unitary events and which patterns of stimulation are unrelated to one another? What enables young perceivers to attend to patterns of stimulation that are relevant and meaningful while ignoring patterns which are less relevant to their actions and needs? In other words, what are the factors that initially organize attention and perception such that its developmental trajectory provides the foundation for the knowledge base and perceptual and conceptual competencies of the adult perceiver?

## Infant Perception of Amodal Information

Research has made some progress in addressing these questions. In the area of intersensory perception, research has now generated a solid data base demonstrating that infants are adept perceivers of multimodal stimulation across a variety of natural events. According to Gibson's (1969) invariant detection view of perceptual development, infants come into the world with a unified perceptual system, capable of detecting amodal, invariant information. Amodal information is information such as synchrony, tempo, rhythm, intensity, and so forth, that is common across several sense modalities. Through development infants differentiate increasingly finer aspects of stimulation (Gibson, 1969). This view has prompted a great deal of research investigating infant capabilities for perceiving amodal, invariant relations and has revealed that infants are adept at perceiving a host of amodal relations uniting the multimodal stimulation across different sense modalities (see Lewkowicz & Lickliter, 1994, for a review). For example, infants detect temporal synchrony, shared rhythm, and spectral information uniting movements of the mouth and the timing and nature of speech sounds (e.g., Dodd, 1979; Kuhl & Meltzoff, 1982, 1984; Lewkowicz, 1996). They detect common auditory-visual information conveying speaker gender and age (Bahrick, Netto, & Hernandez-Reif, 1998; Walker-Andrews, Bahrick, Raglioni, & Diaz, 1991) as well as affect common to the face and voice (e.g., Soken & Pick, 1992; Walker, 1982; Walker-Andrews, 1997). Infants also abstract common temporal information uniting the sights and sounds of moving objects including the synchrony between movements and their impact sounds (Bahrick, 1988, 1992; Lewkowicz, 1992; Spelke, 1979), their common tempo and rhythm (Allen, Walker, Symonds, & Marcell, 1977; Bahrick, Flom, & Lickliter, 2002; Bahrick & Lickliter, 2000; Gogate & Bahrick, 1998; see Lewkowicz, 2000, for a review), and amodal temporal information specifying the composition and substance of moving objects (Bahrick, 1983, 1987, 1988, 1992). Young infants are also adept at perceiving multimodal information specifying the self and their body motion (Butterworth, 1992; Rochat, 1995). They can adjust their posture in response to visual feedback (Butterworth & Hicks, 1977; Lee & Aronson, 1974), and they detect proprioceptive information resulting from their body motion and can relate it to the visual consequences of that motion (Bahrick & Watson, 1985; Rochat & Morgan, 1995). Young infants are adept perceivers of the rich flux of multimodal stimulation.

Although young infants appear to be quite capable of abstracting meaningful information and coherent multimodal events from the flow of sensory stimulation, the origins and nature of this developmental trajectory are still unclear. How do infants initially accomplish this, and what guides attention, perception, and learning such that meaningful, unitary events are abstracted in the first place? Which competencies are derived from earlier ones, and how? What are the principles that guide and constrain perceptual development such that infants develop the competencies of adult perceivers so early and in such an economical and veridical manner?

## Principles of Perceptual Development

Recent evidence now addresses some of these important developmental questions. Consistent with Gibson's (1969) view of perceptual development, research from my laboratory has shown that learning about multimodal events proceeds in order of increasing specificity and this guides and provides important constraints for perceptual development (Bahrick, 1992, 1994, 2001).

In a series of studies, we found support for three basic principles of intersensory learning.

First, global, amodal relations are detected developmentally prior to nested amodal relations (Bahrick, 2001). Global relations include shared temporal synchrony (such as that uniting the sights and sounds of an object's impacts), and rhythm and tempo of intermodal events. Nested amodal relations are more specific and are detectable within each synchronous impact. They convey more detail about the intersensory event such as its substance (rigidity vs. elasticity), composition (that it is comprised of a single vs. an aggregate of elements), its weight or number. Bahrick (2001) habituated infants to naturalistic events depicting single and compound objects striking a surface, producing their natural impact sounds. Visual recovery tests were then given in which the sounds were presented out of synchrony with the objects' impacts, or the sounds and objects were mismatched so that the single object produced the sounds of the compound object at each impact and vice versa. Results (depicted in figure 4.1) demonstrated that infant detection of temporal synchrony was already evident by the age of 4 weeks and remained stable across age, whereas the detection of nested amodal temporal microstructure specifying the object's composition did not emerge until 7 weeks of age and increased dramatically across age such that, by 11 weeks, detection

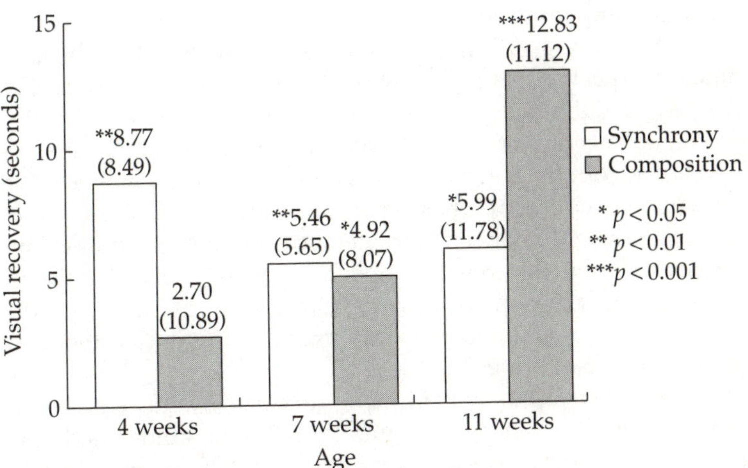


**Figure 4.1** Mean visual recovery and standard deviations (in parenthesis) to test trials depicting a change in temporal synchrony and temporal microstructure specifying the composition of the objects at 4, 7, and 11 weeks of age (from Bahrick, 2001). Reprinted with permission of Elsevier.

of this nested amodal information was significantly greater than detection of global synchrony. Early detection of temporal synchrony is important because temporal synchrony can specify the unity of the audiovisual event. Once infants attend to a unitary event, differentiation of further relations can then proceed in a veridical manner. However, attention to a sound and a sight that do not belong together would be maladaptive and would lead to learning of incongruent intersensory relations.

A second developmental principle is that detection of amodal relations in a given domain developmentally precedes detection of arbitrary, modality-specific relations. Modality-specific information is information that is specified by only a single sense modality. For example, color and pattern are specific to vision, whereas pitch and timber are specific to audition. An intersensory relation between modality-specific information is typically arbitrary and must be learned. For example, the relation between the visual appearance of a woman's face and the particular sound of her voice is arbitrary. So is the relation between the pitch of an impact sound and the color of an object, or that between a speech sound and the appearance of the object it represents, or the relation between the visual appearance of a container and the temperature or taste of its contents. Bahrick (1992, 1994) found that by 3 months of age infants detected amodal temporal synchrony and temporal information specifying object composition in single and compound objects striking a surface. However, it was not until the age of 7 months that they detected the arbitrary, modality-specific relation between the pitch of the sounds and the colors and shapes of the moving objects, even though at 3 months of age infants could discriminate among all the objects and their sounds. Further, it was found that even when the modality-specific properties were made more highly discriminable, the amodal relations were nevertheless perceived developmentally prior to the arbitrary, modality-specific relations (Bahrick, 2000). There appears to be a developmental lag between the detection of amodal and modality-specific audiovisual relations provided by a given event.

A third developmental principle revealed by our research is that the infants' detection of amodal relations guides and constrains perceptual learning about arbitrary relations. For example, if an infant detects the amodal synchrony, rhythm, and/or tempo uniting a person's face and his or her voice, the infant is then likely to learn the unique and arbitrary relation between the pitch/timber of that individual's voice and the particular configuration of his or her face. In contrast, if no common synchrony, rhythm, or tempo is detected, the association between the appearance of the face and sound of the voice is less likely to be learned. This principle was found to apply to intersensory learning about the arbitrary relation between the appearance of an object and the speech sound paired with it (Gogate & Bahrick, 1998), the color/pattern of an object and its tactually experienced shape (Hernandez-Reif & Bahrick, 2001), and the visual appearance of a single or compound object striking a surface and the particular sound it produced (Bahrick, 1988, 1992, 1994). Even newborns show evidence of learning arbitrary audiovisual relations in the presence of amodal information but not in its absence (Slater, Quinn, Brown, & Hayes, 1999). Studies of a variety of events perceived through various sensory modalities now suggest that detection of amodal information such as temporal synchrony can promote further differentiation of the unitary event and lead to learning about nested properties and, finally, about arbitrary, modality-specific relations.

This developmental sequence where learning progresses in order of increasing specificity (from detection of amodal to arbitrary, modality-specific relations) is adaptive because it can promote learning about consistencies and regularities across the senses that are context-independent prior to learning about more context-dependent relations (see Bahrick, 2001). Early detection of amodal relations fosters appropriate, veridical generalizations and minimizes inappropriate generalizations about relations that vary across contexts and are specific to certain events. In this manner, detection of amodal relations can guide and constrain learning about modality-specific relations such that general principles (e.g., voices go with faces; male faces go with deeper voices and female faces go with higher voices; happy faces go with happy voices; single objects make single impact sounds; rigid objects make abrupt impact sounds) are well established prior to learning about more specific details of these events (e.g., John's face goes with a low, raspy voice; a particular speech sound goes with a particular object; the high squeaking sound is made by the yellow duck; the red object makes a musical sound when struck). This progression from global to specific is adaptive and provides a means of organizing, guiding, and constraining perceptual learning in a way that will efficiently lead to the intermodal knowledge of adult perceivers.

The above research has revealed important principles of perceptual development explaining attentional allocation, perception, and learning about events experienced multimodally. These principles were all derived in multimodal research paradigms where infants received simultaneous audible and visible stimulation, as is typical in the natural environment. However, stimulation from a given event does not always reach multiple sense modalities. For example, one might experience a voice from a nearby room, the sounds of unseen hands clapping, or the sight of a silent face. Although less typical in the infant's world, properties of events, including amodal properties (e.g., tempo, rhythm, substance, composition, intensity, etc.) and modality-specific properties (e.g., color, pattern, pitch, timber), can be experienced in the context of unimodal stimulation as contrasted with multimodal sensory stimulation.

Are the principles of perceptual learning derived from the study of multimodal events (described above) applicable to these unimodal contexts as well? Conversely, how does unimodal exploration of events generalize to exploration of the typical multimodal environment? This is not only an important theoretical question; it is significant for practical and methodological reasons as well.

## Unimodal vs. Multimodal Stimulation

Developmental psychologists have traditionally studied the development of specific perceptual or cognitive abilities in one sense modality at a time and eliminated concurrent stimulation to other sense modalities in their research designs. Thus, theories of speech perception and language development have traditionally been formulated by focusing on the auditory stream devoid of the speaking face; theories of face perception have primarily been based on studies of unimodal, visual facial displays; memory has been studied for static visual displays or for auditory information separately; early communication has been studied by examining joint visual attention without the vocal accompaniment, and so forth, to name a few examples (for a review of this type of research, see Kuhn & Siegler, 1998). However, all these capabilities emerge in a primarily multimodal context of people who coordinate speech, gesture, facial movements, and touch, and of objects and events that can typically be seen and heard. As a consequence, we know little from these studies about how perception and cognition actually develop in the context of the multimodal environment (Lickliter & Bahrick, 2001). Because of this nearly exclusive historical focus on the development of capabilities in single sense modalities, and because of the growing appreciation of the "unity of the senses" even in young infants, the area of intersensory perception emerged and has grown into an important area of research in its own right. However, the field of psychology continues to reflect this dichotomy, with "intersensory" research delineated as a separate area, as if it were a content area unto itself. Thus, research on intersensory perception has been for the most part segregated from research on the same questions explored in unimodal stimulation. Research on the development of a particular competence (be it speech or face perception, memory, or categorization, etc.) is likely to be conducted in separate studies of unimodal vs. multimodal perception, and undertaken by separate investigators. Consequently, the research findings from the two areas are not easily integrated and studies of unimodal and multimodal perception are difficult to compare, typically employing methods and measures that differ. Further, few studies actually compare responsiveness in one sense modality to responsiveness in two or more sense modalities, and thus it is not known how detection of properties of events generalize from unimodal to multimodal contexts or from multimodal to unimodal contexts. Moreover, it is not known whether the principles of perceptual learning derived from the study of multimodal events (such as those described above) are generalizable to unimodal contexts and, conversely, whether theories and findings derived from unimodal exposure to events generalize to the typical multimodal environment. Research findings from "multimodal" and "unimodal" studies of the development of attention, perception, cognition, and social competencies are badly in need of integration.

## Insights from Psychobiology and Neuroscience

Research from the area of developmental psychobiology on animal infants provides some insight into this important issue. In comparative studies of perceptual development, conditions of multimodal and unimodal stimulation have typically been included in single designs and compared. Research from this area suggests that unimodal and multimodal stimulation are functionally different for the developing system, and information presented to the different senses interacts in complex ways. For example, at the neural level of analysis, it has been found that visual orienting in cats is dramatically affected by a co-located auditory stimulus (Meredith & Stein, 1986; Stein, Meredith, & Wallace, 1994). Stein and Meredith (1993) proposed a "multiplicative" effect where the magnitude of neural responsiveness from bimodal (audiovisual) stimulation exceeds the magnitude predicted by adding together the responsiveness from each modality alone. At the neural level, unimodal and multimodal stimulation (for a given stimulus location) are responded to differently.

Research at the behavioral level also points out that significantly different consequences result from multimodal vs. unimodal stimulation in the period just following hatching. For example, the pioneering work of Gottlieb and his colleagues on species identification in birds (Gottlieb, 1971a; Johnston & Gottlieb, 1981; Lickliter, Dyer, & McBride, 1993; Lickliter & Gottlieb, 1988) has demonstrated that multimodal experience from conspecifics (i.e., auditory, visual, and tactile) in the period just following hatching is a key component in the development and maintenance of normal perceptual and social preferences underlying species identification. Research with precocial bird embryos and hatchlings has also demonstrated that uncoupling multimodal experience can lead to changes in the young organism's normal developmental pattern (Columbus, Sleigh, Lickliter, & Lewkowicz, 1998; Sleigh, Columbus, & Lickliter, 1998). For example, quail chicks who received only unimodal auditory or visual stimulation just after hatching show abnormal perceptual responsiveness to auditory, visual, and multimodal maternal stimulation during the early postnatal period. Even visual responsiveness (as well as multimodal responsiveness) is delayed if chicks have unimodal visual stimulation just after hatching, demonstrating the complex interdependencies among the developing senses (Sleigh et al., 1998). Further, it has been established that in prenatal development the senses become functional in an invariant sequence across species. First the tactile, vestibular, then chemical senses emerge. Late in gestation, audition becomes functional, and not until after birth or hatching does vision become functional. Researchers (Gottlieb, 1971b; Turkewitz & Kenney, 1982) have proposed that the sequential onset of function of the various senses has important consequences for perceptual development. It allows earlier-developing systems to differentiate and mature without competition from other senses. Consequently, the development of audition occurs *in utero/ovo* without competition from visual input. Just after birth, typically vision becomes functional and this likely creates a sudden increase in the degree and nature of intersensory interactions. This principle underscores that important interdependencies exist among the senses, but it has received little attention from researchers of human infant development.

The neural and comparative findings point out important differences in both behavioral and neural outcomes resulting from unimodal vs. multimodal exposure to events. These differences should be taken as a caution against generalizing research findings from unimodal to multimodal contexts, and vice versa, in human infants without an empirical basis (Lickliter & Bahrick, 2001). They point out the need and importance for researchers of the development of perception and cognition in human infants to limit generalizations to the context (unimodal vs. multimodal) in which the investigation was conducted. Thus, research based on unimodal stimulation (e.g., such as that from speech or from faces) should be limited to generalizations regarding unimodal contexts (e.g., faces in the absence of speech; the speech stream devoid of faces). Conversely, research based on multimodal stimulation (e.g., coordinated faces and voices) should be generalized to multimodal contexts (multimodal faces and voices). Research will be ecologically valid to the extent that generalizations are appropriate to these important contextual differences. Second, the comparative findings point out the need for investigations of human perceptual and cognitive development to incorporate conditions of unimodal and multimodal stimulation into single designs and to examine the nature of resulting interactions.

To this end, and as a first step toward integrating research from the areas of "unimodal" vs. "multimodal" paradigms, we (Bahrick & Lickliter, 2000, 2002) have developed a framework for investigating the development of perception in unimodal and multimodal contexts. This framework is called the "intersensory redundancy hypothesis" and explains how perceptual development unfolds as a consequence of unimodal and multimodal exploration of events. It is a systems perspective in that it takes into account the organism and the nature of its exploratory activity in relation to the environment and the nature of the sensory stimulation it provides for exploration. In the remainder of this chapter, I describe the intersensory redundancy hypothesis, data generated from studies with young infants, and consequences for theories of attention, perception, and cognition of this way of thinking about development.

## The Intersensory Redundancy Hypothesis: Integration of Unimodal and Multimodal Research Paradigms

The "intersensory redundancy hypothesis" (Bahrick & Lickliter, 2000, 2002) holds that in early development, information presented redundantly and in temporal synchrony to two or more sense modalities recruits infant attention and facilitates perceptual differentiation of that information more effectively than does the same information presented to one sense modality at a time. Intersensory redundancy refers to the spatially coordinated and concurrent presentation of the same information (e.g., tempo, rhythm, intensity change, temporal microstructure, etc.) across two or more sense modalities. Only amodal properties of events can be presented redundantly since, by definition, amodal information is information that can be conveyed by more than one type of sensory stimulation. Thus, consistent with Gibson's (1969) invariant detection view, the hypothesis emphasizes that the concurrent pick-up of the same information in two sense modalities is highly salient to young organisms and directs exploration. This causes amodal, redundant stimulus properties to become "foreground" and other properties to become "background," and promotes earlier processing of redundant stimulation than other types of stimulation. Since intersensory redundancy is typically available, this causes perception, learning, and memory for amodal properties to develop prior to other properties. This amodal processing precedence, in turn, has long-range effects on perception, cognition, social, and emotional development.

However, at times, intersensory redundancy is not available, either because the organism is not actively exploring a particular event with multiple senses, or because the environment is not providing redundant stimulation for a particular event at that point in time. In this case, amodal information (e.g., rhythm or rate) from a given event may be available to only a single sense modality (e.g., the sounds of hands clapping an irregular rhythm, or the sight of a light flashing at a rapid rate). The amodal property would then not be redundantly specified, and therefore it would not be expected to be salient. Further, according to the hypothesis, when redundancy is not available, and consequently unimodal stimulation from the event is provided, infant attention is likely to be recruited toward modality-specific properties of the event (color, pattern, orientation, pitch, timber, etc.), at the expense of other properties. This unimodal exploration enhances perceptual differentiation of modality-specific information (as compared with the same information presented in the context of redundancy).

Thus, the nature of the exploration (unimodal vs. bimodal) afforded to the organism interacts with the type of property explored (amodal vs. modality-specific) to determine the attentional salience of various properties. Figure 4.2 depicts this relationship. As can be seen from the figure, there is an advantage given to

| Stimulation available for exploration | Stimulus property: Amodal | Stimulus property: Modality-specific |
|---|---|---|
| Multimodal (auditory-visual) | + | – |
| Unimodal (auditory or visual) | – | + |

**Figure 4.2** Predictions of the intersensory redundancy hypothesis. Facilitation vs. attenuation of attention and perceptual processing for amodal vs. modality-specific properties of stimulation as a function of the type of stimulation (multimodal vs. unimodal) available for exploration (from Bahrick & Lickliter, 2002). Reprinted with permission of Elsevier.

bimodal exploration of amodal properties and to unimodal exploration of modality-specific properties, whereas processing will be disadvantaged for bimodal exploration of modality-specific properties (e.g., listening to the pitch and timber of a voice while also seeing the speaking face), and for unimodal exploration of amodal properties (e.g., seeing a rhythm displayed visually without sound, or hearing a rhythm in sound without visual accompaniment).

Perceptual development is thus characterized by an intercoordination between exploration of amodal and modality-specific properties of events, and because of the prevalence of redundancy, detection of amodal information leads and constrains learning about modality-specific properties of stimulation. It should be noted that the terms "amodal" and "modality-specific" have a broad and context-sensitive meaning in the present framework in the sense that they are dependent on the modality context of stimulation. Thus, in the present framework where the modalities used for exploration are auditory and visual, "modality-specific" refers to properties that are available in visual but not auditory stimulation, and in auditory but not visual stimulation, and "amodal" refers to properties that can be redundantly specified by both auditory and visual stimulation. Some properties, therefore, are classified as modality-specific in the context of audiovisual stimulation, such as texture or direction and orientation of motion, even though they could also be conveyed tactually. In the context of visual-tactile exploration, they would be classified differently.

Intersensory redundancy impacts the organism first at the level of attention. The effects of redundancy on perception, learning, and memory appear to derive from differential attentional allocation to various properties of events as a function of multimodal vs. unimodal stimulation. When redundancy is present, it is highly salient and attention will be promoted to amodal properties of stimulation. It should also be noted, however, that attention can be impacted by a variety of other factors (e.g., the internal state of the organism, sudden movement or changes in intensity of stimulation, violation of expectancies, etc.), and the effects of intersensory redundancy would likely be attenuated or, alternatively, maximized by these factors. However, once attention is captured by intersensory redundancy, exploration of amodal properties of the event is promoted, and this in turn promotes attention to nested amodal properties of the event, and, eventually, to modality-specific properties. Thus, perceptual development proceeds in order of increasing specificity across development (Bahrick, 2001; Gibson, 1969).

Further, this sequence of increasing specificity and the amodal processing precedence observed across development likely has its roots in a similar processing sequence that occurs within a given episode of exploration at any given age. Within an episode of exploration, attention also likely proceeds in order of increasing specificity. If an event provides intersensory redundancy and captures attention, then, according to this hypothesis, attention will first be focused on global amodal relations, followed by nested amodal relations, and, eventually, on modality-specific properties. Once the infant has explored the redundant amodal relations uniting the multimodal stimulation from an event, this promotes continued processing of the unitary event and guides attention to nested, increasingly more specific levels of stimulation. If exploration is not terminated, it may eventually proceed to modality-specific aspects of stimulation. Thus, just as perceptual development proceeds from detection of global to specific aspects of stimulation, perceptual processing within a given episode of exploration may proceed from global to specific aspects of stimulation. A similar global processing precedence within an episode of exploration has been demonstrated for exploration of unimodal visual stimuli (see Freeseman, Colombo, & Coldren, 1993; Frick, Colombo, & Allen, 2000). However, if exploration is interrupted, the event changes or terminates, or the infant disengages, then the more specific levels of stimulation will remain unexplored and greater processing time will have been devoted to more global levels of stimulation. Consequently, in early phases of development, when attention is more limited and it takes longer to process information, it is the global, amodal relations that will receive maximum attention. This is hypothesized to lead to the developmental pattern of increasing specificity observed in our studies (e.g., Bahrick, 2001). This global processing advantage is adaptive in very young organisms and promotes veridical perceptual development. However, these are important empirical questions and should be tested across a variety of domains. If the global to specific sequence reflects a general pattern of multimodal processing, according to the intersensory redundancy hypothesis, the advantage of intersensory redundancy should be most evident and pronounced during early phases of exploration or processing a particular event. Research is currently underway to test this prediction.

It should also be emphasized that the facilitating effects of intersensory redundancy on differentiation of amodal properties will be most apparent when infants or organisms are first learning a skill and when detection of the information is difficult. Once the skill is mastered or the perceptual discrimination is easier, the information in question (e.g., a rhythmic sequence) can be detected rapidly and can likely be discriminated in both unimodal and bimodal stimulation. At this point, results generated from unimodal and bimodal conditions would be indistinguishable due to this ceiling effect. Thus, the effects of intersensory redundancy should be most apparent when the organism is first learning to differentiate information. That the effects of redundancy appear to be most pronounced in early development has important implications for attention, perception, learning, and memory. Since these capabilities emerge primarily in a multimodal context, and initial conditions can have important influences on the trajectory and organization of development, the effects of intersensory redundancy are likely to have lasting effects on the nature and course of later development across a variety of areas. Because sensitivity to intersensory redundancy occurs so early in development and so pervasively, it can create a cascading effect across development such that its consequences manifest in an ever-widening trajectory across a variety of domains during the course of ontogeny (see Michel & Moore, 1995, and Moore, 1990, for examples of such cascading effects). The intersensory redundancy hypothesis can thus potentially serve as a model to guide appropriate interventions for developmental delays in a variety of areas as a function of the type of property in question (amodal vs. modality-specific) and the likely basis of the developmental delay.

## Empirical Support for the Intersensory Redundancy Hypothesis

The intersensory redundancy hypothesis has received recent empirical support from a variety of studies. The attentional salience of intersensory redundancy and ability of redundancy to direct the flow of attention are illustrated in an early study of selective attention in infancy (Bahrick et al., 1981). Infants were shown two films of naturalistic events (hands clapping, a toy slinky being manipulated, or a xylophone being played). The films were shown superimposed upon one another and accompanied by the natural soundtrack to one of them. When adults viewed the superimposed events silently, they appeared to be like two ghostly images passing through one another (see figure 4.3). However, when the soundtrack was turned on, the sound-specified film seemed to jump out from the background of the silent event, creating a strong impression of figure and ground. When the other soundtrack was played, the second event immediately became figure and the other, background. Attention seemed compelled by the sound. The addition of sound created intersensory redundancy for properties such as the rhythm, tempo, intensity shifts, and synchrony of the visible and audible events. In the experiment, we explored

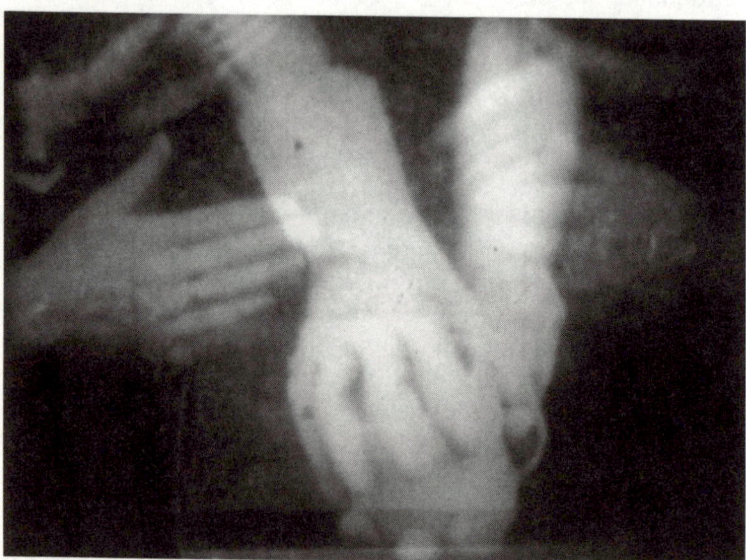

**Figure 4.3** Photograph of two superimposed images (from Bahrick et al., 1981). Reprinted with permission of Elsevier.

whether infant attention was similarly directed by the soundtrack and the redundancy it created. Infants viewed the superimposed events along with a soundtrack, and then received test trials where the films were separated and played silently side by side. Infants demonstrated that they had attended to the sound-specified event and ignored the silent one by showing a visual preference for the novel, previously "unseen" event during test trials. A second study confirmed this interpretation. When infants were shown only one centrally projected film along with its soundtrack, and then received silent, side-by-side test trials as before, they again showed a novelty preference of the same magnitude (figure 4.4

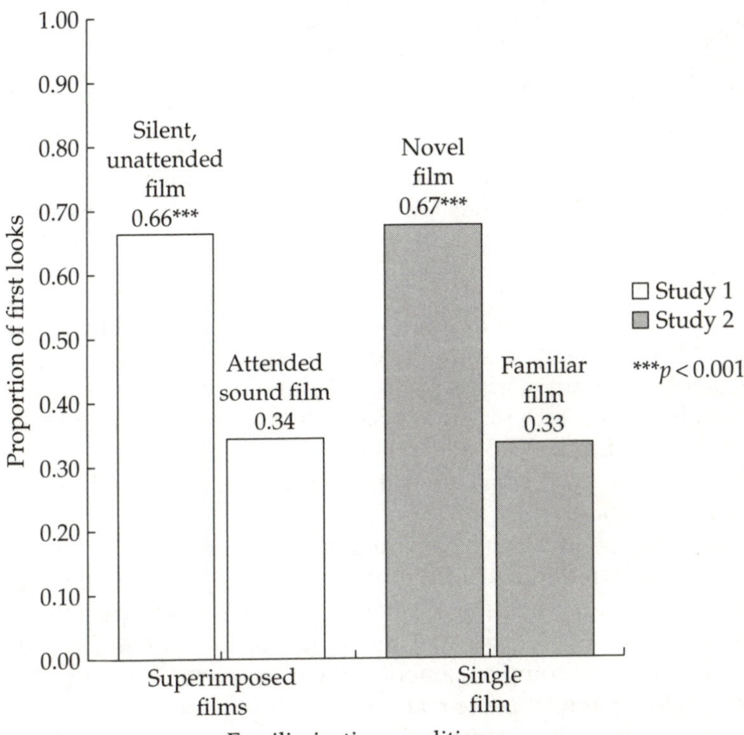


**Figure 4.4** Proportion of first looks during the test trials when the films were presented separately and side by side as a function of the infant's familiarization condition. In one condition, familiarization was conducted to two superimposed films along with a soundtrack that belonged with one of them, and in the other condition, familiarization was conducted to a single film along with its soundtrack. Results indicate novelty preferences for the silent, unattended, superimposed film and for the novel, unseen film (from Bahrick et al., 1981).

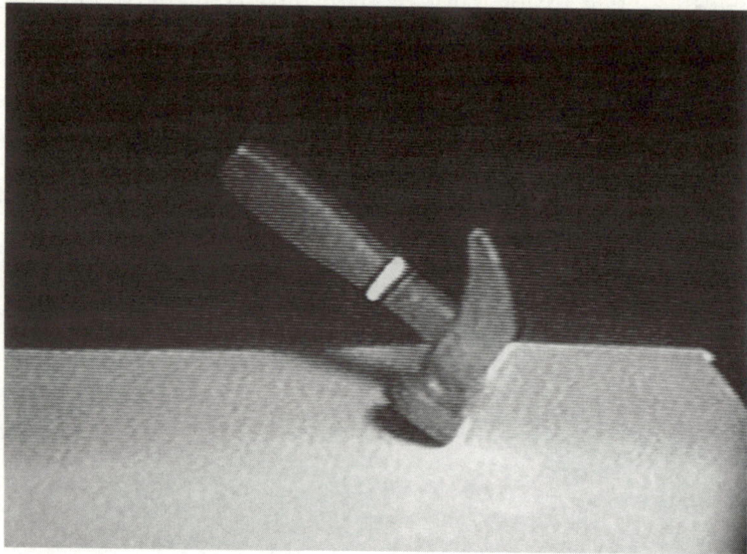

**Figure 4.5** Photograph of the red hammer used to display the rhythmic sequences (from Bahrick & Lickliter, 2000).

depicts the results of these two studies). Infants appeared to respond to the events in the way adults did, by attending to the sound-specified film, even though another event was visually superimposed upon it. Intersensory redundancy across vision and audition can direct the flow of attention, allowing redundancy to become foreground and other visual stimulation to become background, even when all visual stimulation occupies the same spatial location.

Several recent studies have demonstrated the effectiveness of intersensory redundancy for promoting attention and facilitating perceptual differentiation of amodal properties of events. Bahrick and Lickliter (2000) assessed the ability of 5-month-old infants to discriminate complex, amodal, rhythmic patterns in bimodal, redundant stimulation as compared with unimodal stimulation. Infants were habituated to videos of a red plastic hammer (depicted in figure 4.5) tapping out a distinctive rhythm under conditions of bimodal, redundant stimulation (they could see and hear the hammer), unimodal visual stimulation (they could only see the hammer moving), or unimodal auditory stimulation (they could only hear the soundtrack to the hammer). Infants then received test trials depicting a new rhythm. Results are depicted in figure 4.6. They indicated that infants who received the bimodal,

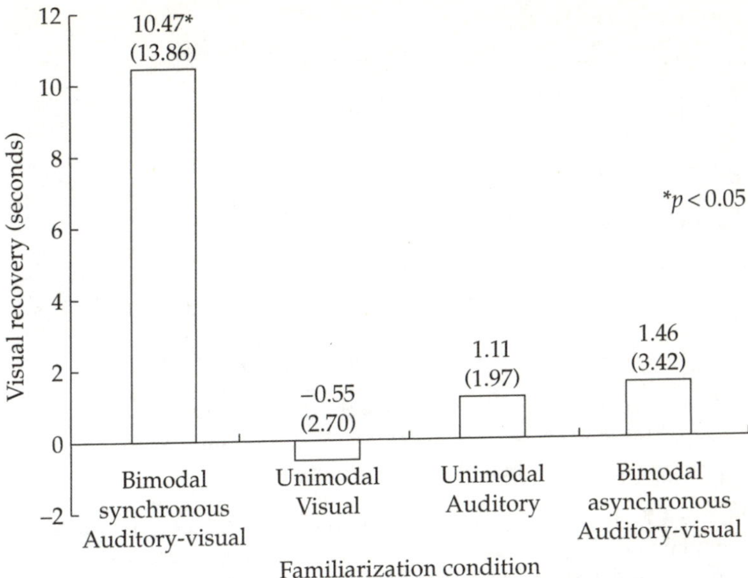


**Figure 4.6** Infants' visual recovery to a change in rhythm following bimodal synchronous audiovisual habituation, asynchronous audiovisual habituation, unimodal visual, and unimodal auditory habituation (from Bahrick & Lickliter, 2000).

redundant stimulation showed robust, significant visual recovery to the change in rhythm, whereas those who received unimodal visual and those who received unimodal auditory stimulation showed no recovery to the change in rhythm. These findings demonstrated that only infants who received redundant, bimodal stimulation from a rhythm were able to perceive the rhythm and discriminate it from a similar one, whereas those who received unimodal stimulation were not. A further study assessed rhythm discrimination for bimodal, nonredundant stimulation (asynchronous films and soundtracks of the hammers tapping) and found no evidence of rhythm discrimination (see figure 4.6). Infants required redundancy in the form of temporal synchrony between the visual and acoustic stimulation for discrimination of rhythm.

A second study replicated and extended the findings of Bahrick and Lickliter (2000) documenting the facilitating effects of intersensory redundancy for the detection of amodal information, by testing detection of a different amodal property with infants of a younger age. Bahrick, Flom, and Lickliter (2002) assessed

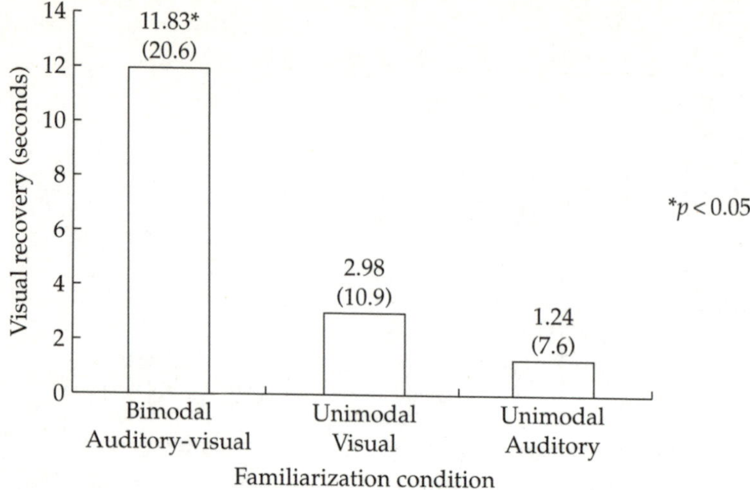


**Figure 4.7** Infants' visual recovery to a change in tempo following bimodal audiovisual habituation, unimodal visual, or unimodal auditory habituation (from Bahrick, Flom, & Lickliter, 2002).

discrimination of tempo in 3-month-old infants, in a similar paradigm. Infants were habituated to films of the red hammer tapping out a rhythmic sequence in one of two tempos (55 bpm vs. 120 bpm). The same tempo could be detected visually by watching the hammer, or acoustically by listening to its impact sounds. Infants received bimodal, redundant, audiovisual stimulation, unimodal visual stimulation, or unimodal auditory stimulation during habituation. Then they received test trials depicting a novel tempo. Results are depicted in figure 4.7, and are remarkably similar to those of the prior study assessing rhythm discrimination with older infants. They demonstrated discrimination of the tempos following bimodal, audiovisual stimulation, but not following unimodal visual or unimodal auditory stimulation. These findings converge with those of rhythm discrimination and demonstrate the facilitating effects of intersensory redundancy for guiding attentional selectivity and fostering perceptual differentiation in early infancy. It should be noted that the stimulus events in these studies were chosen to be difficult for infants of the ages tested. The five-element rhythms differed only in relative timing (the arrangement of elements) and were chosen to be difficult for 5-month-olds. Tests of tempo were considered easier than rhythm and thus 3-month-olds were tested since these tests were likely to challenge infants of this age. Together, these studies suggest that when infants first learn to differentiate specific amodal properties, differentiation is facilitated by intersensory redundancy. However, it was not known to what extent the facilitating effects of intersensory redundancy would persist across development. According to the intersensory redundancy hypothesis, the advantage of intersensory redundancy should be most pronounced when infants are first learning a skill, and attenuated later in development. That is, once infants become proficient at detecting a particular property, perception of that property should become increasingly flexible and should no longer require redundancy. An amodal property may then be detected in unimodal stimulation.

Bahrick, Lickliter, and Flom (2002) tested this hypothesis. We assessed the ability of 8-month-old infants to discriminate complex rhythms in a task just like that experienced by the 5-month-olds in our prior study. Infants received videos of the hammer tapping out one of the two rhythms, as before. Infants were habituated to the rhythmic sequences in the context of bimodal, redundant audiovisual stimulation or unimodal, visual stimulation. Test trials depicted a novel rhythm. Results indicated that infants in both the redundant audiovisual and the unimodal visual condition showed significant visual recovery to the change in rhythm. These findings contrast with those of the 5-month-olds and demonstrate that by 8 months, infants no longer required intersensory redundancy for discriminating complex rhythmic sequences. Together, they support the intersensory redundancy hypothesis and our developmental prediction, that perception of amodal properties emerges in the context of redundancy and is later extended to nonredundant, unimodal contexts. Further research is underway to determine whether, once infants detect amodal relations in unimodal stimulation, there still exists a facilitating effect of redundancy. It is expected that if the task is made more difficult, or the processing time shortened, the advantage of redundancy would become apparent. In any event, the facilitating effects of redundancy are apparently most pronounced when infants are younger and first learning a particular skill. This initial salience of redundancy has important implications for the development of perception and cognition. It creates a developmental precedence for detection of properties that are amodal and redundantly specified and this guides early attention, perception, and learning.

Additional research has also focused on the perception of modality-specific properties of events perceived in unimodal vs. bimodal, redundant stimulation (the right-hand quadrants of figure 4.2). According to the intersensory redundancy hypothesis, information experienced in one sense modality selectively recruits attention to modality-specific properties of events and facilitates perceptual differentiation of those properties at the expense of other properties. To evaluate this hypothesis, we again tested 5-month-old infants, this time assessing detection of orientation, a property available visually but not acoustically. We expected that infants would discriminate changes in orientation during unimodal visual, but not bimodal audiovisual, stimulation. Infants were again habituated to films of the hammer tapping out a rhythm; however, this time the movements of the hammer were depicted in one of two orientations (upward vs. downward). Either the hammer hit downward against a wooden floor, or it hit upward against a wooden ceiling. Infants received habituation to videos of the hammers in one of the two orientations in the bimodal, audiovisual condition (where they could see and hear the hammer moving) or the unimodal, visual condition (where they could only see the hammer moving). Then infants received test trials, under their respective conditions, where the orientation of the hammer was changed. Results indicated significant visual recovery to the change in orientation following unimodal visual habituation, but not following bimodal audiovisual habituation. Thus, consistent with predictions of the intersensory redundancy hypothesis, 5-month-olds discriminated changes in orientation, a visual property, following unimodal visual exposure, but not following redundant, bimodal exposure. Apparently, the addition of the soundtrack created intersensory redundancy and selectively recruited attention away from unimodally conveyed properties and toward redundantly specified properties of stimulation (as in Bahrick & Lickliter, 2000, and Bahrick, Flom, & Lickliter, 2002). In contrast, the unimodal, visual stimulation promoted attention to visual properties of the event without competition from salient redundant properties. Thus, attention to modality-specific or nonredundantly specified properties is likely best fostered in the context of unimodal exploration when competition from concurrent redundantly specified properties is minimized.

This observation is consistent with insights gained from comparative studies regarding the sequential onset of the functioning of the senses (Gottlieb, 1971b; Turkewitz & Kenney, 1982). In prenatal development, earlier-developing senses are able to differentiate without competition from later-developing senses. Thus, auditory perception develops during the last trimester of gestation without competition from visual stimulation. Similarly, competition appears to play an important role in regulating attentional allocation to different properties of events during postnatal development. Our research suggests that after birth, unimodal exploration (of a face or voice, for example) is promoted when there is little competition from concurrent, amodal, redundant stimulation. This unimodal exploration likely fosters differentiation of auditory or visual information in a manner that is not supported when redundant stimulation is available. Thus, differentiation of the appearance of a face would be best promoted when the face is silent and relatively still, whereas when the individual is speaking and moving, competition from audiovisual redundancy would be more likely to focus attention on amodal properties such as prosody, rhythm, tempo, and intensity variations common to the speech and facial movement.

The attentional salience of intersensory redundancy and its facilitation of perceptual learning have also been observed recently in comparative studies of animal infants. Lickliter et al. (2002) found that intersensory redundancy facilitates prenatal auditory learning in bobwhite quail chicks. Bobwhite quail embryos were exposed to an individual maternal call for 6, 12, or 24 hours, under conditions of unimodal auditory stimulation, concurrent but asynchronous auditory and visual stimulation, or redundant and synchronous auditory and visual stimulation. They were then tested one day after hatching to determine if they preferred the familiar maternal call over an unfamiliar version of the maternal call. Results are depicted in figure 4.8. They indicated that chicks who received the redundant audiovisual exposure significantly preferred the familiar maternal call following all exposure durations, whereas those who received the nonredundant audiovisual exposure showed no preference for the familiar call after any exposure duration. Chicks who received the unimodal auditory familiarization showed eventual learning and preferred the familiar call following the longest period (24 hours) of prenatal exposure. These results demonstrate that bobwhite quail chicks show greatly enhanced learning of the maternal call when amodal information (tempo, rhythm, duration) is presented redundantly, across two sense modalities. These findings extend the facilitating effects of intersensory redundancy to the prenatal period and to a different species.

This converging evidence across species, developmental periods, and properties of events highlights the fundamental importance of intersensory redundancy for promoting attention and fostering perceptual differentiation of amodal properties of events. Further, it explains how, in a predominantly multimodal

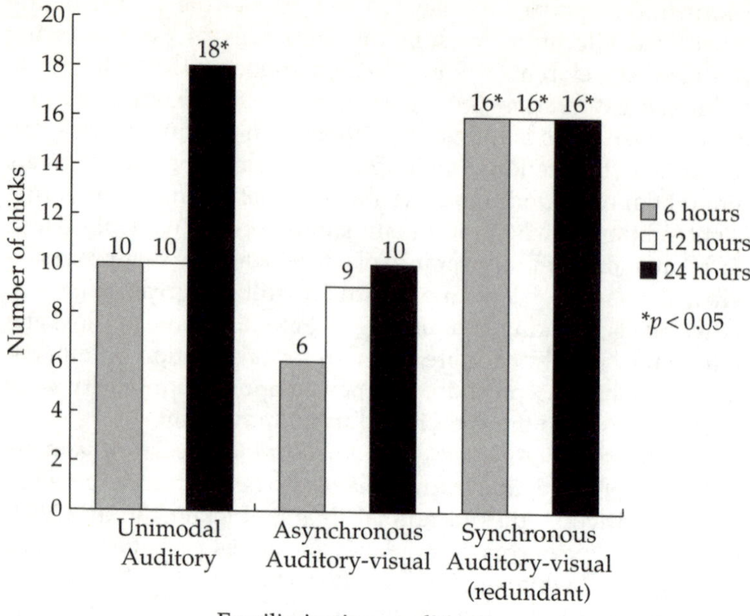


**Figure 4.8** Number of chicks showing a preference for the maternal call with which they were familiarized during prenatal development under conditions of unimodal auditory stimulation, concurrent but asynchronous audiovisual stimulation, or redundant and synchronous audiovisual stimulation. Note: in each group 26 chicks were tested and their data were classified into one of three categories, a preference for the familiar call (shown here), a preference for the novel call, or a preference for neither/both calls (from Lickliter et al., 2002).

environment, perceptual learning is guided and constrained by detection of amodal relations. These findings also converge to demonstrate that there are conditions under which attention to amodal properties is not facilitated, and attention to modality-specific properties and nonredundant aspects of stimulation is favored. That is, when a given event provides stimulation to only a single sense modality, attention and learning about unimodally specified properties of events are enhanced. Modality-specific properties are best differentiated when competition from intersensory redundancy is not present. This important interaction between attention to amodal vs. modality-specific properties in unimodal vs. multimodal stimulation underlies the concurrent and interrelated course of development of intersensory and unimodal perceptual capabilities across the period of infancy.

## Conclusion

In this chapter, I have described a number of basic principles underlying the development of attention, perception, and cognition as it emerges in a multimodal environment. The intersensory redundancy hypothesis provides a working framework for viewing the allocation of attention and its effects on the development of perception and learning in an environment that provides both redundancy across the senses and modality-specific information about objects and events in an interdependent system. The intersensory redundancy hypothesis highlights an important and previously unexplored interaction (depicted in figure 4.2) between the stimulation provided by an event for infant exploration (unimodal vs. multimodal) and the selective processing of different properties of stimulation (amodal vs. modality-specific). Under conditions of multimodal stimulation where redundancy is routinely available, attention is likely to be initially and primarily focused on amodal properties of stimulation. Since multimodal stimulation is typical, this creates a processing priority for amodal stimulation and promotes earlier perceptual differentiation, learning, and memory for properties of events that are amodal (e.g., synchrony, intensity, rhythm, tempo, temporal microstructure). In contrast, when an event provides stimulation to only a single sense modality, the infant's attention to modality-specific and nonredundant properties of stimulation is likely to be promoted. This fosters attention to and differentiation of properties such as color, pattern, timber, pitch, and orientation, without competition from the more salient redundantly specified properties. Together, these principles portray a developmental trajectory where differentiation of amodal and modality-specific properties emerges in a coordinated and interdependent manner, with detection of amodal properties leading and constraining learning about more specific properties of events. These principles have now received support from a number of recent studies (e.g., Bahrick, 1992, 1994, 2001; Gogate & Bahrick, 1998; Hernandez Reif & Bahrick, 2001).

The perceptual precedence of amodal stimulation and the intercoordinated exploration of amodal and modality-specific properties of events are adaptive for perceptual development in several respects. First, the prevalence and salience of intersensory redundancy fosters attention to unitary multimodal events. This facilitates further processing of visual, acoustic, and tactile stimulation that belong together. Perceptual differentiation can thus proceed in order of increasing specificity, with attention to global, amodal relations, followed by nested amodal relations, and finally modality-specific, arbitrary relations, as demonstrated in recent research (Bahrick, 1992, 1994, 2001). Second, the salience of redundancy and detection of amodal relations serves as a buffer against premature learning of specific details that vary from one context or event to another. Relations between modality-specific properties across the senses are often arbitrary and not generalizable across contexts or events. For example, the color or shape of an object does not consistently go with the pitch or timber of its sound. The salience of redundancy focuses attention on amodal intersensory relations that are global and invariant across events and contexts. For example, single objects produce single impact sounds; faces go with voices; happy faces go with happy voices. Thus, learning about specific details is likely to be delayed until the organism has a multimodal framework from which to make sense of the details, and therefore, generalizations based on specific details are likely to be appropriately constrained.

Thus, the advantage of intersensory redundancy should be most apparent in early development when new skills and knowledge first emerge. Clearly, though, infants eventually become skilled at detecting amodal and modality-specific properties in both unimodal and multimodal stimulation and thus, later in development, the facilitating effects of redundancy would be less apparent. However, even in later development when individuals first learn a new skill or when a task is difficult, redundancy may also benefit learning. For example, adults learning to speak a new language or disambiguate speech sounds in a noisy environment may benefit from detection of amodal, audiovisual information (Massaro, 1998).

These findings regarding the salience of intersensory redundancy and its importance for learning about global aspects of events are consistent with the recent body of research from comparative studies (e.g., Lickliter et al., 2002; Sleigh et al., 1998) and from neural studies demonstrating the existence of multisensory neurons and the heightened neural responsiveness to redundant, multimodal stimulation (e.g., Stein & Meredith, 1993). Thus, converging evidence across species and across levels of analysis points to the attentional salience of intersensory redundancy and its importance for perceptual learning.

In response to the question posed in the introduction concerning which factors initially organize attention and perception such that its developmental trajectory provides the foundation for the knowledge base and competencies of the adult perceiver, several answers have been put forth in this chapter. In brief, detection of amodal relations in the context of redundancy provides an economical and effective avenue for initiating and organizing perceptual development along a trajectory that can effectively lead to the knowledge of adult perceivers. It guides and constrains detection of more specific information so that unitary events are explored in a coordinated manner and specific details are perceived in the context of more general principles that organize those details. This amodal processing precedence in turn has an effect on the development of perceptual, conceptual, social, and linguistic competence.

The intersensory redundancy hypothesis and the empirical findings that support it also provide a basis and a framework for integrating the bodies of research generated from studies of unimodal perception with those of multimodal perception. Typically, research in these areas has been conducted by different investigators with different methods and has enjoyed little cross-fertilization. The present framework suggests several important generalizations and avenues for cross-fertilization. In an environment that provides both redundancy across the senses and modality-specific information about properties of objects and events, the intersensory redundancy hypothesis provides a framework for understanding how unimodal and multimodal exploration of our environment interacts with and differentially affects perceptual learning. Multimodal exploration promotes attention and learning of amodal properties, whereas unimodal exploration promotes attention and learning of modality-specific aspects of stimulation. Given the prevalence of multimodal stimulation, detection of amodal information typically leads and constrains learning about modality-specific stimulation. Thus, detection of amodal and modality-specific properties of events progresses as part of an interrelated system that is dependent on the nature of the organism's exploration and the nature of stimulation provided by the event.

This insight calls for more research that includes both unimodal and multimodal conditions in single designs. It points out the need for sensitivity to variables such as the nature of infant exploration (unimodal or multimodal) and the type of stimulus properties explored (amodal vs. modality-specific). This insight also underscores the importance of limiting generalizations of research findings to contexts and factors that closely resemble those of the research setting. Thus, research on unimodal stimulation (such as that from speech or faces) should be limited to generalizations regarding unimodal stimulation (faces in the absence of speech, and speech in the absence of moving faces). Similarly, research on the perception of multimodal stimulation (e.g., coordinated face–voice stimulation) should be generalized to conditions of multimodal stimulation (coordinated faces and voices). Attention to the importance of modality and context in research settings, and limiting generalizations appropriately, will foster a more meaningful integration of the bodies of research generated from unimodal vs. multimodal perception (Lickliter & Bahrick, 2001).

## REFERENCES

Allen, T. W., Walker, K., Symonds, L., & Marcell, M. (1977). Intrasensory and intersensory perception of temporal sequences during infancy. *Developmental Psychology*, 13, 225–9.

Bahrick, L. E. (1983). Infants' perception of substance and temporal synchrony in multimodal events. *Infant Behavior and Development*, 6, 429–51.

Bahrick, L. E. (1987). Infants' intermodal perception of two levels of temporal structure in natural events. *Infant Behavior and Development*, 10, 387–416.

Bahrick, L. E. (1988). Intermodal learning in infancy: Learning on the basis of two kinds of invariant relations in audible and visible events. *Child Development*, 59, 197–209.

Bahrick, L. E. (1992). Infants' perceptual differentiation of amodal and modality-specific audio-visual relations. *Journal of Experimental Child Psychology*, 53, 180–99.

Bahrick, L. E. (1994). The development of infants' sensitivity to arbitrary intermodal relations. *Ecological Psychology*, 6, 111–23.

Bahrick, L. E. (1995). Intermodal origins of self-perception. In P. Rochat (Ed.), *The self in early infancy: Theory and research* (pp. 349–73). Amsterdam: North Holland-Elsevier.

Bahrick, L. E. (2000, July). The role of attentional salience in infants' detection of arbitrary intermodal relations. Paper presented at the International Conference on Infant Studies, Brighton, UK.

Bahrick, L. E. (2001). Increasing specificity in perceptual development: Infants' detection of nested levels of multimodal stimulation. *Journal of Experimental Child Psychology*, 79, 253–70.

Bahrick, L. E., Flom, R., & Lickliter, R. (2002). Intersensory redundancy facilitates discrimination of tempo in 3-month-old infants. *Developmental Psychobiology*, 41, 352–63.

Bahrick, L. E., & Lickliter, R. (2000). Intersensory redundancy guides attentional selectivity and perceptual learning in infancy. *Developmental Psychology*, 36, 190–201.

Bahrick, L. E., & Lickliter, R. (2002). Intersensory redundancy guides early perceptual and cognitive development. In R. Kail & H. Reese

(Eds.), *Advances in child development and behavior* (Vol. 30, pp. 153–87). New York: Academic Press.

Bahrick, L. E., Lickliter, R., & Flom, R. (2002, April). Intersensory redundancy is most effective when skills are first learned. Paper presented at the International Conference on Infant Studies, Toronto, Canada.

Bahrick, L. E., Netto, D., & Hernandez-Reif, M. (1998). Intermodal perception of adult and child faces and voices by infants. *Child Development*, 69, 1263–75.

Bahrick, L. E., Walker, A. S., & Neisser, U. (1981). Selective looking by infants. *Cognitive Psychology*, 13, 377–90.

Bahrick, L. E., & Watson, J. S. (1985). Detection of intermodal proprioceptive-visual contingency as a potential basis of self-perception in infancy. *Developmental Psychology*, 21, 963–73.

Butterworth, G. (1992). Origins of self-perception in infancy. *Psychological Inquiry*, 3 (2), 103–11.

Butterworth, G., & Hicks, L. (1977). Visual proprioception and postural stability in infancy: A developmental study. *Perception*, 6, 255–62.

Butterworth, G., & Hopkins, B. (1988). Hand–mouth coordination in the new-born baby. *British Journal of Developmental Psychology*, 6, 303–14.

Columbus, R. F., Sleigh, M. J., Lickliter, R., & Lewkowicz, D. J. (1998). Unimodal sensory experience interferes with responsiveness to the spatial contiguity of multimodal maternal cues in bobwhite quail chicks. *Infant Behavior and Development*, 21, 397–409.

Dodd, B. (1979). Lip reading in infants: Attention to speech presented in- and out-of-synchrony. *Cognitive Psychology*, 11, 478–84.

Freeseman, L. J., Colombo, J., & Coldren, J. T. (1993). Individual differences in infant visual attention: Four-month-olds' discrimination and generalization of global and local stimulus properties. *Child Development*, 64, 1191–1203.

Frick, J. E., Colombo, J., & Allen, J. R. (2000). Temporal sequence of global–local processing in 3-month-old infants. *Infancy*, 1, 375–86.

Gibson, E. J. (1969). *Principles of perceptual learning and development*. New York: Appleton-Century-Crofts.

Gogate, L. J., & Bahrick, L. E. (1998). Intersensory redundancy facilitates learning of arbitrary relations between vowel sounds and objects in seven-month-old infants. *Journal of Experimental Child Psychology*, 69, 1–17.

Gogate, L. J., Bahrick, L. E., & Watson, J. D. (2000). A study of multimodal motherese: The role of temporal synchrony between verbal labels and gestures. *Child Development*, 71, 878–94.

Gottlieb, G. (1971a). *Development of species identification in birds*. Chicago: University of Chicago Press.

Gottlieb, G. (1971b). Ontogenesis of sensory function in birds and mammals. In E. Tobach, L. Aronson, & E. Shaw (Eds.), *The biopsychology of development* (pp. 67–128). New York: Academic Press.

Hernandez-Reif, M., & Bahrick, L. E. (2001). The development of visual-tactile perception of objects: Amodal relations guide learning about arbitrary relations. *Infancy*, 2, 51–72.

Jaffee, J., Beebe, B., Feldstein, S., Crown, C. L., & Jasnow, M. D. (2001). Rhythms of dialogue. *Monographs of the Society for Research in Child Development*, 66 (2, Serial No. 265), 1–132.

Johnston, T., & Gottlieb, G. (1981). Development of visual species identification in ducklings: What is the role of imprinting? *Animal Behaviour*, 29, 1082–99.

Kuhl, P. K., & Meltzoff, A. N. (1982). The bimodal perception of speech in infancy. *Science*, 218, 1138–41.

Kuhl, P. K., & Meltzoff, A. N. (1984). The intermodal representation of speech in infants. *Infant Behavior and Development*, 7, 361–81.

Kuhn, D., & Siegler, R. S. (Eds.). (1998). *Handbook of child psychology. Vol. 2. Cognition, Perception, and Language*. New York: Wiley.

Lee, A. N., & Aronson, E. (1974). Visual proprioceptive control of standing in human infants. *Perception and Psychophysics*, 15, 529–32.

Lewkowicz, D. J. (1992). Responsiveness to auditory and visual components of a sounding/moving compound stimulus in human infants. *Perception and Psychophysics*, 52, 519–28.

Lewkowicz, D. J. (1996). Perception of auditory-visual temporal synchrony in human infants. *Journal of Experimental Psychology: Human Perception and Performance*, 22, 1094–1106.

Lewkowicz, D. J. (2000). The development of intersensory temporal perception: An epigenetic systems/limitations view. *Psychological Bulletin*, 126, 281–308.

Lewkowicz, D. J., & Lickliter, R. (Eds.). (1994). *The development of intersensory perception: Comparative perspectives*. Hillsdale, NJ: Erlbaum.

Lickliter, R., & Bahrick, L. E. (2001). The salience of multimodal sensory stimulation in early development: Implications for the issue of ecological validity. *Infancy*, 2, 451–67.

Lickliter, R., Bahrick, L. E., & Honeycutt, H. (2002). Intersensory redundancy facilitates prenatal perceptual learning in bobwhite quail embryos. *Developmental Psychology*, 38, 15–23.

Lickliter, R., Dyer, A. B., & McBride, T. (1993). Perceptual consequences of early social experience in precocial birds. *Behavioral Processes*, 30, 185–200.

Lickliter, R., & Gottlieb, G. (1988). Social specificity: Interaction with own species is necessary to foster species-specific maternal preference in ducklings. *Developmental Psychobiology*, 21, 311–21.

Massaro, D. W. (1998). *Perceiving talking faces: From speech perception to a behavioral principle*. Cambridge, MA: Harvard University Press.

Meredith, M. A., & Stein, B. E. (1986). Spatial factors determine the activity of multisensory neurons in the cat superior colliculus. *Brain Research*, 365, 350–4.

Michel, G. R., & Moore, C. L. (1995). *Developmental psychobiology*. Cambridge MA: MIT Press.

Moore, C. L. (1990). Comparative development of vertebrate sexual behavior: Levels, cascades, and webs. In D. A. Dewsbury (Ed.), *Contemporary issues in comparative psychology* (pp. 278–99). Sunderland, MA: Sinauer.

Rochat, P. (1993). Hand–mouth coordination in the newborn: Morphology, determinants, and early development of a basic act. In G. Savelsbergh (Ed.), *The development of coordination in infancy* (pp. 265–88). Amsterdam: Elsevier.

Rochat, P. (Ed.). (1995). *The self in infancy: Theory and research.* Amsterdam: Elsevier.

Rochat, P., & Morgan, R. (1995). The function and determinants of early self-exploration. In P. Rochat (Ed.), *The self in early infancy: Theory and research* (pp. 395–415). Amsterdam: North Holland-Elsevier.

Schmuckler, M. A. (1995). Self-knowledge of body position: Integration of perceptual and action system information. In P. Rochat (Ed.), *The self in early infancy: Theory and research* (pp. 221–41). Amsterdam: North Holland-Elsevier.

Slater, A., Quinn, P. C., Brown, E., & Hayes, R. (1999). Intermodal perception at birth: Intersensory redundancy guides newborn infants' learning of arbitrary auditory-visual pairings. *Developmental Science,* 2, 333–8.

Sleigh, M. J., Columbus, R. F., & Lickliter, R. (1998). Intersensory experience and early perceptual development: Postnatal experience with multimodal maternal cues affects intersensory responsiveness in bobwhite quail chicks. *Developmental Psychology,* 34, 215–23.

Soken, N., & Pick, A. (1992). Intermodal perception of happy and angry expressive behaviors by seven-month-old infants. *Child Development,* 63, 787–95.

Spelke, E. S. (1979). Perceiving bimodally specified events in infancy. *Developmental Psychology,* 15, 626–36.

Stein, B. E., & Meredith, M. A. (1993). *The merging of the senses.* Cambridge, MA: MIT Press.

Stein, B. E., Meredith, M. A., & Wallace, M. (1994). Development and neural basis of multisensory integration. In D. J. Lewkowicz & R. Lickliter (Eds.), *The development of intersensory perception: Comparative perspectives* (pp. 81–105). Hillsdale, NJ: Erlbaum.

Trevarthen, C. (1993). The self born of intersubjectivity: The psychology of an infant communicating. In U. Neisser (Ed.), *The perceived self: Ecological and interpersonal sources of self-knowledge* (pp. 121–73). New York: Cambridge University Press.

Turkewitz, G., & Kenney, P. A. (1982). Limitations on input as a basis for neural organization and perceptual development: A preliminary theoretical statement. *Developmental Psychobiology,* 15, 357–68.

van der Meer, A. L. H., van der Weel, F. R., & Lee, D. N. (1995). The functional significance of arm movements in neonates. *Science,* 267, 693–5.

Walker, A. S. (1982). Intermodal perception of expressive behaviors by human infants. *Journal of Experimental Child Psychology,* 33, 514–35.

Walker-Andrews, A. (1997). Infants' perception of expressive behaviors: Differentiation of multimodal information. *Psychological Bulletin,* 121 (3), 437–56.

Walker-Andrews, A. S., Bahrick, L. E., Raglioni, S. S., & Diaz, I. (1991). Infants' bimodal perception of gender. *Ecological Psychology*, 3, 55–75.

Zukow-Goldring, P. (1997). A social ecological realist approach to the emergence of the lexicon: Educating attention to amodal invariants in gesture and speech. In C. Dent-Read & P. Zukow-Goldring (Eds.), *Evolving explanations of development: Ecological approaches to organism-environment systems* (pp. 199–252). Washington, DC: American Psychological Association.

# 5

# Neuroscience Perspectives on Infant Development

*Mark H. Johnson and Annette Karmiloff-Smith*

## Biology and Cognitive Development

Throughout the history of developmental psychology the field has been influenced by thinking and findings from the biological sciences, particularly developmental neuroscience and evolutionary theory. Why has developmental psychology been so closely related to these areas of biology? One reason is that underlying both disciplines is the fundamental question about how complex organic structures, such as the human brain and mind, can arise from apparently much simpler matter – such as a mere bunch of undifferentiated cells. Ideas regarding the mechanisms of evolution influenced leaders in developmental psychology from early on, the clearest example of which can be found in the writings of Piaget (Piaget, 1954, 1971). In addition to his own training as a biologist, Piaget was heavily inspired by the developmental biologist C. H. Waddington (Piaget, 1971). It was from observation of embryological growth that Waddington developed his concept of the "epigenetic landscape" (e.g., Waddington, 1975). Interestingly, some of Waddington's concepts have recently been resurrected by researchers interested in nonlinear dynamic

We wish to thank the Medical Research Council (UK) and our host institutions for financial support, and the editors for their comments on an earlier version of this chapter.

systems approaches to cognitive development (Butterworth, 1998; Butterworth & Jarrett, 1991; Elman, Bates, Johnson, Karmiloff-Smith, Parisi, & Plunkett, 1996; Thelen & Smith, 1994). By this view, many adaptations to the natural environment are discovered afresh by each developing individual.

In contrast to the above application of evolutionary theory in developmental psychology is the notion that much of ontogeny essentially reduces to phylogeny. This line of thinking has recently been labeled "evolutionary psychology" or EP (Baron-Cohen, 1998; Tooby & Cosmides, 1992), although a long tradition in evolutionary psychology already exists. EP places on center stage the assumption that many aspects of human cognition can be directly attributed to species adaptations, such that the human infant is born with specialized subsystems which function independently of one another.

In parallel with these two divergent approaches to incorporating evolutionary thinking into developmental psychology are two ways in which evidence from developmental neuroscience has been imported. This is the primary focus of the present chapter. Here again there are two different approaches to relating brain development to cognitive and behavioral change in infants and children. The predominant one is based on assumptions about the maturation of different brain regions. This "maturational" approach assumes that neural development is largely under genetic control, though perhaps can be accelerated or decelerated by experience. A second, contrasting approach that we term neuroconstructivism or "interactive specialization" (Johnson, 2000, 2001; Karmiloff-Smith, 1998; see also Elman et al., 1996) emphasizes the activity-dependent nature of brain development. By this view, many changes in brain structure during later prenatal and postnatal development are reactions to patterns of electrical activity, some of which are induced by input through sensory systems. In this chapter, we will discuss the merits of this latter approach as applied to both typical and atypical human development over the first years of life. Just prior to his untimely death, George Butterworth's longstanding interest in typical infant development had extended to atypical development in infants and toddlers with genetic disorders (Laing, Butterworth et al., 2002).

## Human Brain Development

It is outside the scope of this chapter to review all that is known about primate brain development (see Johnson, 1993, 1997, 2001, for reviews). However, what follows is a number of important summary statements drawn from our own and others' reviews of this literature.

- In a recent review of pre- and postnatal brain development, Nelson and Bloom (1997) summarize as follows: "An unfortunate misconception of developmental neurobiology is that most aspects of brain development during the pre- and immediate post-natal periods reflect rigidly deterministic, genetic programs that are implemented at different points in time. . . . this view is inappropriate for even the very earliest stages of brain development" (p. 979).
- During both pre- and postnatal life, neural circuits – especially those within the cerebral cortex – are remodeled in interaction with their input. Recent evidence indicates during prenatal life much of this input comes from internally generated spontaneous activity (see Katz & Shatz, 1996, for review). With maturation of the sense organs and input from the environment in postnatal life, there is a gradual shift to taking account of effects of the input from the external environment.
- Human brains do not contain any new structures or parts not found in other primates. Rather, our brain development is characterized by (1) greater volume, particularly in the cerebral cortex, and (2) vastly slowed development, and in particular an extended period of postnatal plasticity (see Johnson, 1997, 2001, for review). This relatively delayed sequence of brain development makes our species more open to influence by interactions with the postnatal environment. In addition, the slowed developmental timetable may increase the volume of later-developing structures such as the cerebral cortex, and especially prefrontal cortex.

Thus, recent reviews of pre- and postnatal brain development have come to the conclusion that brain development is not merely a process of the unfolding of a genetic plan, or a passive response to environmental input, but is an activity-dependent process at the molecular, cellular, and organismal levels involving probabilistic epigenesis (bidirectional relations between genes, brain, and behavior). In humans, this process extends further into postnatal life than in any other primates.

While this general characterization is attractive to many, it is too underspecified in the face of specific models of how regional maturation enables behavioral changes. However, we are now beginning to develop a more precise model of the processes underlying the postnatal specialization of the human brain.

## Interactive Specialization

Many of the efforts to relate brain to typical behavioral development have hitherto entailed a maturational framework. Within this, it is assumed that as particular regions of the brain develop, they allow or enable new sensory, motor, and cognitive functions to appear. Such a position leads to a further assumption, i.e., that functional development closely follows patterns of neuroanatomical regional maturation within cortex. This, it is claimed, reflects a general progression of maturation from posterior to anterior regions, with the primary sensory areas being functional from around the time of birth, and the frontal lobes and prefrontal cortex argued to be the last parts of cortex to become functional.

An example of such assumptions can be seen in the progression within the frontal lobes themselves which has been used to explain developments in the ability to reach for coveted objects toward the end of the first year. Specifically, infants younger than 8 months often fail to accurately retrieve a hidden object after a short delay period, if the object's location is visibly changed from the one where it was successfully retrieved on previous trials. Rather, infants tend to perseverate by reaching to the location where the object was found on the preceding trials. This "A-not-B" error, originally identified by Piaget (1954), is strikingly similar to errors made by human adults with frontal lesions and by monkeys with lesions to the dorsolateral prefrontal cortex (Diamond & Goldman-Rakic, 1986, 1989). These findings led to the proposal that the simple maturation of this specific region in human infants enables them to retain information over space and time and to inhibit prepotent responses (Diamond, 1991). In turn, these brain developments are claimed to allow successful performance in object-retrieval paradigms. While converging evidence for this claim comes from associations with resting frontal electroencephalogram (EEG) responses (Bell & Fox, 1992) as well as deficits in children with a neurochemical deficit in the prefrontal cortex resulting from phenylketonuria (Diamond, 1991), as yet no direct functional imaging on human infants during retrieval tasks has been possible.

Despite the intuitive appeal of the maturational approach, there are serious reasons to believe that it will be far from explaining all aspects of functional brain development in human infants. An alternative approach is based on the idea that there are bidirectional interactions between brain and behavioral development. Gottlieb (1992) distinguished between two approaches to the study of development. On the one hand, he identifies "deterministic epigenesis" in which it is assumed that there is a unidirectional causal path from genes to structural brain changes to psychological function. The second approach is termed "probabilistic epigenesis," in which interactions between genes, structural brain changes, and psychological function are viewed as bidirectional, dynamic, and emergent. Integral to the latter approach is the importance of activity-dependent development. As discussed above, some current theorizing on the neural basis of sensory, motor, and cognitive change assumes that the maturation of particular neocortical regions or pathways allows or enables new functions to appear. This is clearly based on a predetermined epigenetic view in which the primary cause of a cognitive change can be attributed to neural maturation. By contrast, a number of recent reviews of pre- and postnatal brain development have concluded that probabilistic epigenesis is a more appropriate way to view postnatal brain development (e.g., Johnson, 1997; Nelson & Bloom, 1997). Further, probabilistic epigenesis has provided a basis for "dynamical systems" approaches to behavioral development (Thelen & Smith, 1994). Explaining developmental change when there are bidirectional interactions between brain structure and (psychological) function is, however, more challenging. When adopting a probabilistic epigenesis viewpoint, the aim is still to unite developmental neuroanatomical observations with functional development. However, a probabilistic epigenetic approach emphasizes the need for notions of *partial functioning* of neural pathways. This is because, in order for bidirectional interactions between brain structure and function to work, there needs to be early partial functioning which then shapes subsequent structural developments. From this viewpoint, then, structural and functional changes in regions of the brain *co-develop*. Cortical regions are not functionally silent before they abruptly become activated in their mature state, nor is their development totally isolated one from another.

In further contrast to the maturational approach, an alternative perspective is based on the assumption that postnatal functional brain development, at least within cerebral cortex, is partly a process of organizing intra- and interregional interactions (Johnson, 2000, 2001). Referring to adult brain imaging data, Friston and Price (2001) point out that it may be an error to assume that particular functions can be localized within a certain cortical region. Rather, they suggest, the response properties of a region are determined by its patterns of connectivity to other regions as well as by their current activity states. By this view, "the cortical infrastructure supporting a single function may involve many specialized areas whose union is mediated by the functional integration among them" (Friston & Price, 2001, p. 276). Similarly, in discussing the design and interpretation of adult functional magnetic resonance imaging (fMRI) studies, Carpenter and collaborators have argued that: "In contrast to a localist assumption of a one-to-one mapping between cortical regions and cognitive operations, an alternative view is that cognitive task performance is subserved by large-scale cortical networks that consist of spatially separate computational components, each with its own set of relative specializations, that collaborate extensively to accomplish cognitive functions" (Carpenter, Just, & Reichle, 2000, p. 360).

These notions about adult processing resonate well with the developmental perspective that we have advanced elsewhere (Elman et al., 1996; Karmiloff-Smith, 1998), in which different cortical regions and pathways become increasingly specialized as a result of being recruited for specific tasks over developmental time. Within the neuroconstructivist framework, Johnson (2000, 2001) specifically advanced an "interactive specialization" view of human postnatal functional brain development. By this view, cortical pathways in the newborn differ from each other by virtue of their particular pattern of inputs and outputs to other brain structures as well as biases in their information-processing properties. The latter refers to slight differences such as those in the detailed patterns of intrinsic connectivity, the balance of neurotransmitters, or synaptic density. Such differences correspond to those that Elman et al. (1996) referred to as "architectural constraints." The following hypothesis was put forward: in the newborn there are slight biases on an overall very similar, general neocortical architecture. These initial biases are argued to be sufficient to ensure that particular types of sensory input, or input–output pairings, are more efficiently, although not necessarily exclusively, processed by a subset of the pathways. There is thus a gradual process of progressive "recruitment" of particular pathways and structures for certain functions (Elman et al., 1996). One manifestation of this recruitment process is that cortical pathways and structures go through a process of specialization. By specialization, Johnson (2000) referred to the extent that a given cortical region is selective in its response properties such that it progressively becomes responsive only to one class of stimuli. In other words, while early in development a cortical region may respond to a wide variety of stimuli and tasks, with specialization it progressively becomes engaged only by a subset of these. This process may be akin to the tuning of response properties of single neurons.

A number of authors have described developmental changes in the spatial extent of cortical activation in a given situation during postnatal life. Event-related potential experiments with infants have indicated that both for word learning (Neville, 1991) and face processing (DeHaan, Oliver, & Johnson, 1998), there is increasing localization of processing with age and particularly with experience of a stimulus class. That is, scalp recording leads reveal a wider area of processing for words or faces in younger infants than in older ones whose processing has become more specialized and localized. Within the present framework, such developmental changes are accounted for in terms of more pathways initially being partially activated in younger infants prior to experience with a class of stimuli. With increasing experience, the specialization of one or more of those pathways occurs over time. In the example of word recognition, processing is initially found over widespread cortical areas in both hemispheres. This narrows to left temporal leads after children's vocabularies have reached a certain level, irrespective of maturational age (Neville, 1991). Changes in the extent of localization can be viewed as a direct consequence of specialization. Initially, multiple pathways are activated for most stimuli. With increasing experience, fewer pathways become activated by each specific class of stimuli. Pathways become tuned to specific functions and are therefore no longer engaged by the broad range of stimuli as was the case earlier in development. Additionally, there may be inhibition from pathways that are becoming increasingly specialized for that function. In this sense, then, there is competition between pathways to recruit functions, with the pathway best suited for the function (by virtue of its initial biases) usually winning out.

According to the interactive specialization view, the onset of a new behavioral competence during infancy will be matched by changes in activity over several regions, and not just by the onset of activity in one or more additional region(s) (Johnson, 2001). Further, and in contrast to the maturational approach, we would predict that during development, patterns of cortical activation will be as extensive as, or even more extensive than, those observed in adults. However, the patterns of regional activation in a given task could potentially be different in the infant or child compared to adults. In this way, acquiring a new skill in development does not entail the maturation of a new structure, but rather the reorganization of interactions between existing, partially active structures.

## *An example of interactive specialization: Face processing*

Several authors have proposed that we have an innate cortical module for face processing (Farah, Rabinowitz, Quinn, & Liu, 2000). This claim is usually based on one or more of the following lines of evidence: (1) adults have dedicated cortical tissue for face processing, supported by neuropsychological evidence from brain-damaged adults suffering from prosopagnosia (inability to recognize faces); (2) newborn infants preferentially orient to faces; and (3) there are cases of developmental prosopagnosia. As will be evident from the discussion above, the fact that specific regions of cortex, such as the "fusiform face area" (Kanwisher, McDermott, & Chun, 1997), are normally activated by faces in adults does not constitute evidence that this is the state of affairs in infants. Noteworthy is the fact that such specializations can, and do, vary between different adults (most fMRI studies on face processing only present results from a selected group of adults who show activation of the "fusiform face area"), and are likely to be the end product of a nondeterministic process of specialization. The fact that newborn infants tend to orient to faces indicates that they have some, albeit primitive, representation of a face-like form from birth (what Johnson & Morton, 1991, termed "CONSPEC"). However, most commentators agree that this newborn tendency is unlikely to be mediated by the same cortical structures as those engaged in face recognition in adults (DeHaan, Humphreys, & Johnson, 2002). Finally, while there have been some reports of individuals with "developmental prosopagnosia" resulting from early brain damage (Bentin, Deouell, & Soroker, 1999; Farah et al., 2000; Jones & Tranel, 2001; Nunn, Postma, & Pearson, 2001), studies involving larger samples have failed to dissociate face deficits from more general visual object-processing problems. For example, in one study of face-processing abilities in 5- to 14-year-olds who had experienced perinatal unilateral lesions, the effects were fairly mild: less than half the children showed impaired performance relative to controls on tests of face or object identity recognition. Furthermore: (1) face-processing deficits were no more common than object-processing deficits following a right hemisphere lesion; (2) face-processing deficits were no more common after right-sided than left-sided damage; and, most importantly, (3) a face-processing deficit never occurred in the absence of an object-processing deficit. This general pattern is similar to that reported in other studies (Ballantyne & Trauner, 1999; Mancini, Deschonen, Deruelle, & Massoulier, 1994) and suggests that the infant's face-processing system is more widely distributed and/or more plastic following damage than is the adult system.

Given that the evidence for an innate cortical module for face processing is, at best, weak, we considered it worthwhile to explore whether dynamic processes of localization and specialization could be observed during infancy. To do this, Johnson, DeHaan, and colleagues have used high-density event-related potentials (ERPs) to trace the patterns of cortical activation elicited by faces at different ages during infancy (DeHaan, Humphreys, & Johnson, 2002; DeHaan, Pascalis, & Johnson, 2002). The method provides a measure of electrical activity at the scalp caused by the simultaneous firing of banks of neurons within cortex. In particular, Johnson and colleagues focused on a spatiotemporal component of the event-related potential known as the "N170." The N170 has been shown by several laboratories to be sensitive to faces in adults. For example, the N170 is influenced by disruption of configural encoding of the face such as inversion or scrambling: it is of larger amplitude and longer latency to faces that are inverted or have the features scrambled (Bentin, Allison, Puce, Perez, & McCarthy, 1996; DeHaan, Pascalis, & Johnson, 2002; Eimer, 2000; George, Evans, Fiori, Davidoff, & Renault, 1996; Rebai, Poiroux, Bernard, & Lalonde, 2001; Taylor, Edmonds, McCarthy, & Allison, 2001). This is specific to faces and not simply a general effect of inversion. This is clear from the fact that there is no difference in the N170 elicited by monkey faces whether upright or inverted (DeHaan et al., in press) or upright compared to inverted objects (Rebai et al., 2001; Rossion et al., 2000). These results suggest that the N170 elicited by the human face is not simply a reaction to the basic configuration of eyes–nose–mouth (since this is also present in monkey faces), but has become tuned more specifically to characteristics of the upright, human face.

The question we have addressed is whether this pattern already holds for face processing in infants. Does the N170 show the same degree of specificity in infants as observed in adults? Six-month-olds elicit a component of similar morphology to the adult N170 but with a longer peak latency and smaller amplitude (DeHaan et al., in press). At this age, the component shows some sensitivity to the human face in that it differs in amplitude for human compared to monkey faces. However, unlike adults, 6-month-olds show no effect of face inversion on this ERP component. This is not because infants of this age cannot detect the difference between upright and inverted faces, as a longer-latency ERP component (P400) was affected by orientation. By contrast, by 12 months of age a more adult-like response is seen: like adults, 12-month-olds show a larger N170 for inverted than for upright faces. Moreover, also like adults, this effect of inversion was specific to human faces and was not observed for monkey faces. These results are consistent with the idea that the infants' processing of faces becomes gradually more specific to the upright human face over the course of the first year of life.

In addition to this increasing specialization of responses, Johnson and colleagues observed a tendency for increasing localization. While most (but not all) adults show a greater (more specific) response to upright human faces over the right hemisphere, infants tend to show a more bilateral response. If this finding is replicated, it supports the work on word recognition mentioned earlier in demonstrating an increasing pattern of localization with age/experience.

## Atypical Development and Interactive Specialization

The neuroconstructivist framework of interactive specialization is of particular relevance to atypical development (Johnson, Halit, Grice, & Karmiloff-Smith, 2002; Karmiloff-Smith, 1998; Paterson, Brown, Gsödl, Johnson, & Karmiloff-Smith, 1999). Yet the field is replete with assumptions derived from adult neuropsychology that ignore the dynamics of development over time (e.g., Baron-Cohen, 1998; Temple, 1997). Many authors argue that certain forms of atypical development offer the prime example of how infants are born with brains that already have innate specialization, some parts of which are intact and others impaired. But the idea that the brain of a child with a genetic disorder develops as a series of independently functioning modules is, in our view, highly unlikely. More plausible is the assumption that the atypical brain shows subtle abnormality across multiple regions as it progressively structures itself over time. We examine this assumption for two developmental disorders, one a single-gene disorder, Fragile-X syndrome, the other a multiple-gene disorder, Williams syndrome.

## *Fragile-X syndrome*

Fragile-X syndrome is amongst the most common forms of inherited mental retardation (DeVries et al., 1997) and has been of particular interest to cognitive neuroscientists because it is a single-gene disorder on the X chromosome. The hope was that Fragile-X children would present with a pattern of intact and impaired abilities, allowing a one-to-one mapping between the mutated gene and a specific cognitive outcome. However, this turned out not to be the case. Not only is there wide individual variation in Fragile-X patients, with IQs falling in the mild to severe levels of mental retardation (Turk, 1998), but subtle impairments are found across multiple cognitive domains. This is because the Fragile-X gene contributes to synaptic plasticity with widespread effects (Karmiloff-Smith, Scerif, & Thomas, 2002). The Fragile-X profile is characterized by weaknesses in attention (Munir, Cornish, & Wilding, 2000), in visuospatial cognition (Cornish, Munir, & Cross, 1999), in short-term memory and sequential information processing, alongside (relative) strengths in language, long-term memory, and holistic information processing (Freund & Reiss, 1991). But these latter are not "intact"; they are simply *relatively* better than other domains because the effects of the mutated genes are more subtle in these domains. In addition, many individuals with Fragile-X display hyperactive/attention-deficit disorder, hyperacusis, and autistic-like behaviors (Hagerman & Cronister, 1996).

To fully understand the nature of the Fragile-X syndrome, it is important to recall that at the molecular, cellular, and system levels, *experience-dependent* synaptic plasticity is critical in determining the phenotypic outcome (see review in Karmiloff-Smith et al., 2002). As we stressed earlier, experience and learning are key factors in shaping the structure of the brain, so the effects on individuals with Fragile-X has to be considered in the context of a dynamically developing cognitive system rather than merely in terms of the anomalous adult outcome. Focus on the (static) adult system alone will not explain how restrictions in low-level synaptic plasticity in early development result in the pattern of deficits in the adult phenotype. In other words, because of early synaptic plasticity in establishing neural networks across the developing brain, it is likely that numerous circuits in which this low-level process is involved will, to some extent, develop atypically. But this widespread effect may not be visible in the adult outcome, because some cognitive domains may be far less reliant on the particular low-level process than others. So only some domains will show obvious impairment in overt behavioral tasks. However, once more in-depth tasks are used to probe seemingly "intact" areas, these often reveal subtle impairments too (Cornish et al., 1999). In other words, the process of development itself will be a crucial factor in governing atypical phenotypic outcome across and within domains of both relative strength and weakness (Karmiloff-Smith, 1998). In sum, Fragile-X syndrome should be characterized in terms of the effects of the single gene mutation on the development of the whole brain, such that numerous cognitive domains are likely to have *developed* atypically to some extent. As we shall see in our second example, Williams syndrome, it is crucial to probe in depth the very domains that seem, at first sight, to be "intact." The usual focus of research with clinical populations on domains of very apparent deficit should never overshadow atypicalities, however subtle, in other domains. This is because it is highly unlikely that the rest of a system will develop normally when part is seriously impaired, due to compensatory activity in the less impaired parts.

Finally, it is worth noting that even in the case of a disorder like phenylketonuria, it was originally thought that if children were kept under a strict diet early in infancy, development was normal. But recent research (Diamond, 2001) has revealed subtle impairments across several domains in this disorder too, because the whole of the system had originally developed atypically.

## *Williams syndrome*

Williams syndrome (WS) is another genetic disorder that has attracted much attention from those interested in the organization of the human brain and the relationship between genotype and phenotype. Unlike Fragile-X syndrome, WS is not a single-gene disorder but involves the deletion of 16 genes of one copy of chromosome 7. Initial excitement stemmed from the fact that individuals with WS seemed to present with proficient language, face-processing, and social skills alongside deficient visuospatial cognition, number, and problem-solving. Researchers were rapid to characterize the syndrome along the lines of adult neuropsychology, suggesting that the WS brain started out with some components intact and others impaired. Some researchers have indeed characterized WS as a juxtaposition of impaired and intact mental capacities (Bellugi, Lichtenberger, Jones, Lai, & St. George, 2002; Rossen, Klima, Bellugi, Bihrle, & Jones, 1996), where language, face-processing, and social skills are viewed as the intact components, and number, problem-solving, and visuospatial cognition the impaired components.

Focus on the ostensibly intact domains of WS functioning paints a very different picture, however. In a series of studies of face processing in WS, it was found that infants, older children, and adults all show atypical patterns of behavior. Unlike typically developing infants and toddlers, those with WS, although able to notice both featural and configural changes in faces, preferred to focus on featural changes (Humphreys, Ewing, & Karmiloff-Smith, 2002). The normal control infants looked longer at configural changes. In childhood and adulthood, a number of studies have now revealed that, in contrast to both mental age- and chronological age-matched controls, patients with WS analyze the featural components of faces both more accurately and more rapidly than configural changes (Deruelle et al., 1999; Humphreys et al., 2002; Karmiloff-Smith, 1997). These behavioral differences are also displayed in measures of brain electrophysiology (Mills, Alvrez, St. George, Appelbaum, Bellugi, & Neville, 2002; Neville 1991). Moreover, age-matched controls display a pattern of differentiation between human upright faces and all other stimuli, with upright human faces being processed in terms of both latency and amplitude significantly differently to inverted faces, monkey faces, and cars. Not only do adolescents and adults with WS show a very reduced N170 over the temporal electrodes, but for them there is no difference in amplitude between upright and inverted human faces, nor between human faces, monkey faces, and cars (Grice, 2002; Grice et al., 2001). Finally, when frontal electrodes were assessed for gamma-band oscillatory activity, again the patients with WS looked very different to both age-matched normal controls and to a group of individuals with high-functioning autism (Grice et al., 2001). Thus, despite scores in the normal range on some standardized face-processing tasks, people with WS actually go about face processing in a different way to normal controls. This, we suggest, is the result of an atypical developmental pathway from infancy onwards.

Similar studies have been carried out in the other two areas which are reported to be intact in Williams syndrome: language and social cognition. Whether it be speech segmentation, lexical development, semantics, syntax, morphology, pragmatics, or reading, subtle impairments were consistently found in all ages of people with WS (Karmiloff-Smith, Grant, Berthoud, Davies, Howlin, & Udwin, 1997; Nazzi, Paterson, & Karmiloff-Smith, 2003; Paterson et al., 1999; Thomas et al., 2001). The same applies to social development in this syndrome. Despite superficially good social interaction, in fact once again subtle impairments are found in infants, toddlers, children, and adults (Laing et al., 2002; Sullivan & Tager-Flusberg, 1999; Tager-Flusberg & Sullivan, 2000). It is in the domain of social interaction that George Butterworth made a significant contribution to atypical development.

Anecdotally, young children with WS had been claimed to be intact in social interaction. Our neuroconstructivist framework led us to challenge this assumption and to join forces with George Butterworth, who had made in-depth studies of the dyadic and triadic aspects of social interaction in typically developing infants (Butterworth & Cochran, 1980). George had demonstrated the importance during infancy of referential pointing (Franco & Butterworth, 1996) and the ability to follow others' pointing (Butterworth & Grover, 1989; Butterworth & Jarrett, 1991). Using a procedure similar to that of Franco and Butterworth (1996), we employed large dolls that moved by remote control, placed far enough away from the child so that pointing behaviors are essential. The study took place in a curtained room, with the child sitting in a high chair in the middle of one wall. In front of the child, in a semicircular formation, were six remotely controlled dolls. Two video cameras were positioned between dolls 1 and 2 and between dolls 5 and 6. A chair was placed either side of the child to enable the experimenter to sit on either the left- or the right-hand side of the child.

A second experimenter sat in an adjacent room and watched the child on a split-screen video. A lightbox behind the child indicated which doll was active. This second experimenter activated the dolls from this adjacent room. The experiment consisted of two conditions: a set of six production trials and a set of six comprehension trials. In the production trials the experimenter stared straight ahead. The doll was activated and its arms and legs moved in a repetitive cycle lasting 7 seconds. In this condition, the doll also squeaked and "talked" to get the child's attention. The experimenter was instructed to respond to the child, but not to lead the child's direction of gaze in any way. In the comprehension trials, the experimenter pointed to one of the dolls using an index finger point. This pointing was done with either the left or right hand, depending on which doll was activated in each item, with the pointing never crossing the body. The doll was only activated (without sound effects in the comprehension condition) when the second experimenter could see on the video screen that the child had turned his or her head to follow the experimenter's point.

The findings showed that children with WS produced pointing significantly less than typically developing children of the same mental age, and also showed a tendency to follow pointing less than controls. Furthermore, the lack of pointing behavior was observed in an experimentally controlled situation in which typically developing children and children with Down's syndrome (DS) have been shown to display pointing behavior. While few of the children with WS produced even a single point across all trials, all were already producing referential language, a pattern not displayed in typical or DS development where pointing precedes referential language. Toddlers with WS also had problems with the comprehension of pointing, suggesting that social referencing is deviant in function for children with WS. Our results reveal intriguing differences in preverbal communication skills of young children with WS. Particularly striking was the marked difference between controls and clinical group in terms of dyadic and triadic interaction, with the WS children displaying significant impairment in the latter, and the failure of the WS toddlers to understand the referential function of pointing.

The finding that similar overt behaviors like dyadic interaction may differ in function across typical and atypical development is important. It suggests that equivalent behaviors may result from different brain processes (Karmiloff-Smith, 1998). As we mentioned above, in studies of face processing, individuals with WS have been shown to reach behavioral scores equivalent to those of normal controls. However, they solve face-processing tasks via different cognitive processes (Karmiloff-Smith, 1997; Grice et al., 2001). The study that we carried out with George Butterworth suggests that many aspects of nonlinguistic communication differ in function for the WS toddlers compared to the normal controls. It is thus crucial to explore alternative developmental pathways, instead of focusing on behavioral outcome alone (Karmiloff-Smith, 1998).

The finding that the WS group had relatively good dyadic social interaction skills can usefully be related to the results of Tager-Flusberg and Sullivan (2000) with older children and adults with WS. These authors argue for two distinct components of social communication: a sociocognitive component and a socioperceptual component. The sociocognitive component refers to the representational understanding of minds, is related to language acquisition, and is thought to be dependent on prefrontal cortex. The socioperceptual component is considered less related to other cognitive and language abilities, appears earlier than the sociocognitive component, and is thought to be dependent on the limbic system, particularly the amygdala. In a series of tasks related to theory of mind, Tager-Flusberg and Sullivan demonstrated that children with WS are impaired on the sociocognitive but not on the socioperceptual component. Our study with George Butterworth on much younger children with WS also suggests that the socioperceptual component (rooted in dyadic interaction) is a relative strength in WS, whereas those aspects of joint attention which require representational skill and triadic interaction are particularly problematic for this clinical group.

The work with George Butterworth demonstrated experimentally for the first time that despite relatively good language skills and superficially good social skills in later childhood and adulthood, toddlers with WS are impaired in several aspects of early communication that are normally related to language. Two aspects of prelinguistic development – pointing and triadic joint attention – are impaired in toddlers with WS and are likely to contribute to the delay in their language (Laing et al., 2002).

Once one considers developmental pathways across time, it is not surprising that areas that appear at first blush to be intact turn out to display subtle impairments due to their atypical trajectories of learning. In general, in contrast to the view that developmental disorders can be characterized by a pattern of intact and impaired modules, the neuroconstructivist approach turns out to be more appropriate for analyzing such disorders in terms of atypical developmental pathways developing under different constraints.

## Conclusion

We have argued that thinking and findings from biology, and especially from neuroscience, are critical to the future of developmental psychology. However, we cautioned against evolutionary psychology and maturational approaches to human development. Instead, we advanced a neuroconstructivist framework that places activity-dependent development center stage. This new approach sheds light on both typical and atypical developmental processes, and we believe that it offers an exciting future for the field. We know that, at least in general terms, George Butterworth shared and even anticipated our vision some 20 years ago. In his own words, "The tasks for the future are to describe how qualitative transformations in cognitive growth come about through interaction with the world, and to relate them to their neurological substrate" (Butterworth, 1981, p. 165).

## REFERENCES

Ballantyne, A. O., & Trauner, D. A. (1999). *Neuro-psychological profiles of infants and children with early focal brain damage.* Joint Institute for Neural Sciences, 5, 145.

Baron-Cohen, S. (1998). Modularity in developmental cognitive neuropsychology: Evidence from autism and Gilles de la Tourette syndrome. In J. A. Burack, R. M. Hodapp, & E. Zigler (Eds.), *Handbook of mental retardation and development* (pp. 334–8). Cambridge: Cambridge University Press.

Bell, M. A., & Fox, N. A. (1992). The relations between frontal brain electrical activity and cognitive development during infancy. *Child Development*, 63 (5), 1142–63.

Bellugi, U., Lichtenberger, L., Jones, W., Lai, Z., & St. George, M. (2002). The neurocognitive profile of Williams syndrome: A complex pattern of strengths and weaknesses. *Journal of Cognitive Neuroscience*, 12 (Supplement), 7–29.

Bentin, S., Allison, T., Puce, A., Perez, E., & McCarthy, G. (1996). Electrophysiological studies of face perception in humans. *Journal of Cognitive Neuroscience*, 8 (6), 551–65.

Bentin, S., Deouell, L. Y., & Soroker, N. (1999). Selective visual streaming in face recognition: Evidence from developmental prosopagnosia. *NeuroReport*, 10 (4), 823–7.

Butterworth, G. (1981). Object permanence and identity in Piaget's theory of infant cognition. In G. Butterworth (Ed.), *Infancy and epistemology* (pp. 137–69). Brighton: Harvester.

Butterworth, G. (1998). Origins of joint visual attention in infancy. *Monographs of the Society for Research in Child Development*, 63 (4), 144–66.

Butterworth, G., & Cochran, E. (1980). Towards a mechanism of joint visual attention in human infancy. *International Journal of Behavioural Development*, 3, 253–72.

Butterworth, G. E., & Grover, L. (1989). Joint visual attention, manual pointing and preverbal communication in human infancy. In M. Jeannerod (Ed.), *Attention and performance XII* (pp. 605–24). Hillsdale, NJ: Erlbaum.

Butterworth, G., & Jarrett, N. (1991). What minds have in common is space: Spatial mechanisms serving joint visual attention in infancy. *British Journal of Developmental Psychology*, 9, 55–72.

Carpenter, P., Just, M. A., & Reichle, E. D. (2000). Working memory and executive function: Evidence from neuroimaging. *Current Opinion in Neurobiology*, 10 (2), 195–9.

Cornish, K. M., Munir, F., & Cross, G. (1999). Spatial cognition in males with Fragile-X syndrome: Evidence for a neuropsychological phenotype. *Cortex*, 35, 263–71.

DeHaan, M., Humphreys, K., & Johnson, M. H. (2002). Developing a brain specialised for face perception: A converging methods approach. *Developmental Psychobiology*, 40, 200–12.

DeHaan, M., Oliver, A., & Johnson, M. H. (1998). Electrophysiological correlates of face processing by adults and 6-month-old infants. *Journal of Cognitive Neuroscience*, 36 (Annual Meeting Supplement).

DeHaan, M., Pascalis, O., & Johnson, M. H. (2002). Specialization of neural mechanisms underlying face recognition in human infants. *Journal of Cognitive Neuroscience*, 14 (2), 199–209.

DeHaan, M., Pascalis, O., & Johnson, M. H. (submitted). Spatial and temporal characteristics of cortical activation in adults and infants viewing faces.

Deruelle, C., Mancini, J., Livet, M., Casse-Ferot, C., & DeSchonen, S. (1999). Configural and local processing of faces in children with Williams syndrome. *Brain and Cognition*, 41, 276–98.

DeVries, B. B., van den Ouweland, A. M., et al. (1997). Screening and diagnosis for the Fragile-X syndrome among the mentally retarded: An epidemiological and psychological survey. Collaborative Fragile-X Study Group. *American Journal of Human Genetics*, 61, 660–7.

Diamond, A. (1991). Frontal lobe involvement in cognitive changes during the first year of life. In K. R. Gibson & A. C. Petersen (Eds.), *Brain maturation and cognitive development: Comparative and cross-cultural perspectives* (pp. 127–80). New York: Aldine de Gruyter.

Diamond, A. (2001). A model system for studying the role of dopamine in prefrontal cortex during early development in humans. In M. H. Johnson, Y. Munakata, & R. Gilmore (Eds.), *Brain development and cognition: A reader* (pp. 441–93). Oxford: Blackwell.

Diamond, A., & Goldman-Rakic, P. S. (1986). Comparative development of human infants and infant rhesus monkeys of cognitive functions that depend on prefrontal cortex. *Neuroscience Abstracts*, 12, 274.

Diamond, A., & Goldman-Rakic, P. S. (1989). Comparison of human infants and rhesus monkeys on Piaget's A-not-B task: Evidence for dependence on dorsolateral prefrontal cortex. *Experimental Brain Research*, 74, 24–40.

Eimer, M. (2000). Effects of face inversion on the structural encoding and recognition of faces: Evidence from event-related brain potentials. *Cognitive Brain Research*, 10, 145–58.

Elman, J. L., Bates, E. A., Johnson, M. H., Karmiloff-Smith, A., Parisi, D., & Plunkett, K. (1996). *Rethinking innateness: A connectionist perspective on development*. Cambridge, MA: MIT Press.

Farah, M. J., Rabinowitz, C., Quinn, G. E., & Liu, G. T. (2000). Early commitment of neural substrates for face recognition. *Cognitive Neuropsychology*, 17 (1–3), 117–23.

Franco, F., & Butterworth, G. (1996). Pointing and social awareness: Declaring and requesting in the second year of life. *Journal of Child Language*, 23 (2), 307–36.

Freund, L., & Reiss, A. L. (1991). Cognitive profiles associated with the Fragile-X syndrome in males and females. *American Journal of Medical Genetics*, 38, 542–7.

Friston, K. J., & Price, C. J. (2001). Dynamic representation and generative models of brain function. *Brain Research Bulletin*, 54 (3), 275–85.

George, N., Evans, J., Fiori, N., Davidoff, J., & Renault, B. (1996). Brain events related to normal and moderately scrambled faces. *Cognitive Brain Research*, 4 (2), 65–76.

Gottlieb, G. (1992). *Individual development and evolution*. New York: Oxford University Press.

Grice, S. (2002). The electrophysiology of face perception in Williams syndrome. Unpublished PhD thesis, Neurocognitive Development Unit, Institute of Child Health, University College London.

Grice, S., Spratling, M. W., Karmiloff-Smith, A., Halit, H., Csibra, G., DeHaan, M., & Johnson, M. H. (2001). Disordered visual processing and oscillatory brain activity in autism and Williams syndrome. *NeuroReport*, 12, 2697–2700.

Hagerman, R. J., & Cronister, A. (1996). *Fragile-X syndrome: Diagnosis, treatment, and research*. Baltimore: Johns Hopkins University Press.

Halit, H., DeHaan, M., & Johnson, M. H. (2000). Modulation of event-related potentials by prototypical and atypical faces. *NeuroReport*, 11, 1–5.

Humphreys, K., Ewing, S., & Karmiloff-Smith, A. (2002, April). Face processing in Williams syndrome: Infant precursors in developmental disorders. Paper presented at the International Conference on Infant Studies, Toronto, Canada.

Johnson, M. H. (Ed.). (1993). *Brain development and cognition: A reader*. Oxford: Blackwell.

Johnson, M. H. (1997). *Developmental cognitive neuroscience: An introduction*. Oxford: Blackwell.

Johnson, M. H. (2000). Functional brain development in infants: Elements of an interactive specialization framework. *Child Development*, 71, 75–81.

Johnson, M. H. (2001). Functional brain development in humans. *Nature Reviews Neuroscience*, 2, 475–83.

Johnson, M. H., Halit, H., Grice, S., & Karmiloff-Smith, A. (2002). Neuro-imaging and developmental disorders: A perspective from multiple levels of analysis. *Development and Psychopathology*, 14, 521–36.

Johnson, M. H., & Morton, J. (1991). *Biology and cognitive development: The case of face recognition*. Oxford: Blackwell.

Jones, R. D., & Tranel, D. (2001). Severe developmental prosopagnosia in a child with superior intellect. *Journal of Clinical and Experimental Neuropsychology*, 23 (3), pp. 265–73.

Kanwisher, N., McDermott, J., & Chun, M. M. (1997). The fusiform face area: A module in human extrastriate cortex specialized for face perception. *Journal of Neuroscience*, 17 (11), 4302–11.

Karmiloff-Smith, A. (1997). Crucial differences between developmental cognitive neuroscience and adult neuropsychology. *Developmental Neuropsychology*, 13, 513–24.

Karmiloff-Smith, A. (1998). Development itself is the key to understanding developmental disorders. *Trends in Cognitive Sciences*, 2, 389–98.

Karmiloff-Smith, A., Grant, J., Berthoud, I., Davies, M., Howlin, P., & Udwin, O. (1997). Language and Williams syndrome: How intact is "intact"? *Child Development*, 68 (2), 246–62.

Karmiloff-Smith, A., Scerif, G., & Thomas, M. (2002). Different approaches to relating genotype to phenotype in developmental disorders. *Developmental Psychobiology*, 40 (3), 311–22.

Katz, L. C., & Shatz, C. J. (1996). Synaptic activity and the construction of cortical circuits. *Science*, 274, 1133–8.

Laing, E., Butterworth, G. E., Ansari, D., Gsödl, M., Longhi, E., Panagiotaki, G., Paterson, S., & Karmiloff-Smith, A. (2002). Atypical development of language and social communication in toddlers with Williams syndrome. *Developmental Science*, 5, 233–46.

Mancini, J., Deschonen, S. D., Deruelle, C., & Massoulier, A. (1994). Face recognition in children with early right or left brain damage. *Developmental Medicine and Child Neurology*, 36 (2), 156–66.

Mills, D. L., Alvrez, D., St. George, M., Appelbaum, G., Bellugi, U., & Neville, H. (2002). Electrophysiological studies of face processing in Williams syndrome. *Journal of Cognitive Neuroscience*, 12 (Supplement), 47–64.

Munir, F., Cornish, K., & Wilding, J. (2000). A neuropsychological profile of attention deficit in young males with Fragile-X syndrome. *Neuropsychologia*, 38, 1261–70.

Nazzi, T., Paterson, S., & Karmiloff-Smith, A. (2003). Early word segmentation by infants and toddlers with Williams syndrome. *Infancy*, 4 (2).

Nelson, C. A., & Bloom, F. E. (1997). Child development and neuroscience. *Child Development*, 68, 970.

Neville, H. J. (1991). Neurobiology of cognitive and language processing: Effects of early experience. In K. R. Gibson & A. C. Petersen (Eds.), *Brain maturation and cognitive development: Comparative and cross-cultural perspectives* (pp. 355–80). New York: Aldine de Gruyter.

Nunn, J. A., Postma, P., & Pearson, R. (2001). Developmental prosopagnosia: Should it be taken at face value? *Neurocase*, 7, 15–27.

Paterson, S. J., Brown, J. H., Gsödl, M. K., Johnson, M. H., & Karmiloff-Smith, A. (1999). Cognitive modularity and genetic disorders. *Science*, 286, 2355–8.

Piaget, J. (1954). *The construction of reality in the child* (Trans. M. Cook). New York: Basic Books.

Piaget, J. (1971). *Biology and knowledge*. Chicago: University of Chicago Press.

Rebai, M., Poiroux, S., Bernard, C., & Lalonde, R. (2001). Event-related potentials for category-specific information during passive viewing of faces and objects. *International Journal of Neuroscience*, 106 (3–4), 209–26.

Rossen, M., Klima, E. S., Bellugi, U., Bihrle, A., & Jones, W. (1996). Interaction between language and cognition: Evidence from Williams syndrome. In J. H. Beitchman, N. Cohen, M. Konstantareas, & R. Tannock (Eds.), *Language learning and behaviour* (pp. 367–92). New York: Cambridge University Press.

Rossion, B., Gauthier, I., Tarr, M. J., Despland, P., Bruyer, R., Linotte, S., & Crommelinck, M. (2000). The N170 occipito-temporal component is delayed and enhanced to inverted faces but not to inverted objects: An electrophysiological account of face-specific processes in the human brain. *NeuroReport*, 11 (1), 69–74.

Sullivan, K., & Tager-Flusberg, H. (1999). Second-order belief attribution in Williams syndrome: Intact or impaired? *American Journal on Mental Retardation*, 104 (6), 523–32.

Tager-Flusberg, H., & Sullivan, K. (2000). A componential view of theory of mind: Evidence from Williams syndrome. *Cognition*, 76 (1), 59–89.

Taylor, M. J., Edmonds, G. E., McCarthy, G., & Allison, T. (2001). Eyes first! Eye processing develops before face processing in children. *NeuroReport*, 12 (8), 1671–6.

Temple, C. (1997). *Developmental cognitive neuropsychology*. Hove: Psychology Press.

Thelen, E., & Smith, L. B. (1994). *A dynamical systems approach to development of cognition and action*. Cambridge, MA: Bradford Books, MIT Press.

Thomas, M. S. C., Grant, J., Barham, Z., Gsödl, M., Laing, E., Lakusta, L., Tyler, L. K., Grice, S., Paterson, S., & Karmiloff-Smith, A. (2001). Past tense formation in Williams syndrome. *Language and Cognitive Processes*, 2 (16), 143–76.

Tooby, J., & Cosmides, L. (1992). The psychological foundations of culture. In J. Barkow, L. Cosmides, & J. Tooby (Eds.), *The adapted mind: Evolutionary psychology and the generation of culture* (pp. 19–136). New York: Oxford University Press.

Turk, J. (1998). Fragile-X syndrome and attentional deficits. *Journal of Applied Research in Intellectual Disabilities*, 11 (3), 175–91.

Waddington, C. H. (1975). *The evolution of an evolutionist*. Ithaca, NY: Cornell University Press.

# Part II Cognitive Development

Contents

# 6

# The Case for Developmental Cognitive Science: Theories of People and Things

*Andrew N. Meltzoff*

## Introduction

A hundred years ago few scientists studied infants. Scholars interested in the brain (the forerunner of today's neuroscience) and those interested in epistemology and experimental psychology (the forerunners of cognitive science) did not perceive infants as a key population for psychological research. Attention was devoted to rodents and undergraduates. This has begun to change. Neuroscientists and cognitive scientists now turn to

This chapter is dedicated to my friend and colleague, George Butterworth. George and I spent many days discussing the topics that have made it into this chapter. He was a pioneer in object permanence and joint visual attention and thought deeply about imitation and intentionality. Every conversation with George sparked an idea; every interaction was a joy. I miss him. I am deeply indebted to Alan Slater and Gavin Bremner for their extreme patience and help as I composed this chapter. Thanks also to three collaborators with whom I've discussed many of the ideas presented here: Keith Moore, Alison Gopnik, and Rechele Brooks. Pat Kuhl provided useful insights on the writing, and Craig Harris and Calle Fisher helped in putting the chapter together. Work on the chapter was provided by a grant from NIH (HD-22514).

infancy to sharpen their understanding of mind, brain, and evolution (e.g., Diamond, Casey, & Munakata, in preparation; Meltzoff & Decety, 2003; Johnson & Karmiloff-Smith, chapter 5 in this volume).

Popular though it is, infancy is not a settled field. Piagetian theory no longer reigns. Modularity-nativism gained adherents in the 1990s, but is now being challenged. There is uncertainty about how to explain the new data pouring out of laboratories. This chapter discusses this theoretical ferment with particular reference to infants' knowledge of people and things. I conclude by sketching foundations for a *developmental* cognitive science that may allow us to escape from between a rock (Piagetian theory) and a hard place (nativism).

## Infant Theories: Standard Model and New Proposals

The Piagetian view of infancy was built on two fundamental axioms: the *action* assumption and the *invisibility* assumption. The former holds that infant knowing is rooted in their taking action. To know an object is to use it, and the acquisition of new knowledge requires motor exploration. Preverbal infants are confined to "knowing how," not "knowing that." The invisibility assumption proposes that when young infants lose sensory contact with an object, the object ceases to exist for the infant. To the young infant, an object is nothing more than "a mere image which re-enters the void as soon as it vanishes" (Piaget, 1954, p. 11). It does not have an independent, stable existence in external space.

The classic designation of infancy as the "sensorimotor period" codifies these two axioms. Infant intellectual growth is based on increasingly elaborate sensorimotor connections (practical habits), without mediating mental representations. The crowning achievement of the sensorimotor period is the birth of representation at about 18 months of age. Representation allows children to go beyond sensorimotor hookups and resonances with perceptually present stimuli. Representation allows infants to escape the eternal present. It undergirds their ability to perform deferred imitation and solve complex object permanence problems involving serial invisible displacements (Piaget, 1952, 1954, 1962).

The classic sensorimotor view of infancy has not received overwhelming empirical support. The action assumption was undermined by results showing that infants recognize familiar vs. novel displays they have never manipulated (Bower, 1982; Cohen,

Chaput, & Cashon, 2002; Fantz, 1964; Haith, 1998; Quinn, 2002; Slater, 1989, 1997). Infants learn, remember, and categorize without the necessity for motor involvement.[1] Research has also been directed at the invisibility assumption. Studies of deferred imitation and object occlusion discovered that young infants link objects and events across temporal gaps involving disappearances. Contrary to Piaget, the evidence shows that the absence of sensory contact does not terminate *mental* contact (e.g., Baillargeon, 1993; Meltzoff & Moore, 1998; Spelke, 1998).

Several alternative theoretical approaches have been suggested to replace Piaget. In this chapter I will suggest that the infant is not a sensorimotor organism but a representational one right from the neonatal period. Infants never go through a purely sensorimotor period, in which they operate solely with habit knowledge. Such a stage was postulated but does not exist.

However, moving beyond Piaget does not mandate acceptance of the modern-day nativism of Fodor (1983) or Spelke (1994, 1998). Although a young infant is more than a bundle of reflexes and sensorimotor habits, it does not follow that infants possess adult knowledge. The newborn's conception of persons and objects undergoes radical conceptual change as a function of the input received. What we need is a non-Piagetian theory of conceptual change in infancy.

Table 6.1 outlines four theories of infancy. This 2 × 2 table casts theories according to their views on two dimensions: the status of *representation* at birth and the reality of *conceptual change* in infancy. Obviously, a more complex description could be envisioned, but this suffices to capture critical points on which modern theories of infancy differ.

The classical Piagetian position occupies the "No–Yes" cell. It holds that infants have no representational system at birth and that there is a profound cognitive difference between newborns and 18-month-olds. Spelke's core knowledge thesis is the opposite:

**Table 6.1** Four theories of infancy

| *Representation at birth* | *Conceptual change in infancy* | *Example theorist* | *Theory* |
|---|---|---|---|
| No | Yes | Piaget | Sensorimotor |
| Yes | No | Spelke | Core knowledge |
| No | No | Thelen & Smith | Dynamic systems |
| Yes | Yes | Meltzoff, Moore, & Gopnik | Theory theory |

it couples innate representation (a "yes" to Piaget's "no") with no conceptual change; the core concepts of adults are present in infants in mature, unchanging form (Spelke, 1994, 1998; Spelke, Breinlinger, Macomber, & Jacobson, 1992). Thelen and Smith's (1994) dynamic systems theory shares the Piagetian view that there is no innate representation, but differs from Piaget in eschewing infant conceptual development. Thelen and Smith do not see sensorimotor coordinations as precursors to infant mentation and believe that explaining infant behavior at a conceptual level is misguided. On this view, the theoretical account of infants' response to problems should be in terms of the perceptual-motor demands and habitual responses involved in each specific situation. Children are limited to "know how" from birth to 3 (and possibly beyond). There is behavioral reorganization but not conceptual change because there are no infant concepts to work with.

Meltzoff and Moore (1998) incorporated both an initial representational capacity and conceptual change in a model of infancy. This position is a particular instance of a more general formulation of cognitive and semantic development called "theory theory." This view holds that infants understand the world in ways that change according to the data obtained and the experiments they perform (Gopnik & Meltzoff, 1997; Gopnik, Meltzoff, & Kuhl, 1999). In short, the theory is that infants have changeable theories of the world – not sensorimotor reactions (Piaget; Thelen & Smith) or adult theories that are masked by performance constraints or uncoordinated with action (Spelke).[2]

In this chapter I provide examples of how the theory-theory approach can be cashed out. I will consider four "hot topics": representation, joint visual attention, intentionality, and object permanence. The view presented is not a familiar one. I will argue that young infants have innate representational capacities and will discuss what this means. I will show that they can perform deferred imitation, but do not have a notion of object permanence in the first half-year of life. I will further sketch ideas about how object permanence, joint attention, and intentionality may develop with experience.

## Innate Representation

### *What's at stake*

Piaget thought that representation first emerged at 18 months of life. Both facial imitation and deferred imitation were used to buttress this view. Facial imitation was thought to be a late attainment, because the child's face was invisible to him or her. Deferred imitation was impossible because the target-to-copy was absent from view. These behaviors simply could not be early developments, and it took elaborate theoretical work to explain their appearance in the second year of life. It was critical for theory that deferred imitation first became possible at about 18 months of age in synchrony with higher-order symbolic behaviors such as language, pretend play, and the understanding of invisible displacements.

Piaget's theory does not conform to the modern empirical research (Meltzoff, 1999; Meltzoff & Prinz, 2002; Nadel & Butterworth, 1999). It has been shown, for example, that young infants perform deferred imitation. Evidently, invisibility is not an insurmountable problem. Infants can recall the past and use the past to guide their present actions.

## *Empirical findings*

In assessing the new data on deferred imitation and its impact on classical theory, it is important to distinguish between (1) forming a representation of an event from observation alone without motor involvement and (2) repeating one's own behavior or motor habits after a delay. For Piaget (1962), only the former qualified as deferred imitation. At stake is whether infants must motorically produce the act at Time-1 for it to be preserved at Time-2.

Meltzoff (1985, 1995) addressed this issue by introducing an "observation-only" design to explore early deferred imitation. In this paradigm infants were shown target acts on objects but not allowed to touch or handle the objects at Time-1. A delay was then imposed. After the delay, the objects were presented to the infants, and deferred imitation was assessed. Thus, infants could not be repeating their own actions with the objects, because interaction with them had been barred at Time-1. Using this design, deferred imitation of actions on objects has now been documented in infants as young as 6 to 9 months of age (Barr, Dowden, & Hayne, 1996; Heimann & Meltzoff, 1996; Meltzoff, 1988b).

Even if deferred imitation is possible, there are other hurdles to overcome before the theoretical implications are clear. For example, if deferred imitation in the pre–18-month-olds was restricted to highly familiar behaviors, it would sharply limit the implications for representation. Several experiments have addressed these issues using novel acts. Meltzoff (1988a) showed infants an adult who leaned forward and pressed a panel with his forehead. The infants were not allowed to play with the panel and were sent home for a 1-week delay interval. The baseline rate of producing this novel act was 0 percent for the control groups who did not see the adult display. However, 67 percent of the infants who saw the display reproduced the act after the week's delay. Gergely, Bekkering, and Király (2002) replicated this imitation of the novel head-touch act and showed it is not an automatic response, because there were conditions under which infants choose to duplicate the adult's odd behavior and conditions where they did not. Infants also imitate novel event sequences after a delay (e.g., Barr & Hayne, 1996; Bauer & Hertsgaard, 1993; Bauer & Mandler, 1992).

Researchers have investigated the length of delay that can be tolerated by young infants, with surprising results. Infants as young as 6 to 9 months of age successfully imitate after delays of 24 hours (Barr et al., 1996; Heimann & Meltzoff, 1996; Meltzoff, 1988b), 12-month-olds perform deferred imitation after 1-month delays (Klein & Meltzoff, 1999), and infants in the second year can imitate from memory after 4 months or longer (e.g., Bauer & Wewerka, 1995; Mandler & McDonough, 1995; Meltzoff, 1995). Once formed, representations evidently tend to persist and can be used as the basis of subsequent action.

In light of the evidence so far presented, there might be a temptation to tinker slightly with the classic theory to allow deferred imitation and representation at about 6 to 12 months old instead of 18 months. However, these capacities seem to be part of the initial state, at least when simple body actions are presented. Infants soon after birth can perform deferred imitation of facial gestures. Such facial imitation is representationally mediated: it has been demonstrated using an observation-only design, with novel gestures, and over long delays. Thus we infer that neonates have some primitive form of representation that allows them to organize action based on stimuli no longer in the perceptual field.

One early study used the observation-only design with neonates. Infants sucked on a pacifier while an adult demonstrated mouth opening and tongue protrusion (Meltzoff & Moore, 1977). This technique blocked infants from imitating while the display was in the perceptual field. The adult then stopped the demonstration, assumed a neutral face, and only then removed the pacifier. The results showed that 3-week-old infants imitated the gestures in the subsequent response period, despite the fact that the target gesture was no longer visible. Other studies have also reported early facial imitation when the gesture was no longer visible (Fontaine, 1984; Heimann, Nelson, & Schaller, 1989; Heimann & Schaller, 1985; Legerstee, 1991; Meltzoff & Moore, 1989).

Young infants have also been shown to imitate across longer delays. In one study, four groups of 6-week-old infants saw different gestures on Day 1 and returned on Day 2 to see the adult with a neutral pose (Meltzoff & Moore, 1994). The results showed that 6-week-old infants differentially imitated the gestures they saw 24 hours earlier. They imitated based on their representation of things past.

Finally, 6-week-old infants are able to imitate a somewhat novel gesture, a tongue-protrusion-to-the-side (Meltzoff & Moore, 1994, 1997). It is interesting that such young infants do not imitate this novel act on first try but modify their behavior over successive efforts, without feedback from the adult. We interpret this to mean that imitation is an active process in which infants cross-modally compare their own motor productions to a stored representation of the absent stimulus and correct the behavior to bring the two into register, as described by the active intermodal matching (AIM) model of imitation (see Meltzoff & Moore, 1997, for further analysis of the mechanisms underlying early imitation).

### *Larger implications*

These findings impact theories of representational development (Hayne, 2002; Slater, 2002). Three inferences can be drawn: (1) representations can be formed from observation alone, without concomitant motor action; (2) representations are durable mental entities in the preverbal period; and (3) they are a sufficient basis on which to organize action. The modern data suggest that young infants are not confined to sensorimotor coordination and motor habits. It is too conservative to build a theory of infancy that does not impute innate representational capacities. This weighs against the Piagetian and dynamic system theories (table 6.1). A richer starting state is needed.

## Joint Visual Attention

### *What's at stake*

In the adult psychological framework, head and eye movements have special significance. Adults realize that others direct their attention toward objects, picking up information about them from afar, despite the spatial gap between attender and target. We ascribe intentionality to the perceiver who turns his or her head. Do infants? Or are headturns interpreted as physical motions with no notion that they are *directed toward* the external object?

It is already known that young infants follow another's gaze, but there is a debate about mechanism (Butterworth, 2001). Nativists propose that infants have an innately specified shared attention module (Baron-Cohen, 1995). Others argue that this overinterprets gaze following. One proposal is that such behavior is based on infants being attracted to the spatial hemifield toward which the adult's head is moving. The infant visually tracks the adult and thereby swings his or her own head to the correct half of space without processing the adult's gaze or attention to an object (e.g., Butterworth & Jarrett, 1991; Moore & Corkum, 1994). On this view, infants do not understand the adult as a perceiver but simply process the salient movements regardless of what the organs of attention, the eyes, are doing.

## *Empirical findings*

A recent study zeroed in on whether infants understand the object directedness or referential value of adult attentive movements (Brooks & Meltzoff, 2002). Two identical objects were used, and the adult turned to look at one of them with no verbal or emotional cues. The infants were 12, 14, and 18 months of age. The interesting manipulation was that the adult turned to the target object with *eyes open* for one group and with *eyes closed* for

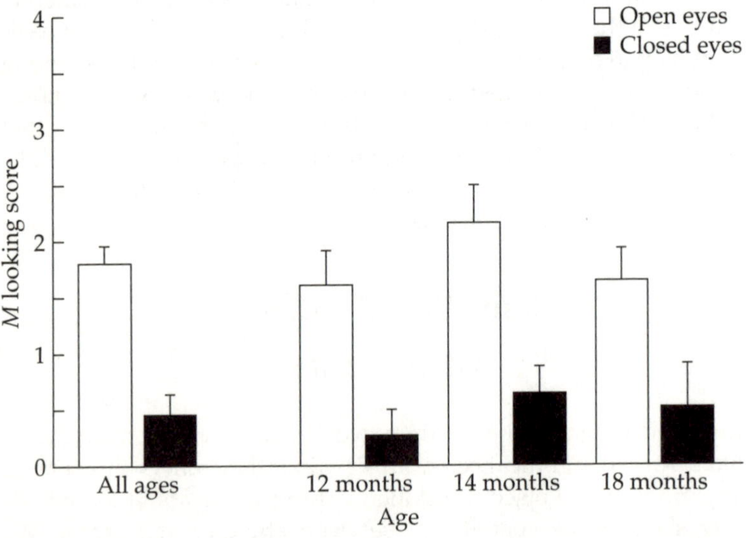


**Figure 6.1** Mean looking score (+ SE) for open-eyes and closed-eyes groups at each age ($n$ = 32 per age) (from Brooks & Meltzoff, 2002).

the other group. In each case infants interacted contingently with the adult before the trial. If infants rely simply on gross head motions, they should turn in both cases. If they rely on an abstract rule to look in the same direction as a "contingent interactant" (Johnson, Slaughter, & Carey, 1998), they should also look whether the adult's eyes were open or closed, because the adult's interactive behavior was identical in both groups.

The findings showed that the infants at all three ages turned selectively (figure 6.1). They seem to realize that a person may either be looking or not, depending on the status of his or her perceptual systems. This is sophisticated behavior for a 1-year-old, but it is not based on innate knowledge. Recent research shows that 9-month-olds turn just as readily in the direction of the adult's turn, regardless of whether the adult's eyes are open or closed (Brooks & Meltzoff, 2003). As Butterworth predicted, these young infants seem to be governed by the adult's gross head movements and do not take into account whether or not the adult is actually gazing at the object. We are currently studying this important developmental transition (see also Carpenter, Nagell, & Tomasello, 1998).

Brooks and I also noticed two responses that have not been systematically investigated in the joint visual attention literature. First, we found that infants pointed to the target object significantly more often if the adult looked at it with open vs. closed eyes. The infant's response involved a different motor movement than the adult's. The goal was the same, making reference to an object, but the means were different. Second, we discovered that

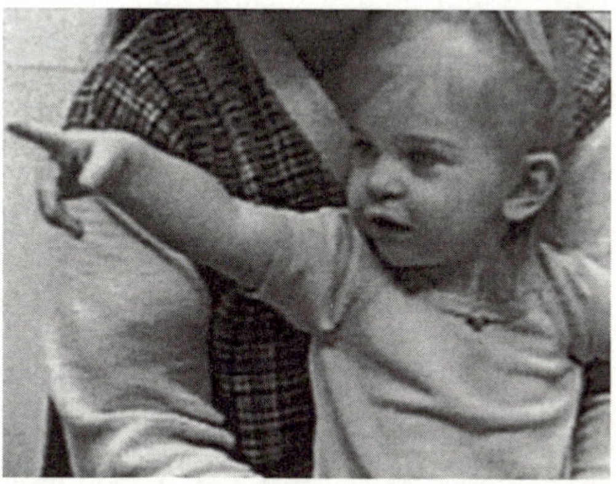

**Figure 6.2** An 18-month-old pointing to the correct target (from Brooks & Meltzoff, 2002).

infants visually inspected the object longer when they followed the adult's open eyes. This is significant because the object, in itself, is the same whether the adult turns with open or closed eyes. This suggests that the inanimate object takes on special valence because it is referenced by another person. It becomes more interesting to infants, and they visually inspect it for a longer period of time.

### *Larger implications*

Taken together, the pointing and visual examination data suggest that infants are not simply observing meaningless motions. Infants are not simply coding physical motions, but making a psychological attribution to the perceiver. The findings do not prove that infants ascribe to the adult an "internal experience of attending," but they move beyond the leanest interpretations of gaze following. At minimum, they suggest that by 12 months of age, infants represent the object directedness of adult gaze. They see head movements as directed toward the external world and not mere bodily movements without significance (Butler, Caron, & Brooks, 2000; Johnson, 2000; Wellman & Phillips, 2001; Woodward, in press).

In the conclusions of this chapter I show how infants' experience with their *own* eye opening–closing – cutting off and reaccessing the world through it – may contribute to their understanding the visual perception of others. My hypothesis is that they see others as "like me" and use the experience gained through their own self-action to help them interpret the behavior of others. This "like-me" framework, I will suggest, may be an engine for developmental change in infants' understanding of gaze and other acts as well (Woodward, Sommerville, & Guajardo, 2001).

## Intention

### *What's at stake*

Persons are more than dynamic bags of skin whose actions can be represented and imitated and whose direction of gaze can be followed. In the mature adult notion, persons have beliefs, desires, and intentions that predict and explain human actions. One cannot see, hear, or taste others' mental states, but it is an essential part of our commonsense psychology that we believe people have them. So-called "theory-of-mind" research addresses the development of this understanding of people.

A strong nativist view was provided by Fodor (1987, p. 132): "Here is what I would have done if I had been faced with this problem in designing *Homo sapiens*. I would have made a knowledge of commonsense *Homo sapiens* psychology innate; that way nobody would have to spend time learning it." Leslie (1994, 1995) also laid out the case for an innately specified theory of mind module. What do the recent data say about the development of infants' understanding of other minds and especially the intentions of others?

## Empirical findings

To begin to tackle this issue, Meltzoff (1995) developed a procedure called the behavioral reenactment technique. The procedure capitalizes on imitation, but it uses this proclivity in a new, more abstract way. It investigates infants' ability to read below the visible surface behavior to the underlying goals and intentions of the actor.

One study involved showing 18-month-old infants an unsuccessful act, a failed effort (Meltzoff, 1995). For example, the adult "accidentally" under- or overshot his target, or he tried to perform a behavior but his hand slipped several times; thus the goal-state was not achieved. To an adult, it was easy to read the actor's intention although he did not fulfill them. The experimental question was whether infants also read through the literal body movements to the underlying goal of the act. The measure of how they interpreted the event was what they chose to reenact. In this case the correct answer was not to copy the literal movement that was actually seen, but to copy the actor's goal, which remained unfulfilled.

The study compared infants' tendency to perform the target act in several situations: (1) after they saw the full target act demonstrated, (2) after they saw the unsuccessful attempt to perform the act, and (3) after it was neither shown nor attempted. The results showed that 18-month-olds can infer the unseen goals implied by unsuccessful attempts. Infants who saw the unsuccessful attempt and infants who saw the full target act both produced target acts at a significantly higher rate than controls. Evidently, young toddlers can understand our goals even if we fail to fulfill them.

At what age does this understanding of others emerge? My research suggests that it is not available innately. I have found that 15-month-olds behaved much like the 18-month-olds in the original 1995 study, but 9-month-olds did not respond above baseline levels to the unsuccessful-attempt demonstrations (Meltzoff, 1999). Importantly, control conditions indicated that 9-month-olds succeeded if the adult demonstrated successful acts. The 9-month-olds imitated visible acts on objects, but gave no evidence of inferring intentions beyond the visible behavior itself. This finding of developmental change in infants' understanding of others' goals and intentions has also been documented in other studies (Bellagamba & Tomasello, 1999), so there is converging evidence for an important developmental change between 9 and 15 months. We have also shown that children's understanding of goals continues to change and influence behavior in the 3- to 6-year-old age range (e.g., Gleissner, Meltzoff, & Bekkering, 2000), and many have argued that making sense of others' goals and intentions is a lifelong enterprise (Bruner, 1999).[3]

In the adult psychological framework, people and other agents have goals and intentions, but inanimate devices do not. Do infants carve the world in this way? In order to assess this, Meltzoff designed an inanimate device made of plastic and wood (Meltzoff, 1995, Exp. 2). The device had poles for arms and mechanical pincers for hands. It did not look human, but it traced the same spatiotemporal path that the human actor traced and manipulated the object much as the human actor did. The results showed that infants did not attribute a goal or intention to the movements of the inanimate device when its pincers slipped off the ends of a dumbbell that it was "trying" to pull apart. Infants were no more (or less) likely to pull the toy apart after seeing the failed attempt of the inanimate device than they were in baseline levels when they saw nothing. This was the case despite the fact that infants pulled the dumbbell apart if the inanimate device successfully completed this act. Evidently, infants can pick up certain information from the inanimate device, but not other information: they can understand successes, but not failures. This makes sense because successes lead to a change in the object, which gives them an endstate to achieve, whereas failures leave the object intact and therefore must be interpreted at a deeper level.

## Larger implications

The research shows that infants distinguish between what the adult meant to do and what he actually did. They ascribe goals to human acts; indeed, they infer the goal of an act even when the goal is not attained. This differentiation lies at the core of our commonsense psychology. It underlies communication as well as moral judgments. Thus, infants already exhibit an essential aspect of our commonsense psychology: the acts of persons (but not the motions of unambiguously mechanical devices) are understood within a psychological framework involving goals and intentions.[4]

## Object Permanence

### *What's at stake*

Before 8 months of age infants do not search for objects hidden by an occluder. Piaget interpreted this as evidence that they had not yet developed the concept of a permanent object. Object permanence is the notion that material objects are not annihilated by virtue of their occlusion. They continue to exist in a spatial location behind the screen and are simply hidden from view. The fact that burning, melting, and explosion destroy objects does not violate the adult notion of object permanence. Object permanence does not mean that we think objects are forever permanent and cannot be destroyed. The essential point is that we do not think that an *occlusion* event, in and of itself, destroys an object. We would be shocked (and disbelieve) evidence that an object "disappeared into thin air" by virtue of being occluded by a screen.

The problem that has bedeviled developmentalists is that the failure of pre-8-month-olds to search for occluded objects may not reveal a deficit in understanding object permanence. Search errors may be due to other factors such as a lack of motor skill, memory, and/or means-ends coordination (e.g., Bremner, 1994; Butterworth & Jarrett, 1982; Diamond, 1985; Harris, 1987; Moore & Meltzoff, 1999; Munakata, 1998; Munakata et al., 1997). Researchers have attempted to circumvent this by measuring infants' visual response to object occlusions. Infants' preferential looking to novelty after habituation/familiarization has been used to investigate object permanence. Typically, these findings are interpreted as showing that infants as young as 3.5 months of age, and perhaps from birth, exhibit object permanence (e.g., Baillargeon, 1993; Spelke et al., 1992).

Recently, the attribution of early object permanence based on looking-time studies has been questioned (Bogartz, Shinskey, & Schilling, 2000; Cashon & Cohen, 2000; Haith, 1998, Meltzoff & Moore, 1998). In particular, Meltzoff and Moore (1998) suggested that infants' representational capacity itself, in the absence of permanence, would be sufficient to generate increased looking times. Infants could represent the pre-hiding event and compare this scene with the post-hiding situation. Pre-post discrepancies would recruit increased looking without requiring an understanding of the object's continued existence *in a specific location behind the occluder while it is out of sight*. Meltzoff and Moore (1998) reviewed looking-time studies and found they could be accounted for by the operation of infant representation and identity rules alone, without the notion of object permanence. Whether this view provides a complete account of all the early permanence work (e.g., Baillargeon, 2002) is an issue that will continue to be debated, but we think we have accounted for the classic studies based on different (less developmentally mature) mechanisms than permanence.

Recently, we returned to the gold standard of manual search. Our reasoning was as follows. If infants actively search for an occluded object, this is good evidence for permanence. They are searching in the invisible place precisely because they think the object exists in that spatial location even though the object is not in sight. The problem has always been that failures were hard to interpret. We designed a new study in which failures as well as successes were interpretable. The results suggest that object permanence develops through a progressive understanding and is not innately fixed.

## Empirical findings

In Moore and Meltzoff (1999) infants were shown two different types of total occlusion in which the *same* toy is hidden in the *same* place behind the *same* screen. If young infants solve one hiding but not the other, this task dissociation cannot be attributed to differences in motor skill, means-ends coordination, or other ancillary factors, because the same response is needed to find the toy in both. In other words, the tasks controlled for the ancillary factors that are often invoked to account for search errors. The tasks differed only in the type of cognitive problem they posed to the infant (in ways that will be described below).

In these experiments, we adopted three criteria for isolating permanence-governed search:

1 Infants were precluded from reaching until the occlusion was complete. If search is based on permanence, infants should be able to initiate search after the disappearance event has

terminated. Search acts that start before occlusion is complete do not necessitate permanence, because they could be planned and launched from direct perception.

2 A strict criterion for the form of the search act was adopted. If infants represent a hidden object as spatially localized, for example under a cloth, the aim of search should be to uncover that space and thus the object. Pointing at or even touching the occluder do not unequivocally index a hidden location; they may simply mark where the last perceptual change occurred in the visual field.

3 The infant's gaze during the act of uncovering was measured. If search is permanence-governed, the infant's gaze should be directed toward the hidden location as uncovering begins, because they are looking for the object under the occluder. (The last two points help distinguish infant play with occluders from permanence-governed search, as discussed by Butterworth, 1977; Willatts, 1984.)

Experiment 1 involved 10-, 12-, and 14-month-old infants. Each infant was given both hiding tasks in a counterbalanced order. Figure 6.3 displays the two occlusion events. They differed in a subtle way – so subtle that existing theories do not predict any difference between them. In the hiding by screen, the occlusion is accomplished by putting the object in a place on the table top,

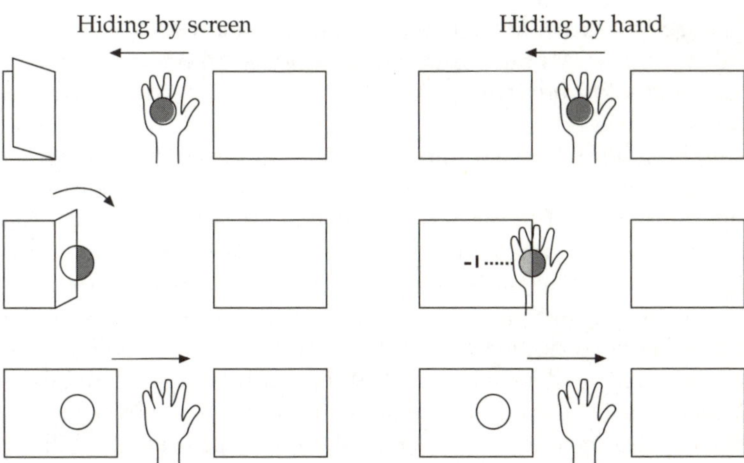


**Figure 6.3** Object permanence is not an all-or-none acquisition. There is a significant dissociation in infants' performance on the two tasks; see text for details (from Moore & Meltzoff, 1999).

**Table 6.2** Number of infants succeeding/failing as a function of type of occlusion

| | | *Hiding by hand* | |
|---|---|---|---|
| | | *Fail* | *Succeed* |
| *Hiding by screen* | *Succeed* | **15** | 36 |
| | *Fail* | 20 | **1** |

and then covering it with the screen. In the hiding by hand, the occlusion is accomplished by putting the object on a platform (the hand) and moving the platform under the screen to deposit the object underneath the screen. Piaget made no distinction between these: in his scheme they are both simple, complete occlusions at one location (indeed in Piaget, 1954, he sometimes hides objects one way and sometimes another, without discrimination).

The results showed that the hiding by screen was systematically solved earlier than the hiding by hand. The data are displayed in a 2 × 2 table showing how many infants solve both tasks, neither task, or one vs. the other. The crucial cells fall on the diagonal (table 6.2, bold cells), because they show a change in performance from one task to the other. As shown, 15 infants solve hiding-by-screen but not hiding-by-hand, vs. only one infant who does the reverse ($p < 0.001$, McNemar test). Further analyses showed that this task dissociation was strongly exhibited in both the 10- and 12-month-olds, but that almost all of the 14-month-olds succeeded on both tasks.[5]

Experiment 2 tested the generality of these findings with 10-month-olds. We hid the objects under pillows on one side of the room, far out of reach of the infants. In order to recover the object, they first needed to crawl/walk across the room to lift up the occluder. The mean length of time to navigate across the room after the hiding and before recovery was 11 seconds, so the delay between occlusion and recovery was not negligible. The results replicated Experiment 1: 9 infants solved the hiding-by-screen but not the hiding-by-hand, and 0 did the converse.

Ancillary factors such as motivation, memory, motor skill, or means-ends coordination cannot explain the task dissociation, because these were equated in the two tasks. Piagetian theory cannot explain the dissociation, because both tasks were occlusions in one location. Nor does nativism fare well: if adult object permanence is part of core knowledge, infants should search for the object for *both* occlusions (if they have the skill) or *neither* occlusion (if there are performance constraints or knowledge–action disconnects).[6]

Some development in object permanence *per se* seems to occur between 10 and 14 months of age, inasmuch as 14-month-olds solve both tasks, whereas 10- to 12-month-olds can solve only one of them. The question is how to characterize this development.

## Larger implications

Moore and Meltzoff use these results to support the idea that object permanence is not innately specified and fixed. We hypothesize that at the ages studied here, the object permanence rule used by infants is: "an object continues to exist in the *place* it disappeared." In the hiding-by-screen, this rule leads to success. The object is on the table, in the place it resided when it was occluded. Conversely, hiding by hand is more challenging because the place the object disappeared and now should be (the hand) is empty. This confronts infants with perceptual evidence that the object no longer exists, according to their rules (not in the place of disappearance). The empty hand leads young infants to interpret this type of hiding as one that does not preserve permanence. Thus the same rule that allows infants to understand one hiding leads them astray for the other.

Moore and Meltzoff's shorthand for this is that the concept of object permanence develops, or more strictly, the range of hidings over which permanence is understood becomes increasingly comprehensive, over age and experience. Infant object permanence is not a once-and-for-all attainment. Young infants at first interpret the world as showing that certain transformations preserve the permanence of objects and others do not. Permanence is *occlusion-dependent* in infancy.

The idea that permanence depends on the type of disappearance, rather than being all-or-none, should not surprise developmentalists. In the adult's theory, certain disappearances do not preserve the permanence of objects, e.g., burning, melting, exploding (Michotte, 1962). Adults believe that the object is annihilated in these cases. The difference, however, is that adults understand that all *occlusions* preserve permanence. Infants only gradually come to the adult view that material objects, qua objects, are permanent across any and all occlusions – that occlusions prevent perceptual access to objects but do not remove them from the external world. There is a series of logically ordered steps that infants go through as they acquire this adult concept of object permanence (see Moore & Meltzoff, 1999, for a more comprehensive developmental theory).

## Elements of a Developmental Cognitive Science

In this chapter we explored four issues in infancy: representation, joint visual attention, intention, and object permanence. It would be overreaching to say that the debates in each are identical. Nonetheless, we can profit from the commonalities. Each domain has boosters and scoffers – those who claim infant knowledge is equal to adults' and those who seek to reduce infant reactions to motor habits, hardly worthy of the name knowledge at all. In this chapter I have tried to advocate a developmental view that endorses a rich innate state but still embraces conceptual change. Consider infants' developing understanding of people and things from this developmental perspective.

### *Developing knowledge of objects*

Object permanence and imitation stand out as test cases of infant theories. Young infants were supposed to fail on tests of object permanence and deferred imitation, according to sensorimotor theory. Both involve removal of perceptual contact. Although infants were thought to respond adaptively to the perceptual world (they categorize, reach, track, etc.), invisibility was said to be an insurmountable hurdle. Infants could adapt their actions to the current situation, but could not represent the invisible – hence, they must fail on object permanence and deferred imitation tests.

In both cases, research challenged this standard model, and a lively debate ensued. This chapter interprets the evidence in a somewhat novel way, by suggesting that deferred imitation is innately present but object permanence is not. Most theories assume that if infants represent absent stimuli and engage in deferred imitation, they will also have a notion of object permanence. But this is not a logical entailment.

If we are to make headway in constructing a new developmental theory, we must differentiate the concepts of representation and permanence.

There is a crucial distinction between:

1 *existence of a representation of absent objects* and
2 *representation of the existence of absent objects.*

Manual search for occluded objects relies on the latter; deferred imitation (and the looking-time studies of "early permanence") rely on the former.

An example may help bring this conceptual distinction into sharper focus. Crudely put, think of a balloon. If the balloon explodes, we maintain a mental representation of it, but we do not think that the balloon still exists in the world. The representation persists, but we do not think the object does. Maintaining a representation of the object is not the same as representing it *as* permanent. Meltzoff and Moore (1998) systematically reviewed the "early permanence" literature and concluded that the preferential-looking results rely on representation but not object permanence.

We define object permanence as representing an object as continuing to exist in a hidden location during the time that it is invisible. In order to investigate object permanence defined in this way, Moore and Meltzoff (1999) used manual search. Importantly, the study instituted new controls that rendered both failure to search and successful search more interpretable. The results showed that infants responded to two types of occlusions in different ways. Occlusion of an object by movement of a screen over it was solved at an earlier age (about 10 months old) than occlusion in which an object was carried under the screen (about 14 months old). This dissociation cannot be explained by ancillary factors such as motivation, motor skill, or means-ends coordination, because for both tasks the same object was hidden in the same place under the same screen and required the same uncovering response. In contrast to the nativist position, the 10-month-olds' understanding of occlusions is not equivalent to the adult's understanding, and moreover, it is not even fixed in an all-or-none fashion within infancy, because there is evidence for a sharp developmental shift over a 4-month interval.

However, rejecting a strong nativist account of object permanence does not send us back to Piaget. Piaget's only explanatory tools were the sensorimotor schemes (e.g., competing motor habits, means-ends coordination, etc.) that were demanded by one hiding or another. Moore and Meltzoff (1999) propose that object permanence develops from simpler beginnings involving maintaining the numerical identity of objects (based on spatiotemporal parameters involving place and trajectory). We propose that permanence is an interpretation infants impose to make sense of multiple appearances of the numerically *same* individual over occlusion events. In the absence of identity rules for maintaining numerical identity and experience with disappearance–reappearance events, infants would have no basis to infer the permanence of objects. Permanence is a concept infants develop to "bridge the gap" between two visual appearances of the same thing. (This identity-based theory of object permanence development is fleshed out in more detail in Meltzoff & Moore, 1998; Moore & Meltzoff, 1999; Moore, Borton, & Darby, 1978.)

## *Developing knowledge of persons: The "like-me" mechanism*

Philosophers have long wondered how we come to ascribe beliefs, desires, and intentions to others – in short, where our ability to understand other minds comes from. The empirical work shows that 18-month-olds have already adopted an essential aspect of the adult intentional framework. However, this framework does not come out of nowhere. It has developmental roots.

My thesis is that imitation provides a foundation for developing our understanding of other minds. Below is a sketch of a three-step developmental process.

1 *Innate foundations.* Infants recognize equivalences between acts they perceive in others and produce themselves. They have neural machinery that allows them to code others as "like me" (Meltzoff & Decety, 2003). This is the starting state as documented by motor imitation in newborns (Meltzoff & Moore, 1997).
2 *Self-learning.* As infants perform particular bodily acts they have certain mental experiences. Behaviors are regularly related to mental states. For example, when infants produce certain emotional expressions (e.g., smiling) or bodily activity (e.g., struggling to obtain an out-of-reach toy), they also experience their own mental states (happiness, thwarted desire). Infants register this systematic relation between their own behaviors and underlying mental states. They construct a detailed map linking bodily acts and mind.
3 *Attributions to others "like me."* When infants see others behaving "like me" – producing the same expressions and bodily acts – they hypothesize/infer/project that others have

> the mental experiences that are linked to those behaviors in the self. This gives infants purchase on understanding other minds until spoken language can be used. This "like me" projection is most compatible with mental states that have relatively reliable outward bodily expressions – such as emotion, intentional action, visual perception, and desires. These are, in fact, the mental states that infants first attribute to others. The attribution of false belief is, admittedly, not as easily accomplished by the above mechanism, and interestingly is a later acquisition. Thus, the foregoing mechanism may be key for the earliest construal of other minds, with further development needed to flesh out the fully mature adult state (Flavell, 1999; Goldman, 1992, 2000; Gordon, 1995; Meltzoff, Gopnik, & Repacholi, 1999; Taylor, 1996; Wellman, 2002).

Let us examine how the foregoing model provides infants leverage on understanding the intentions and visual perspective of others.

According to the model, infants may come to understand others' intentions in part because they have experience with their own intentionality. Infants have experienced their own desires and acts of "try and try again." When an infant sees another act in this same way, the infant's own experience would suggest that there is a goal beyond the surface behavior; the surface behavior would be seen as a familiar type indicating effortfulness, purposiveness, or striving, rather than as an end in itself.

The "like-me" mechanism could also help explain how younger infants come to understand the attentional acts of others. Infants in the first year of life can imitate head movements (Meltzoff, 1988a; Meltzoff & Moore, 1989; Piaget, 1962). These data indicate that infants can map between their own head movements and those they see others perform. Because they recognize that the other person's headturn is similar to their own, infants could use their own subjective experiences gained from "turning in order to see" to make sense of the head movements of others. Moreover, infants know something about the effects of eye closures. The infant's own experience is that eye closure cuts off his or her own visual access to objects. Because an infant can map his or her own eye closure onto those of others (as manifest in imitating blinking; Piaget, 1962), he or she can give felt meaning to the eye closures of others. Rather than interpreting the adult's head and eye movements as a purely physical motion (a physical analysis), infants have the tools for interpreting them within a psychological framework that connects gazer and object, as a primitive act of "seeing" rather than meaningless "lateral motion in space."

The more general point is that the basic human tendency to construe others as sentient beings with intentions, desires, perceptions, and emotions need not be preloaded into the infant's mind. Rather, the "like-me-ness" of others, first manifest in imitation, may be the wellspring of more mature forms of social cognition and an engine for its development. At first infants realize that others can act like me; from this foundation they develop the more abstract idea that others who act like me also have mental states like me. Without the neural machinery and social interaction provided in early infancy, the adult notion of other minds would not take the form that it does.

## *The value of staying open-minded*

Empirical work over the past 25 years revealed a much richer innate state than Piaget assumed. One might say that the nativists have prevailed. Two distinct schools of nativism have been offered, however, and they have profound differences. One view, final-state nativism (Fodor, 1983; Spelke et al., 1992), argues that the initial state is equivalent to the final state. The other, starting-state nativism, argues that radical conceptual revision begins at birth (e.g., Gopnik & Meltzoff, 1997; Meltzoff & Moore, 1998).

Fodor advocates final-state nativism for social cognition. He thinks the newborn innately possesses the mature theory of mind: it is culturally universal and adaptive, so why waste time learning it? Spelke advocates final-state nativism concerning material objects. She argues that age-related changes in infants' response to object occlusions are due to the lifting of performance constraints that block the expression/use of innate core knowledge.

In contrast, the starting-state view does not portray infants' similarity to adults in terms of unchanging core knowledge but in the striving for a coherent interpretation of the behavior of people and things. Infants do not begin life with adult concepts, but rather with discovery procedures that lead them to develop adult concepts. The regularities infants use come from many sources, including the laws of physics, the actions of others, and experience of the self as an intentional agent.

Development is thus an open-ended process. Early concepts are used to interpret the behavior of people and things and are revised in light of data. The benefit is social and cognitive adaptability. Human babies are special. What makes them special is not that they are born so intelligent but that they are designed to change their minds when faced with the data.

## NOTES

1 Piagetians often respond to this challenge by arguing that visual perception is itself action. Thus, they argue that visual preference-for-novelty in the absence of manipulative experience does not violate Piagetian theory.

2 Table 6.1 does not offer a survey of all positions in infancy. Baillargeon (2002) argues for innate object permanence but developmental changes in other aspects of physical knowledge in infancy. Carey (1985, 1991, 1995) largely endorses Spelke's model of infancy, but proposes conceptual changes in childhood. Other theorists have considered only one dimension of the 2 × 2 table, or offered positions not fully captured by the two dimensions of this table (Bertenthal, 1996; Karmiloff-Smith, 1992; Munakata, McClelland, Johnson, & Siegler, 1997).

3 Researchers have used visual habituation and preferential-looking-to-novelty to investigate 6- to 12-month-olds' understanding of goal-directed actions (e.g., Gergely, 2002; Gergely, Nádasdy, Csibra, & Bíró, 1995; Wellman & Phillips, 2001; Woodward, 1998, 1999). It is a subtle point, but useful for theory, to acknowledge that the infant looking-time measures and action measures (behavioral reenactment technique) do not always ask identical questions. For example, Woodward constructed a stimulus that involved an adult grasping an object in one of two locations. The question was whether infants treated the object as the goal of the reach even if the object was moved to a new location. In this case the "goal of the reach" is the *seen* physical object (a toy ball or bear). Similarly, the goals in the Gergely work are spatial locations, physical endpoints (such as "next to the large circle" or "in the left-hand corner of the screen") seen during the habituation phase. This kind of "goal" differs from an *unseen* goal that was never visually presented to the infant, as was tested in Meltzoff (1995). Consistent with the viewpoint of this chapter, I do not think understanding goals and intention is all-or-none in infancy. There is development in infants' understanding of goals. The development may be from external, visible endstates to invisible, internal states of mind in the actor. A value of the behavioral reenactment approach is that it allows us to assess something like the bridge from the former to the latter (Meltzoff, 1995). Both habituation and action techniques are useful and provide complementary evidence for mapping the entire developmental pattern.

4 In certain circumstances infants seem to make intentional attributions to pretend humans (stuffed animals and puppets; Johnson, 2000) and dynamic displays that are ambiguous as to animacy (e.g., 2D spots that leap and move spontaneously; Gergely, 2002; Gergely et al., 1995). This does not contradict the proposals made here. On the one hand, even adults make mistakes and overattributions in some contexts (acting as though the light "doesn't want" to come on). On the other hand, the Meltzoff study used a wood/plastic display that was clearly inanimate and not acting like a psychological agent, whereas

the Johnson/Gergely displays capture aspects of animacy and agency. Experiments are needed that manipulate the stimulus within one paradigm to explore the boundary conditions. One must also be attentive to developmental change: younger infants may assign goals/intentions to either a narrower *or* broader range of entities than older infants. These are empirical questions.

5 The journal paper includes further details that will interest object permanence aficionados, some of which are these. Two screens, laid out in a left–right orientation, were used for each *S*. For each *S*, both tasks were administered on the same side (counterbalanced across *S*s), thus there was no change of location (pp. 627–8). The vast majority of the unsuccessful searches were due to infants not initiating recovery efforts; only a few infants searched in the wrong location (p. 631). Infant looking behavior was tightly coupled to their reaching behavior (p. 631). We proposed ideas about the developmental relation between object *identity* and object *permanence* (pp. 638–41) and distinguished these tasks from Piaget's more complex serial invisible displacements (p. 640).

6 Moore and Meltzoff (1999) and Munakata (1998; Munakata et al., 1997) agree that object permanence is not an innate given and develops with experience. But the theories are not identical. Munakata's view is that development entails a gradual strengthening of the representation of the hidden object. As currently formulated, this does not predict the task dissociation, observed here, because there is no reason why the object representation should be stronger or weaker in one hiding or the other. The same object and occluder were used in both hidings. Meltzoff and Moore think that the spatiotemporal parameters (place and trajectory) embodied in the hiding are key to understanding this task dissociation and developmental change, rather than a more generic "strengthening" of representations. The two views are not wholly incompatible and a hybrid model would be possible.

## REFERENCES

Baillargeon, R. (1993). The object concept revisited: New directions in the investigation of infants' physical knowledge. In C. Granrud (Ed.), *Visual perception and cognition in infancy* (pp. 265–315). Hillsdale, NJ: Erlbaum.

Baillargeon, R. (2002). The acquisition of physical knowledge in infancy: A summary in eight lessons. In U. Goswami (Ed.), *Handbook of childhood cognitive development* (pp. 47–83). Oxford: Blackwell.

Baron-Cohen, S. (1995). The eye detection detector (EDD) and the shared attention mechanism (SAM): Two cases for evolutionary psychology. In C. Moore & P. J. Dunham (Eds.), *Joint attention: Its origins and role in development* (pp. 41–59). Hillsdale, NJ: Erlbaum.

Barr, R., Dowden, A., & Hayne, H. (1996). Developmental changes in deferred imitation by 6- to 24-month-old infants. *Infant Behavior and Development*, 19, 159–70.

Barr, R., & Hayne, H. (1996). The effect of event structure on imitation in infancy: Practice makes perfect? *Infant Behavior and Development*, 19, 253–7.

Bauer, P. J., & Hertsgaard, L. A. (1993). Increasing steps in recall of events: Factors facilitating immediate and long-term memory in 13.5- and 16.5-month-old children. *Child Development*, 64, 1204–23.

Bauer, P. J., & Mandler, J. M. (1992). Putting the horse before the cart: The use of temporal order in recall of events by one-year-old children. *Developmental Psychology*, 28, 441–52.

Bauer, P. J., & Wewerka, S. S. (1995). One- to two-year-olds' recall of events: The more expressed, the more impressed. *Journal of Experimental Child Psychology*, 59, 475–96.

Bellagamba, F., & Tomasello, M. (1999). Re-enacting intended acts: Comparing 12- and 18-month-olds. *Infant Behavior and Development*, 22, 277–82.

Bertenthal, B. I. (1996). Origins and early development of perception, action, and representation. *Annual Review of Psychology*, 47, 431–59.

Bogartz, R. S., Shinskey, J. L., & Schilling, T. H. (2000). Object permanence in five-and-a-half-month-old infants? *Infancy*, 1, 403–28.

Bower, T. G. R. (1982). *Development in infancy* (2nd ed.). San Francisco: W. H. Freeman.

Bremner, J. G. (1994). Processes underlying young children's spatial orientation during movement. *Journal of Experimental Child Psychology*, 57, 355–76.

Brooks, R., & Meltzoff, A. N. (2002). The importance of eyes: How infants interpret adult looking behavior. *Developmental Psychology*, 38, 958–66.

Brooks, R., & Meltzoff, A. N. (2003, April). Gaze following at 9 and 12 months: A developmental shift from global head direction to gaze. Poster presented at the Society for Research in Child Development, Tampa, FL.

Bruner, J. S. (1999). The intentionality of referring. In P. D. Zelazo, J. W. Astington, & D. Olson (Eds.), *Developing theories of intention: Social understanding and self-control* (pp. 329–39). Mahwah, NJ: Erlbaum.

Butler, S. C., Caron, A. J., & Brooks, R. (2000). Infant understanding of the referential nature of looking. *Journal of Cognition and Development*, 1, 359–77.

Butterworth, G. (1977). Object disappearance and error in Piaget's stage IV task. *Journal of Experimental Child Psychology*, 23, 391–401.

Butterworth, G. (2001). Joint visual attention in infancy. In G. Bremner & A. Fogel (Eds.), *Blackwell handbook of infant development* (pp. 213–40). Oxford: Blackwell. Reprinted as chapter 12 in this volume.

Butterworth, G., & Jarrett, N. (1982). Piaget's stage 4 error: Background to the problem. *British Journal of Psychology*, 73, 175–85.

Butterworth, G., & Jarrett, N. (1991). What minds have in common is space: Spatial mechanisms serving joint visual attention in infancy. *British Journal of Developmental Psychology*, 9, 55–72.

Carey, S. (1985). *Conceptual change in childhood*. Cambridge, MA: MIT Press.

Carey, S. (1991). Knowledge acquisition: Enrichment or conceptual change? In S. Carey & R. Gelman (Eds.), *The epigenesis of mind: Essays on biology and cognition* (pp. 257–91). Hillsdale, NJ: Erlbaum.

Carey, S. (1995). On the origins of causal understanding. In D. Sperber, D. Premack, & A. Premack (Eds.), *Causal cognition* (pp. 269–302 Oxford: Clarendon.

Carpenter, M., Nagell, K., & Tomasello, M. (1998). Social cognition, joint attention, and communicative competence from 9 to 15 months of age. *Monographs of the Society for Research in Child Development*, 63 (4, Serial No. 255).

Cashon, C. H., & Cohen, L. B. (2000). Eight-month-old infants' perceptions of possible and impossible events. *Infancy*, 1, 429–46.

Cohen, L. B., Chaput, H. H., & Cashon, C. H. (2002). A constructivist model of infant cognition. *Cognitive Development*, 17, 1323–43.

Diamond, A. (1985). Development of the ability to use recall to guide action, as indicated by infants' performance on AB. *Child Development*, 56, 868–83.

Diamond, A., Casey, B. J., & Munakata, Y. (in preparation). *Textbook of developmental cognitive neuroscience.*

Fantz, R. L. (1964). Visual experience in infants: Decreased attention to familiar patterns relative to novel ones. *Science*, 146, 668–70.

Flavell, J. H. (1999). Cognitive development: Chidren's knowledge about the mind. *Annual Review of Psychology*, 50, 21–45.

Fodor, J. A. (1983). *The modularity of mind: An essay on faculty psychology.* Cambridge, MA: MIT Press.

Fodor, J. A. (1987). *Psychosemantics: The problem of meaning in the philosophy of mind.* Cambridge, MA: MIT Press.

Fontaine, R. (1984). Imitative skills between birth and six months. *Infant Behavior and Development*, 7, 323–33.

Gergely, G. (2002). The development of understanding self and agency. In U. Goswami (Ed.), *Handbook of childhood cognitive development* (pp. 26–46). Oxford: Blackwell.

Gergely, G., Bekkering, H., & Király, I. (2002). Rational imitation in preverbal infants. *Nature*, 415, 755.

Gergely, G., Nádasdy, Z., Csibra, G., & Bíró, S. (1995). Taking the intentional stance at 12 months of age. *Cognition*, 56, 165–93.

Gleissner, B., Meltzoff, A. N., & Bekkering, H. (2000). Children's coding of human action: Cognitive factors influencing imitation in 3-year-olds. *Developmental Science*, 3, 405–14.

Goldman, A. I. (1992). Empathy, mind, and morals: Presidential address. *Proceedings and Addresses of the American Philosophical Association*, 66, 17–41.

Goldman, A. I. (2000). The mentalizing folk. In D. Sperber (Ed.), *Metarepresentations: A multidisciplinary perspective.* New York: Oxford University Press.

Gopnik, A., & Meltzoff, A. N. (1997). *Words, thoughts, and theories.* Cambridge, MA: MIT Press.

Gopnik, A., Meltzoff, A. N., & Kuhl, P. K. (1999). *The scientist in the crib: Minds, brains, and how children learn.* New York: William Morrow.

Gordon, R. M. (1995). Sympathy, simulation, and the impartial spectator. *Ethics*, 105, 727–42.

Haith, M. M. (1998). Who put the cog in infant cognition? Is rich interpretation too costly? *Infant Behavior and Development*, 21, 167–79.

Harris, P. L. (1987). The development of search. In P. Salapatek & L. Cohen (Eds.), *Handbook of infant perception* (Vol. 2, pp. 155–207). New York: Academic Press.

Hayne, H. (2002). Thoughts from the crib: Meltzoff and Moore (1994) alter our views of mental representation during infancy. *Infant Behavior and Development*, 25, 62–4.

Heimann, M., & Meltzoff, A. N. (1996). Deferred imitation in 9- and 14-month-old infants: A longitudinal study of a Swedish sample. *British Journal of Developmental Psychology*, 14, 55–64.

Heimann, M., Nelson, K. E., & Schaller, J. (1989). Neonatal imitation of tongue protrusion and mouth opening: Methodological aspects and evidence of early individual differences. *Scandinavian Journal of Psychology*, 30, 90–101.

Heimann, M., & Schaller, J. (1985). Imitative reactions among 14–21-day-old infants. *Infant Mental Health Journal*, 6, 31–9.

Johnson, S. C. (2000). The recognition of mentalistic agents in infancy. *Trends in Cognitive Sciences*, 4, 22–8.

Johnson, S. C., Slaughter, V., & Carey, S. (1998). Whose gaze will infants follow? The elicitation of gaze-following in 12-month-olds. *Developmental Science*, 1, 233–8.

Karmiloff-Smith, A. (1992). *Beyond modularity: A developmental perspective on cognitive science*. Cambridge, MA: MIT Press.

Klein, P. J., & Meltzoff, A. N. (1999). Long-term memory, forgetting, and deferred imitation in 12-month-old infants. *Developmental Science*, 2, 102–13.

Legerstee, M. (1991). The role of person and object in eliciting early imitation. *Journal of Experimental Child Psychology*, 51, 423–33.

Leslie, A. M. (1994). ToMM, ToBY, and agency: Core architecture and domain specificity. In L. A. Hirschfeld & S. A. Gelman (Eds.), *Mapping the mind: Domain specificity in cognition and culture* (pp. 119–48). New York: Cambridge University Press.

Leslie, A. M. (1995). A theory of agency. In D. Sperber, D. Premack, & A. J. Premack (Eds.), *Causal cognition: A multidisciplinary debate* (pp. 121–49). New York: Oxford University Press.

Mandler, J. M., & McDonough, L. (1995). Long-term recall of event sequences in infancy. *Journal of Experimental Child Psychology*, 59, 457–74.

Meltzoff, A. N. (1985). Immediate and deferred imitation in fourteen- and twenty-four-month-old infants. *Child Development*, 56, 62–72.

Meltzoff, A. N. (1988a). Infant imitation after a 1-week delay: Long-term memory for novel acts and multiple stimuli. *Developmental Psychology*, 24, 470–6.

Meltzoff, A. N. (1988b). Infant imitation and memory: Nine-month-olds in immediate and deferred tests. *Child Development*, 59, 217–25.

Meltzoff, A. N. (1995). Understanding the intentions of others: Re-enactment of intended acts by 18-month-old children. *Developmental Psychology*, 31, 838–50.

Meltzoff, A. N. (1999). Origins of theory of mind, cognition, and communication. *Journal of Communication Disorders*, 32, 251–69.

Meltzoff, A. N., & Decety, J. (2003). What imitation tells us about social cognition: A rapprochement between developmental psychology and cognitive neuroscience. *Transactions of the Royal Society B*, 358, 491–50.

Meltzoff, A. N., Gopnik, A., & Repacholi, B. M. (1999). Toddlers' understanding of intentions, desires, and emotions: Explorations of the dark ages. In P. D. Zelazo, J. W. Astington, & D. Olson (Eds.), *Developing theories of intention: Social understanding and self-control* (pp. 17–41). Mahwah, NJ: Erlbaum.

Meltzoff, A. N., & Moore, M. K. (1977). Imitation of facial and manual gestures by human neonates. *Science*, 198, 75–8.

Meltzoff, A. N., & Moore, M. K. (1989). Imitation in newborn infants: Exploring the range of gestures imitated and the underlying mechanisms. *Developmental Psychology*, 25, 954–62.

Meltzoff, A. N., & Moore, M. K. (1994). Imitation, memory, and the representation of persons. *Infant Behavior and Development*, 17, 83–99.

Meltzoff, A. N., & Moore, M. K. (1997). Explaining facial imitation: A theoretical model. *Early Development and Parenting*, 6, 179–92.

Meltzoff, A. N., & Moore, M. K. (1998). Object representation, identity, and the paradox of early permanence: Steps toward a new framework. *Infant Behavior and Development*, 21, 201–35.

Meltzoff, A. N., & Prinz, W. (Eds.). (2002). *The imitative mind: Development, evolution and brain bases*. Cambridge: Cambridge University Press.

Michotte, A. (1962). *Causalité, permanence, et réalité phénoménales*. Louvain: Publications Universitaires.

Moore, C., & Corkum, V. (1994). Social understanding at the end of the first year of life. *Developmental Review*, 14, 349–72.

Moore, M. K., Borton, R., & Darby, B. L. (1978). Visual tracking in young infants: Evidence for object identity or object permanence? *Journal of Experimental Child Psychology*, 25, 183–98.

Moore, M. K., & Meltzoff, A. N. (1999). New findings on object permanence: A developmental difference between two types of occlusion. *British Journal of Developmental Psychology*, 17, 563–84.

Munakata, Y. (1998). Infant perseveration and implications for object permanence theories: A PDP model of the AB task. *Developmental Science*, 1, 161–84.

Munakata, Y., McClelland, J. L., Johnson, M. H., & Siegler, R. S. (1997). Rethinking infant knowledge: Toward an adaptive process account of successes and failures in object permanence tasks. *Psychological Review*, 104, 686–713.

Nadel, J., & Butterworth, G. (1999). *Imitation in infancy*. Cambridge: Cambridge University Press.

Piaget, J. (1952). *The origins of intelligence in children*. New York: International Universities Press.

Piaget, J. (1954). *The construction of reality in the child* (Trans. M. Cook). New York: Basic Books.

Piaget, J. (1962). *Play, dreams and imitation in childhood*. New York: W. W. Norton.

Quinn, P. C. (2002). Early categorization: A new synthesis. In U. Goswami (Ed.), *Handbook of childhood cognitive development* (pp. 84–101). Oxford: Blackwell.

Slater, A. (1989). Visual memory and perception in early infancy. In A. Slater & G. Bremner (Eds.), *Infant Development* (pp. 43–71). Hillsdale, NJ: Erlbaum.

Slater, A. (1997). Visual perception and its organisation in early infancy. In J. G. Bremner, A. Slater, & G. Butterworth (Eds.), *Infant development: Recent advances* (pp. 31–53). Hove: Psychology Press.

Slater, A. (2002). An article for all seasons: Commentary on Meltzoff and Moore (1994). *Infant Behavior and Development*, 25, 68–71.

Spelke, E. S. (1994). Initial knowledge: Six suggestions. *Cognition*, 50, 431–45.

Spelke, E. S. (1998). Nativism, empiricism, and the origins of knowledge. *Infant Behavior and Development*, 21, 181–200.

Spelke, E. S., Breinlinger, K., Macomber, J., & Jacobson, K. (1992). Origins of knowledge. *Psychological Review*, 99, 605–32.

Taylor, M. (1996). A theory of mind perspective on social cognitive development. In R. Gelman & T. Au (Eds.), *Handbook of perception and cognition. Vol. 13. Perceptual and cognitive development* (pp. 283–329). New York: Academic Press.

Thelen, E., & Smith, L. B. (1994). *A dynamic systems approach to the development of cognition and action*. Cambridge, MA: MIT Press.

Wellman, H. M. (2002). Understanding the psychological world: Developing a theory of mind. In U. Goswami (Ed.), *Handbook of childhood cognitive development* (pp. 167–87). Oxford: Blackwell.

Wellman, H. M., & Phillips, A. T. (2001). Developing intentional understandings. In B. F. Malle, L. J. Moses, & D. A. Baldwin (Eds.), *Intentions and intentionality: Foundations of social cognition* (pp. 125–48). Cambridge, MA: MIT Press.

Willatts, P. (1984). Stages in the development of intentional search by young infants. *Developmental Psychology*, 20, 389–96.

Woodward, A. L. (1998). Infants selectively encode the goal of an actor's reach. *Cognition*, 69, 1–34.

Woodward, A. L. (1999). Infants' ability to distinguish between purposeful and non-purposeful behaviors. *Infant Behavior and Development*, 22, 145–60.

Woodward, A. L. (in press). Infants' developing understanding of the link between looker and object. *Developmental Science*.

Woodward, A. L., Sommerville, J. A., & Guajardo, J. J. (2001). How infants make sense of intentional action. In B. F. Malle, L. J. Moses, & D. A. Baldwin (Eds.), *Intentions and intentionality: Foundations of social cognition* (pp. 149–69). Cambridge, MA: MIT Press.

# 7
# Theories of Development of the Object Concept

*Scott P. Johnson*

## Introduction

We inhabit a world of objects, an environment cluttered with autonomous, solid bodies that occupy unique locations in space. We are able to engage in object-oriented activities by virtue of perceptual and cognitive systems that are exquisitely tuned to solving the problem of keeping track of objects. These systems function under challenging conditions. Consider our ability to track effortlessly almost any object of our choosing. The immediate visual array (i.e., the light that is reflected to the visual system from visible object surfaces in the environment) may change with every head or eye movement, and objects themselves frequently go out of sight and subsequently return to view. Yet our experience is not a visual world of fleeting, disembodied shapes, but rather one of substance, volume, and depth.

The developmental origins of this experience have fascinated philosophers for centuries, and there has long been fierce debate as to the best characterization of its emergence in infants and children. These debates have often centered on the extent to which knowledge of objects is gained from visual or manual experience, or arises from an internally generated system of thought. Until the last century, arguments were limited to philosophical discussions, because systematic empirical approaches to these

Support for preparation of this chapter was provided by NSF grant BCS-0094814 and NIH grant R01-HD40432.

vital questions were unavailable. This changed with the publication of a succession of texts by Jean Piaget, who introduced a series of tasks posed to his own children in an attempt to gain access to development of object representations, and cognition more generally, across infancy. Some of these tasks are described subsequently in this chapter. Also described are two theories that provide alternative views to Piaget's account, *nativist theory* and *information-processing theory*. Following presentation of these three theories, I consider the possibility of reconciling their core tenets and views, in light of evidence from several decades of research.

First, some matters of terminology and scope. I will restrict discussion in this chapter to a determinate topic: the developmental origins, in humans, of the ability to represent objects in the absence of direct perceptual support, which, following Piaget, I refer to as the *object concept*. I suggest that an object concept in this context implies some (internal) cortical activity that registers the presence of a hidden object or hidden object part beyond what is available via sensory input, as well as some (external) behavioral manifestation of the representation. Most research on infant cognitive development has relied on evidence from age-related changes in behavior to reveal ontogenetic development of object concepts, due to restrictions in available technology to record cortical activity in infants. The limited scope of this chapter necessarily omits many interesting literatures on other topics related to mature object knowledge, such as object identity, numerosity, animacy, object-based attention, and so forth. Nevertheless, there has been much research effort directed at object concept development, and these investigations continue to bear on the debate by providing an increasingly rich base of empirical evidence.

## Piagetian Theory

### *The theory*

Piaget (1954), following the philosopher Immanuel Kant, organized a theory of infant cognitive development around four broad themes: object, space, time, and causality (Kant, 1934). Knowledge of these domains developed in tandem, and although it is possible to discuss them in isolation, in actuality they were thought to be wholly interdependent. For example, a co-requisite for an object concept is a complementary concept of spatial relations: one cannot perceive or act on an object accurately without awareness of its position in space relative to other objects.

The principal explanandum of Piagetian theory was *objectification,* the knowledge of the self and external objects as distinct entities, spatially segregated, persisting across time and space, and obeying certain commonsense causal constraints. Piaget suggested that objectification is rooted in the child's recognition of her own body as an independent object and her own movements as movements of objects through space, akin to movements of other objects she sees. This constitutes a transition from *egocentric* to *allocentric* reasoning. Things are detached from actions, and actions are placed on the ongoing, observed series of surrounding events, all encapsulated in the broader construction of the reality of time and space. The progression from egocentric to allocentric spatial reasoning and to a mature object concept was revealed by changes in infants' behavior in the normal, day-to-day flow of activities, and when confronted with a series of tasks that Piaget devised (described fully in Piaget, 1952, 1954, and sketched out below).

Objectification was thought to be an outcome of coordination of *schemes,* or action repertoires. Initially, schemes were rehearsed and repeated, and then infants progressed to exploration of novelty, as when trying new schemes, or using familiar schemes with no clear prediction of outcome. These behaviors are evident in everyday play activities, as when Piaget observed his daughter repeatedly hide, and reveal, a toy under a blanket. These simple games led the child to establish cognitive "groups" (e.g., spatial relations among objects, such as above, below, and behind) largely by manual experience. For example, infants who are learning to reach (at 4 to 6 months) soon discover which objects are within reach and which are not, imparting a kind of depth perception. Parallax perception, achieved by moving the head back and forth, was reported to achieve some systematicity by 8 to 10 months, and this is an excellent way of seeing relative depth. On this view, therefore, both direct experience (to learn when search is successful or not) and deduction (reasoning from general principles to specific instances) contribute to the constructive process.

Development of schemes, spatial concepts, and the object concept was organized into six stages that corresponded to six stages of general cognitive development in infancy (Piaget, 1952). Initially (during Stages 1 and 2), infants exhibited a kind of recognition memory, for example, seeking the mother's breast after losing contact shortly after birth, and within several months, continuing to look in the direction of a person's exit from the room. These behaviors were not systematic, however, and Piaget considered them more passive than active. For Piaget, active search, initiated by the child, was a critical feature of object concepts.

More active search behavior emerged after 4 months and marked the beginnings of "true" objectification during Stage 3. Piaget outlined five examples, in roughly chronological order (i.e., the order in which they could be elicited across the third stage). The first of these was "visual accommodation to rapid movements," when an infant would respond to a dropped object by looking down toward the floor, behavior that became more systematic when the infant himself dropped it. A second behavior, "interrupted prehension," refers to the infant's attempts to reacquire an object that was dropped or taken from her hand if it is out of sight momentarily and within easy reach. (There is no search, however, if the object is fully occluded.) "Deferred circular reactions" describes the infant's repetitive gestures when interrupted during some object-oriented play activity, resuming the game after some delay (necessitating memory of the object, the actions, and their context). "Reconstruction of an invisible whole from a visible fraction" was evinced, for example, by retrieval of an object from a cover when only a part of the object was visible. Finally, the infant became capable of "removal of obstacles preventing perception," as when he pulls away a cover from his face during peekaboo, or withdraws a fully hidden toy from beneath a blanket. This behavior marked the transition to Stage 4.

During Stage 4, beginning at about 8 months, the infant will search actively for a hidden object under a variety of circumstances. Search may fail to be systematic, however, when the object is hidden first at a single location followed by (successful) search, and then hidden successively in multiple locations, as the infant watches. Here, the infant often removes the obstacle at the first location visited by the object, even though she saw it hidden subsequently somewhere else. This response has come to be known as the *A-not-B error*, or the perseverative error, or simply the Stage 4 error. Piaget described as well an interesting incident when one of his daughters, aged 15 months, saw her father in the garden. Yet when asked "Where is papa?" she pointed to the window of his office in the home, as if there were *two* papa Piagets: "papa at his window" and "papa in the garden." These intriguing behaviors certainly marked active search for a vanished object, but their erroneous nature, according to Piaget, indicated a fundamental characteristic of the incipient object concept: there is not yet true objectification during Stage 4. Rather, to the infant, the object is considered an extension of her own behavior, and identity of objects is not preserved across perceptual contacts. That is, if an object appears at a particular place at the child's whim (i.e., her activity), so to speak, there is no concept yet of continuity across time and space.

The transition to full objectification is completed across the next two stages as the infant first solves the problem of multiple visible displacements, searching at the last location visited by the object (Stage 5), and then multiple invisible displacements (Stage 6). Finally, then, the infant searches systematically at all potential hiding locations visited by the object (perhaps, for example, remaining hidden in Piaget's hand between occluders). For Piaget, this type of mature search revealed detachment of the object from the action, and knowledge of the infant's body itself as merely one object among many, and brought into an allocentric system of spatially organized objects and events.

## The evidence

Piagetian theory has received a great deal of interest since translations in English of the original work began to appear in the 1950s, and with the publication of a landmark summary of the theory by John Flavell (1963). Much of this attention has been conspicuously biased toward examinations of the A-not-B error, due no doubt to the compelling and continued puzzlement that this phenomenon has elicited among cognitive development theorists, but a number of researchers have explored earlier developmental patterns as well (described subsequently). The theory has received mixed reviews. It enjoys strong support for many of the details of behavior that Piaget so assiduously captured. The reasoning behind the developmental changes in behavior, however, has not seen the same level of enthusiasm.

Turning first to the A-not-B error, there have been hundreds of successful attempts to replicate the effect in 8- to 12-month-old infants, some of which are reviewed in Bremner (1985), Marcovitch and Zelazo (1999), Thelen, Schöner, Scheier, and Smith (2001), and Wellman, Cross, and Bartsch (1986). Nevertheless, the basis for the error, and what it reveals about object concept development, remain a matter of relentless debate. Three examples of research paradigms that have examined Piagetian claims help to illustrate this controversy. Diamond (e.g., 1990) has used the A-not-B error as an index of cortical development, specifically an area known as prefrontal dorsolateral cortex, which is thought to be important in working memory function and inhibitory control. According to Diamond, the A-not-B error arises in infants because there is a difficulty in maintaining a short-term representation of the object and its location, plus a difficulty in inhibiting a tendency to reach at a "primed" location. Baillargeon (1993) has suggested that the A-not-B error is a poor index of infants' object concepts, because of a general lack of coordinated manual search behavior in infants who are still learning to reach appropriately. Baillargeon cited evidence (some of which is described subsequently) for veridical object knowledge when assessed with paradigms that do not require directed reaches. Finally, Smith, Thelen, Titzer, and McLin (1999) have claimed that the A-not-B error tells us nothing at all about object concepts, because the error is a function of task demands, reaching history, and the experimental context. Infants can even produce perseverative responses in the absence of hidden toys!

Turning next to other evidence of early object concepts, numerous experiments have revealed that by 2 to 4 months, infants appear to maintain representations of partly and fully hidden objects across short delays. These experiments rely on visual preference paradigms, using techniques developed by Bower (1974) and further refined by Spelke and colleagues (1985). These paradigms built on methods pioneered by Fantz (1964), who discovered that infants tend to lose interest in repetitive visual patterns, and recover interest to novel stimuli. Some researchers, in addition, have devised a variant of the novelty-preference paradigm known as the "violation-of-expectation" method, which relies on the assumption that infants will look preferentially in general at odd or unusual events. A well-known example was described by Baillargeon, Spelke, and Wasserman (1985), who showed 5-month-old infants a stimulus consisting of a rotating screen that appeared to move through the space occupied by a previously seen object. This event was reported to recruit increased visual attention relative to an event in which the screen stopped at the object's location (see figure 7.1). The first event, then, seemed to violate the previously seen object's solidity, but the second event was consistent with an "expectation" of solidity. These methods, too, are not free of controversy (e.g., Cohen & Marks, 2002; Rivera, Wakeley, & Langer, 1999). Nevertheless, there are dozens of related findings supporting the thesis that young infants perceive objects as persistent and whole across short intervals of time and space. Some of these are reviewed in Baillargeon (2001), Carey and Xu (2001), Johnson (2001b), and Spelke and van de Walle (1993). Notably, interpretation of these findings as revealing

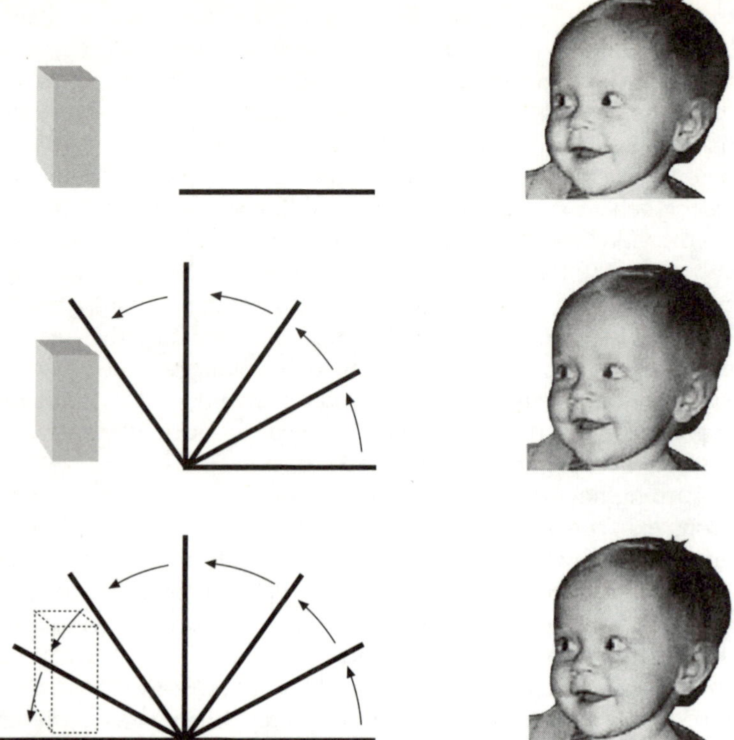

**Figure 7.1** Schematic depiction of the events employed by Baillargeon et al. (1985) to probe young infants' object representations across short intervals of occlusion. *Top*: The infant sees a box and a screen that is flat on the table. *Center*: The screen rotates up to the box and stops, a so-called "possible" event. *Bottom*: The screen appears to rotate through the space seen to have been occupied by the box, an "impossible" event. Infants were reported to look longer at the impossible event than at the possible event, leading to the conclusion that the infants viewed it as a violation of the expectation that the box continued to exist while occluded.

developing object concepts is rooted in behavioral evidence rather than in evidence of cortical activity or change.

## *Evaluation: Piagetian theory*

Piaget's theory may be evaluated in terms of both his reported observations of changes with development in object-oriented behavior and his theoretical account of these changes. There is now little doubt that there are striking transformations across infancy in visual responses to events that feature partly and fully occluded objects. It seems most parsimonious to analyze these findings in terms of underlying perceptual and cognitive change, consistent with the emergence of object representations early in infancy. Some simple reaching measures are consistent as well with this interpretation, such as reaching in the dark toward previously seen locations (e.g., Clifton, Rochat, Litovsky, & Perris, 1991; Hood & Willatts, 1986). The outcomes of these experiments may be interpreted as broadly consistent with Piaget's claims: evidence for the rudiments of object concepts, in place early in infancy, which are elaborated with learning and experience. Reaching errors in the context of multiple hiding locations, however, are rather more difficult to interpret, and at present it is unclear what such tasks reveal. Also in question is a central tenet of Piaget's theory of object concept development: the idea that nascent object concepts are subjective, not objective, and a function of the child's own behavior. Few active theoreticians would appear to agree with this notion, and the evidence that Piaget offered in support of this proposal seems weak relative to other aspects of the theory. The evidence concerning the centrality of action to development of the object concept is limited solely to the A-not-B error; there are no independent behavioral observations that provide corroborative evidence.

In sum, Piaget set the stage for decades of fruitful research that have established clearly the availability of functional object concepts within several months after birth. These concepts are, at minimum, sufficient to guide visual behaviors in such a way as to reveal detection of anomalous stimuli when compared to some occlusion event. Despite this progress, fundamental questions remain in the extent to which object representations develop with experience, learning, and general maturation. These questions are considered in subsequent sections of the chapter.

## Nativist Theory

### *The theory*

A central tenet of nativist theory is that some kinds of initial knowledge form a central core around which more diverse, mature cognitive capacities are elaborated. That is, some kinds of knowledge, including the object concept, are *innate*. An understanding of a nativist theory therefore necessitates an understanding of what it means for some perceptual, motor, or cognitive competence to be innate. This term has been used, variously, to refer to anatomical structure or representational content that is purported to be (a) present at birth, (b) genetically mediated, (c) "central" (as opposed to "peripheral"), (d) "biological" (as opposed to "environmental"), (e) outside perceptual experience, (f) constant across development, (g) culturally universal, (h) domain-specific, or some combination of these possibilities (cf. Cowie, 1999; Elman, Bates, Johnson, Karmiloff-Smith, Parisi, & Plunkett, 1996). Clearly, such a lack of standard usage threatens to render the term ineffectual.

Philosophical discussions of innateness are ancient; historically, these discussions have centered around the extent to which human knowledge must necessarily be rooted in, or is independent of, postnatal experience, and this is the kind of innateness that I will consider in this section of the chapter. Plato and Descartes, for example, proposed that some ideas were universal and available innately because they were elicited in the absence of any direct tutoring or instruction, or were unobservable in the world, and thus unlearnable (e.g., concepts of geometry or God). With the advent of rigorous testing methods in the last century, the debate began to shift from the role of innate *concepts* to the role of innate *process* in shaping knowledge acquisition. Hebb (1949), for example, noted the "intrinsic organization" that characterized the neonate's electroencephalogram, which he postulated as a contributing mechanism of subsequent perceptual development, based primarily on associative learning. Innate process was an important facet of Gestalt perceptual theory as well: "dynamic forces" of electrical activity in the brain were thought to guide general perceptual organization, alongside experience with specific object kinds (Koffka, 1935).

More recently, theories of innate concepts have again become more common: concepts of objects as obeying certain real-world, physical constraints, such as persistence and numerical identity across occlusion, and nonpenetrability or solidity. Developmental psychologists of a nativist persuasion have offered three arguments for these hypothesized innate object concepts. First, veridical object knowledge can be elicited in very young infants under some circumstances, suggesting that early concepts emerge too quickly to have derived from postnatal learning. Second, infants' acquisition of "physical knowledge" (i.e., detection of apparent violations of simple events) has been proposed to arise from experience weighing *contrastive evidence*, or opportunities to observe conditions under which an object behaves in a manner consistent or inconsistent with a particular concept (Baillargeon, 1994). If this is the principal mechanism of development of object knowledge, so goes the reasoning, then a concept of persistence across occlusion must be innate, because it cannot have been acquired from observing contrastive evidence: there simply are no available opportunities to observe conditions under which an object goes out of existence (Aguiar & Baillargeon, 1999). (Other concepts, however, such as "support," are posited to be acquired when infants gain experience placing small objects on larger surfaces and noting when the smaller object falls, as when there is insufficient contact with the bottom surface.) Third, there is evidence from nonhuman animals and anatomical specialization in humans for commonality of function across species, and commonality of structure across individuals. This suggests a kind of inevitability of certain concepts that is "programmed" via evolutionary pressure. These arguments are explicated most fully, perhaps, in the area of mathematical reasoning (e.g., Dehaene, 1997; Wynn, 1998).

A fourth argument that has been made recently for nativist theory is geared less toward concepts and more toward process, and comes from evidence showing how cortical structure emerges from intrinsic molecular and chemical mechanisms prior to birth (Spelke & Newport, 1998). For example, neural connectivity patterns in early visual cortex (i.e., area V1) originate in part from spontaneous activity in retinal cells that passes, wavelike, to neighboring cells (Wong, 1999). This semi-structured activity is conveyed, in turn, through to higher stages of subcortical processing until reaching cortex, imparting a close correspondence between activation of spatial layout of retina and the circuitry of V1. The result is a cortical map that encodes spatial position in the environment, ready to encode the locations of visual stimuli once the infant is born.

## *The evidence*

The majority of evidence for early object concepts comes from experiments in which looking times are recorded to novel or ostensibly unexpected events, relative either to a familiarization stimulus or to some aspect of object knowledge that the infant is purported to bring to the task. As noted previously, there is now compelling evidence from a variety of laboratories and experimental settings for representations of objects as solid bodies that are spatiotemporally coherent and persistent, representations that appear to be functional by 2 to 4 months after birth. Nevertheless, the question of concern for this chapter, the *origins* of object concepts, cannot be addressed merely by noting competence in these experiments at a young age. Unequivocal evidence for *innate* object concepts must address one or more points raised previously: functionality at birth, emergence in the absence of experience, stable across development, and so on. At present the issue is unsettled, but experiments on infants' perception of partly occluded objects, reviewed in brief next, cast doubt on the viability of many of these varieties of innateness as the best descriptor of the development of object concepts.

Bower (1967) devised a task to examine "phenomenal identity," or the perceptual equivalence of two identical forms, one of which was partially occluded. An operant conditioning procedure was employed, with sucking rate as the operant response: reduced sucking rates were interpreted as evidence of perceptual discrimination, after the infants had received training with a partly occluded triangle. One-month-olds were tested. The infants maintained sucking rates in response to a complete (unoccluded) triangle, taken as evidence for phenomenal identity, and perception of the partly occluded triangle (the training stimulus) as having a definite form behind the occluder. Presentation of triangle parts (separated by a gap) resulted in a response decrement, taken as evidence that these incomplete forms were perceived as different than the partly occluded triangle. In a series of follow-up experiments with 4-month-olds, Kellman and Spelke (1983) were unable to replicate the finding of perceptual completion on the basis of static information (see figure 7.2). Using an habituation paradigm (with appropriate controls), Kellman and Spelke reported that only motion was effective in specifying unity: after habituation to a partly occluded rod, the infants looked longer at two rod parts than at a complete object, but only when the rod parts moved relative to the occluder. These experiments challenge the conclusion that young infants perceive unitary objects on the basis of Gestalt perceptual information such as good continuation, but leave open the question of development of phenomenal identity in infancy.

This question was addressed by Slater, Morison, Somers, Mattock, Brown, and Taylor (1990), who replicated the methods of Kellman and Spelke (1983) with neonates, who were tested in the hospital less than 3 days after birth. Slater et al. found that neonates, in contrast to 4-month-olds, responded to a partly occluded object display solely on the basis of its visible parts,

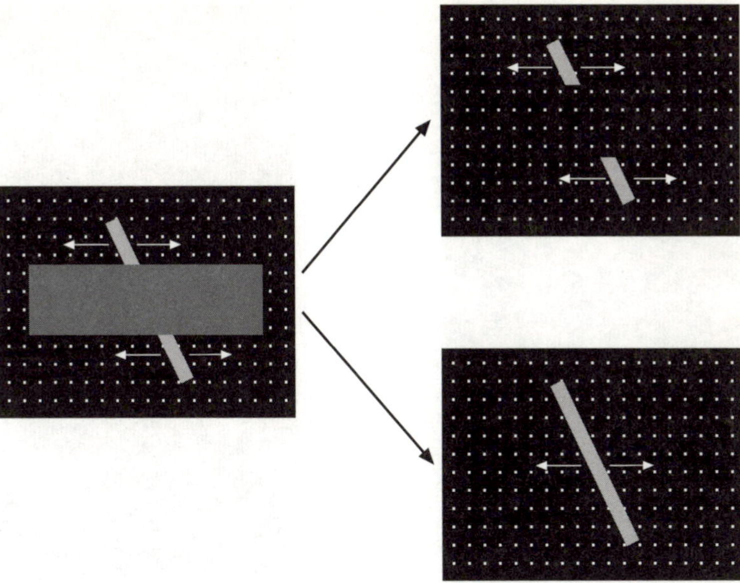

**Figure 7.2** Events presented to young infants in investigations of perception of partial occlusion. After habituation to the partly occluded rod at left, infants view displays depicting either the rod segments that were formerly visible (top), or a complete version of the rod (bottom). Neonates look longer at the complete rod display, suggesting that it is relatively novel and the rod segments familiar, and fail to achieve perceptual completion during habituation. Four-month-olds' perceptual completion is more robust, evinced by a switch in preference toward the rod segments. Adapted from Johnson and Aslin (1996).

failing to perceive completion behind the occluder. Johnson and Aslin (1995) found that under some conditions, 2-month-olds would perceive object unity, as when the occluder is made narrow and the distance of perceptual interpolation is reduced, relative to a display in which older infants are able to achieve perceptual completion. A parallel pattern of responses was reported recently by Johnson, Bremner, Slater, Mason, Foster, and Cheshire (2003) in a series of studies examining perception of object persistence when fully occluded (i.e., an object moving back and forth, becoming completely hidden for a short time before reemerging; see figure 7.3). Four-month-olds perceived persistence of the object only when it was out of sight for a very brief interval; when out of sight for a more extended duration, the infants appeared

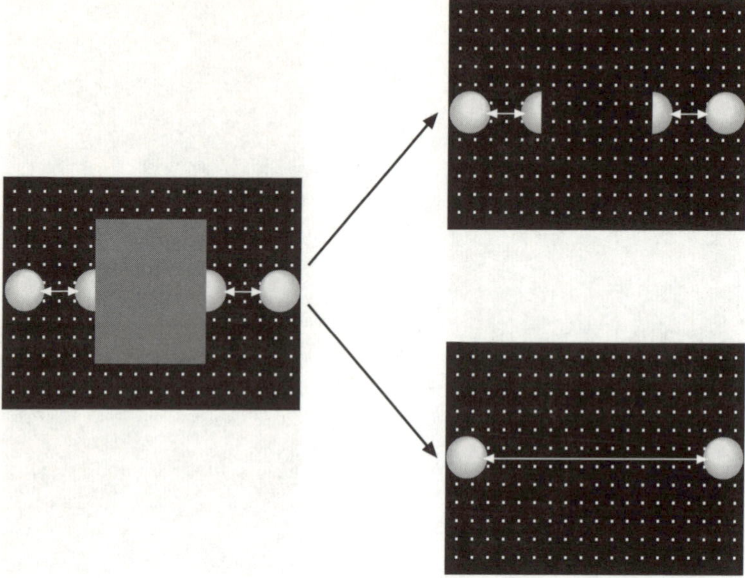

**Figure 7.3** Events presented to young infants in investigations of perception of object persistence under occlusion. After habituation to the partly occluded object trajectory at left, infants view displays depicting either the trajectory segments that were formerly visible, without the occluder present (top), or a continuous version of the trajectory, again with no occluder (bottom). Four-month-olds look longer at the continuous trajectory, implying perception of the partly occluded trajectory not as continuous, but rather as consisting of disconnected path segments. Six-month-olds, in contrast, exhibit the reverse preference, suggesting perception of trajectory continuity in the habituation display. When 4-month-olds view a version of the habituation display in which the occluder size (and thus occlusion time) is reduced, however, their preferences too show a reversal. This may indicate that easing the cognitive load imposed by a longer duration out of sight leads to perception of the object trajectory as continuous (adapted from Johnson, Bremner et al., 2003).

to perceive only the visible segments of the object trajectory, failing to perceive persistence. In other words, they behaved in like manner to neonates viewing a partly occluded object, responding on the basis of what is directly visible only. Six-month-olds seemed to perceive persistence even under the longer occlusion duration.

Consider this pattern of empirical results in light of the claims for innateness outlined previously. All evidence to date indicates that perception of occlusion is not available at birth. Without perception of occlusion, of course, a functional object concept is impossible. Veridical object percepts emerge rapidly, but the point remains that *there is not continuity across development* in this most fundamental domain of object knowledge. It would appear difficult, therefore, to defend any level of object concept in an organism, such as the human newborn, that cannot parse an array of visible surfaces into coherent units. How the change occurs toward perception of objects as unified and persistent is unknown at present. (It is likely that exposure to contrastive evidence plays little role, although this type of learning may be central in acquiring other kinds of object knowledge.) It is important to note, nevertheless, that these data rule out certain kinds of innateness as contributing to the object concept, but not others. Some potential mechanisms of development have been proposed that are consistent with, and indeed rely on, innate structure and process. These are presented in subsequent sections of the chapter.

## *Evaluation: Nativist theory*

Nativist theory draws praise for the cultivation of exciting, alternative perspectives on questions of cognitive development and for serving as the inspiration for the generation of an abundance of data. Support for some kinds of innateness is strong: fundamental object concepts are, as far as we know, universal across individuals and societies, and emerge early in infancy. In another sense, however, claims of innate object knowledge would appear to be overreaching and even inaccurate, because there is a clear pattern of change in the foundations of object knowledge within several months after birth. We do not know whether these changes are inevitable, arising, for example, from the natural course of neural maturation, or whether they depend on exposure to the normal flow of activities and events in the everyday surroundings (there is evidence for both these possibilities, discussed subsequently). There is certainly a range of mechanisms that provide a structured cortex at birth in humans, but their contributions to the neural circuits necessary for veridical object concepts are also unknown (see Elman et al., 1996). One possibility is that prenatal development results in a cortex without the fine-grained neural microcircuitries necessary to support object concepts (Johnson, 1997). On this view, object concepts are acquired, in part, by viewing objects in the environment, subsequent to onset of exposure to patterned light. The distinction between what is innate and what is learned becomes blurred at this level of analysis, and highlights a broader criticism of nativist theory: proposing that object concepts emerge in the absence of experience provides little explicit information about how developmental change might take place.

In sum, it is unclear precisely what nativist theory contributes to the quest for specific mechanisms of development of object concepts. Development is always a matter of building new structure upon the old, whether the structures under consideration are concrete, such as arrangements of neural connections, or more abstract, such as object concepts (in the words of Elman et al., 1996, "interactions all the way down"). The ultimate value of nativist theory, instead, may be the attention it calls to the potential role of more general developmental processes that may operate outside experience, even while lacking specific proposals for how this might occur in the case of object knowledge. The infant is delivered to the world outside the womb an active perceiver, endowed with the readiness and ability to acquire information, prepared to discover the patterns and regularities in the events she views in the surrounding environment. An understanding of the state of neonates' perceptual systems may be a more well-defined question under the purview of nativism than is development of object concepts.

## Information-Processing Theory

### *The theory*

In many respects information-processing theory is the polar opposite of nativist theory. Rather than presuppose an unchanging, innate core of cognitive capacities, information-processing theorists posit a set of sensory, perceptual, and (nonconceptual) cognitive processes that are constant across development (Cohen, 1998; Cohen, Chaput, & Cashon, 2002). These processes include perceptual sensitivities to auditory and visual input, memory, attention, and categorization. On this view, complex and mature concepts are constructed from these more primitive mechanisms, and the principal developmental changes occur in the *content* of information, and what constitutes a *unit* of information. These units naturally expand with improvements in information-processing skills: initially, the information that is accessed is relatively simple, but with development, infants become able to integrate the lower-level units of information into a more complex, higher-level unit, these higher-level units serve as the components for even more complex units, and so on. Concepts are thus formed incrementally in a bottom-up fashion. This hierarchical approach to cognitive development is repeated across domains, underlying skill acquisition and proficiency over a range of tasks, and throughout the lifespan.

Experiments that examine early form perception provide evidence for this approach. Cohen and Younger (1984) presented 6- and 14-week-old infants with two lines joined at an angle, either 45 degrees or 135 degrees. After habituation, the infants viewed test stimuli designed to determine whether the infants attended primarily to the individual line segments, or to the angle itself. This was accomplished by arranging the line segments in test stimuli in familiar orientations but a novel angle, or in novel orientations but a familiar angle. The younger infants tended to look longer at the novel orientations, but not the novel angles, suggesting that during habituation they did not attend to the relations between the line segments (i.e., the angle itself). In contrast, the older infants tended to prefer the novel angles over the novel orientations, suggesting that during habituation they attended to angles rather than the orientations of the angles' components. That is, there was a change with development in the units of information that the infants processed, from the lower-level orientations of individual line segments to the higher-level relations between segments after integrating the components into a more complex form. Slater, Mattock, Brown, and Bremner (1991) demonstrated subsequently that very young infants would respond to angles in a category-like fashion if they were viewed in varying orientations during habituation, implying that processing of compounds is a function of testing method as well as age (but see Cohen, 1998, for an alternative perspective).

Experiments that demonstrate more clearly the dynamic shifting between processing of higher-level concepts and processing of lower-level components were reported by Cohen and colleagues (Cohen & Amsel, 1998; Cohen & Oakes, 1993; Oakes & Cohen, 1990). Infants between 4 and 10 months of age were tested with stimuli in which an object moves across the display into the vicinity of a second object. If the objects make contact, and the second object moves away abruptly, adults report a causal relation between the two, a "launching" event. This kind of causality is not perceived, however, if there is no contact between the two objects, or if there is a temporal delay between contact and launch. The likelihood of causal perception at any particular age is a function of the complexity of the events. For example, 6.5-month-olds responded to causality, and not merely the movements of the individual components of the event, if the objects were simple shapes. If more complex objects participate in such events, infants at this age provide no evidence of causality perception, but rather respond solely on the basis of the spatial and temporal characteristics of the objects in the displays. Ten-month-olds can process causality in displays with more intricate objects, yet fail to detect causality when the objects themselves changed from trial to trial but a causal relation was maintained. Presumably, the infants were compelled to process the events under these circumstances at a perceptual rather than a conceptual level, due to increased constraints presented by the added complexity of the stimuli.

## *The evidence*

In experiments on stimulus compounds and causality, and others (see Cohen et al., 2002, for review), the developmental pattern is one of initial processing of constituents of stimulus displays, and later combining the components into conjunctions and concepts. This pattern pertains as well to studies that have explored the development of perception of object trajectories, and perception of partly occluded objects (introduced previously in the chapter).

A key principle of information-processing theory is a developmental progression from perception of lower-level to higher-level units in a particular stimulus configuration. Consider a simple display, similar to those described by Piaget to explore object permanence in his children, in which an object (such as a ball) moves back and forth repeatedly. In the center of a display is an occluding screen, which the ball passes behind, as it continues on its trajectory. Adults would remark that the ball continues to exist during its hidden passage, and would forecast its reemergence from behind the screen at a particular time and place. Consider now a set of predictions that would arise from information-processing theory concerning infants. In the present example, the lower-level stimulus components are the directly visible components of the stimulus: the portions of the trajectory during which the ball is in view, and the occluder. An important higher-level component is the notion of the trajectory as continuous – that is, the addition of an object concept, to complete the path of motion. Information-processing theory, therefore, predicts that young infants would respond only to the visible path segments, and older infants would respond as if they perceived the trajectory as continuous. Such a developmental progression, consistent with information-processing theory (and Piagetian theory), is clearly at odds with a nativist view. Which is the better account?

Recall the evidence, presented previously in brief, that 4-month-olds do not achieve perceptual completion of a partly occluded trajectory when the occluder is relatively wide (Johnson, Bremner et al., 2003). Rather, the infants provided evidence of processing of path segments only, as follows from the precepts of the information-processing viewpoint. The additional load imposed by the extended time of occlusion, on this account, forced the infants into the lower-level mode of processing. In contrast, when this load was eased by reducing occlusion time, the infants were able to perceive the ball's trajectory as continuous. Here the unit of processing, in other words, was path continuity, not just path segments. Older infants (6-month-olds) perceived continuity even under the additional demands of the wide occluder, whereas younger infants (2-month-olds) failed to perceive continuity even when the demands were minimized via a narrow occluder (and thus, presumably, they were unable to perceive completion under any circumstances). All these results are consistent with the information-processing view.

The findings on trajectory continuity are not necessarily inconsistent with nativist theory, however. It is possible, for example, that infants have a latent tendency to respond to occluded objects as persistent but this tendency is masked and remains unexpressed under demanding situations precisely *because of* poor information-processing skills. On this view, an information-processing "bottleneck" constrains crucial inputs to the conceptual system that is responsible for reconciling visual input with underlying knowledge. If the visual input is insufficient, so goes the argument, access to veridical object concepts is blocked.

This argument has been used to explain two effects in the object unity literature (see Jusczyk, Johnson, Spelke, & Kennedy, 1999; Smith, Johnson, & Spelke, in press). The first, described previously, is the pattern of development across the first several months after birth: neonates respond to a partly occluded rod in terms of its visible surfaces only, whereas 2-month-olds respond to unity in a narrow occluder display. Four-month-olds perceive unity even when the occluder is relatively wide. The second effect is the attenuation of unity perception when the rod parts are not aligned across the occluder, as when an *angled* object is partly hidden at the point of intersection of the rod segments. This effect obtains in both infants and adults (Johnson & Aslin, 1996;

Jusczyk et al., 1999; Smith et al., in press). The importance of "good continuation," to use the Gestalt term, is highlighted by these findings. An important question is why misalignment would reduce unity perception, especially if the rod parts moved together, providing a powerful unifying cue.

Nativist and information-processing theories furnish opposing explanations of these findings. On a nativist view, infants achieve unity percepts on the basis of common motion, which has been identified as a potential "core principle" upon which a comprehensive system of object concepts is elaborated (Spelke & van de Walle, 1993). If access to common motion of object parts is hindered, on this account, then the object parts cannot be perceptually unified. Occluder size and edge alignment play a role in sensitivity to common motion: when the rod parts are too far apart, or are misaligned, it is difficult for very young infants to detect them as moving together. This view predicts, therefore, that whenever infants can discern the motions and orientations of rod segments in an occlusion display, and these segments move together, they will necessarily be perceived as unified. On an information-processing view, in contrast, infants will be sensitive to the motions and orientations of stimulus components such as rod segments, yet very young infants, nevertheless, may not perceive unity. This is because unity perception itself develops, the formation of a higher-level unit of analysis.

I recently examined these opposing explanations in two experiments (Johnson, 2003). In the first experiment, 2-month-old infants were tested for unity perception under one of three conditions: (1) a narrow occluder display in which rod parts were aligned above and below the box; (2) a wide occluder display with similarly aligned rod parts; and (3) a narrow occluder display in which the rod parts were misaligned. In all three displays, the rod parts underwent common motion. The infants provided evidence of unity perception in the first condition only, a result that replicates past findings of the attenuating effects on unity by occluder width and misalignment. In the second experiment, I asked whether the infants failed to perceive unity because they could not detect the motions and orientations of the rod segments in the second and third displays; that is, if common motion was perceived only when the rod parts were aligned and in close proximity. This was accomplished by habituating groups of 2-month-olds with rod-and-box displays in which the rod segments moved together in the same direction (i.e., *corresponding motion* displays) or in which the rod segments moved in opposite directions (i.e., *converse motion* displays). There were three corresponding motion displays, which were identical to the three habituation displays employed in the first experiment (i.e., narrow occluder/aligned rod parts, wide occluder/aligned rod parts, and narrow occluder/misaligned rod parts). There were three converse motion displays as well, in which these three stimulus configurations were modified so that the rod parts moved in opposite directions. In all then, there were six habituation displays. After habituation, the infants were presented with the display containing the same stimulus components but the differing motion pattern, alternating with the display they had viewed during habituation. In other words, the infants were tested for their ability to detect the difference between corresponding motion and converse motion, under conditions in which occluder width and alignment were manipulated. Nativist theory predicts that motion discrimination would obtain only when facilitated by the proximity afforded by the narrow occluder, and by alignment. Information-processing theory predicts, in contrast, that the infants would discriminate the motion patterns under all conditions. The outcome was clear in its support for the information-processing account: the infants showed reliable posthabituation recovery of interest to the new motion, no matter which type of motion was novel, and no matter the specific stimulus configuration (i.e., occluder width or edge orientation). These experiments are compatible with the hypothesis, therefore, that there is a time in infancy when infants process visible components only in occlusion displays, and that what develops is the ability to go beyond what is seen directly. In other words, occlusion perception itself develops.

## *Evaluation: Information-processing theory*

The bulk of evidence from experiments that investigate developmental origins of object concepts would appear to be consistent with the stipulations of an information-processing view: infants analyze motion patterns and configurations of stimulus components prior in development to organizing these components into higher-level structures or concepts. Information-processing theory provides an appropriate description of this developmental progression, which is a necessary step on the way to a complete account, but leaves missing a more explicit characterization of how it occurs. How, exactly, do infants come to perceive connectedness of two visible parts of a scene, and how, exactly, do infants come to perceive persistence of an object that has gone out of view? We know now that these two processes reach maturity postnatally, a crucial advance contributed by evidence consistent with information-processing theory, but it remains unknown at an explanatory level what mechanisms underlie successful performance at occlusion tasks, and how these mechanisms develop. These questions are considered in the next section of the chapter.

In sum, information-processing theory contributes clarity in the search for development of object concepts. This search must focus on *prenatal* developmental processes that provide a functional visual system with which the infant begins to parse the optic array, and on *postnatal* developmental processes that use this information as inputs to higher-level structure, such as an object concept.

## Moving Forward: Integrating Piagetian, Nativist, and Information-Processing Theories

In the previous sections of the chapter I presented and critiqued three theories, each of which captures a piece of the puzzle of development of the object concept. None is adequate on its own to complete this puzzle, but each contributes important ideas to this goal. From Piagetian theory comes the notion that full object permanence likely takes many months to mature, from an initial response to a missing object part to the ability to solve complex hiding tasks. In addition, the idea that the infant's own behaviors have a direct role in concept development is appealing, but at present this idea is largely unsupported and remains speculative. Nativist theory stresses the importance of development that occurs outside experience, and we know that this must be right for some skills, because some important visual and cognitive functions develop prenatally (see Slater, 1995): infants are born with the ability to distinguish between separate regions of visual space that constitute visible surface fragments (e.g., figure–ground segregation), they are able to retain information for short intervals (i.e., a kind of short-term memory), and there are distinct visual preferences at birth (e.g., preferences for moving over stationary stimuli, and for edges over homogeneous regions). These three innate abilities may provide the foundations for subsequent emergence of object concepts, a possibility for which I provide more detail subsequently. Nevertheless, there is strong evidence against the thesis that infants are born with object representations or concepts. Finally, information-processing theory motivates research that documents the postnatal progression toward integrating and retaining lower-level information across space and time, imparting a view of the visual environment as consisting of objects rather than simply visible surface fragments. These mechanisms of integration and retention, and how they may develop, will be the focus of the rest of the chapter.

I will explicate the claim that object concepts emerge early in infancy from a foundation of perceptual and memory skills that are available at birth, via a combination of endogenous and exogenous mechanisms. There are several candidate mechanisms that are attractive, but it is unlikely that any single mechanism can account for all kinds of early concept formation. I will suggest, furthermore, that mature object concepts are elaborations of simple "perceptual filling-in," a phrase that captures both perception of object unity and perception of object persistence (i.e., trajectory continuity) under short durations of occlusion. How, then, does the infant develop the capacity for perceptual filling-in?

## *Integrating information over time and space: The role of eye movements*

Piaget (1954) proposed that infants acquire the object concept from object manipulation: manual exploration of objects, gauging their properties, and learning the outcomes of simple hiding events that they themselves create. Object manipulation is surely a vital part of the acquisition of object knowledge (i.e., objects' physical characteristics; see Baillargeon, 1994), but it cannot contribute in any meaningful way to the origins of perceptual filling-in, because these origins appear earlier in development than does skilled manual exploration. But this is not to deny the role of another action system in the process: exploration of objects via eye movements. The oculomotor system is largely functional at birth and matures rapidly (Johnson, 2001a), and even neonates scan the environment in a systematic fashion, attending more, for example, to edges than to homogeneous regions of visual space (Haith, 1980; Slater, 1995). There are important developments between 2 and 4 months in the extent of scanning some kinds of stimuli, such as displays of partly occluded objects: younger infants scan less "efficiently," tending to fixate specific parts of the display rather than all the visible surfaces (Johnson

& Johnson, 2000). It remains unknown, however, how scanning patterns contribute to unity perception directly. It could be, for example, that infants learn about unity by frequent alternating fixations of the visible regions of partly occluded objects. Current research in my laboratory is examining this possibility.

## *Learning and experience*

Learning about occlusion and perceptual filling-in might be a deductive process: repeated exposure to many instances of objects becoming occluded and reemerging, and subsequent identification of partly occluded objects as continuous, via an associative process. Occlusion and disocclusion are ubiquitous: all sighted observers, including young infants, are exposed to multiple instances of such events routinely in the normal visual environment, and young infants are remarkably adept at rapid associative learning (e.g., Kirkham, Slemmer, & Johnson, 2002). Recently, Denis Mareschal and I asked whether associative learning may be a viable mechanism by which an observer could learn to perceive object unity (Mareschal & Johnson, 2002). We created several connectionist models that were presented with input representing moving objects and an occluder, and subsequently tested the models for their response to a partly occluded object. During training, the models were exposed to events in which a complete object was seen to become occluded and then emerge again, so that the model received information for the identity of views of a single object (i.e., a single object seen both in its entirety and as partly occluded). The models were successful at responding to a partly occluded object as being continuous, despite the occlusion, providing evidence for the possibility that a similar associative process might be at work in human infants in building object representations from multiple exposures of objects. This possibility remains to be tested in infants.

A second demonstration of learning from experience was completed recently in my laboratory. We tested young infants' perception of the persistence of a moving object under occlusion by recording anticipatory eye movements to an event in which a ball moved back and forth, the center of its trajectory momentarily occluded by a box (Johnson, Amso, & Slemmer, 2003). We reasoned that perception of the ball as persistent despite occlusion, and perception of the trajectory as continuous, would be evinced by a pattern of consistent anticipations (i.e., moving the point of gaze to the place of the object's reemergence from the occluder while it was still out of sight). We had two predictions. First, 4-month-olds were expected to exhibit fewer anticipations than would 6-month-olds, because of earlier evidence of marked changes in perception of trajectory continuity across this age range (Johnson, Bremner et al., 2003). Second, 4-month-olds were expected to benefit from a short time of exposure to an unoccluded trajectory event, as reflected in a greater proportion of anticipations when subsequently viewing the partly occluded trajectory. Six-month-olds, in contrast, were expected to receive no special benefit from this kind of experience, because the older infants are already capable of perceiving trajectory continuity (Johnson, Bremner et al., 2003). Both predictions were supported. Infants in the younger age group produced far fewer anticipations than did the older infants when viewing the partly occluded trajectory displays. When first presented with events in which the ball moved on an unoccluded trajectory (the "training" condition), however, the number of anticipatory eye movements made by 4-month-olds was roughly equivalent to the number made by the 6-month-olds who had viewed the partly occluded trajectories only. In other words, given a particular kind of experience, the 4-month-olds' performance was boosted to the level of the older infants. The 6-month-olds in the enrichment condition, however, did not produce more anticipations than did the 6-month-olds who had seen only the partly occluded trajectories. This may indicate that 6-month-olds are immune to the potential effects of experience in enhancing performance on this task, because they come to the task with the ability to form object concepts.

## *Neurophysiological development*

A complete account of cortical development is beyond the scope of this chapter, of course, and excellent recent reviews are available (e.g., Atkinson, 2000; Johnson, 1997; Nelson & Luciano, 2001). For the sake of the present discussion of developmental origins of object concepts, it is worth highlighting some of what is known about cortical mechanisms of perceptual filling-in, and how such mechanisms might develop in infancy (see Johnson, in press, for further consideration of these possibilities). Perception of edge connectedness across a spatial gap may be accomplished with relatively low- and mid-level mechanisms (i.e., cortical areas V1 through inferotemporal cortex; see Nakayama, He, & Shimojo, 1995), and development consists of at least two kinds of neural maturation. First, long-range cell-to-cell interactions in early visual areas connect neural circuits coding for common edge orientations may reach sufficient maturity within several months after birth to support unity perception under some circumstances (cf. Burkhalter, 1993; Burkhalter, Bernardo, & Charles, 1993). Second, there are improvements in firing patterns of cell assemblies across the brain by reduction of neural "noise" (Singer, 1995; Skoczenski & Norcia, 1998). Perception of object persistence under occlusion may be accomplished by somewhat higher-level mechanisms (i.e., centered in inferotemporal and perirhinal cortex) that support neural activity coding for objects that have become occluded, and that guide overt behavioral responses. These behaviors include anticipatory eye movements in young infants, and reaching behaviors in older infants. This progression toward appropriate search in the context of complex hiding tasks is consistent with a view positing age-related strengthening of neural representations, such that with development, stronger representations support success at enacting appropriate behaviors across a wide range of situations involving occlusion (Munakata, 2001). One candidate mechanism that may promote development of many kinds of organized cortical activity (such as binding of object features or coordination of object representations and object-oriented action) is *neural synchrony*: neural circuits that participate in a common goal engage in synchronized activity, firing in brief bursts in the 40 Hz range (Singer & Gray, 1995). Evidence has emerged that there are changes in synchronized activity in infants that accompany perceptual changes (Csibra, Davis, Spratling, & Johnson, 2000).

In sum, development of the object concept likely arises from a host of mechanisms: the infants' own (self-directed) means of information uptake, associative and other kinds of learning, fundamental changes in cortical activity across infancy, and perhaps others. I hope the reader will now agree that the distinction between theories is rather obscure when an explicit characterization of these mechanisms is undertaken, as I have tried to do in this chapter.

## Conclusion

I have presented a close examination of claims and evidence from three theories of development of the object concept: Piagetian theory, nativist theory, and information-processing theory. Careful consideration of this evidence reveals that no one account can embrace the multitude of cortical and behavioral changes that underlie the emergence of object concepts in infancy. Significant progress, nevertheless, has been realized. We now know where to look for answers: the rudiments of veridical object concepts are evident in the first 6 months after birth. We know also the kinds of tools to use: assessments of eye movements, for example, and cortical development (e.g., recording event-related potentials) have revealed important hints to behavioral and physiological changes that accompany development of object concepts in young infants. Finally, the multi-pronged approach advocated in this chapter rejects polemic debates between the roles of "nature" or "nurture," debates which, I hope I have made clear, are ultimately meaningless. There is no pure case of development caused in the absence of either intrinsic or external influences (Elman et al., 1996; Quartz & Sejnowski, 1997). The question is what mechanisms are responsible for perceptual and cognitive development. There are many mechanisms, and, therefore, no one correct approach to the question of development of the object concept.

## REFERENCES

Aguiar, A., & Baillargeon, R. (1999). 2.5-month-old infants' reasoning about when objects should and should not be occluded. *Cognitive Psychology*, 39, 116–57.

Atkinson, J. (2000). *The developing visual brain*. New York: Oxford University Press.

Baillargeon, R. (1993). The object concept revisited: New directions in the investigation of infants' physical knowledge. In C. Granrud (Ed.), *Visual perception and cognition in infancy* (pp. 265–315). Hillsdale, NJ: Erlbaum.

Baillargeon, R. (1994). How do infants learn about the physical world? *Current Directions in Psychological Science*, 3, 133–40.

Baillargeon, R. (2001). Infants' physical knowledge: Of acquired expectations and core principles. In E. Dupoux (Ed.), *Language, brain, and cognitive development: Essays in honor of Jacques Mehler* (pp. 341–61). Cambridge, MA: MIT Press.

Baillargeon, R., Spelke, E. S., & Wasserman, S. (1985). Object permanence in five-month-old infants. *Cognition*, 20, 191–208.

Bower, T. G. R. (1967). Phenomenal identity and form perception in an infant. *Perception and Psychophysics*, 2, 74–6.

Bower, T. G. R. (1974). *Development in infancy*. San Francisco: W. H. Freeman.

Bremner, J. G. (1985). Object tracking and search in infancy: A review of the data and a theoretical evaluation. *Developmental Review*, 5, 371–96.

Burkhalter, A. (1993). Development of forward and feedback connections between areas V1 and V2 of human visual cortex. *Cerebral Cortex*, 3, 476–87.

Burkhalter, A., Bernardo, K. L., & Charles, V. (1993). Development of local circuits in human visual cortex. *Journal of Neuroscience*, 13, 1916–31.

Carey, S., & Xu, F. (2001). Infants' knowledge of objects: Beyond object files and object tracking. *Cognition*, 80, 179–213.

Clifton, R. K., Rochat, P., Litovsky, R. Y., & Perris, E. E. (1991). Object representation guides infants' reaching in the dark. *Journal of Experimental Psychology: Human Perception and Performance*, 17, 323–9.

Cohen, L. B. (1998). An information-processing approach to infant perception and cognition. In F. Simion & G. Butterworth (Eds.), *The development of sensory, motor, and cognitive capacities in early infancy: From perception to cognition* (pp. 277–300). Hove: Psychology Press.

Cohen, L. B., & Amsel, G. (1998). Precursors to infants' perception of causality. *Infant Behavior and Development*, 21, 713–31.

Cohen, L. B., Chaput, H. H., & Cashon, C. H. (2002). A constructivist model of infant cognition. *Cognitive Development*, 17, 1323–43.

Cohen, L. B., & Marks, K. S. (2002). How infants process addition and subtraction events. *Developmental Science*, 5, 186–201.

Cohen, L. B., & Oakes, L. M. (1993). How infants perceive simple causality. *Developmental Psychology*, 29, 421–33.

Cohen, L. B., & Younger, B. A. (1984). Infant perception of angular relations. *Infant Behavior and Development*, 7, 37–47.

Cowie, F. (1999). *What's within? Nativism reconsidered*. New York: Oxford University Press.

Csibra, G., Davis, G., Spratling, M. W., & Johnson, M. H. (2000). Gamma oscillations and object processing in the infant brain. *Science*, 290, 1582–5.

Dehaene, S. (1997). *The number sense: How the mind creates mathematics*. New York: Oxford University Press.

Diamond, A. (1990). The development and neural basis of memory functions as indexed by the AB and delayed response tasks in human infants and adult monkeys. *Annals of the New York Academy of Sciences*, 608, 267–317.

Elman, J. L., Bates, E. A., Johnson, M. H., Karmiloff-Smith, A., Parisi, D., & Plunkett, K. (1996). *Rethinking innateness: A connectionist perspective on development*. Cambridge, MA: MIT Press.

Fantz, R. L. (1964). Visual experience in infants: Decreased attention to familiar patterns relative to novel ones. *Science*, 146, 668–70.

Flavell, J. H. (1963). *The developmental psychology of Jean Piaget*. Princeton, NJ: Van Nostrand.

Haith, M. M. (1980). *Rules that babies look by: The organization of newborn visual activity*. Potomac, MD: Erlbaum.

Hebb, D. O. (1949). *The organization of behavior: A neuropsychological theory*. Mahwah, NJ: Erlbaum.

Hood, B., & Willatts, P. (1986). Reaching in the dark to an object's remembered position: Evidence for object permanence in 5-month-old infants. *British Journal of Developmental Psychology*, 4, 57–65.

Johnson, M. H. (1997). *Developmental cognitive neuroscience*. Cambridge, MA: Blackwell.

Johnson, S. P. (2001a). Neurophysiological and psychophysical approaches to visual development. In A. F. Kalverboer & A. Gramsbergen (Series Eds.) & J. B. Hopkins (Section Ed.), *Handbook of brain and behaviour in human development. IV. Development of perception and cognition* (pp. 653–75). Amsterdam: Elsevier.

Johnson, S. P. (2001b). Visual development in human infants: Binding features, surfaces, and objects. *Visual Cognition*, 8, 565–78.

Johnson, S. P. (2003). Perceptual filling-in in infancy: Implications for development of object perception. Manuscript in preparation.

Johnson, S. P. (in press). Building knowledge from perception in infancy. In L. Gershkoff-Stowe and D. Rakison (Eds.), *Building object categories in developmental time*. Mahwah, NJ: Erlbaum.

Johnson, S. P., Amso, D., & Slemmer, J. A. (2003). Development of object concepts in infancy: Evidence for early learning in an eye tracking paradigm. Manuscript submitted for publication.

Johnson, S. P., & Aslin, R. N. (1995). Perception of object unity in 2-month-old infants. *Developmental Psychology*, 31, 739–45.

Johnson, S. P., & Aslin, R. N. (1996). Perception of object unity in young infants: The roles of motion, depth, and orientation. *Cognitive Development*, 11, 161–80.

Johnson, S. P., Bremner, J. G., Slater, A., Mason, U., Foster, K., & Cheshire, A. (2003). Infants' perception of object trajectories. *Child Development*, 74, 94–108.

Johnson, S. P., & Johnson, K. L. (2000). Early perception–action coupling: Eye movements and the development of object perception. *Infant Behavior and Development*, 23, 461–83.

Jusczyk, P. W., Johnson, S. P., Spelke, E. S., & Kennedy, L. J. (1999). Synchronous change and perception of object unity: Evidence from adults and infants. *Cognition*, 71, 257–88.

Kant, I. (1934). *Critique of pure reason* (Trans. J. M. D. Meikeljohn). London: J. M. Dent and Sons. (Original work published 1787.)

Kellman, P. J., & Spelke, E. S. (1983). Perception of partly occluded objects in infancy. *Cognitive Psychology*, 15, 483–524.

Kirkham, N. Z., Slemmer, J. A., & Johnson, S. P. (2002). Visual statistical learning in infancy: Evidence for a domain-general learning mechanism. *Cognition*, 83, B35-B42.

Koffka, K. (1935). *Principles of Gestalt psychology*. London: Routledge & Kegan Paul.

Marcovitch, S., & Zelazo, P. D. (1999). The A-not-B error: Results from a logistic meta-analysis. *Child Development*, 70, 1297–1313.

Mareschal, D., & Johnson, S. P. (2002). Learning to perceive object unity: A connectionist account. *Developmental Science*, 5, 151–85.

Munakata, Y. (2001). Graded representations in behavioral dissociations. *Trends in Cognitive Sciences*, 5, 309–15.

Nakayama, K., He, Z. J., & Shimojo, S. (1995). Visual surface representation: A critical link between lower-level and higher-level vision. In D. N. Osherson (Series Ed.) & S. M. Kosslyn & D. N. Osherson (Vol. Eds.), *Visual cognition. Vol. 2. An invitation to cognitive science* (2nd ed., pp. 1–70). Cambridge, MA: MIT Press.

Nelson, C. A., & Luciano, M. (2001). *Handbook of developmental cognition neuroscience*. Cambridge, MA: MIT Press.

Oakes, L. M., & Cohen, L. B. (1990). Infant perception of a causal event. *Cognitive Development*, 5, 193–207.

Piaget, J. (1952). *The origins of intelligence in children* (Trans. M. Cook). New York: International Universities Press. (Original work published 1936.)

Piaget, J. (1954). *The construction of reality in the child* (Trans. M. Cook). New York: Basic Books. (Original work published 1937.)

Quartz, S. R., & Sejnowski, T. J. (1997). The neural basis of cognitive development: A constructivist manifesto. *Behavioral and Brain Sciences*, 20, 537–96.

Rivera, S. M., Wakeley, A., & Langer, J. (1999). The drawbridge phenomenon: Representational reasoning or perceptual preference? *Developmental Psychology*, 35, 427–35.

Singer, W. (1995). Development and plasticity of cortical processing architectures. *Science*, 270, 758–64.

Singer, W., & Gray, C. M. (1995). Visual feature integration and the temporal correlation hypothesis. *Annual Review of Neuroscience*, 18, 555–86.

Skoczenski, A. M., & Norcia, A. M. (1998). Neural noise limitations on infant visual sensitivity. *Nature*, 391, 697–700.

Slater, A. (1995). Visual perception and memory at birth. In C. Rovee-Collier & L. P. Lipsitt (Eds.), *Advances in infancy research* (Vol. 9, pp. 107–62). Norwood, NJ: Ablex.

Slater, A., Mattock, A., Brown, E., & Bremner, J. G. (1991). For perception at birth: Cohen and Younger (1984) revisited. *Journal of Experimental Child Psychology*, 51, 395–406.

Slater, A., Morison, V., Somers, M., Mattock, A., Brown, E., & Taylor, D. (1990). Newborn and older infants' perception of partly occluded objects. *Infant Behavior and Development*, 13, 33–49.

Smith, L. B., Thelen, E., Titzer, R., & McLin, D. (1999). Knowing in the context of action: The task dynamics of the A-not-B error. *Psychological Review*, 106, 235–60.

Smith, W. C., Johnson, S. P., & Spelke, E. S. (in press). Motion and edge sensitivity in perception of object unity. *Cognitive Psychology*.

Spelke, E. S. (1985). Preferential-looking methods as tools for the study of cognition in infancy. In G. Gottlieb & N. A. Krasnegor (Eds.), *Measurement of audition and vision in the first year of postnatal life: A methodological overview* (pp. 323–63). Norwood, NJ: Ablex.

Spelke, E. S., & Newport, E. (1998). Nativism, empiricism, and the development of knowledge. In W. Damon (Series Ed.) & R. M. Lerner (Vol. Ed.), *Handbook of child psychology. Vol. 1. Theoretical models of human development* (pp. 275–340). New York: Wiley.

Spelke, E. S., & van de Walle, G. A. (1993). Perceiving and reasoning about objects: Insights from infants. In N. Eilan, R. McCarthy, & B. Brewer (Eds.), *Spatial representation: Problems in philosophy and psychology* (pp. 132–61). Cambridge, MA: Blackwell.

Thelen, E., Schöner, G., Scheier, C., & Smith, L. B. (2001). The dynamics of embodiment: A field theory of infant perseverative reaching. *Behavioral and Brain Sciences*, 24, 1–86.

Wellman, H. M., Cross, D., & Bartsch, K. (1986). Infant search and object permanence: A meta-analysis of the A-not-B error. *Monographs of the Society for Research in Child Development*, 54 (1, Serial No. 214).

Wong, R. O. L. (1999). Retinal waves and visual system development. *Annual Reviews in Neuroscience*, 22, 29–47.

Wynn, K. (1998). An evolved capacity for number. In D. Cummins Dellarosa & C. Allen (Eds.), *The evolution of mind* (pp. 107–26). New York: Oxford University Press.

# 8

# Remembering Infancy: Accessing Our Earliest Experiences

*Alan Fogel*

## Introduction

The oldest-known written description of infant development is from St. Augustine (354–430 CE). In the *Confessions* (1991), Augustine gives a remarkably detailed and developmentally appropriate report of his own infancy, describing how he sucked from the breast and his patterns of quieting and crying. He reports that his first smiles occurred during sleep, which can be observed in infants today. Augustine established the source of his data in the following way: "This at least is what I was told, and I believed it since that is what we see other infants doing. I do not actually remember what I then did" (St. Augustine, 1991, p. 8).

Augustine's description reveals that infantile amnesia, the apparent loss of memory about one's own infancy, has been accepted as fact for at least a few thousand years. Events in one's life that

This chapter is based in part on an invited lecture presented at the Associazione Italiana di Psicologia, Sezione di Psicologia dello Sviluppo, Alghero, Sardinia, September 26–28, 2000. This work is supported in part by a grant from the United States National Institute of Mental Health (R01 MH57669). I am grateful to Gavin Bremner, Lynette Cofer, Lisa Diamond, Raymond Kesner, Ilse de Koeyer, Sarah Norgate, Monisha Pasupathi, and Allan Schore for their helpful comments on earlier drafts of this chapter.

occur before the age of 3 or 4 years cannot be explicitly named, cannot be organized into a coherent narrative structure, and appear to be lost to the self (Rubin, 2000). Infantile amnesia has been explained by the onset of *autobiographical memory*, sometime during the third year of life (Fivush, 1994; Harley & Reese, 1999). In this view, children need to acquire conventional and symbolic language, and its cognitive prerequisites, in order to describe themselves to other members of their linguistic community and, in so doing, to remember themselves.

In this chapter, I shall review research – on infant and adult memory, infant neurobehavioral development, working models of attachment, recollections of documented early childhood trauma, and clinical work with adults and children – suggesting that children and adults may in fact remember some aspects of their first few years of life. In addition to the distinction typically made between implicit and explicit memory systems, I suggest that there is a third type of memory, which I call participatory memory – the experience of reliving or reenacting the past – that can help to explain both contemporaneous infant memory and child and adult memories for infancy. I describe some of the conditions under which individuals may access participatory memories of infancy. I argue that this is a necessary pathway bridging unconscious and conscious processes and one pathway for therapeutic processes aimed at resolving trauma from early childhood. I conclude by discussing the research and clinical implications of accessing infantile memories.

## Varieties of Memory

Memory researchers distinguish two memory systems. *Explicit memories* (also called conceptual or declarative memories) are composed of specific categories for types of event, times, and places. Explicit memory is recall *about* an event. *Implicit memory* (also called procedural or nondeclarative) "is concerned with unique, concrete personal experiences dated in the rememberer's past" (Tulving, 1983, p. 1). Implicit memory is self-relevant, context specific, and "concrete." These two types of memory are believed to be centered in different neurological structures located in different hemispheres of the brain (Schacter, 1992; Squire & Knowlton, 1995; Wheeler, Struss, & Tulving, 1997).

The differences between explicit and implicit memory can be extended to distinguish between two types of cognitive system:

a rational system and an experiential system. The rational system is analytical, marked by conscious appraisal processes, encoded in symbols, and it operates in the realm of conscious control. The experiential system, on the other hand, is emotional, concrete, experienced passively, and mediated by "vibes" from past experiences rather than by explicit judgments and appraisals (Epstein, 1991). This is similar to William James's distinction between knowledge by description (explicit) and knowledge by acquaintance (implicit).

Implicit memories have been used to explain skill learning, such as driving a car or playing a musical instrument. In this case, the memories are specific to the context (sitting behind a steering wheel or at a piano keyboard) and they are embodied, requiring the activation of specific sensory and motor systems. These memories are not memories "about" driving an automobile or performing music. Rather, the memory is constituted in the performance itself, not separate from it. A conceptual memory of driving is an armchair experience, thinking back on a specific incident. The conceptual memory requires a verbal narrative and does not necessarily require nonverbal actions. Implicit memories are from the past but may not correspond to a specific source event, time, or location (Schacter, 1996).

Both explicit and implicit memories are relational in the sense that not all the information required to remember is "in the head" (Fogel, 1993; Pasupathi, 2001). Compared to explicit memories which are relatively context-free, implicit memories require a specific type of context in order to be substantiated, a context similar to one in which the memory was acquired. In this case, the memory occurs spontaneously when the relationship between the subject and context is reconstituted. Some implicit memories are social relational because the contexts in which they were acquired and those in which the memory recurs are interpersonal situations, a process called *implicit relational knowing* (Beebe, 1998; Lyons-Ruth, 1998; Siegel, 2001).

All explicit memories are intrinsically relational because they are substantiated via socially shared cultural conventions such as words and images. This is true even for memories that occur when a person is alone because solitary thought takes the form of these same cultural words and images (Fogel, 1993; Vygotsky, 1978). Explicit memories are told and retold in social narratives. Evidence suggests that the explicit memories people retain are those which have been told to other people, making the process of memory formation and development inherently social (Pasupathi, 2001).

Research on infant memory suggests that, probably from birth, infants have both implicit and explicit forms of relational memories. Explicit memory, for example, is shown when infants recognize their mother's face or voice without necessarily demonstrating any enactive behavior (Howe, 2000). On the other hand, both types of memory have a different developmental course. Implicit memories are more prevalent and salient in early infancy. Explicit memory grows with increasing cognitive sophistication and with the ability to share autobiographical experiences with others via language (Fivush, 1993; Howe & Courage, 1993; Lewis, 1991).

Underlying verbal autobiographical memory, however, there is a memory for a preverbal sense of self, a "primary consciousness" or "ecological self" or "core self" consisting of sensing, feeling, and acting (Damasio, 1999; Rochat, 1995; Stern, 1985). Recent research on infant behavioral and neurophysiological development suggests that from the late fetal period, long before infants can recognize themselves in a mirror, infants have direct access to and implicit memories for their bodily states. Infants and late-term fetuses can experience their body's movements and senses. They also have access to the direct neural monitoring of the internal milieu of the body: the bowel and bladder, the heart beat, the breath, and other bodily functions that are linked to psychophysiological well-being (Butterworth, 1995; Damasio, 1999; Fifer, Monk, & Grose-Fifer, 2001; Rochat, 1995; Stern, 1985, 2000).

The remainder of this chapter is an account of the types of memory that are likely to be retained long term from the preverbal period and the conditions under which that memory may be accessed. I also suggest that there is a third type of memory, participatory memory, that forms a bridge between implicit (unconscious) and explicit (conscious) experience and may be one of the primary pathways for integrating infancy experience into the autobiographical self.

## *Implicit memory as regulatory memory*

Implicit memory is primarily *regulatory*, automatized, and unconscious (Bargh & Chartrand, 1999). Implicit memories do most of the work of mediating between perception and action, as when stimuli are unconsciously evaluated, approached, or avoided. Implicit memories are operating all the time and account for the organization and regulation of most of our adaptive behavior.

There is a growing amount of evidence from neurodevelopmental research suggesting that early experiences alter neural pathways and structures to create patterns of responding to everyday events. These patterns are primarily emotional (that is, evaluations regarding harms or benefits) and serve to regulate behavior at a preconscious level, one's "primary" or "core" self that begins to be established in early infancy (Damasio, 1999; Stern, 1985).

Because most infant experience occurs in interpersonal relationships, the infant brain is particularly attuned to faces, voices, and social information. Multiple, repeated experiences of social interaction become embodied in neuromotor pathways to create implicit relational knowing, implicit memories of how to do things with intimate others (Beebe, 1998; Lyons-Ruth, 1998; Siegel, 2001). The brain of the infant is experience-dependent and learns, via social experience, to view the social environment as fundamentally threatening or fundamentally friendly (Panksepp, 2001).

> Although we may never recall "explicitly" what happened to us as infants, the experiences we had with our caregivers have a powerful and lasting impact on our implicit processes. These experiences . . . involve our emotions, our behaviors, our perceptions, and our mental models of the work of others and of ourselves. Implicit memories encode our earliest forms of learning about the world. Implicit memories directly shape our here-and-now experiences without clues to their origins from past events.
> (*Siegel, 2001, p. 74*)

One of the most salient organizing factors of regulatory implicit memory is the infant's history of communication and emotion with significant others (Schore, 2001a,b). A number of attachment theorists have reconceptualized Bowlby's "internal working model" of attachment, which regulates communication with significant others, as a form of regulatory implicit relational memory. This memory is acquired through experience with separation, reunion, and mutual availability issues in relation to attachment figures from infancy and early childhood.

The experience-dependent maturation of the brain creates an intuitive, unconscious sense of one's ability to regulate flows of emotion, either alone or in interpersonal relationships. With a sense of security, infants are more likely to regulate their experiences of a variety of both positive and negative emotions because their social relational experience of these emotions has a history of effective resolution. The right hemisphere specifically provides the unconscious regulation of one's emotional synchrony with others.

> This capacity involves the abilities to nonconsciously yet efficiently read faces and tones and therefore intentionalities . . . to empathically resonate with states of others, to communicate emotional states and regulate interpersonal affects, and thus to cope with the ambient interpersonal stressors of early childhood.
>
> (*Schore, 2001a, p. 45*)

An example of a regulatory implicit memory comes from one of the most comprehensive chronicles of everyday memory, Marcel Proust's *Remembrance of Things Past*. The hero, Swann, is responding to the new coldness of his former lover, Odette.

> This new manner, indifferent, offhand, irritable, which Odette now adopted with Swann, undoubtedly made him suffer; but he did not realize how much he suffered . . . this change was his deep, secret wound, which tormented him day and night, and whenever he felt that his thoughts were straying too near it, he would quickly turn them into another channel for fear of suffering too much. He might say to himself in an abstract way: "There was a time when Odette loved me more," but he never formed any definite picture of that time. (*Proust, 1981, p. 350*)

Regulatory implicit memories, then, seem to be composites of repeated early experiences rather than accurate records of single incidents (Epstein, 1991; Stern, 1985). These generalizations create an unconscious predisposition to act or feel in particular ways in particular situations. These memories serve to regulate the links between self and other by altering the possibility for emotional response before an emotion is ever experienced. They are unconscious and, under ordinary conditions, unable to be explicitly accessed.

## *Participatory memories*

In addition to regulatory implicit memories and explicit verbal memories, there is another type of memory. It is a form of memory that can enter into the conscious experience of the remembering individual (similar to explicit memory), but the memory is behavioral and emotional rather than verbal or conceptual (similar to implicit memory). *Participatory memories are lived reenactments of personally significant experiences that have not yet become organized into a verbal or conceptual narrative.* Participatory memories are conscious experiences in the present that are not *about* a past experience, meaning that the past experience is not represented as an image or concept divorced from emotional significance. Rather, participatory memories are emotionally experienced as a *being with* or a *reliving of* past experiences (Bråten, 1998; Fogel, 1993, 2001; Heshusius, 1994). When experiencing a participatory memory, one is not thinking about the past. One is directly involved in a past experience as if it were occurring in the present.

I will argue in the following sections of this chapter that participatory memories arise from unconscious implicit memories and, under certain social relational conditions (during psychotherapy, for example), may become transformed into explicit verbal memories. In that process, implicit memories of unresolved and unconscious traumas from early childhood may become resolved and reintegrated into a more complex and expanded autobiographical sense of self through time.

Some contemporaneous memories of late-term fetuses and young infants appear to be participatory. In one type of memory study, for example, 3-month-old infants are taught to display a series of limb movements or headturns in order to activate the movement of a mobile suspended over their crib. Infants as young as 2 months of age can remember for up to 2 weeks without reminders the specific actions they learned to initiate the movement of a mobile. When infants are given periodic reminders, however, they can remember the procedures indefinitely.

Infant participatory memory, therefore, is *embodied* because when *reenacting* and probably *reexperiencing* a procedure, infants can be said to remember it (Fogel, 1993). The body, moving in relation to the context, is actively involved in the substantiation of the remembered experience.

> efforts at understanding the subjective world of the infant have focused primarily on mental representations as the building blocks of inner experience. The baby's body, with its pleasures and struggles, has largely been missing from this picture.
>
> (***Lieberman, 1996, p. 289***)

Infant participatory remembering is also situated in the context where initial learning occurs. Forgetting occurs when babies are retested in different cribs, in the same cribs with different-colored bumpers, with different mobiles, with different odors in the room, or with different music playing. In these situations, infants are less likely to show a participatory memory of activating the mobile (Butler & Rovee-Collier, 1989; Fagen, Prigot, Carroll, Pioli, Stein, & Franco, 1997; Rubin, Fagen, & Carroll,

1998). Participatory memories are also shown, after the age of 6 months, when infants reenact something via deferred imitation after delays of hours or days (Howe, 2000). Implicit memory is shown if infants at any time activate a mobile or perform some other action, having learned to do so in the past. The memories shown in these experimental studies are embodied in a specific sequence in a specific context, thus recreating the entirety of the prior experience.

Proust gives many examples of participatory memories. The novel's narrator, as a young child, had become intrigued by the name "Swann." Whenever he later heard the name, he would not have an explicit memory of Swann as an image in the mind. The remembering was comprised of a reenactment of relevant emotional experiences.

> I would be obliged to catch my breath, so suffocating was the pressure, upon that part of me where it was for ever inscribed, of that name which, at the moment when I heard it, seemed to me fuller, more portentous than any other, because it was heavy with the weight of all the occasions on which I had secretly uttered it in my mind. (***Proust, 1981, p. 157***)

In this passage, the writer describes the sensory and emotional manifestations in the present moment that form what he recognizes as a memory of his prior experiences. This memory is not conceptual or abstract, nor is it merely regulatory and unconscious. Rather, the memory is literally and realistically relived. Each time it recurs, the same feelings of portent create the experience of suffocation.

## *Participatory memory for trauma*

Post-traumatic stress disorder (PTSD) in humans involves participatory memory experiences including strong and unexplained emotions, somatic sensations, and visual images such as nightmares and flashbacks, all of which are reenactments of trauma-related responses. Traumatic participatory memories are behavioral reenactments of earlier experiences and are associated with specific changes in the right limbic system, particularly the hippocampus and amygdala (Schore, 2001a,b; van der Kolk, 1996a).

Participatory memories associated with PTSD have a number of notable characteristics. First, they are not transformed as a result of subsequent experiences. Typically, people do not remember autobiographical events veridically. Rather, everyday memory is altered by the developmental and social processes that occur in the interim between the original experience and the remembering of the experience, usually with another person (Pasupathi, 2001). Trauma memories, however, are "timeless and unmodified by further experience" (van der Kolk, 1996a, p. 232). Individuals may have the same traumatic nightmares or reexperience the same recurrent flashbacks for many years, such as being suddenly intensely afraid and breaking into a cold sweat for no apparent reason (Smyth & Pennebaker, 1999; Terr, 1994; van der Kolk, 1996b).

One of the reasons why this may occur in PTSD is:

> that emotional memories can be established without any conscious evaluation of incoming information by the neocortex, and that a high degree of activation of the amygdala and related structures can facilitate the generation of emotional responses and sensory impressions based on fragments of information, rather than full-blown perceptions of objects and events.
>
> (*van der Kolk, 1996a, p. 234*)

Participatory memories for human infancy in older children and adults may be preserved in more or less complete experiential form because the infant limbic system is more developmentally mature than the neocortex. Thus, situations from infancy, especially if they are salient – which would certainly be the case for trauma – could become "timeless."

A second characteristic of participatory memories is that they are primarily emotional and perceptual rather than explicit. Beside the apparent vividness of the participatory reenactment is the common observation that trauma victims display a selective amnesia for the actual events of the trauma. They may not even be aware that their flashbacks have a specific origin in time and place (van der Kolk, 1996b). Pierre Janet (1904) reported cases in which patients experienced overwhelming emotions that were seemingly traumatic but for which they had no explicit memory. Freud and Breuer (1966) reported on patients who were troubled by emotional and behavioral symptoms, apparently participatory memories, that the patients could not explain.

This feature of traumatic participatory memories appears to be explained by the same neurological processes as the previous feature. Because traumatic events cannot be assimilated into a coherent verbal narrative, they are remembered primarily by the areas of the brain that process sensory, motor, and iconic information. When traumatic memories are provoked in PTSD victims, there is a decreased activation in Broca's area (identified with some aspects of language processing) and right-hemisphere activation in the amygdala and hippocampus (see van der Kolk, 1996b, for a review of this literature).

All autobiographical memories, both implicit and explicit, partake of cortical and limbic processes, as well as neural connections vertically into the body (Fink, Markowitsch, Reinkemeier, Bruckbauer, Kessler, & Heiss, 1996; Tucker, 2001). The emotional and perceptual aspects of traumatic memories, however, are dissociated from cortical processing and thus become split off from the narrative part of the autobiographical self. This again suggests a similarity between memories for trauma and memories from infancy, where cortical and narrative processes are developmentally less available. While this lack of verbal memory for infancy has been the explanation for infantile amnesia, the trauma research suggests that the emotional and sensorimotor components of some infancy experiences may indeed be preserved and available for recall under certain conditions.

There are a growing number of well-documented studies showing that adults and young children retain an ability to reenact some experiences of trauma that occurred during their own infancy, that is, to show participatory memory for trauma. Long-term memory for pain in infancy has been shown in rats who, as newborns, were given a painful injection on either their right or their left rear paws. When tested as adults, the injected paw was more sensitive to pain compared to the noninjected paw, and compared to nontreated control rats. In addition, there was a higher density of nerve endings in the injected paws of the adult rats. At least in rats, these memories of trauma are localized to specific regions of the body and may last until adulthood (Ruda et al., 2000). This memory is participatory in the sense that the adult rat seems to contemporaneously reexperience the early pain in the same location that it was inflicted. This is not a memory about pain (not an explicit conceptual memory of having the pain inflicted to the paw during infancy), nor is it an unconscious favoring of the affected paw without a contemporaneous psychological experience (not a regulatory implicit memory).

Early stress and deprivation in rats and monkeys can create long-term behavioral changes that could be considered participatory memories, such as fear and behavioral inhibition in novel contexts and higher levels of anxiety and stress reactivity. These apparent reenactments of trauma-specific behavior are associated with neurological changes in the hypothalamic-pituitary-adrenocorticol (HPA) axis (Gunnar, 2001; Posner, Rothbart, Farah, & Bruer, 2001). In a potentially analogous way, human children who had been institutionalized in infancy because of parental death or absence are more likely than nondeprived children to show behaviors such as being resentful or aggressive when corrected, irritability, and fighting with peers (Ames, 1997; Hodges & Tizard, 1989). These behaviors are not explicit memories of being treated a certain way in early childhood. They are activated in the present, have emotional force, and probably replicate in the body the interpersonal conditions of early experiences.

It may be theoretically useful to reconsider the concept of working models of attachment from the perspective of participatory memories as distinct from implicit memories. Children and adults with insecure attachment histories, for example, are more vigilant for signs of abandonment, gaining approval, and avoiding rejection (Goodman & Quas, 1997; Main, 1999). This vigilance is manifested in body postures of holding back, withdrawing, and in lived emotional experiences of shame and anxiety. Anxious styles of attachment are seen in clinging, reaching, and a hunger for body contact, while avoidance is seen as pushing away and aversion to interpersonal closeness. These are probably participatory memories because they tend to be reenacted with close friends, parent figures, romantic and sexual partners but not necessarily with other people, that is, in emotional and postural situations (e.g., lying down, close holding) in which the original experiences may have occurred (Lisa Diamond, personal communication).

Long-term memories of pain trauma in human infants also have been investigated in children who had a traumatic injury that brought them to the hospital emergency room some time during their first 2 years of life (Peterson, 1999; Peterson & Bell, 1996; Peterson & Rideout, 1998). If the injury occurred around the age of 2 years or after, children could recall the situation verbally up to 2 years later. One such child had burned his hand on a lawnmower exhaust pipe when he was just under 2 years old. A year and a half later, he could state that he burned his hand, who was there, why it happened, and that he saw a doctor. These are explicit, conceptual, autobiographical memories.

Children who were injured before 18 months were different. At 16 months, a child fell and cut his forehead. His emergency room visit was traumatic for him, since he had to be tightly wrapped in a blanket to keep him from moving during the stitching of the cut. For the next few months, he showed sleep disturbances, fear of strangers, did not want to leave the house, and became hysterical when blankets were put on him. He was interviewed by the researchers when he was 22 months old. At that time he still did not have verbal skills sufficient to describe the situation, but when he heard the word *hospital* he pointed to the place on his forehead where he had received the stitches. When interviewed 18 months after the accident (at 34 months of age), he still had no verbal memory of it but his parents said he still refused to be wrapped in a smock when getting his hair cut.

These memories are not explicit because there is no verbal memory and the child cannot stand outside the experience and reflect upon it. Nor are these memories simply regulatory, controlling the feelings before they occur by an unconscious avoidance of the situation. Rather, these memories are relived experiences in the present: they are participatory.

One of the most dramatic studies on participatory memories comes from clinical research on children who were under the age of 5 years at the time they were exposed to documented traumas such as sexual abuse, physical injuries, witnessing the death of a family member, or accidents (Terr, 1988). All children in the study had what Terr calls "behavioral memories," but only children older than 28 months at the time of the trauma were capable of retaining partial or full verbal memory for the trauma.

Of interest to this chapter are the behavioral memories, some of which appear to satisfy the criteria for participatory memory. These include post-traumatic play or reenactment and trauma-specific fears. In one play therapy episode, a child poked at her abdomen and talked about spears pointed at her during a visit to Disneyland. The spot she touched was exactly the place where videotapes of her sexual abuse (made by the perpetrators) revealed a man's erect penis jabbing her and not, as might be presumed, in her genital area.

Terr also groups "personality changes," such as persistent sadness or anger, under the category of behavior memories. These personality changes, however, appear to be regulatory implicit memories, confined to the background of psychological functioning. Under the cover of sad or angry moods, the potential for reenacting the trauma remains in the unconscious background.

While accurate verbal memories of documented trauma are not surprising for children older than 3 years at the time of the incident,

> The surprise comes when one looks at behavioral memories, at how early they appear, how long they continue, and how accurately

> they reflect what happened to the child. Behavioral memory appears to operate by different rules from those governing verbal remembrance. For instance, behavioral recall allows for repetition of action in multiple, variable, and long-lasting abuses, even when the verbal descriptions of these abuses seem forever lost to consciousness. (*Terr, 1988, p. 103*)

## *Participatory memories for nontraumatic experiences*

There seems to be a consistent clinical, neurological, and theoretical explanation for why some traumatic memories are participatory and relatively unmodified by later experience, even when those memories occur before the age of 18 months. Can nontraumatic events from infancy also be retained as participatory memories? Given that the infant brain tends to monitor primarily emotional and sensorimotor occurrences, and given that there is no verbal mediation of such experiences, highly salient positive experiences from infancy may be preserved in the emotional right hemisphere. Since such salient events would have occurred prior to language acquisition, they may become "timeless" in the same way that we have seen for traumatic memories.

Participatory memories have been documented for nontraumatic experiences, but at the present time there is less convincing evidence than the evidence for traumatic memories. Compared to rat pups who received relatively little maternal attention, pups who received higher levels of licking and grooming from their mothers were less fearful and showed lower levels of stress both behaviorally and in the HPA-axis response (Liu, Dioro, Tannenbaum, Caldji, Francis, Freedman et al., 1997; Posner et al., 2001). Secure attachment behavior, the participatory reenactment of approaching and comfort seeking in humans, is believed to be affected by infancy experience as mediated through the effective regulation of the HPA axis, the right limbic system, and the parasympathetic nervous system, especially vagal tone (Diamond, 2001; Schore, 2001a,b). Preferences for food and other sensory pleasures may also be interpreted as participatory memories. These are rather general assertions, however, and research is lacking on the specificity of nontraumatic memories from infancy.

There are a few exceptions. In one study, children who were 2.5 years old were retested in a procedure that had required them to reach for objects in the dark when they were 6 months of age. Compared to infants who did not have the 6-month experience of reaching in the dark, the children who had the experience were better at the task at 2.5 years even though they had no verbal/conceptual memory of having done the task when they were younger (Perris, Myers, & Clifton, 1990). In this study, it is difficult to say whether the memory for reaching in the dark is implicit, i.e., a general automaticity, or participatory.

In another study, a sample of 8- to 10-year-old participants were shown pictures of their preschool classmates, children who they knew when they themselves were 3 years old. In comparison to pictures of 3-year-olds who the participants did not know, the participants had reliable skin conductance responses even though they could not reliably identify verbally which of the pictures were of their former classmates (Newcombe & Fox, 1994). Although there were physiological effects, this memory did not appear to become part of the participant's conscious experience in the present. Thus, this study may show evidence for implicit regulatory memory rather than for participatory memory.

A clinical case study of nontraumatic participatory memory followed a group of singletons and twins from the late fetal period until the age of 3 years (Piontelli, 1992). Piontelli observed the fetuses in the company of the parents and physicians during ultrasound imaging of the fetus. She later conducted naturalistic observations of the children in their families. One set of dizygotic twins, for example, stroked each other between the walls of their separate amniotic sacs. After birth, they liked to touch and stroke each other, more so than the other twins in the study who did not show this behavior prenatally. At the age of 1 year, they developed a game of stroking each other from opposite sides of a silk curtain. Another set of fraternal twins was prone to hitting each other prenatally and continued to show violence and dislike toward each other for many years. A singleton who "wildly" licked her placenta and umbilical cord during the fetal period developed an eating disorder in infancy and an insatiable need for sensory pleasure.

Though suggestive of nontraumatic participatory memories from early infancy, the studies reviewed here are insufficient to make a strong case. There are, however, good theoretical reasons to suppose that such memories exist and can be revealed by future research. On the other hand, a much stronger case can be made at the present time for the preservation of participatory memories of infant trauma well into childhood and possibly for a lifetime.

## Infant to Adult, Adult to Infant

The previous section suggested that there are situations in which previously unconscious implicit regulatory memories can be brought to life in the form of a participatory memory. The play therapy situation used by Terr is one such example. Can we say something general about the conditions under which participatory memories of infancy are likely to emerge?

Participatory memories are more likely to occur when the situation in the present has similarities to a salient situation in the past, one that is not explicitly remembered. A variety of studies on nonhuman animals show that fears conditioned during infancy can be reinstated when the older animals are placed under stress. Rats who were fear-conditioned at 21 days showed no retention 2 weeks later, a form of infantile amnesia. When given an injection of epinephrine or other stress hormones, the conditioned fears returned. The form of behavior shown by the stressed animals was infantile in appearance, involving stilling and freezing (Jacobs & Nadel, 1985; Nijenhuis, Vanderlinden, & Spinhoven, 1998). These findings suggest that under neurological conditions similar to the initial learning situation, the animals had a participatory memory of the conditioned stimulus.

In humans, emotional memories for abuse, trauma, and stress related to infantile attachment history are linked to the relatively nonverbal right hemisphere (Brake, Sullivan, & Gratton, 2000; Fink et al., 1996; Schore, 2001a,b). As in the case of fear-conditioned rats, these stressful and traumatic early experiences, because they are based in the right brain, lead to an inability to talk about emotions and internal states related to the trauma, that is, to dissociations of explicit memory (Schore, 2001a,b). It seems reasonable to suspect that reinstatement of the neurobehavioral conditions of infancy – primarily sensory, motor, and emotional situations – may create opportunities for the emergence of infantile participatory memories.

Similar to the research with rats, when humans with traumatic early histories are under physiological or psychosocial stress, their amnesia for early experiences becomes manifested as enactive "symptoms" (Fox & Card, 1999). The majority of reported symptoms involve heightened sensory and motor states, such as inability to feel emotions or excessive emotionality, gastric and eating disorders, sensitivity to touch, and the like (Krueger, 1989). It may be clinically and theoretically useful to consider these symptoms as examples of participatory memories.

## Therapeutic transformations from implicit to participatory to explicit memory

Participatory memories that manifest as symptoms under stress do not necessarily become explicit because they lack an interpersonal context that facilitates integration into the autobiography of the self. These memories, though participatory, remain split off, dissociated from the conscious self. A number of therapeutic methods have been devised that evoke participatory memories and then facilitate their integration into the autobiographical self.

Freud, for example, was aware of the need to get adults out of their habitual and conceptual cognition in order to access childhood experiences for the purpose of treating symptomatic complaints. He experimented first with an early form of hypnosis and then later discovered a method that he called *free association*. Freud realized that thinking and reasoning about oneself is important for therapeutic integration, self-control, and appropriate social behavior. On the other hand, these ego functions – according to Freud – also serve to defend against awareness of the original trauma. One of the goals of psychotherapy is to free up the unconscious memories of emotionally laden experiences. In the company of an emotionally available therapist, these memories can be reexperienced and understood.

> The co-construction of a coherent narrative of the trauma may emerge in a relational contact which promotes a callosal transfer of affective information from the right to left orbitofrontal regions. This structural advance allows for left hemispheric retrieval and explicit semantic processing of right hemispheric emotional states encoded in implicit-procedural memory. (*Schore, 2001b, p. 245*)

I suggest that one pathway from implicit to explicit remembering is the temporary manifestation of the implicit memories as participatory memories. These so-called regressions to earlier experiences that occur during psychotherapy, for example, provide a fertile ground for this process to occur.

> The vividness and immediacy of regressed states of experience become the core of an active reorganization of the interpersonal self, and one aspect of the analytic situation is the creation of a relational environment that permits, rather than induces, therapeutic regression. This environment allows the individual partially to surrender the role of protecting ego stability because he feels safe enough to share the responsibility with the analyst. By

> doing so, the patient permits the emergence of regressed states of experience, along with intense reenactment in the transference of early and sometimes developmentally fragmented modes of thinking, feeling, and behaving. (*Bromberg, 1991, p. 416*)

The "vividness and immediacy" of regressed states seems to be a description of the lived experiential nature of participatory memories, awakened into being relived in conscious experience in the midst of a particular type of therapeutic relationship.

Bromberg (1991) suggests that language alone is inadequate to create such therapeutic opportunities: they cannot arise via interpretation, they are permitted rather than induced. Such opportunities occur when patient and therapist move into a play-like communication that is founded upon a history of trust built through the relationship. The participatory memories must be communicated to and witnessed by another person who is prepared to accept them and to help regulate the emotions as the client revises his or her autobiographical narrative to include not only the early experience, but the ability to cognitively regulate the emotions surrounding it.

Bromberg's idea of permitting and allowing rather than inducing participatory memories is reminiscent of models of early mother–infant communication associated with secure attachments. Rather than inducing affective states in their infants, mothers match infant emotions and engage in moments of dynamic sharing of emotions. This has been called attunement, interpersonal affective resonance, dyadic states of consciousness, or co-regulation. These moments are typically associated with positive transformations of social and emotional behavior (Fogel, 1993; Schore, 1991; Stern, 1985; Tronick, 1998).

Similar moments have been observed during psychotherapeutic encounters. They have been called "now moments" (Sander, 1995; Stern, 1998). When they occur, clients experience novel insights and heightened emotions. These insights are fundamentally new forms of self-experience. The sense of the truth of the moment and its importance for the self is related to the fact that it can be *recognized as part of the self* (Beebe, 1998; Lyons-Ruth, 1998; Sander, 2000). A now moment is a "hot moment of truth" in which participants are caught "off guard," requiring some unpredictable and ultimately creative act (Stern, 1998). This is also similar to Winnicott's (1971) concept of the potential space between partners that arises when each is completely open to the possibilities that arise in relation to the other. Tronick's (1998) concept of "dyadic states of consciousness" is similar: "Dyadic states of consciousness between the patient and therapist do not involve interpretation . . . they are purely emotional and procedural (implicit)." These descriptions from the therapy literature strongly suggest that what comes up during now moments are personally relevant, surprising, emotional, creative experiences. Because of their emotional aliveness, these experiences are very likely to be participatory memories from early childhood.

Another possible route into participatory memories of early childhood and infancy and their therapeutic transformation is somatic awareness therapies and somatic psychotherapies. These are forms of adult therapy that may use free associative talking and also body movement, body awareness, and touch as a way to access the memories of early childhood and reintegrate them into the self. Since infants experience their world via movement, touch, and embodied self-awareness, for many somatic awareness practitioners, this seems to be a more direct route to an adult's infant experience than merely talking. Somatic awareness approaches may use soft music and low lighting. Awareness is enhanced as the practitioner helps the client to pay attention not only to their words but to their body movements, emotions, and sensations (Ogden & Minton, 2000; Schofield & Abbuhl, 1975).

Sylvan Tomkins, well known for his pioneering theoretical work on emotions, reported the reactivation of emotional memories from infancy and early childhood by means of creating a current situation that is similar to the physical and/or emotional conditions of early life.

> If we place the adult in the milieu of the infant or child, bombard him with messages peculiar to the milieu, and permit, require, and urge him to emit the behaviors characteristic of infancy and childhood, we should be able to activate traces that have been dormant for most of the individual's lifetime.
>
> (***Tomkins, 1992, p. 214***)

Tomkins (1992) advocated creating oversize rooms, leaving the adult in darkness, being rocked, sucking on a pacifier, imitating the unstable walk of infants, hearing lullabies, and the like.

Clinicians practicing a variety of somatic awareness methods including somatic psychotherapy and Rosen Method Bodywork have written case reports documenting that participatory memories, self-relevant and immediate, can be part of a therapeutic transformational process. Rosen Method Bodywork uses gentle touch and words to help the client reexperience sensory and emotional states that had been held back since infancy and childhood (Wooten, 1995). Like Bromberg's approach to psychotherapy, the Rosen Method focuses on permitting and allowing clients to have participatory experiences in the context of a trusting therapeutic relationship. This is illustrated by one Rosen Method practitioner.

> I was curious throughout my Rosen training as well as in my early-on private practice and teaching about the physical, emotional and attitudinal changes that occurred in my clients. I had experienced it myself time and time again. Often it seemed, my body remembered something which no words or images could convey, and the result was that my posture and the way I moved changed in significant ways: I stood up straighter without effort and with hips more relaxed, my stride became longer. I became more relaxed altogether and learned to notice the images that unexpectedly came to my mind, both as I was being worked on and after. Sometimes it was several days after a session when a significant memory would emerge from my unconscious.
>
> (*Wooten, 1995, p. 41*)

I became personally convinced about the possibility for both traumatic and nontraumatic participatory memories of infancy in my own experience receiving and practicing Rosen Method Bodywork during the past 4 years. This clinical work, coupled with 30 years of research expertise on the development of infant relational and embodied cognition and emotion, has opened new areas of research, clinical practice, and education in my career.

To take one example, participatory memories from infancy and childhood have been activated in college students who enroll in my infant development classes. With Mark Reese, a certified Feldenkrais Method practitioner and teacher, we developed infant-like self-awareness lessons that simulate such infant movements as sucking, smiling, rolling over, crawling, and balancing. These lessons, their theoretical background, links to infant development, and reports of student experiences doing them, can be found in one of my books (Fogel, 2001). Students are led first through relaxation exercises and then step by step through infant movements, repeated slowly and deliberately, until the sensorimotor processes of primary consciousness predominate the students' awareness.

In the sucking lesson, for example, all the students who reported negative feelings or body tensions when sucking found out from their parents that they had problems with sucking or eating during infancy. One student who was especially distressed by her adult sucking experience learned that she had been fed through a tube as a baby. These students were unaware of having these early feeding difficulties until the participatory experience of the lesson led them to confirm their infancy experiences by interviewing their parents. Students who had a sense of peace, calm, and relaxation during the sucking – the most common participatory experience doing this lesson – discovered that their early feeding had been normal (Fogel, 2001).

In methods such as these, access to participatory memory is aided by the creation of a deep state of relaxation that decreases sympathetic nervous system activity, which has the effect of creating a relaxation response and enhanced inner self-awareness. This state is similar to that produced during psychotherapy, bodywork, hypnosis, yoga, meditation, and prayer. It has parallels to artistic and scientific creativity, play, and dreaming, in which the individual breaks free from the ordinary boundaries of implicit regulatory processes and awakens to an experience of direct participation (Rossi, 1993; Varela, Thompson, & Rosch, 1991; Winnicott, 1971).

## Conclusion

This chapter makes a case for the existence of at least two kinds of memory for early childhood prior to the acquisition of language: implicit memory and participatory memory. Implicit memory forms the core self, the unconscious processes that regulate our response to the sensory and motor aspects of the environment, the interpersonal world, and emotion. Participatory memory occurs when implicit memory comes alive in such a way that the person directly experiences something in the present that is recognized as being part of the self at some time in the distant past.

Participatory memories – at the moment when they are experienced – are unexpected, nonrational, spontaneous, and emotional. We are not likely to experience them during ordinary conversation (explicit memory) or during everyday patterns of living (implicit memory). When participatory memories arise, they reveal the locations and processes in the body that were part of the formation of the original experience. Recent studies of the brain suggest that virtually all cognitive functions are organized vertically with connections in the midbrain directly into the motor and regulatory systems of the body (Seitz, 2000; Tucker, 2001; Varela et al., 1991). While conceptual systems serve to regulate narrative autobiographical memory, they do not act alone but rather with respect to the substrate of primary consciousness, the ongoing monitoring of embodied experience that forms the foundation of self-awareness (Damasio, 1999; Tucker, 2001). Symptoms typically have some embodied link to the original event.

Participatory memories are likely to occur during periods of stress or during particular kinds of therapeutic situations. When they occur in therapy, they open the possibility for a healing change to occur. The participatory memory, recognized as part of the self but unconnected to particular times and places, can become transformed into a coherent narrative for the reintegrated autobiographical self. There is relatively little systematic data on therapeutic processes from the perspective of participatory memory. Nevertheless, a number of hypotheses may be suggested as grounds for further study.

*All moments of change – "now moments" in spiritual, meditative, somatic awareness or psychotherapeutic practices – involve participatory memories.* The clinical evidence suggests that now moments have the possibility to evoke participatory memories. I suggest that a closer examination of such moments will reveal that their particular salience for the participants can be accounted for by the sense of "truth" or "rightness" that occurs. This sense of truth occurs because the personal experience is immediately recognized as part of the self. The individual cannot pin down the exact location of the experience in time or space and at the same time feels a powerful sense of familiarity that is unusually compelling. If human change and transformation is connected to the reexperiencing of self-relevant memories from very early in one's lifetime, the therapeutic moment is fundamentally a rejuvenation (Fogel, 2001). When the early past is brought to life in a participatory memory, it is like grafting a stem cell of the psyche into the adult mind-body system, yielding new pathways for growth.

*Participatory memories do not need to be accurate to be therapeutic and transformational.* Whenever memory for early childhood is discussed, there is the tendency to ask about its accuracy. Did these things actually happen to the person? When the issue is brought into a legal case, such as recovered memories of child abuse, there is good reason to ask about accuracy. Although there are documented cases of both true and false recovered memories, from a young age children appear to have the ability to edit and reject false memories (Brainerd & Reyna, 2002). In therapeutic situations, however, accuracy is not an issue. Because participatory memories are not localized to a particular event, and because they are so personally compelling, individuals and cultures have devised many ways to make explicit sense out of them. They have been attributed to the prenatal or infancy periods, to past lives, or to a spiritual connection. Regardless of whether these narratives are correct or accurate, they are almost always transformational because of their emotional force for the individual. Since all memory is gist-like, there may be fragments of actual experience that coalesce with cultural and personal stories and myths to create a sense of participatory memory. Recognizing these kinds of experiences as participatory memories may facilitate research into their origins.

*Methods that heighten the possibility for experiencing participatory memories can be used for both therapeutic and scientific purposes.* When researchers of infancy and early childhood approach the subject from only a verbal/conceptual epistemological stance, there is a profound barrier to what can be understood about babies. Should we be satisfied with shaping our view of infancy according to our own adult conceptual framework? Is it reasonable to describe a nonconceptual being in conceptual terms? Or, shall we take steps to reshape ourselves in the image of infants by using participatory and embodied epistemologies – such as somatic awareness practices – in our research and our everyday life? At a minimum, by doing this we will become more self-aware, more relaxed, and healthier. In addition, as researchers dare to adopt such methods, especially in collaboration with psychotherapists and somatic awareness practitioners, we shall open windows of opportunity on our understanding of infancy and the contribution of infant experience to the adult psyche.

*The scientific study of participatory memory for infant experience can shed new light on therapeutic processes that seek to heal infant trauma and integrate the person into a cohesive sense of self across the life course.* Research problems include the conditions under which participatory memories may arise, how they are best transformed into autobiographical integration, and the plasticity of the brain to reorganize following such experiences. What is the relationship between mind and body, infant and adult, in the transformation of trauma into health? The theoretical plausibility of participatory memories from infancy and childhood may provide the impetus for new research.

## REFERENCES

Ames, E. (1997). *The development of Romanian orphanage children adopted to Canada*. (Final Report to the National Welfare Grants Program: Human Resources Development Canada). Burnaby, British Columbia: Simon Fraser University.

Baddeley, A. (1994). The remembered self and the enacted self. In U. Neisser & R. Fivush (Eds.), *The remembering self: Construction and accuracy in the self-narrative* (pp. 236–42). New York: Cambridge University Press.

Bargh, J., & Chartrand, T. (1999). The unbearable automaticity of being. *American Psychologist*, 54 (7), 462–79.

Beebe, B. (1998). A procedural theory of therapeutic action: Commentary of the symposium, "Interventions that effect change in psychotherapy." *Infant Mental Health Journal*, 19 (3), 333–40.

Brainerd, C. J., & Reyna, V. F. (2002). Recollection rejection: How children edit their false memories. *Developmental Psychology*, 38, 156–72.

Brake, W., Sullivan, R., & Gratton, A. (2000). Perinatal distress leads to lateralized medial prefrontal cortical dopamine hypofunction in adult rats. *Journal of Neuroscience*, 20 (14), 5538–43.

Bråten, S. (1998). Infant learning by altercentric participation: The reverse of egocentric observation in autism. In S. Bråten (Ed.), *Intersubjective communication and emotion in early ontogeny. Studies in emotion and social interaction* (2nd series, pp. 105–24). New York: Cambridge University Press.

Bromberg, P. (1991). On knowing one's patient inside out: The aesthetics of unconscious communication. *Psychoanalytic Dialogues*, 1 (4), 399–422.

Butler, J., & Rovee-Collier, C. (1989). Contextual gating of memory retrieval. *Developmental Psychobiology*, 22, 533–52.

Butterworth, G. E. (1995). An ecological perspective on the origins of self. In J. L. Bermudez, A. Marcel, & N. Eilan (Eds.), *The body and the self* (pp. 87–105). Cambridge, MA: Bradford.

Damasio, A. (1999). *The feeling of what happens: Body and emotion in the making of consciousness*. San Diego, CA: Harcourt.

Diamond, L. (2001). Contributions of psychophysiology to research on adult attachment: Review and recommendation. *Personality and Social Psychology Review*, 5 (4), 27–95.

Epstein, S. (1991). Cognitive-experiential self theory: Implications for developmental psychology. In M. R. Gunnar & L. A. Sroufe (Eds.), *Self processes and development. The Minnesota symposium on child development* (Vol. 23, pp. 79–123). Hillsdale, NJ: Erlbaum.

Fagen, J., Prigot, J., Carroll, M., Pioli, L., Stein, A., & Franco, A. (1997). Auditory context and memory retrieval in young infants. *Child Development*, 68 (6), 1057–66.

Fifer, W., Monk, C., & Grose-Fifer, J. (2001). Prenatal development and risk. In G. Bremner & A. Fogel (Eds.), *Blackwell handbook of infant development* (pp. 505–42). Cambridge, MA: Blackwell.

Fink, G., Markowitsch, H., Reinkemeier, M., Bruckbauer, T., Kessler, J., & Heiss, W. (1996). Cerebral representation of one's own past: Neural networks involved in autobiographical memory. *Journal of Neuroscience*, 16 (13), 4275–82.

Fivush, R. (1993). Developmental perspectives on autobiographical recall. In G. S. Goodman & B. L. Bottoms (Eds.), *Understanding and improving children's testimony* (pp. 1–24). New York: Guilford Press.

Fivush, R. (1994). Constructing narrative, emotion, and self in parent–child conversations about the past. In U. Neisser & R. Fivush (Eds.), *The remembering self: Construction and accuracy in the self-narrative* (pp. 136–57). New York: Cambridge University Press.

Fogel, A. (1993). *Developing through relationships*. Chicago: University of Chicago Press.

Fogel, A. (2001). *Infancy: Infant, family and society* (4th ed.). Belmont, CA: Wadsworth.

Fox, N., & Card, J. (1999). Psychological measures in the study of attachment. In J. Cassidy & P. Shaver (Eds.), *Handbook of attachment theory, research and clinical applications* (pp. 226–45). New York: Guilford Press.

Freud, S., & Breuer, J. (1966). *Studies on hysteria* (Trans. J. Strachey). New York: Avon.

Goodman, G., & Quas, J. (1997). Trauma and memory: Individual differences in children's recounting of a stressful experience. In N. Stein, P. Ornstein, B. Tversky, & C. Brainerd (Eds.), *Memory for everyday and emotional events* (pp. 267–94). Hillsdale, NJ: Erlbaum.

Gunnar, M. (2001). Effects of early deprivation: Findings from orphanage-reared infants and children. In C. A. Nelson & M. Luciana (Eds.), *Handbook of developmental cognitive neuroscience* (pp. 617–29). Cambridge, MA: MIT Press.

Harley, K., & Reese, E. (1999). Origins of autobiographical memory. *Developmental Psychology*, 35 (8), 1338–48.

Heshusius, L. (1994). Freeing ourselves from objectivity: Managing subjectivity or turning toward a participatory mode of consciousness? *Educational Researcher*, 23 (3), 15–22.

Hodges, J., & Tizard, B. (1989). Social and family relationships of ex-institutional adolescents. *Journal of Child Psychology and Psychiatry*, 30, 77–97.

Howe, M. L. (2000). *The fate of early memories: Developmental science and the retention of childhood experiences*. Washington, DC: American Psychological Association.

Howe, M. L., & Courage, M. L. (1993). On resolving the enigma of infantile amnesia. *Psychological Bulletin*, 113, 305–26.

Jacobs, W., & Nadel, L. (1985). Stress-induced recovery of fears and phobias. *Psychological Review*, 92 (4), 512–31.

Janet, P. (1904). L'amnésie et la dissociation des souvenirs par l'émotion [Amnesia and the dissociation of memories by emotion]. *Journal de Psychologie Normale et Pathologique*, 1, 417–53.

Krueger, D. (1989). *Body self and psychological self: A developmental and clinical integration of disorders of the self*. New York: Brunner/Mazel.

Lewis, M. (1991). Ways of knowing: Objective self-awareness or consciousness. *Developmental Review*, 11 (3), 231–43.

Lieberman, A. (1996). Aggression and sexuality in relation to toddler attachment: Implications for the caregiving system. *Infant Mental Health Journal*, 17 (3), 276–92.

Liu, D., Dioro, J., Tannenbaum, B., Caldji, C., Francis, D., Freedman, A., et al. (1997). Maternal care, hippocampal gluco-corticoid receptors, and hypothalamic-pituitary-adrenal responses to stress. *Science*, 277, 1659–61.

Lyons-Ruth, K. (1998). Implicit relational knowing: Its role in development and psychoanalytic treatment. *Infant Mental Health Journal*, 19 (3), 282–9.

Main, M. (1999). Attachment theory: Eighteen points with suggestions for future studies. In J. Cassidy & P. Shaver (Eds.), *Handbook of attachment: Theory, research and clinical applications* (pp. 845–87). New York: Guilford Press.

Newcomb, N., & Fox, N. (1994). Infantile amnesia: Through a glass darkly. *Child Development*, 65 (1), 31–40.

Nijenhuis, E., Vanderlinden, J., & Spinhoven, P. (1998). Animal defensive reactions as a model for trauma-induced dissociative reactions. *Journal of Traumatic Stress*, 11 (2), 243–60.

Ogden, P., & Minton, K. (2000). Sensorimotor sequencing: One method for processing traumatic memory. *Traumatology*, 6 (3), article 3.

Panksepp, J. (2001). The long-term psychobiological consequences of infant emotions: Prescriptions for the twenty-first century. *Infant Mental Health Journal*, 22 (1–2), 132–73.

Pasupathi, M. (2001). The construction of the personal past and its implications for adult development. *Psychological Bulletin*, 127 (5), 651–72.

Perris, E. E., Myers, N. A., & Clifton, R. K. (1990). Long-term memory for a single infancy experience. *Child Development*, 61, 1796–1807.

Peterson, C. (1999). Children's memory for medical emergencies: 2 years later. *Developmental Psychology*, 35 (6), 1493–1506.

Peterson, C., & Bell, M. (1996). Children's memory for traumatic injury. *Child Development*, 67, 3045–70.

Peterson, C., & Rideout, R. (1998). Memory for medical emergencies experienced by 1- and 2-year-olds. *Developmental Psychology*, 34 (5), 1059–72.

Piontelli, A. (1992). *From fetus to child: An observational and psychoanalytic study*. New York: Routledge.

Posner, M., Rothbart, M., Farah, M., & Bruer, J. (2001, August). The developing human brain. [Special Issue]. *Developmental Science*, 4 (3).

Proust, M. (1981). *Remembrance of things past. Vol. 3* (Trans. S. K. Scott-Moncrieff & T. Kilmartin). New York: Random House.

Rochat, P. (1995). Early objectification of the self. In P. Rochat (Ed.), *The self in early infancy: Theory and research* (pp. 53–72). Amsterdam: Elsevier.

Rossi, E. (1993). *The psychobiology of mind-body healing: New concepts of therapeutic hypnosis*. New York: W. W. Norton.

Rubin, D. (2000). The distribution of early childhood memories. *Memory*, 8, 265–9.

Rubin, G. B., Fagen, J. W., & Carroll, M. H. (1998). Olfactory context and memory retrieval in 3-month-old infants. *Infant Behavior and Development*, 21 (4), 641–58.

Ruda, M. A., et al. (2000). Altered nocioceptive neuronal circuits after neonatal peripheral inflammation. *Science*, 289, 628–30.

St. Augustine (1991). *Confessions* (Trans. H. Chadwick). New York: Oxford University Press.

Sander, L. (1995). Identity and the experience of specificity in a process of recognition. *Psychoanalytic Dialogues*, 5, 579–93.

Sander, L. (2000). Where are we going in the field of infant mental health? *Infant Mental Health Journal*, 21 (1–2), 5–20.

Schacter, D. (1992). Understanding implicit memory: A cognitive approach. *American Psychologist*, 47 (4), 559–69.

Schacter, D. (1996). *Searching for memory: The brain, the mind, and the past.* New York: Basic Books.

Schofield, L. J., & Abbuhl, S. (1975). The stimulation of insight and self-awareness through body movement exercise. *Journal of Clinical Psychology*, 31, 745–6.

Schore, A. (1991). Early superego development: The emergence of shame and narcissistic affect regulation in the practicing period. *Psychoanalysis and Contemporary Thought*, 14 (2), 187–250.

Schore, A. (2000). Attachment and the regulation of the right brain. *Attachment and Human Development*, 2 (1), 23–47.

Schore, A. (2001a). Effects of a secure attachment on right brain development, affect regulation, and infant mental health. *Infant Mental Health Journal*, 22 (1–2), 7–66.

Schore, A. (2001b). The effects of early relational trauma on right brain development, affect regulation, and infant mental health. *Infant Mental Health Journal*, 22 (1–2), 201–69.

Seitz, J. (2000). The bodily basis of thought. *New Ideas in Psychology*, 18 (1), 23–40.

Siegel, D. (2001). Toward an interpersonal neurobiology of the developing mind: Attachment relationship, "mindsight," and neural integration. *Infant Mental Health Journal*, 22 (1–2), 67–94.

Smyth, J. M., & Pennebaker, J. W. (1999). Sharing one's story. In C. R. Snyder (Ed.), *Coping: The psychology of what works* (pp. 70–89). Oxford: Oxford University Press.

Squire, L., & Knowlton, B. (1995). Memory, hippocampus, and brain systems. In M. S. Gazzaniga (Ed.), *The cognitive neurosciences* (pp. 825–37). Cambridge, MA: MIT Press.

Stern, D. N. (1985). *The interpersonal world of the infant: A view from psychoanalysis and developmental psychology.* New York: Basic Books.

Stern, D. N. (1998). The process of therapeutic change involving implicit knowledge: Some implications of developmental observations for adult psychotherapy. *Infant Mental Health Journal*, 19 (3), 300–8.

Stern, D. N. (2000). Putting time back into our considerations of infant experience: A microdiachronic view. *Infant Mental Health Journal*, 21 (1–2), 21–8.

Terr, L. (1988). What happens to early memories of trauma? A study of twenty children under age of five at the time of documented traumatic events. *Journal of the American Academy of Child and Adolescent Psychiatry*, 27 (1), 96–104.

Terr, L. (1994). *Unchained memories.* New York: Basic Books.

Tomkins, S. (1992). *Affect, imagery, consciousness. Vol. 4. Cognition: Duplication and transformation of information.* New York: Springer.

Tronick, E. (1998). Dyadically expanded states of consciousness and the process of therapeutic change. *Infant Mental Health Journal*, 19 (3), 290–9.

Tucker, D. M. (2001). Motivated anatomy: A core-and-shell model of corticolimbic architecture. In G. Gainotti (Ed.), *Handbook of neuropsychology* (2nd ed.). *Vol. 5. Emotional behavior and its disorders.* Amsterdam: Elsevier.

Tulving, E. (1983). *Elements of episodic memory*. Oxford: Oxford University Press.

van der Kolk, B. (1996a). The body keeps the score: Approaches to the psychobiology of traumatic stress disorder. In B. A. van der Kolk, A. C. McFarlane, & L. Weisaeth (Eds.), *Traumatic stress: The effects of overwhelming experience on mind, body, and society* (pp. 214–41). New York: Guilford Press.

van der Kolk, B. (1996b). Trauma and memory. In B. A. van der Kolk, A. C. McFarlane, & L. Weisaeth (Eds.), *Traumatic stress: The effects of overwhelming experience on mind, body, and society* (pp. 279–302). New York: Guilford Press.

Varela, F. J., Thompson, E., & Rosch, E. (1991). *The embodied mind: Cognitive science and human experiences*. Cambridge, MA: MIT Press.

Vygotsky, L. S. (1978). *Mind in society*. Cambridge, MA: Harvard University Press.

Wheeler, M. A., Struss, D. T., & Tulving, E. (1997). Toward a theory of episodic memory: The frontal lobes and autonoetic consciousness. *Psychological Bulletin*, 121, 331–54.

Winnicott, D. (1971). *Playing and reality*. New York: Basic Books.

Wooten, S. (1995). *Touching the body, reaching the soul: How touch influences the nature of human beings*. Sante Fe, NM: Rosen Method Center Southwest.

# Part III
# Social Development and Communication

Contents

# 9

# Maternal Sensitivity and Infant Temperament in the Formation of Attachment

*Marinus H. van IJzendoorn and Marian J. Bakermans-Kranenburg*

## Introduction

Bowlby (1969, 1973) proposed that all primates are born with an innate bias to become attached to their mother or to another primary attachment figure to whom the infant could stay close, in particular in dangerous territories or stressful circumstances. On the basis of Darwinist theory, Bowlby saw this bias emerging from millions of years of variation and selection of behavioral systems in the environment of evolutionary adaptedness: proximity to a protective caregiver results in an increase in the chances of survival. He thus credited the attachment behavioral system with the same evolutionary value as, for instance, the need for food. However, individual differences in the quality of the attachment relationship with the primary attachment figure do exist. Already in her Uganda study, Mary Ainsworth (1967) suggested that parental sensitivity may be considered the crucial

The work on this chapter was facilitated by a Fellowship from the Netherlands Institute for Advanced Study in the Humanities and Social Sciences (NIAS) for Marinus H. van IJzendoorn.

factor in the development of secure or insecure attachments. As an alternative, infant temperament has been advanced as linked to the quality of attachment (see Vaughn & Bost, 1999). Infant temperament may affect interaction and is a plausible co-determinant of the formation of attachment security.

In this chapter, the thesis will be defended that parental sensitivity shapes the child's attachment security and is an important causal factor in the development of the infant–parent attachment relationship. Nevertheless, much remains to be explained by other parenting, contextual, and constitutional factors. A role for temperament as a co-determining factor appears completely compatible with the tenets of attachment theory, which always implied the reciprocal nature of infants' first tie to their parents (Bowlby, 1969). We will argue, however, that the empirical evidence is still insufficient to document the causal role of temperament in the development of attachment security (Sroufe, 1985; Vaughn & Bost, 1999).

In investigating the relative contributions of sensitivity and temperament to the formation of attachment relationships, we will rely mainly on the outcomes of a series of recent meta-analyses in order to make sense of the complicated research literature in this area. Vaughn and Bost (1999) have discussed the association between attachment and temperament in a narrative way. The current theoretical review integrates several separately published meta-analyses on specific aspects of the association between attachment and temperament. Meta-analysis is the quantitative analysis and synthesis of a series of studies in a specific domain (Cooper & Hedges, 1994; Mullen, 1989). Traditional, narrative reviews sometimes produce rather vague and disappointing statements, such as the following: "Taken together, these studies offer some suggestion that B group infants are more sociable . . . although this difference is not highly reliable, since more than one investigator has failed to find this effect" (Lamb, Thompson, Gardner, & Charnov, 1985). In any interesting area of research, studies supporting a certain hypothesis will be mixed with studies showing null results or even negative evidence. The narrative reviewer will easily be perplexed by the multitude of seemingly diverging findings and conclude that no firm conclusions can be drawn – except, of course, the unsurprising statement that more research is needed.

Meta-analysis has advantages over narrative reviews or single empirical studies in evaluating theoretical claims and in bringing persistent controversies to a satisfactory conclusion. Especially in domains in which small samples provide insufficient power for statistically reliable conclusions, we have to rely on synthesized study outcomes. The area of attachment research is such a domain in which the time-consuming observational methods prevent investigators from including large numbers of participants.

## Attachment

We will first describe very briefly the well-known procedure to assess infant attachment – the Strange Situation – and the attachment classifications derived from this assessment (Ainsworth, Blehar, Waters, & Wall, 1978), as they are central to the current topic. In the Strange Situation, infants are confronted with three stressful components: a strange environment, interaction with a stranger, and two short separations from the caregiver. This stressful situation elicits attachment behavior and on the basis of infants' reactions to the reunion with the parent or other caregiver three patterns of attachment can be distinguished. Infants who actively seek proximity to their caregivers upon reunion, communicate their feelings of stress and distress openly, and then readily return to exploration are classified as secure (B) in their attachment to that caregiver. Infants who seem nondistressed, and ignore or avoid the caregiver following reunion (although physiological research shows that their arousal during separation is similar to other infants; see Spangler & Grossmann, 1993), are classified as insecure-avoidant (A). Infants who combine strong proximity-seeking and contact-maintaining with contact resistance, or who remain unsoothable, without being able to return to play and explore the environment, are classified insecure-ambivalent (C). The main attachment classifications are divided into several subclassifications (A1, A2, B1, B2, B3, B4, C1, C2; see Ainsworth et al., 1978, for details).

An overview of all American studies with nonclinical samples (21 samples with a total of 1,584 infants) conducted in the years 1977 to 1990 shows that about 67 percent of the infants are classified secure, 21 percent are classified as insecure-avoidant, and 12 percent are classified insecure-ambivalent (van IJzendoorn, Goldberg, Kroonenberg, & Frenkel, 1992). Some children (about 15 percent in typical middle-class samples; van IJzendoorn, Schuengel, & Bakermans-Kranenburg, 1999) show a momentary breakdown of their strategy to deal with the stresses of the Strange Situation procedure by freezing or stilling, or by the display of contradictory behavior patterns (Main & Solomon, 1990). These children receive the additional classification "disorganized" (D), but are also classified as secure, insecure-avoidant, or insecure-resistant, indicating their overall attachment strategy.

## *Sensitivity and attachment*

In Mary Ainsworth's short-term longitudinal field study (Ainsworth, 1967), carried out in 1954–5, she discovered the three (A, B, and C) patterns of attachment in a small sample of 28 infants, and she also found that three antecedents appeared to be especially important: (1) infants of mothers who enjoyed breastfeeding were more often securely attached; (2) when mothers provided much maternal care and took their babies along wherever they went, babies developed secure attachments; (3) mothers who served as good, nonidealizing informants about their babies seemed "to be free enough of preoccupations and anxieties of their own, that they are sensitively perceptive" (pp. 397–8) of their infants' specific expressions of emotions to foster a secure bond. These mothers appeared to enjoy talking about the baby and to be attentive to his or her needs and wishes. The crucial antecedent seemed to be the sensitivity of the mother in perceiving the baby's attachment signals, and the promptness and appropriateness of her responses. The communicative intent of infants' signals has been underlined repeatedly by Butterworth's research (Butterworth, 1998; Franco & Butterworth, 1990, 1996); the mother's adequate response to these signals makes sure that the child feels understood and fosters the dyad's smooth interaction.

The causal role of parental sensitivity in the formation of attachment security is now a firmly established fact, thanks to painstaking and time-consuming efforts on the part of several hundred researchers. Three meta-analyses can be cited to substantiate this suggestion. They provide correlational evidence, experimental evidence, and methodological evidence.

### CORRELATIONAL EVIDENCE

A meta-analysis of 66 studies with more than 4,000 families summarizes the association between parenting and attachment security (DeWolff & van IJzendoorn, 1997). The 66 studies focused on different dimensions of parenting, one of them being "sensitivity," defined as the adequate perception of, and appropriate and prompt response to, infants' attachment signals (Ainsworth et al., 1978). The effect size for the association between sensitivity and attachment was comparable to a correlation of 0.24 ($n$ = 1,099). Other parenting dimensions were also included in the meta-analysis. Through an expert sorting task, the set of studies was divided in several conceptually homogeneous subsets and the combined strength of the associations between these parenting dimensions and attachment was computed. For instance, contiguity of response, that is, the promptness of parental reactions to their infants' signals, appeared to be much less effective in shaping attachment security than sensitive responses ($r$ = 0.10). This was also true of the frequency of physical contact without weighting the quality of the contact ($r$ = 0.09). This points to the importance of carefully distinguishing between sensitivity, on the one hand, and responsivity or contiguity of response, on the other hand, both on the empirical and on the conceptual level. Stronger associations are to be found in domains in which the reciprocal nature of the parent–infant interaction is taken into account, for example synchrony (the extent to which interaction appears to be reciprocal and rewarding for both parent and child) or mutual interactive sequences (positive exchanges where parent and child attend to the same thing). These reciprocal assessments of parenting correlated 0.26 and 0.32, respectively, with attachment security.

Is the correlation of 0.24 for sensitivity and attachment security large enough to support the claim that sensitivity is a crucial factor in the formation of attachment security, or is it disappointingly small? On the basis of a binomial effect size display (BESD; Rosenthal, 1991), it could be argued that the association between sensitivity and attachment is remarkably strong, and theoretically as well as practically of great significance. In medical science and in medical practice, drugs are recommended for the prevention of important diseases on the basis of effect sizes much smaller than the value that we found for the association between attachment and sensitivity. If someone is at risk for cardiovascular diseases, for example, it is considered perfectly rational to take a daily dose of the famous drug aspirin, although the use of aspirin correlates only −0.03 with the occurrence of cardiovascular diseases. It nevertheless leads to thousands of saved lives: using daily doses of aspirin increases the survival percentage of patients at risk from 48.5 percent to 51.5 percent. Three percent represents a substantial increase in absolute numbers of saved lives if we consider it against the background of the huge population at risk (Rosenthal, 1991).

The BESD depicts an effect size ($r$) in terms of the improvement rate that is attributable to the predictor variable. Applying this approach to the association of $r = 0.24$ between sensitivity and attachment, it means that infants whose mothers respond sensitively to their signals improve their chance of developing a secure relationship from 38 percent to 62 percent. In other words, if we manage to increase parental sensitivity, the success rate in enhancing attachment security will be 24 percent. The sensitivity success rate in improving attachment security is eight times larger than that of aspirin in preventing heart attacks. Insecure attachment is not, of course, a lethal disease, but insecurity entails unnecessary strains and stresses to the children involved. In the long run, it may be one of the factors leading to developmental risks. Why do we tend to ignore correlations of 0.24 because of their small size? One of the reasons is that in single empirical studies, medium-size correlations usually show broad confidence boundaries and appear difficult to replicate. We have learned to interpret this type of outcome cautiously, and for good reasons. But we should refrain from generalizing this tendency beyond the single study. Small or medium effect sizes can be important if they are reliable and based on a multitude of replications.

It should also be noted that the association between sensitivity and attachment is not restricted to western industrialized societies with specific western family constellations and childrearing practices. In fact, the first empirical evidence for the relation between sensitivity and attachment came from Ainsworth's (1967) Ganda study, and later cross-cultural data from nonwestern cultures strongly supports the finding as well (van IJzendoorn & Sagi, 1999). In African cultures like the Gusii (Kermoian & Leiderman, 1986), the !Kung (Konner, 1977), and the Efe (Morelli & Tronick, 1991), the relation between attachment and sensitivity has been documented. The same goes for studies in Beijing (China; Ping & Zhaolan, 1996), Tokyo (Japan; Durrett, Otaki, & Richards, 1984; Vereijken, 1996), and in Indonesia (Zevalkink, 1997). In fact, only one cross-cultural study (carried out in Sapporo, Japan) did not find the predicted association between sensitive parenting and attachment security (Nakagawa, Lamb, & Miyake, 1992), but several problems in the design of this study preclude any firm conclusions regarding the cross-cultural validity of the sensitivity hypothesis (van IJzendoorn & Sagi, 1999, 2001).

## EXPERIMENTAL EVIDENCE

In the past few years several experimental intervention studies on attachment have been published that provide evidence for the causal nature of the link between sensitivity and attachment.

Intervention studies can be distinguished on the basis of their approach. Some interventions are directed at parental sensitivity, that is, at the behavioral level. Other interventions focus on the parents' representation of attachment, in order to pave the way for subsequent behavioral changes. Interventions also differ in the amount of social support offered to the parent (see Egeland, Weinfield, Bosquet, & Cheng, 2000; Juffer, Bakermans-Kranenburg, & van IJzendoorn, in press). An example of the behavioral approach is the Anisfeld, Casper, Nozyce, and Cunningham (1990) study. They provided mothers from deprived immigrant families with soft baby carriers to carry their babies during the first months. The idea was to promote close physical contact between parent and infant. Carrying the baby leads to prompt responses to attachment signals such as crying behavior and would thereby stimulate feelings of security in the infant. The authors included a control group of mothers who received plastic baby seats. The outcome was dramatic: in the experimental group, 83 percent of the infants appeared to be securely attached at 1 year, whereas in the control group only 38 percent were secure.

The second approach is often modeled after Fraiberg's (Fraiberg, Adelson, & Shapiro, 1975) infant–mother psychotherapy in which the parent is enabled to discuss her "ghosts" of the past, that is, her childhood experiences with insecure attachments, and their influence on the interactions with the child. The intervention study of Lieberman, Weston, and Pawl (1991) is an example of this approach. The intervenors provided support and therapy for the mothers during a year, with the goal of enhancing their empathy for the affective and developmental needs of their children. The mothers came from deprived immigrant families. Insecure dyads were randomly assigned to intervention and control group. The intervention started immediately after the Strange Situation assessment at 1 year of age, and continued throughout the second year of life with unstructured home visits taking place weekly. After a year, security of attachment was assessed again. There were no group differences on attachment security.

In a recent meta-analysis, we were able to trace 61 published papers presenting 75 interventions (Bakermans-Kranenburg, van IJzendoorn, & Juffer, 2003). Intervention effects on sensitivity were available for 81 studies, involving 7,636 families. The effect size *d* or standardized difference between the sensitivity means of the experimental and control groups was 0.44. This effect size is comparable to a correlation of about 0.22. Intervention effects on attachment quality were reported in 29 studies, involving 1,503 families. For infant attachment security the effect size was 0.19

in favor of the experimental groups, comparable to a correlation of 0.10.

In 24 intervention studies (with 1,280 families), both maternal sensitivity and children's attachment security were assessed as outcome measures. Our hypothesis was that more effective sensitivity interventions would also be somewhat more effective in enhancing children's attachment security, due to the association between sensitivity and attachment. If maternal sensitivity is an important determinant of infant attachment, stimulating sensitivity should lead to changes in attachment security, and parallel changes in sensitivity and attachment should be expected. The association between sensitivity and attachment effect sizes indeed confirms the hypothesis of a causal link between sensitivity and attachment security. In particular, in the subset of randomized studies (19 studies), we found that sensitivity interventions with larger effect sizes ($d > 0.40$) were also most effective in enhancing infant attachment security ($d = 0.35$). Less effective sensitivity interventions did not manage to bring about changes in attachment security. Thus, interventions that appeared to be more effective in enhancing maternal sensitivity were more effective in enhancing children's attachment security, in particular in randomized studies.

In general, attachment insecurity is more difficult to change than maternal insensitivity, as is documented by the differences in effect sizes for sensitivity and attachment. However, if an intervention is rather successful in enhancing maternal sensitivity, this change appears to be accompanied by a parallel positive change in infant attachment security. Therefore, the correlational evidence for a causal relation between sensitivity and attachment security is now corroborated by experimental evidence as well.

## METHODOLOGICAL EVIDENCE

The correlational and experimental evidence for the causal relation between sensitivity and attachment discussed so far is based mainly on the Strange Situation procedure for assessing attachment security. Infant temperament certainly seems to be associated with attachment behaviors in the Strange Situation procedure, that is, negative reactivity will be related to more fussing and crying in stressful situations such as the Strange Situation (Vaughn & Bost, 1999). But this observation leaves open the question whether temperament is causally related to attachment classifications or attachment security. In earlier studies on Strange Situation classifications and temperament, negative reactivity appeared to be related to the split between the subclassifications A1/A2/B1/B2 vs. B3/B4/C1/C2 (Vaughn & Bost, 1999), but it was only weakly related to the secure–insecure split (A1/A2/C1/C2 vs. B1/B2/B3/B4). The empirical evidence for a causal role of temperament for security or insecurity of attachment as assessed with the Strange Situation procedure appears to be insufficient and inconsistent (Vaughn & Bost, 1999). As an example, Kemp (1987) found that avoidant children were described by their mothers as temperamentally easier than were secure and resistant children. In another study, however, the avoidant children were found to be described as the more temperamentally difficult children (Frodi, Bridges, & Schonk, 1989), as in van den Boom's (1988) study on irritable infants, where the avoidant category was overrepresented. In one study the prototypical secure (B3) children were perceived by their mothers as temperamentally more difficult than other secure and avoidant infants (Rieser-Danner, Roggman, & Langlois, 1987).

As an alternative to the traditional laboratory assessment of attachment security, the home-based Attachment Q-Sort (AQS) has been developed (Vaughn & Waters, 1990; Waters & Deane, 1985). A meta-analysis on the Attachment Q-Sort also points to the more powerful role of parental sensitivity (vs. infant temperament) in the formation of attachment relationships. The Attachment Q-Sort consists of 90 behavioral descriptions that have to be sorted from very adequate to very inadequate descriptions of children's attachment behaviors displayed during 3 or more hours of home observations. The Q-sort of a target child is correlated with a criterion Q-sort, which is the Q-sort of an ideally securely attached child as perceived by experts (Vaughn & Waters, 1990). Originally, independent observers were meant to sort the behavioral descriptions, but recently parents have also been asked to complete the sorting.

In a recent meta-analysis on seven studies with the Attachment Q-Sort descriptions sorted by trained observers, attachment security appeared to be strongly related to parental sensitivity. The combined effect size amounted to a correlation of 0.50 ($n$ = 397). However, in 13 studies with the Attachment Q-Sort sorted by the mother rather than a trained observer, the AQS showed a weaker association with maternal sensitivity, $r = 0.27$ ($n = 845$). Furthermore, the observer Attachment Q-Sort (5 studies, $n = 285$) correlated −0.19 with temperament, i.e., negative reactivity, whereas the mother Attachment Q-Sort correlated −0.31 with negative reactivity (12 studies, $n = 890$; van IJzendoorn, Vereijken, & Riksen-Walraven, in press).

The observer Attachment Q-Sort thus confirms the association between sensitivity and attachment, and it also clearly shows discriminant validity in its relation to parental sensitivity and to infant temperament. The correlation with temperament (0.19) is modest, but somewhat higher than correlations of temperament with the categorical Strange Situation, due to the fact that the Attachment Q-Sort is a continuous measure, blurring the boundaries between secure and insecure attachment classifications.

In the case of the mother version of the Attachment Q-Sort, with mothers sorting the behavioral descriptions of their own child, discriminant validity is lacking. In the eyes of mothers, attachment security is in fact more strongly related to temperament than it is related to sensitivity (van IJzendoorn et al., in press). This finding suggests that naive observers who are asked to report on the attachment relationship with their own child are not able to differentiate between attachment and temperament. Insensitive mothers are inclined to rate their children as secure, presumably because they are not able to observe subtle signs of insecurity in their own child (DeWolff & van IJzendoorn, 1997). The observer Attachment Q-Sort points to a more important role of parental sensitivity than of infant temperament in the development of the attachment relationship. These results confirm the link between parental sensitivity and security of attachment as assessed with the Strange Situation procedure, using a different methodology.

So, to summarize, numerous studies in many parts of the world have examined the association between maternal sensitivity and security of the infant–mother attachment relationship; together they show that this association is real. Intervention studies demonstrate that enhanced maternal sensitivity tends to go together with higher percentages of infant–mother attachment security, providing experimental evidence for the link between sensitivity and attachment. Studies that did not use the standard Strange Situation procedure to measure attachment but used the Attachment Q-Sort, involving prolonged home-based observations, confirm the results of studies with the Strange Situation: they indicate a strong relationship between parental sensitivity and attachment security scores.

## *Parent vs. child influences on attachment distributions*

A different approach of weighing the influence of parenting and infant temperament makes use of the distributions of attachment classifications in various samples. A meta-analytic comparison of attachment security in samples with problematic parents and in samples with children with problems is of interest for the question whether parental or child characteristics are decisive for the quality of infant–parent attachment relationships (van IJzendoorn et al., 1992).

This comparison shows that in families with problematic parents or parents in adverse circumstances, for example depressive parents, the percentage of securely attached children is much lower than in families with handicapped children, for example children with serious physical or mental malfunctions. Furthermore, samples with handicapped infants show similar percentages of secure infants compared to samples with healthy infants. One might argue that communicative handicaps in the parents such as depression are incomparable to physical communication barriers in the handicapped children. In the latter case, however, the comparison is based only on a difference in the children (handicapped or not).

Healthy parents thus appear to be able to compensate for their children's handicaps by sensitive parental behavior, whereas healthy children are not able to compensate for their parents' problems (van IJzendoorn et al., 1992). Disorganized attachment is quite frequent in groups of handicapped children, but even when we account for the occurrence of disorganization, similar numbers of securely attached children can be found in the groups in which the parent is free of serious troubles and the child is handicapped or not. In groups with troubled mothers, however, the percentage of securely attached children is dramatically lower. Further correlational and experimental studies are necessary to document the boundaries within which parental sensitivity is still able to compensate for temperamental difficulties and other communicative handicaps in the infants.

Infant attachment classifications have also been linked with parental attachment representations. In these studies parental attachment representations were assessed with the Adult Attachment Interview (AAI; George, Kaplan, & Main, 1985; Main, Kaplan, & Cassidy, 1985). The AAI is a semi-structured interview that probes alternately for descriptions of the past relationships with parents, specific supportive or contradictory memories, and descriptions of current relationships with parents. An important criterion for the classification is the interview's coherence. Coherence is defined in terms of Grice's (1975) maxims of quality, quantity, relevance, and manner. Coding leads to three classifications, indicating three types of attachment representations: insecure-dismissing, secure-autonomous, and insecure-preoccupied. *Dismissing* adults often offer a very positive evaluation of their attachment experiences, without being able to illustrate their positive evaluations with concrete events demonstrating secure interaction. This makes the narrative of dismissing adults incoherent. *Autonomous* adults are able to describe attachment-related experiences coherently, whether these experiences were negative (e.g., parental rejection or overinvolvement) or positive. *Preoccupied* adults are still very much involved and preoccupied with their past attachment experiences and are therefore not able to describe them coherently. Passivity and vagueness may characterize their biography, or they may express anger when they discuss the present relationship with their parents.

The first 18 studies (with 854 families involved) on the correspondence between infant attachment and adult attachment have been included in a meta-analysis (van IJzendoorn, 1995). The association between infant and parent attachment security appeared to be strong and comparable to a correlation of 0.47. It is of interest that in several studies parental attachment representation was assessed before the infant's birth, with the assessment of infant attachment behavior in the Strange Situation about 15 months later (Benoit & Parker, 1994; Fonagy, Steele, & Steele, 1991; Radojevic, 1994; Ward & Carlson, 1995). These studies did *not* yield smaller effect sizes than the other studies, suggesting an overriding importance of the parent's representation of attachment, and at most a marginal effect of the infant's input on the developing attachment relationship. Because parental attachment representations have been shown to be unrelated to adult temperament (Crowell & Treboux, 1995; DeHaas, Bakermans-Kranenburg, & van IJzendoorn, 1994), the association between parent and infant attachment cannot be explained by shared temperamental characteristics. Parents appear to be more powerful in shaping the bond with their infants, and they may be able to override the influence of infant characteristics such as temperament.

## INFANT–MOTHER/INFANT–FATHER ATTACHMENT

In 1991, Nathan Fox and his co-workers reported a strong relation between infant–mother and infant–father attachment security across 11 studies, amounting to a correlation of 0.31 (Fox, Kimmerly, & Schafer, 1991). This finding has often been used to demonstrate the temperamental basis of attachment: if quality of attachment is relationship-specific, it should show only weak associations across relationships. Otherwise, the *child's* temperament may be the cause of the similarity of the infant's attachments with his or her two parents.

A replication and extension of the meta-analysis on infant–mother/infant–father attachment (van IJzendoorn & DeWolff, 1997) yielded a considerably weaker association in the old set of studies as well as in the extended set, including some new studies. In 14 studies on more than 900 families, a correlation of 0.17 between infant–mother and infant–father attachment was found. More importantly, there is a simple and elegant explanation for some overlap between infant–mother and infant–father attachment security. We conducted a meta-analysis concerning the correspondence between the attachment representations (as assessed with the AAI) of husbands and wives within the same family. In a set of five studies ($n$ = 226), we found a significant overlap between husbands' and wives' attachment security (van IJzendoorn & Bakermans-Kranenburg, 1996). Birds of a feather indeed seem to flock together. Assortative mating or the therapeutic influence of a partner may cause similarity in attachment between father and mother within the same family. The correspondence between husbands' and wives' attachment security may easily be translated into some correspondence on the level of the child's attachment with his or her mother and father in that same family. The family is a system of interrelated, intertwined relationships (Cox & Paley, 1997; Hinde & Stevenson-Hinde, 1990), and fathers may also influence the infant–mother bond through their marital attachment relationship (van IJzendoorn & DeWolff, 1997). Recently, good marital support was found to be directly linked to maternal sensitivity in a German study (Pauli-Pott, Mertesacker, Bade, Bauer, & Beckmann, 2000). Temperament may also explain part of the rather modest correspondence between infant–mother and infant–father attachment, but empirical evidence to substantiate this conjecture is lacking. The temperament interpretation, therefore, remains speculative.

## Temperament and Sensitivity

Patterns of caregiving may modify the relations between temperament and attachment (Belsky & Rovine, 1987; Sroufe, 1985), thus leaving no room for a direct association between temperament and attachment. Studies on the association between infant negative emotionality and maternal sensitivity consistently obtain inconsistent results (see Crockenberg, 1986; Pauli-Pott et al., 2000). A number of studies report that high irritability is linked to lower maternal sensitivity, but about the same number of studies suggest the contrary, namely, that temperamentally difficult children have more sensitive mothers. There appears to be no "ideal" temperament independent of context or circumstances. This is convincingly illustrated by DeVries's (1984, 1987) study of temperament among Masai pastoralists in Kenya (see also Hrdy, 1999). DeVries arrived in Kenya at the height of a 10-year drought, when children and infants were the first in a population to starve. During this particular famine, infant mortality rose to 50 percent. Of 15 newborn infants registered in the initial study population, he could locate only six by the end of his study; all others had died. Only one of the six infants with difficult, "fussy" temperaments had died, whereas five of the seven with "easy" temperaments had done so. In this case temperamental difficultness was of vital importance, presumably to attract mother's attention and elicit her reaction to the infant's hunger signals. Hrdy (1999) also points to an anthropological study among the Eipo in Papua New Guinea (Schiefenhövel & Schiefenhövel, 1978) with similar import, quoting the story of a woman who during pregnancy repeatedly and openly stated that she would not accept another baby girl. She had already one daughter and no son, and sons were strongly preferred. (It has been reported that between 1974 and 1978, 41 percent of all live-born Eipo infants were eliminated. Of 20 infants not kept, 15 were female.) Prior to birth, the mother mentally prepared herself not to form any bond with the child, to remain distant at birth. She gave birth to a particularly healthy-looking girl.

> Without cutting the umbilical cord, leaving the placenta still attached, the mother wrapped the newborn in fern leaves laced with rope made from lianas. For a long while, she sat thoughtfully near the bundle. The infant screamed lustily, struggling to live, her pudgy hands and feet bursting out through the leaves. Eventually, the mother departed, leaving the infant where she lay. Yet she did not throw the bundle into the bushes as would be typical in an Eipo infanticide. Two hours later the mother returned, cut the umbilical cord, and took up the baby. Almost apologetically she explained: *This daughter was too strong.*
>
> (***Hrdy, 1999, pp. 455–6; italics hers***)

Hrdy (1999) concludes that under duress, infants do well to toe a fine line between signaling their distress and appearing too needy. Though a certain quantum of distress is likely to trigger a succoring response, signaling distress could prove risky for a baby whose mother is ambivalent. Instead of being classified as "vigorous" or eliciting a rush of compassion, a complaining baby might inspire an aversive reaction in a mother who perceives her baby as overly demanding.

The situations described above can be considered extreme. Nevertheless, in western societies, fruitful hypotheses may also do well to include specific circumstances or characteristics of the mother–child dyad. As an example, Pauli-Pott et al. (2000) found no direct effect of either maternal depression or infant negative emotionality on maternal sensitivity, but the interaction of the two risk factors was highly significant: depressed mothers of temperamentally difficult infants were very insensitive.

Studies may also go beyond the dyadic perspective and include context factors such as social support and the network of attachment relationships as moderators of the influence of sensitivity and temperament on attachment security. Crockenberg (1981) was the first to show the possibility of a difficult neonatal temperament leading to insecure attachment if combined with moderately or low sensitive parenting and low social support, whereas the same difficult temperament would lead to secure attachment if combined with sensitive parenting or with high social support. In fact, Crockenberg's (1981) study confirms the idea that sensitive parenting may compensate the influence of a difficult temperament, and that the influence of insensitive parenting may be compensated by adequate social support. Van den Boom's (1988) intervention study with mothers of irritable infants emphasizes the same contention: intervention mothers, who received adequate training and support, were more sensitive after the intervention, and the distribution of attachment classifications of their children was similar to that of normal groups.

A recent study of attachment in the Israeli kibbutzim shows the need to take the social context into account most clearly (Sagi et al., 1997). In all kibbutzim, children spend a large part of the day in special "infant houses" under the care of professional caregivers; some kibbutzim, however, kept until recently to the practice of communal sleeping as well. In a comparison between the two types of kibbutzim, the distributions of mothers' attachment representations as assessed with the AAI appeared quite similar. However, only 55 percent of the children from the communal kibbutzim were securely attached to their mothers, whereas 80 percent of the children from the family-based kibbutzim appeared to be secure. In the kibbutzim where the children slept at home, the regular correspondence between mothers' and infants' attachment was found (76 percent). In communal kibbutzim the correspondence was only 40 percent, intergenerational transmission of attachment being the exception rather than the rule. Although children from communal kibbutzim may experience sensitive care during the afternoon, during the night their attachment signals remain unanswered. The kibbutz study shows that intergenerational transmission of attachment is dependent on the social context and culture-specific childrearing arrangements. The mother–child dyad is embedded in a wider social context, which may facilitate or inhibit parents' sensitive interactions with their children.

## *Psychophysiological studies*

The psychophysiological studies of temperament and attachment are most impressive in terms of designs and assessments (for an extensive discussion of different temperament approaches, see Vaughn & Bost, 1999; for an overview of psychophysiological measures in the study of attachment, see Fox & Card, 1999). From a methodological perspective, it is important to test whether the Strange Situation procedure does impose the intended stress on children who are classified as avoidant. Research utilizing heart rate or cortisol has attempted to answer this question. Sroufe and Waters (1977) found that all infants showed increased heart rates upon separation, which remained elevated during reunion. Avoidant infants showed an increase in heart rate from the beginning of the separation until long into the reunion, even though they outwardly appeared unaffected by the separation. Gunnar, Mangelsdorf, Larson, and Hertsgaard (1989) measured salivary cortisol as a stress indicator at home, in the laboratory immediately before, and immediately after the Strange Situation. There were no differences among attachment groups in either cortisol level or the degree of cortisol change.

Although psychophysiological studies should be considered the most sophisticated tests of a relation between temperament and attachment, they yielded disappointingly little evidence for a link between temperament and attachment classification. Temperamental traits have been operationalized with psychophysiological indicators, ranging from cortisol assessments (Gunnar et al., 1989) and electroencephalograms (EEG; Dawson, Klinger, Panagiotides, & Spieker, 1992) to several dimensions of infant heart rate (Calkins & Fox, 1992; Izard, Porges, Simons, & Haynes, 1991). In fact, all studies showed nonsignificant results in testing the crucial multivariate difference between the three main attachment classifications or between the secure and insecure classifications. The Izard et al. (1991) study showed some significant univariate associations between infant cardiac activity and secure vs. insecure infant attachment classification, but no significant relation at the multivariate level was found. The authors therefore suggested cautious treatment of univariate differences (p. 435). They only found significant multivariate effects for the regressions of cardiac activity on a continuous measure for attachment security, but continuous assessments may artificially enhance the chance of getting significant associations between temperament and attachment.

Calkins and Fox (1992) also failed to find a main effect for earlier heart-rate indicators and later attachment classifications. The study is one of the most elegant investigations into the complicated area of attachment and temperament to date. Because of the large number of assessments there is, however, a risk of capitalizing on chance in testing all possible associations. For example, they report two significant relations between a measure of temperament (one observational and one parent-report measure) and infant attachment classification. These findings are the only significant tests out of a total of 60 statistical tests involving the relation between temperament (observations, maternal perceptions, and psychophysiological indicators) and attachment (A, B, C; and B vs. non-B). Replications seem necessary to confirm these findings. Calkins and Fox (1992) also found an interaction effect between the infants' reactivity to frustration at 5 months and attachment classification at 14 months, predicting inhibition at 24 months. The interaction effect is somewhat difficult to interpret: infants classified as insecure-resistant at 14 months who had not cried to a frustration procedure at 5 months were the most inhibited at 24 months.

Because in the Calkins and Fox (1992) study inhibition has been measured at a later point in time (24 months) than attachment classification (14 months), one may argue that the interaction effect shows the influence of attachment security on inhibition, or is at least not incompatible with this reversed interpretation. In the same vein, Nachmias, Gunnar, Mangelsdorf, Parritz, and Buss (1996) found no association between behavioral inhibition and security of attachment, but they did find that children with higher behavioral inhibition had higher postsession cortisol levels if they were also insecure. Security of attachment can thus be viewed as a buffer against stress or a moderator of initial physiological disposition. The influence of attachment

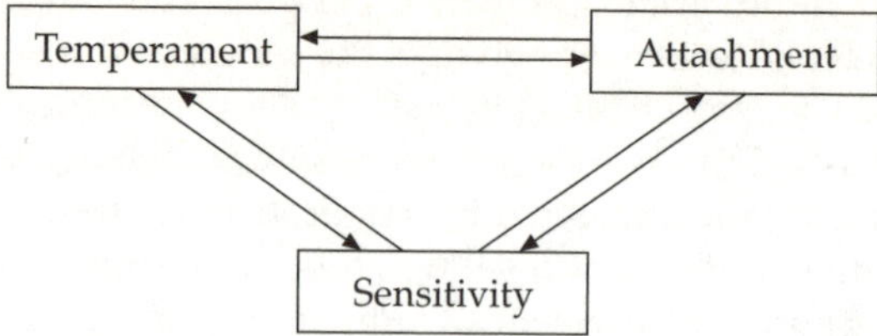


**Figure 9.1** Possible relationships between temperament and attachment.

security on later inhibition, however, does not seem to be compatible with the hypothesis that attachment security is mainly determined by temperament (Kagan, 1995). In figure 9.1 the possible relations between temperament and attachment are presented.

Considering the myriad possible relations, we suggest that further studies on attachment and temperament should try to test alternative directions, including the unexpected influence of attachment on those dimensions of temperament that are associated with the child's interpersonal relationships.

## Why Sensitivity?

Having reviewed the empirical evidence for the idea that maternal sensitivity is a more important factor in the formation of attachment relationships than infant temperament, we may step aside for a moment of reflection on the "why" of the importance of parental sensitivity. In this context we note that evolution plays a role not only in the level of the child's innate attachment system, but also in the level of the parenting system, that is, the parental inclination to respond to the child's quest for protection.

An individual's lifetime reproductive success is dependent on the survival and well-being of the offspring, and is thus boosted by parental sensitivity (although not without limits; see Trivers, 1974). In the ethological literature this innate bias to parent has been called parental investment (Trivers, 1972, 1985) – as parent and child share half of their genes and children generally survive their parent and have offspring of their own, parents are intrinsically motivated to respond to their child's signals. However, the circumstances can compel the parent to be selective. As reported among the Eipo, child survival (parental sensitivity) sometimes depends on a characteristic as trivial as the child's being male or female (which right now also appears to be the case in the People's Republic of China). The child's chances of survival as perceived by the parent may also play a role. In a longitudinal study of seven twin pairs born at extremely low birthweights, Mann (1992) found that 8 months after the twins were brought home from the hospital, all mothers were directing more attention to the healthier twin of the pair, even though in several of these cases remedial care for the sicker of the two twins was also provided (see also Hrdy, 1999). The infant's temperament may be an important factor for the child's survival, but, as mentioned before, there appears to be no ideal temperament independent of context. In some circumstances "easy" children may provoke their parent's sensitive responsiveness, whereas in other circumstances a baby's frequent crying may enhance the chance of a parent's adequate response. On the other hand, one may note that temperament – or actually the diversity of existing temperaments – has evolutionary adaptive value, too, resulting in surviving offspring in diverse conditions of life.

## Conclusion

Several meta-analyses covering hundreds of studies on thousands of participants support the idea that maternal sensitivity is a more important factor in the formation of attachment relationships than infant temperament. However, maternal sensitivity does not provide an exhaustive explanation for individual differences in attachment.

In the current review, mainly direct influences of temperament on the formation of attachment relationships have been discussed. This focus mirrors the state of the empirical research in this area. Several meta-analyses document the orthogonality of temperament and attachment as independent dimensions of children's development. Nevertheless, important questions remain unanswered. In figure 9.1, indirect influences in both directions have been depicted. We propose that in future research these indirect influences should be addressed. In this respect, the following issues are crucial:

1 The development of attachment as well as temperament may be determined in part by similar parenting behaviors or styles.
2 The child's temperament may stimulate or even provoke parental behavior that affects the formation of infant–parent attachment.

3 The child's temperament may influence his or her perception of parental behavior, and indirectly the bond with the parent.
4 The infant-attachment relationship should not only be considered a consequence of parental behavior or children's temperament; attachment may also affect parental interactive behaviors as well as the development and expression of children's temperament.
5 Parental attachment and parental temperament may have to be added to the set of pertinent factors in modeling the complex interactions between attachment, parenting, and temperament.

The closure of the debate on direct influences of temperament on attachment, and the recognition of their separate and unique developmental domains, may open new avenues to a fruitful research program on the interplay between parenting, attachment, and temperament.

In sum, the causal role of maternal sensitivity in the formation of the infant–mother attachment relationship is a strongly corroborated finding. Correlational, experimental, and cross-cultural studies have replicated the association between sensitivity and attachment numerous times, and through different measures and designs. In general, the maternal impact on the infant–mother attachment relationship has been shown to be much larger than the impact of child characteristics such as temperament. During the first few years after birth, parents are more powerful than their children in shaping the child–parent bond. Future research should focus on indirect and reciprocal influences between attachment and temperament.

## REFERENCES

Ainsworth, M. D. (1967). *Infancy in Uganda: Infant care and the growth of love.* Baltimore: Johns Hopkins University Press.

Ainsworth, M. D., Blehar, M. C., Waters, E., & Wall, S. (1978). *Patterns of attachment: A psychological study of the Strange Situation.* Hillsdale, NJ: Erlbaum.

Anisfeld, E., Casper, V., Nozyce, M., & Cunningham, N. (1990). Does infant carrying promote attachment? An experimental study of the effects of increased physical contact on the development of attachment. *Child Development*, 61, 1617–27.

Bakermans-Kranenburg, M. J., van IJzendoorn, M. H., & Juffer, F. (2003). Less is more: Meta-analyses of sensitivity and attachment interventions in early childhood. *Psychological Bulletin*, 129, 195–215.

Belsky J., & Rovine, M. (1987). Temperament and attachment security in the Strange Situation: An empirical rapprochement. *Child Development*, 58, 787–95.

Benoit, D., & Parker, K. C. H. (1994). Stability and transmission of attachment across three generations. *Child Development*, 65, 1444–56.

Bowlby, J. (1969). *Attachment and loss. Vol. 1. Attachment.* London: Penguin.

Bowlby, J. (1973). *Attachment and loss. Vol. 2. Separation: Anxiety and anger.* London: Penguin.

Butterworth, G. E. (1998). Origins of joint visual attention in infancy. *Monographs of the Society for Research in Child Development*, 63 (4), 144–66.

Calkins, S. D., & Fox, N. A. (1992). The relations among infant temperament, security of attachment, and behavioral inhibition at twenty-four months. *Child Development*, 63, 1456–72.

Cooper, H., & Hedges, L. V. (1994). *The handbook of research synthesis.* New York: Russell Sage.

Cox, M. J., & Paley, B. (1997). Families as systems. *Annual Review of Psychology*, 48, 243–67.

Crockenberg, S. B. (1981). Infant irritability, mother responsiveness, and social support influences on the security of infant–mother attachment. *Child Development*, 52, 857–65.

Crockenberg, S. B. (1986). Are temperamental differences in babies associated with predictable differences in caregiving? *New Directions in Child Development*, 31, 53–73.

Crowell, J. A., & Treboux, D. (1995). A review of adult attachment measures: Implications for theory and research. *Social Development*, 4, 294–327.

Dawson, G., Klinger, L. G., Panagiotides, H., & Spieker, S. (1992). Infants of mothers with depressive symptoms: Electroencephalographic and behavioral findings related to attachment status. *Development and Psychopathology*, 4, 67–80.

DeHaas, M. A., Bakermans-Kranenburg, M. J., & van IJzendoorn, M. H. (1994). The Adult Attachment Interview and questionnaires for attachment style, temperament, and memories of parental behavior. *Journal of Genetic Psychology*, 155, 471–86.

DeVries, M. W. (1984). Temperament and infant mortality among the Masai of East Africa. *American Journal of Psychiatry*, 141, 1189–93.

DeVries, M. W. (1987). Cry babies, culture and catastrophe: Infant temperament among the Masai. In N. Scheper-Hughes (Ed.), *Anthropological approaches to the treatment and maltreatment of children* (pp. 165–86). Dordrecht: Reidel.

DeWolff, M. S., & van IJzendoorn, M. H. (1997). Sensitivity and attachment: A meta-analysis on parental antecedents of infant attachment. *Child Development*, 68, 571–91.

Durrett, M. E., Otaki, M., & Richards, P. (1984). Attachment and the mother's perception of support from the father. *International Journal of Behavioral Development*, 7, 167–76.

Egeland, B., Weinfield, N. S., Bosquet, M., & Cheng, V. K. (2000). Remembering, repeating, and working through: Lessons from attachment-based interventions. In J. D. Osofsky & H. E. Fitzgerald (Eds.), *Handbook of infant mental health. Vol. 4. Infant mental health in groups at high risk* (pp. 35–89). New York: Wiley.

Fonagy, P., Steele, H., & Steele, M. (1991). Maternal representations of attachment during pregnancy predict the organization of infant–mother attachment at one year of age. *Child Development*, 62, 891–905.

Fox, N. A., & Card, J. A. (1999). Psychophysiological measures in the study of attachment. In J. Cassidy & P. Shaver (Eds.), *Handbook of attachment: Theory, research, and clinical applications* (pp. 226–45). New York: Guilford Press.

Fox, N. A., Kimmerly, N. L., & Schafer, W. D. (1991). Attachment to mother/attachment to father: A meta-analysis. *Child Development*, 62, 210–25.

Fraiberg, S., Adelson, E., & Shapiro, V. (1975). Ghosts in the nursery: A psychoanalytic approach to the problems of impaired infant–mother relationships. *Journal of the American Academy of Child Psychiatry*, 14, 387–423.

Franco, F., & Butterworth, G. E. (1990, August). Effects of social variables on the production of infant pointing. Poster presented at the Fourth European Conference on Developmental Psychology, University of Stirling, Scotland.

Franco, F., & Butterworth, G. E. (1996). Pointing and social awareness: Declaring and requesting in the second year of life. *Journal of Child Language*, 23, 307–36.

Frodi, A., Bridges, L., & Schonk, S. (1989). Maternal correlates of infant temperament ratings and of infant–mother attachment: A longitudinal study. *Infant Mental Health Journal*, 10, 273–89.

George, C., Kaplan, N., & Main, M. (1985). Adult Attachment Interview. Unpublished manuscript, University of California, Berkeley.

Grice, P. (1975). Logic and conversation. In P. Cole & J. L. Moran (Eds.), *Syntax and semantics. Vol. 3. Speech acts* (pp. 41–58). New York: Academic Press.

Gunnar, M. R., Mangelsdorf, S., Larson, M., & Hertsgaard, L. (1989). Attachment, temperament, and adrenocortical activity in infancy: A study of psychoendocrine regulation. *Developmental Psychology*, 25, 355–63.

Hinde, R. A., & Stevenson-Hinde, J. (1990). Attachment: Biological, cultural and individual desiderata. *Human Development*, 33, 62–72.

Hrdy, S. B. (1999). *Mother Nature: Maternal instincts and how they shape the human species*. New York: Ballantine.

Izard, C. E., Porges, S. W., Simons, R. F., & Haynes, O. M. (1991). Infant cardiac activity: Developmental changes and relations with attachment. *Developmental Psychology*, 27, 432–9.

Juffer, F., Bakermans-Kranenburg, M. J., & van IJzendoorn, M. H. (in press). Enhancing children's socio-emotional development: A review of intervention studies. In D. M. Teti (Ed.), *Handbook of research methods in developmental psychology*. Cambridge, MA: Blackwell.

Kagan, J. (1995). On attachment. *Harvard Review of Psychiatry*, 3, 104–6.

Kemp, V. (1987). Mothers' perception of children's temperament and mother–child attachment. *Scholarly Inquiry for Nursing Practice*, 1, 51–68.

Kermoian, R., & Leiderman, P. H. (1986). Infant attachment to mother and child caretaker in an East African community. Special Issue: Cross-cultural human development. *International Journal of Behavioral Development*, 9, 455–69.

Konner, M. (1977). Infancy among the Kalahari Desert San. In P. H. Leiderman, S. R. Tulkin, & A. Rosenfeld (Eds.), *Culture and infancy: Variations in the human experience* (pp. 287–328). New York: Academic Press.

Lamb, M. E., Thompson, R. A., Gardner, W., & Charnov, E. L. (1985). *Infant–mother attachment: The origins and developmental significance of individual differences in Strange Situation behavior*. Hillsdale, NJ: Erlbaum.

Lieberman, A. F., Weston, D. R., & Pawl, J. H. (1991). Preventive intervention and outcome with anxiously attached dyads. *Child Development*, 62, 199–209.

Main, M., Kaplan, N., & Cassidy, J. (1985). Security in infancy, childhood, and adulthood: A move to the level of representation. *Monographs of the Society for Research in Child Development*, 50, 66–104.

Main, M., & Solomon, J. (1990). Procedures for identifying infants as disorganized/disoriented during the Ainsworth Strange Situation. In M. T. Greenberg, D. Cicchetti, & E. M. Cummings (Eds.), *Attachment in the preschool years: Theory, research, and intervention* (pp. 121–60). Chicago: University of Chicago Press.

Mann, J. (1992). Nurturance or negligence: Maternal psychology and behavioral preference among preterm twins. In J. Barkow, L. Cosmides, & J. Tooby (Eds.), *The adapted mind* (pp. 367–90). New York: Oxford University Press.

Morelli, G. A., & Tronick, E. Z. (1991). Efe multiple caretaking and attachment. In J. L. Gewirtz & W. M. Kurtines (Eds.), *Intersections with attachment* (pp. 41–51). Hillsdale, NJ: Erlbaum.

Mullen, B. (1989). *Advanced basic meta-analysis*. Hillsdale, NJ: Erlbaum.

Nachmias, M., Gunnar, M., Mangelsdorf, S., Parritz, R., & Buss, K. (1996). Behavioral inhibition and stress reactivity: The moderating role of attachment security. *Child Development*, 67, 508–22.

Nakagawa, M., Lamb, M. E., & Miyaki, K. (1992). Antecedents and correlates of the Strange Situation behavior of Japanese infants. *Journal of Cross-Cultural Psychology*, 23, 300–10.

Pauli-Pott, U., Mertesacker, B., Bade, U., Bauer, C., & Beckmann, D. (2000). Contexts of relations of infant negative emotionality to caregiver's reactivity/sensitivity. *Infant Behavior and Development*, 23, 23–9.

Ping, H., & Zhaolan, M. (1996, June). An examination of infant–mother attachment in China. Poster presented at the Meeting of the International Society for the Study of Behavioral Development, Quebec, Canada.

Radojevic, M. (1994). Mental representations of attachment among prospective Australian fathers. *Australian and New Zealand Journal of Psychiatry*, 28, 505–11.

Rieser-Danner, L. A., Roggman, L., & Langlois, J. H. (1987). Infant attractiveness and perceived temperament in the prediction of attachment classifications. *Infant Mental Health Journal*, 8, 144–55.

Rosenthal, R. (1991). *Meta-analytic procedures for social research* (rev. ed.). Newbury Park, CA: Sage.

Sagi, A., van IJzendoorn, M. H., Scharf, M., Joels, T., Koren-Karie, N., Mayseless, O., & Aviezer, O. (1997). Ecological constraints for intergenerational transmission of attachment. *International Journal of Behavioral Development*, 20, 287–99.

Schiefenhövel, G., & Schiefenhövel, W. (1978). Eipo, Iryan Jaya (West-Newguinea): Vorgänge bei der Geburt eines Mädchens und Änderung der Infantizid-Absicht. *Homo*, 29, 121–38.

Spangler, G., & Grossmann, K. E. (1993). Biobehavioral organization in securely and insecurely attached infants. *Child Development*, 64, 1439–50.

Sroufe, L. A. (1985). Attachment classification from the perspective of infant–caregiver relationships and infant temperament. *Child Development*, 56, 1–14.

Sroufe, L. A., & Waters, E. (1977). Heart rate as a convergent measure in clinical and developmental research. *Merrill-Palmer Quarterly*, 23, 3–27.

Trivers, R. L. (1972). Parental investment and sexual selection. In B. Campbell (Ed.), *Sexual selection and the descent of man, 1871–1971* (pp. 136–79). Chicago: Aldine.

Trivers, R. L. (1974). Parent–offspring conflict. *American Zoologist*, 14, 249–64.

Trivers, R. L. (1985). *Social evolution*. Menlo Park, CA: Benjamin Cummins.

van den Boom, D. (1988). Neonatal irritability and the development of attachment: Observation and intervention. Unpublished doctoral dissertation, Leiden University, The Netherlands.

van IJzendoorn, M. H. (1995). Adult attachment representations, parental responsiveness, and infant attachment: A meta-analysis on the predictive validity of the Adult Attachment Interview. *Psychological Bulletin*, 117, 387–403.

van IJzendoorn, M. H., & Bakermans-Kranenburg, M. J. (1996). Attachment representations in mothers, fathers, adolescents, and clinical groups: A meta-analytic search for normative data. *Journal of Consulting and Clinical Psychology*, 64, 8–21.

van IJzendoorn, M. H., & DeWolff, M. S. (1997). In search of the absent father. Meta-analyses on infant–father attachment: A rejoinder to our discussants. *Child Development*, 68, 604–9.

van IJzendoorn, M. H., Goldberg, S., Kroonenberg, P. M., & Frenkel, O. J. (1992). The relative effects of maternal and child problems on the quality of attachment: A meta-analysis of attachment in clinical samples. *Child Development*, 63, 840–58.

van IJzendoorn, M. H., Juffer, F., & Duyvesteyn, M. G. C. (1995). Breaking the intergenerational cycle of insecure attachment: A review of the effects of attachment-based interventions on maternal sensitivity and infant security. *Journal of Child Psychology and Psychiatry*, 36, 225–48.

van IJzendoorn, M. H., & Sagi, A. (1999). Cross-cultural patterns of attachment: Universal and contextual dimensions. In J. Cassidy & P. Shaver (Eds.), *Handbook of attachment: Theory, research, and clinical applications* (pp. 713–34). New York: Guilford Press.

van IJzendoorn, M. H., & Sagi, A. (2001). Cultural blindness or selective inattention? Comment to Rothbaum et al., 2000. *American Psychologist*, 56, 824–5.

van IJzendoorn, M. H., Schuengel, C., & Bakermans-Kranenburg, M. J. (1999). Disorganized attachment in early childhood: Meta-analysis of precursors, concomitants, and sequelae. *Development and Psychopathology*, 11, 225–49.

van IJzendoorn, M. H., Vereijken, C. M. J. L., & Riksen-Walraven, J. M. A. (in press). Is the Attachment Q-Sort a valid measure of attachment security in young children? In B. Vaughn, E. Waters, & D. Posada (Eds.), *Patterns of secure base behavior: Q-Sort perspectives on attachment and caregiving in infancy and childhood*. Hillsdale, NJ: Erlbaum.

Vaughn, B. E., & Bost, K. K. (1999). Attachment and temperament: Redundant, independent, or interacting influences on interpersonal adaptation and personality development. In J. Cassidy & P. Shaver (Eds.), *Handbook of attachment: Theory, research, and clinical applications* (pp. 198–225). New York: Guilford Press.

Vaughn, B. E., Stevenson-Hinde, J., Waters, E., Kotsaftis, A., Lefever, G. B., Trudel, M., Shouldice, A., & Belsky, J. (1992). Attachment security and temperament in infancy and early childhood: Some conceptual clarifications. *Developmental Psychology*, 28, 463–73.

Vaughn, B. E., & Waters, E. (1990). Attachment behavior at home and in the laboratory: Q-Sort observations and Strange Situation classifications of one-year-olds. *Child Development*, 61, 1965–73.

Vereijken, C. M. J. L. (1996). The mother–infant relationship in Japan: Attachment, dependency and amae. Unpublished doctoral dissertation, Catholic University of Nijmegen, The Netherlands.

Ward, M. J., & Carlson, E. A. (1995). Associations among adult attachment representations, maternal sensitivity, and infant–mother attachment in a sample of adolescent mothers. *Child Development*, 66, 69–79.

Waters, E., & Deane, K. E. (1985). Defining and assessing individual differences in attachment relationships: Q-methodology and the organization of behavior in infancy and early childhood. *Monographs of the Society for Research in Child Development*, 50, 41–65.

Zevalkink, J. (1997). Attachment in Indonesia: The mother–child relationship in context. Doctoral dissertation, University of Nijmegen, The Netherlands.

# 10

# Emerging Co-Awareness

*Philippe Rochat*

*"The innateness of the longing for relation is apparent even in the earliest and dimmest age."* **Martin Buber**

## Introduction

Children first and foremost long for social closeness, affiliation, and recognition. They develop to become increasingly dependent on the judgments and views of others. Secondarily, and possibly in a very illusory manner, they develop to become *Descartes's children*: rational and autonomous beings in a social vacuum, endowed with private insights and awareness, presumably capable of independent judgments and tastes.

An autonomous, socially independent awareness is a myth upheld by many developmental theories, in particular theories on infant behavior and development. The idea of an original adualism from which individual awareness would arise by progressive differentiation was promoted by pioneer psychoanalytical theories (Freud, 1962; Mahler, Pine, & Bergman, 1975), but also by pioneer theories on cognitive development such as Piaget's (1936, 1954).

In this chapter, I discuss the origins of awareness and cognition, in particular the developmental origins of self-awareness, from a radically different perspective, one that gives short shrift to the idea of a differentiated and objective awareness that would

This chapter is based on an invited talk at the International Conference on Infant Studies given in Brighton, England, July 2000. A French version of this presentation will appear in the review *Intellectica*.

develop to allow the child to rectify softer and error-prone subjective experiences. I explore the possibility of an inversion of this general rationale that continues to guide most developmental theories, in particular theories on cognitive development. Here I posit that, in fact, from the outset infants develop primarily and foremost a *subjective* outlook on the world, a subjective outlook on the way they relate to others and share experiences with others (i.e., *intersubjectivity*).

Antithetical to the idea of a growing experience of self as a rational entity separated from others and things in the world, I propose here that infants develop primarily a co-awareness of self in relation to others. I will try to illustrate this general idea based on some recent observations suggesting that from the very beginning of psychological life, infants express first and foremost affective passion and irrationality dictated by the inescapable need to be in relation with others. This can amount to the antithesis of reason.

I shall contend here that infants develop in a world inhabited by the gazes of others staring at them. It is an imaginary and ghostly world. As opposed to the physical world, it is a subjective world that is essentially unpredictable and hard to objectify. It is the affective and relational world that develops to become populated with phantasms, fears, and illusions, the world of passion, seduction, selective affinities, love's glories and defeats. This world is not the orderly world of physics. It is the chaotic world of passions we originate from and for which we live, ultimately. From the outset, I assume that it is also against this world that children measure and eventually recognize themselves.

Prior to discussing the developmental origins of co-awareness, it is necessary first to define this concept and demonstrate further how it is opposite to the concept of individual and objective awareness as it is too often construed. Following this preliminary discussion, and on the basis of recent and selected empirical facts, I will present various forms of early co-awareness emerging in succession between birth and 18 months of age. I will conclude with a brief attempt at synthesizing what infancy research tells us about what it means to be self-aware.

## The Myth of Autonomous Awareness and Reality of Co-Awareness

Co-awareness is a neologism which stands literally for being aware or experiencing the world *together* (with others as opposed to solitary and autonomous). The contrary of co-awareness would be an awareness for itself, the awareness putatively expressed, for example, by Descartes in his philosophical meditations. Even in the case of Descartes's meditations, one can argue that rather than the expression of a solitary and autonomous awareness in process, Descartes's cogitation is actually the expression of a solipsistic form of co-awareness, the expression of internal social dialogue. Accordingly, autonomous and solitary awareness could be a myth, if not an illusion. When, for example, Descartes put forth his famous proposition, "I think, therefore I am," one might ask who emits and who receives the message? Who speaks in Descartes's head? Is it a self-addressed message or is it addressed to a fictive audience? In formulating his ideas in written format for eventual public sharing, it is most probable that Descartes is addressing the fictive audience of future readers. In reality, it is difficult to build a case around the existence of an individualistic, autonomous (i.e., nonsocial) awareness that would exist independently of a social dialogue, whether fictive or real. If such autonomous awareness does exist, it is an exception rather than the rule, for it appears that most conscious mental activities have a dialogical format.

Autonomous/individualistic awareness might indeed be just a myth, one that we hold tight to preserve a sense of identity and social independence, not unlike the adolescent's quest for identity via exaggerated ideological and behavioral demarcation. In reality, it is easy to show that even at our most intimate core, we engage in a constant internal dialogue that orchestrates multiple, often explicitly represented, voices. Even in the form of Descartes's written monologue, conscious thoughts express themselves first and foremost in the form of a social dialogue, whether real or fictitious, as in Dostoevsky's novels where heroes are internally torn by dialogical exchanges between good and evil demons. This kind of "pseudo-" or simulated dialogue could well be the actual foundation of most explicit thoughts and awareness, anchored in the dialogical format of an exchange, whether fictive or real. Accordingly, conscious thoughts would always be co-constructed and individuals always become co-aware, even when absorbed in solitary meditations like Descartes's.

This idea is not new. Thinking as internalized dialogues, problem resolution, concept formation, and other theory-building as processes of virtual dialogues orchestrating multiple voices and perspectives is analogous to what forms the core of Bakhtin's (1981) influential treatment of the evolution of genres in literature history. This idea is also proposed by Cole (1985), Fernyhough

(1996), Vygotsky (1962), and Wertsch (1991); see also Rochat (2001b) regarding cognitive development. Finally, and at a more basic level, Fridlund (1994) discusses the effects of real and fictive audiences on the expression of emotions. Nevertheless, the idea of the social format of high-order thought processes is rarely considered in cognitive sciences. Mainstream cognitive scientists keep construing cognitive processes as separable from a social or dialogical format. This is rather surprising since for most of us it is generally difficult not to engage in overt pseudo-dialogue, without any other listener but ourselves, while trying to resolve daily chores such as putting together a piece of furniture delivered unassembled, operating an electronics component based on a poorly written user manual, or writing a letter of resignation to an abusive supervisor.

This uncontrollable behavior which is public yet for the self, a sort of dialogue in the form of an externalized monologue, is anything but a pathological aberration. On the contrary, it reveals how much mental activity is a dynamic process grounded in social transaction and dialogue. Even at the core of our cognitive intimacy, there is the presence of a virtual other.

If thinking and conceiving rest on the dialectic of a simulated dialogue between multiple voices and perspectives, the product of this dialogue is not an autonomous awareness but, on the contrary, a *co-awareness of the world*, whether this awareness refers to physical, social, or self-knowledge, the latter being the particular focus of this chapter. Note, however, that the exact origins and nature of the internal dialogue remain to be specified. As hinted here, it might constitute a conscious activity itself. Alternatively, it might also be a social overlay to other conscious activities that, in essence, are autonomous. In the latter case, the internal dialogue could be the expression of a habit emerging from our social life. In either case, the dialogical nature and social dimension of cognition is emphasized, both accounts giving credence to the concept of *co-awareness*.

But how does this co-awareness emerge early in life? Infancy research provides facts that allow a better understanding of the nature of co-awareness, in particular what it is made of. But also, it provides a better understanding of how much behavior is determined from the outset by the construal of what others perceive of the self, whether this perception is fictitious or real.

In the remainder of this chapter, I attempt to reconstruct what announces and characterizes the emergence of a co-awareness of the self. Based on selected empirical facts, I propose next a natural history of early co-awareness, in particular how it emerges between birth and 18 months.

## Bodily (Corporeal) Self of Neonates

First, there is a body. A physical place of sensuality, the meeting place of the environment whether visual, auditory, olfactory, tactile, or multisensory. From birth and probably already in the womb, infants manifest an implicit knowledge of their own body as a differentiated entity among other entities in the world. Evidently, this knowledge is neither explicit nor reflexive, nor is it unique to our species. Individuals of any other mammal or even avian species manifest such knowledge (Cenami-Spada, Aurelli, Verbeek, & DeWaal, 1995). Nevertheless, this knowledge represents the foundational element that human infants develop in unique ways toward an explicit co-awareness that, as we will see below, blossoms by the second year of life. But what exactly is this implicit knowledge of a differentiated body of the newborn, and what are the empirical proofs of its existence from the outset of development?

The bodily or corporeal self of the neonate is perceived, not yet conceptual. Over a century ago, William James (1890) introduced the distinction between the felt "I" and the identified "Me." The "I" for James represents the experimenter of the body, in other words, what is perceived of the body. The "Me" stands for what is recognized and conceptualized about the self in the world, particularly the social world. Following James's distinction, newborns express primarily an "I" as product of the immediate perceptual experience of the body in action as well as the felt fluctuation of internal states. Nonetheless, this perceptual experience of the body by neonates is not the "blooming, buzzing confusion" assumed by James, who lacked the vast amount of empirical data we have today regarding infants and their behavior.

Recent research shows that from the first minutes of life outside the womb, babies manifest a sense of their own body as a differentiated entity among other entities in the environment (see Rochat, 1998, for a more detailed discussion of experimental facts supporting this assertion). According to Neisser (1991, 1995; see also Rochat, 1997), newborns manifest rudiments of a perceived or "ecological" self.

For example, in recent research (Rochat & Hespos, 1997) we showed that from birth infants manifest a discrimination between tactile stimulation that is self-produced (self-stimulation) and tactile stimulation from a non-self, external origin (allo-stimulation). Comparing the rooting responses of newborns following a stimulation to either the right or left cheek caused by either the finger of an experimenter (allo-stimulation) or the spontaneous transport of the infant's own hand toward the face (self-stimulation), we observed that newborns tend to turn their head and root more toward the experimenter's finger compared to their own hand.

It appears that infants from birth are capable of discriminating information that specifies the own body as a differentiated entity. This observation is not trivial since it is contrary to the long-held idea of an initial state of undifferentiation or confusion between infants and their environment (e.g., Piaget, 1936). Some psychoanalysts went as far as elaborating theories of personality development on the premise that the starting point of such development is an initial state of undifferentiation or "infantile autism" (Mahler et al., 1975).

Recent research indicates that, on the contrary, early on infants process intermodal (polysensory) information that specifies the body as a distinct entity. Researchers have now accumulated numerous data demonstrating the remarkable coordination at birth of visual and postural/vestibular systems. Such coordination allows infants to pick up information that specifies movements of the own body in a stable environment or the reverse, the stability of the body in a moving environment (Bertenthal & Rose, 1995; Butterworth, 1995; Jouen & Gapenne, 1995). Such discrimination, which is based on the processing of perceptual information from multiple modalities, is evident from birth and probably the result of an active prenatal calibration of sensory and motor systems. Fine ultrasonic scanning of fetuses during the last 3 months of pregnancy reveals indeed that most of the behaviors observed immediately after birth in newborns are already functional and well established in the womb (DeVries, Visser, & Prechtl, 1984; Hopkins & Prechtl, 1984).

There is a remarkable continuity between pre- and postnatal behaviors (Prechtl, 1984). This continuity suggests that the implicit knowledge of the body as a differentiated entity expressed in newborns' behavior could well be the product of prenatal learning. This idea is not farfetched. Prenatal learning is now well established in relation to maternal voice discrimination in newborns (DeCasper & Fifer, 1980; DeCasper, LeCanuet, Busnell, et al., 1994), and in relation to olfactory discrimination. Based on prenatal experience, newborns are shown to discriminate within minutes after birth the amniotic fluid of their mother compared to the amniotic fluid of a female stranger (Marlier, Schaal, & Soussignan, 1998).

The perceptual learning of the own body as differentiated from other entities in the world is the main pillar of an ecological sense of self expressed by infants from birth. Although far from a conception of the self as perceived by others, this basic sense of self is a necessary precursor, a *sine qua non* condition for the emergence of co-awareness. Questions remain, however, as to how infants develop co-awareness from this basic, early (perceived) sense of self.

Next, I propose that a marked progress toward co-awareness occurs at around 2 months of age, when infants not only express a sense of their own body as differentiated, but also begin their lover's career as active *seducers* in the context of reciprocal emotional exchanges with others.

## First Explicit Reciprocity at 2 Months

Considering the remarkable continuity between pre- and postnatal behavior, the physical separation of the child from her mother at birth, as dramatic and intense as it might be, is certainly a major event from a biological standpoint, but probably not from a psychological one. Nothing demonstrates that a psychological birth accompanies the physical birth of the infant. There is no clear evidence of a new psychology emerging with the child leaving the maternal womb, no apparent qualitative behavioral step forward. In sharp contrast, we observe by the second month following birth the first clear evidence of a new emerging psychology, a genuine behavioral step forward. This step is indexed by the emergence of socially elicited smiling, a behavior by which parents typically begin to recognize a person in their infant. This is commonly revealed by baby diaries as well as by traditions and beliefs in certain cultures. For example, natives from Tahiti in the South Pacific reportedly do not grieve an infant's death before he or she has shown signs of smiling and affective reciprocation by the second month. Tahitians begin to mourn the loss of infants once they have smiled, not before (Levy, 1973, p. 437).

One can observe a radical behavioral reorganization with the appearance of the social smile at around 6 weeks of age. This reorganization corresponds to a revolution in the way infants relate to the world, in particular how they relate to others via reciprocal exchanges. This revolution is *de facto* the true psychological birth of the infant, the beginning of a sense of shared experience with others, hence the beginning of co-awareness (Rochat, 2001a).

For parents, witnessing the first smile of their child in the context of intimate face-to-face exchanges (as opposed to the automatic smile expressed by neonates during sleep or following feeding) is a major event. Nothing can exaggerate the importance of the emergence of socially elicited smiling in the life of a child and his caretakers. This emergence marks the beginning of the child's relational existence as it is the first explicit manifestation of a shared positive experience. It is the first unmistakable manifestation of an experience of well-being with others. It is also the first message of reciprocity that is not only linked to basic physical cares dispensed by the adult. It is the first message that begins a lifelong conversation with others. With socially oriented smiling, infants affirm their presence in the world *with* others. It is the beginning of co-awareness, and indeed the true psychological birth of the child.

Parallel to the emergence of social smiling, many other aspects of infants' behavior are reorganized. For example, during the second month the capacity of infants' attention changes markedly and in a relatively sudden fashion. Wolff (1987) observes that by 6 weeks infants spend significantly more time in an awake and alert state, spending significantly more time attending to their environment with eyes wide open. It is also by this age that infants begin to scan faces by focusing markedly more on the eyes and the mouth, facial regions that are rich in information regarding the fluctuating emotional states of others. In sharp contrast, neonates tend to focus much more on the periphery of the head (Haith, Bergman, & Moore, 1977; Maurer & Salapatek, 1976; see also the relevant work of Morton & Johnson, 1991). Note, however, that internal features are not merely overlooked by neonates, since they are capable of facial imitation such as tongue protrusion (Meltzoff & Moore, 1977). Note also that because infants are born with low visual acuity, visual fixations in newborns might not correspond to actual processing of information.

At the level of general cognitive development, the second month marks a change in the stance the infants take toward the world that surrounds them. There is some kind of a radical worldview change. From birth, and even prior, infants are capable of complex sensorimotor learning and perceptual discrimination. However, this learning and discrimination do not appear yet to be under anything that resembles voluntary control, still dependent on the here and now or immediacy of perceptual experiences. There is not yet clear evidence of systematic groping or exploration. For example, numerous studies done in the past 30 years demonstrate the stunning capacity of neonates to imitate facial expressions such as mouth opening, tongue protrusion, and even emotional facial displays such as happy or sad expressions (Field, Woodson, Greenberg, & Cohen, 1982; Meltzoff & Moore, 1977). However, this imitation is still rather fragile. It is not very systematic and does not show much flexibility. This led some critics to view neonatal imitation as nothing more than the product of innate automatic release mechanisms (Anisfeld, 1991). By 6 weeks, infants' imitative behavior eludes such interpretation, clearly demonstrating that there is more to it than a prewired automatism. Meltzoff and Moore (1992) showed that by this age infants begin to systematically modify their imitative response to match the adult model. For example, if the experimenter pulls his tongue to the side, the infant might first pull her tongue to the center and slowly bring it to the side to match the target gesture. This behavior shows systematic approximation and what amounts to willful groping.

Recently, we made similar observations comparing newborn and 2-month-olds' sucking behavior on "musical" rubber nipples. In this research (Rochat & Striano, 1999b), every pressure applied by the infant on the nipple was associated with a contingent succession of sounds that were more or less the auditory analogue of the oral pressures generated by the infant on the pacifier. In one condition (analogue), the pitch variation of the successive sounds heard by the infant was proportional to the variations of pressures applied by the infant on the pacifier. In another (nonanalogue) condition, the pitch variation of the sounds was not, varying randomly. We observed that by 2 months, infants manifest a differential modulation of their suction of the pacifier depending on the condition (i.e., analogue or nonanalogue auditory consequence of sucking). In contrast, we tested newborns who did not show any evidence of such differential responding, hence no evidence of systematic exploration of the auditory consequences of their own oral (sucking) activities.

Around 6 weeks of age, babies thus manifest a novel stance toward objects, toward themselves, and toward others. This novel stance is a *contemplative* and *reciprocal stance*, as opposed to the discriminatory and immediate stance of newborns (Rochat, 2001a,b). This new stance is linked to expectations and the systematic exploration of physical events, as well as to the first reciprocal exchanges with others. Affective reciprocity by the second month is a major step toward co-awareness and, I propose, the second *sine qua non* condition of its development. As discussed earlier, it adds to the sense of a differentiated self expressed by infants from birth that was the first *sine qua non* condition for the emergence of co-awareness. We will see now that in adopting a contemplative stance, and in particular by monitoring reciprocal exchanges with others, infants gain access to self-objectification. They have the opportunity to project themselves in others, with the help of others.

## Self-Ejection and the Social Mirror

When by the second month infants begin to manifest an emotional reciprocity with others via smiling and gazing, it is as if they are literally drawn out into what can be called the "social mirror." Parents and caretakers who are finally gratified in their communicative efforts begin to interact with renewed, more frequent, and more protracted presentations of their own face to the infant. In addition, in the course of these facial presentations, the adult is typically compelled to cause infants to smile, or even better, to cause them to burst into laughter by *imitating* and *exaggerating* their facial expressions. In fact, in these first emotional conversations, adults' behavior is typically a running commentary of the actions and of the fluctuating emotional states of the infant. If the infant starts to cry, for example, the mother or any other caretaker will manifest her empathy by adopting a low and sad-sounding voice. On the contrary, if the infant expresses joy and pleasure, the caretaker's voice will typically follow through with higher pitch and joyful tonality contours.

This highly reliable phenomenon of compulsive emotional resonance of the adult toward the infant is striking and possibly unique to our species, regardless of cultural and familial contexts. Certainly, this phenomenon is prominent in western middle-class culture and observable with some variability anywhere in the world. It corresponds to what Gergely and Watson (1999) coined as *affective mirroring* or Stern (1985) described as *affective attunement*.

At the beginning and from the emergence of the social smile, affective mirroring is highly asymmetrical, the adult initiating exchanges while tracking the emotional states of the infant. Affective mirroring, although a bidirectional process, is first heavily weighted by the adult. Metaphorically speaking, the adult caretaker orients a mirror that is *magnifying* back to the infant an image of emotional expressions that are greatly exaggerated.

The question remains, however, as to what might be gained by both infants and caretakers in such a mirroring game. This question is important considering that such reciprocal, face-to-face interaction might be specific to humans and their close relatives, particularly chimpanzees. It is feasible that the process of affective mirroring is a central feature of primate evolution, a fundamental mechanism evolved by humans that could be at the origin of greater potentials for empathy and other prosocial behavior.

Aside from the communicative and proximity maintenance (intimacy) function served by affective mirroring, from a cognitive standpoint I would like to propose that this primitive form of communicative exchange first initiated by caretakers allows infants to distance or *eject from themselves*, a process necessary for co-awareness. The term ejection is borrowed from Baldwin (1925), who coined it to qualify the process by which children start to project themselves into others and become capable of adopting others' views on things, including what they perceive and construe about themselves.

Gergely and Watson (1999), in their discussion of the putative mechanisms underlying affective mirroring, suggest that the exaggerated online affective responses by the adult serve to mark them as a reflecting (mirroring) commentary, in contrast to any other commentaries. In other words, the adult highlights or puts in "quotes" via amplification and exaggeration the emotions that match those expressed by the infant. This highlighting would allow the infant to differentiate between emotions and emotional narratives that are reflecting of the self and those that are not geared toward any kind of mirroring of the infant. This process, instinctively and compulsively initiated by the adult, would be a privileged way to guide the infant toward an objectification of the self. Accordingly, in observing others interacting with them, infants have the opportunity to see themselves in a magnifying mirror. They would see themselves based on an ability to detect the contingency between the proprioception of their own facial movements and the synchronous vision of the social partner's facial expressions. The same contingency detection would apply to vocal exchanges. Note that such contingency detection ability is well established from at least 3 months of age (Bahrick & Watson, 1985; Watson, 1995). To the extent that co-awareness implies some projection of the self into others, we can appreciate the potential role played by adults' affective mirroring in its emergence.

With the onset of social smiling, infants are literally drawn into the affective mirror presented by others. The joy associated with face-to-face exchanges rests on the sharing of moments of emotional harmony, the protagonists tuned into the same affective key, experiencing similar feelings not unlike grown-ups engaged in the pleasure of gossiping or sharing a good meal. In all instances, the goal is to ascertain closeness and affective fusion with others. With the first socially elicited smile, this process is made possible, each protagonist given the means to recognize himself or herself in the other.

Self-ejection and the perception of self in the behaviors of interacting others form another major step in the development of co-awareness: the third *sine qua non* condition of its development. This condition is the product of active scaffolding on the part of infants' caretakers via an instinctive and universal propensity toward affective mirroring. This propensity is provoked by the first signs of a contemplative and reciprocal (smiling) stance detected by the parent or caretaker in the infant. The putative importance of such a process in personality development is evidenced by research showing that young infants of depressed mothers who are typically more placid and less engaged in affective mirroring also show less social engagement when compared to infants of nondepressed mothers (e.g., Field, Healy, Goldstein, & Perry, 1988).

Recent progress in cognitive neuroscience research brings new empirical facts that indirectly validate the importance of social mirroring as a determinant of co-awareness. It appears that underlying the reciprocal imitation of behavior characterizing affective mirroring, there is a vicarious experience process that is deeply anchored at more molecular levels of brain functioning. For example, the existence of mirror neurons have been demonstrated in the cortex of monkeys. These neurons fire when a particular motor action is produced by the monkey, grasping an object for example. Interestingly, these neurons appear to also fire when the monkey *sees* the same action produced by a conspecific (Rizzolati, Fadiga, Gallese, & Fogassi, 1996). In other words, even in relation to brain organization, mechanisms exist that support an equivalence of treatment between performing an action and seeing this action performed by others. This suggests that brain mechanisms are in place to support affective reciprocity via vicarious experience (see also Preston & DeWaal, 2002). Yet, it is not clear whether these brain mechanisms are innate or the product of experience. At the macroscopic level of behavior and in relation to infants, adults instinctively promote reciprocity via active social mirroring. The process itself is triggered by infants taking a contemplative and reciprocal stance at around 2 months.

## Development in the Social Mirror

In the context of mirroring and other face-to-face exchanges between infants and their caretakers, routines, rituals, and other invariant forms of protoconversation arise in which both protagonists can perceive themselves. It is in this context that babies discover their "interpersonal self," as Neisser (1991) calls it. The interpersonal sense of self of infants emerges in the invariance and the expectation of certain patterns of dynamic social exchanges. As presented earlier, others reflect with amplification what the infant expresses publicly (smiles or whines) as well as what the infant might feel privately (joy or displeasure). This social mirror allows infants to objectify themselves by projecting out of the private sphere onto the screen or sounding board offered by the adult. This self-ejection is a kind of deincarnation constrained by the compulsive affective mirroring promulgated by caretakers.

Infants quickly learn to perceive themselves in others, developing a sense of their interpersonal self as specified by affective mirrors. Between 2 and 6 months, infants develop social expectations that index a developing sensitivity to what adults reflect back to them. For example, if the adult suddenly interrupts her affective mirroring by adopting a sudden still face while continuing to stare at the infant, he tends to show clear signs of distress including gaze avoidance, self-comforting behavior, frowning, and sometimes even crying (Rochat, Neisser, & Marian, 1998; Toda & Fogel, 1993; Tronick, Als, Adamson, Wise, & Brazelton, 1978).

In a recent study (Rochat, Querido, & Striano, 1999), we found that 2-month-old infants are as positively engaged toward an adult playing a peekaboo game, whether this game had a clear pattern and kept occurring at regular intervals or was scrambled and disorganized in its occurrence. At this age, the mere presence of an attentive adult is enough to engage the infant positively. In sharp contrast, by 4 and 6 months, infants begin to show differential engagement (more or less sustained gazing and smiling toward the adult) depending on whether the peekaboo game orchestrated by the adult is organized or disorganized, hence predictable or not.

It is interesting to note that, parallel to the development of such social expectancies between 2 and 6 months, infants develop a great infatuation for physical objects that they start to reach and grasp for systematically (e.g., Rochat, 1989). This new infatuation makes face-to-face protoconversations more furtive and adults have typically a harder time capturing the infant's attention. The infant is increasingly distracted by all that is offered by the physical environment in terms of actions and discoveries. However, the strong social and affective demand of infants is not diminishing. Therefore, they develop novel strategies to capture others' attention toward the self while continuing their irresistible foray into the object world.

In general, we observe that the inertia of gazing toward others, namely, the duration of eye-to-eye contacts once established, diminishes markedly and steadily between 2 and 6 months of age (Rochat, Striano, & Blatt, 2002). This probably reflects the developing information-processing and memory power of the infant. These cognitive gains allow novel allocations of attention that can focus more equally on people and physical objects (Ruff & Rothbart, 1996). It is in this general context that expectation about others and representation of others in relation to the self are developing. It is also in this general context that a new triangulation linking the infant, others, and the surrounding physical world of objects arises. From this triangulation originates also the development of symbolic communication, in particular the use of more or less arbitrary conventional signs to communicate with others in reference to things and events in the world (Bates, Benigni, Bretherton, Camaioni, & Volterra, 1979; Bruner, 1983; Tomasello, 1999).

The processes leading infants eventually to function symbolically remain probably the most controversial topic of developmental psychology and many divergent theories have been proposed, from strong nativist views (e.g., Pinker, 1994) to more functionalist and neo-Vygotskian views (e.g., Bruner, 1983; Tomasello, 1999). Here, my modest foray into this controversial issue will be to suggest that the divided attention toward others and objects expressed by the infant starting at 4 to 6 months of age is an important factor in the emergence of co-awareness. We will see next that to combine the pull toward physical objects and the continuing need to maintain proximity with others, infants are constrained to integrate both attention pulls via co-awareness. It is from this point on that infants begin to have others constantly in mind, even when others are absent. This trait will shape the psychology of the child for life.

## The 9-month-old's Dilemma and Origins of Social Referencing

How do infants come to solve the dilemma of maintaining proximity with others while discovering the expanse of their physical environment? It appears that they solve it by *integrating others* in their exploration of objects and their foray of larger regions of the physical environment. Accordingly, by 9 months and with the onset of locomotion, infants become jointly attentive to objects and events in the world, in other words, attentive *with* others. If an infant plays with an object, she will start to check with quick back-and-forth glances between the object and the social partner, actively monitoring whether they are both interested in the same thing. These signs of joint attention announce the referential and symbolic communication by gestures or by words that blossoms by the second year (Bates et al., 1979; Bruner, 1983; Tomasello, 1995; Tomasello & Farrar, 1986). The integration of others' attention in the exploration of objects by the infant is probably an important factor in the emergence of social referencing, the infant actively attempting to incorporate others' looks and attention in what she is doing for herself. On one hand, the infant begins to lose her independence by becoming increasingly preoccupied by others' attention toward her and her actions. On the other hand, the infant gains control of others, in particular of their proximity, without compromising the infatuation with object exploration that they had no problem expressing on their own at an earlier age.

We will see next that by the end of the first year or the beginning of the second, the drive to control the proximity of others becomes a priority for the child. By 18 months, infants typically have a harder time entertaining themselves on their own with toys or other physical objects for long periods of time. They quickly search for caretakers' assistance and attention. At a later age, children will eventually tend to organize their exploration and play with physical objects sometimes in a recreated or virtual social context in the form of imaginary dialogues and other symbolic plays (Tomasello, Striano, & Rochat, 1999; Striano, Tomasello, & Rochat, 2001).

It is interesting to note that with the emergence of social referencing and attempts at capturing and monitoring others' attention, there is a corresponding emergence of novel overt anxiety: anxiety over separation from familiar figures and the uncontrollable fear of strangers (so-called *eighth-month anxiety*, according to Spitz, 1965). This developmental coincidence is not fortuitous. It is another expression of the 9-month-old's dilemma between novelty exploration and intimacy maintenance with close ones. If from now on the exploration of novelty and its experience needs to be shared, it cannot however be shared with anyone. It is as if infants at this developmental juncture always need to be reassured by the exclusive presence of those individuals who can share experience with them. As I will suggest in the conclusion, the fear of rejection is indeed the mother of all anxieties.

If the fear of rejection and affective exclusivity is exacerbated by 9 months, this is accompanied by new cognitive strategies to use others as informational resources about the states of things and of the environment, such as dangers and other potential risks. Accordingly, by 9 months infants begin to refer feelings of joy, attractions, or fears to the feelings of others. For example, they begin to systematically monitor the facial expressions of others to disambiguate a novel situation, such as the sudden barking of a mechanical dog (Striano & Rochat, 1999), or when crawling toward the edge of a high platform that could lead to a harmful fall (i.e., the visual cliff experiment; see Campos, Anderson, Barbu-Roth, Hubbard, Hertenstein, & Witherington, 2000, for a review). It is indeed at around 9 months that infants begin to monitor the facial expressions of others, referring to them as the emotional theater that reflects not only the resources of the environment, but also its threats and other potential dangers.

By integrating the gazing of others in their foray of the environment, infants manifest at a cognitive level the first signs of a quest for instructions from others. But more importantly, at an affective level, this new development marks the beginnings of a quest for *social approbation*. This quest is probably the core motif of psychology in general, and not only of human psychology (see, for example, DeWaal, 2001). It is the core motif of children when they begin to talk and function symbolically. It is the core motif of the psychology of adolescents in their (often paradoxical) pursuit of a social identity. It is also the core motif of any individual in his or her adult choices.

## Charm, Seduction, and the Growth of Irrationality

The reference to others' view starts a process that rapidly becomes a major determinant of infants' and toddlers' behavior. It leads the child toward a growing awareness of the self in relation to others. At the level of behavior, the emergence of this novel (self-conscious) awareness manifests itself most blatantly in the form of a proactive and systematic enterprise of seduction, leading the child to behave in increasingly irrational and phantasmal ways. It is the dawn of the complex system of representations that children generate as to how they relate to others, how they are perceived and ultimately valued by them. These representations range from the longed sense of being loved and affiliated to the most dreaded sense of being rejected and disenfranchised.

The elaboration of these representations brings the social dependence of the young child to new, much more complex levels of meaning. These new levels of meaning are indexed by the blossoming of behaviors that defy reason and common sense. These include coy behavior, embarrassment, excessive and defiant behavior, irrational fears and anxieties in pretend plays as well as in the form of nightmares during sleep.

At the level of exchanges with others, this psychological "revolution" also translates into the emergence of a whole range of proactive behaviors driven by the irresistible need to maintain affective proximity with others. This marks the beginning of young children's active and selective seduction of the people they encounter, rather than the reverse (adults actively seducing infants), which up to this stage has dominated their life. As we know, games of seduction often defy reason! It is in this sense that parallel to the progress in logic and the rational conception of the physical world as described by Piaget and followers, by the second year children develop also, and probably more decisively, a capacity for seduction that leads them to irrationality. This development pertains to a world that is essentially subjective and phantasmal: it is the represented world regarding how others perceive, value, and eventually judge our selves.

Beyond their first birthday, infants manifest a dependence toward others that more and more defies common sense and straight understanding. When their child begins to walk and even to run, it is common for parents to notice how toddlers seem systematically attracted by the most dangerous obstacles in the environment: stairs, roads, stoves, and other threatening features. These kinds of behavior quickly become means by which infants express defiance and gain renewed attention from the caretakers by controlling their panic intervention. Under the threat of defiant behaviors, parents are coerced into the undivided attention and exclusivity the infant is longing for.

Undivided attention of others on the self is indeed the ultimate expression of closeness and affective fusion that the young child is now actively seeking in others. Defiant behaviors mark the beginning of active seduction as a process of appropriation of others, in particular the appropriation of their undivided love and attention. In this process, children begin actively and systematically to coerce others into co-awareness. Note that this process is not unlike caretakers' drive at coercing younger infants' attention and positive emotions in silly games in an attempt to create a sense of shared experience.

To illustrate and give some empirical ground to this developmental account, I report below three observations that point to the beginning of active seduction at around the first birthday. In an investigation of the developmental origins of instructional learning, we recently studied the impact of the presence and interventions of others in a problem-solving situation with various levels of difficulty (Goubet, Leblond, Poss, & Rochat, 2001; Rochat, Goubet et al., 2002). We systematically observed infants aged between 9 and 18 months presented with an attractive toy placed at a distance on a blanket in front of them. Infants sat on their mother's lap and an experimenter sat to the right of the infant. To grasp the toy, the infant had first to pull the blanket toward her to bring it within reach, a classic Piagetian means-end task that is solved at around 8 months (Piaget, 1936; Frye, 1991).

Our observations confirm that the great majority of 9-month-olds manage with no hesitation to pull the blanket and bring the toy toward them for further exploration and play. Curiously and rather unexpectedly, we found that this simple means-end performance tends to *deteriorate* by 14 and 18 months! At these older ages, about half of the infants do not try to pull the blanket. Rather, they desperately try to reach directly toward the distal toy by stretching and whining while looking at the experimenter. They request help and do not even seem to consider that they could manage to get to the object on their own. This behavior defies reason and does not reflect what infants at this age and following Piaget's account are clearly capable of doing in terms of means-end coordination. In fact, it appears that the physical meaning of a simple means-end task is now transformed into a more complex social and relational problem. It is as if others rather than the toy are becoming the game's end. The infant seems to construe the task as an opportunity to gain proximity with and the undivided attention of others. The goal of the child is to commune and ascertain closeness with others, not to get to the toy. By the middle of the second year, the toy becomes a means to a social end, the end of creating co-awareness.

Another example indexing the emergence of an active process of seduction by the second year is illustrated with another observation we made with infants aged 9, 11, 14, and 18 months. Infants were facing an experimenter who systematically imitated the kind of actions they spontaneously performed on a toy (Agnetta & Rochat, 2003; see also the original study reported by Meltzoff, 1990). By 11 months, but particularly by 18 months, infants begin systematically to test the imitation of the experimenter by accelerating or suddenly stopping their own actions while staring at the experimenter and sometimes smiling at her. With this subtle mutual imitation game, infants attempt to ascertain control of the experimenter's behavior by probing imitative responses. Again, with these actions, infants convey a sense of co-awareness. They play on the same key with the experimenter, equally engaged in trying to be the imitator rather than the imitated. With this kind of development, infants reach new, more reciprocal levels of affective fusion and complicity with others.

Finally, further clear evidence of a major step toward co-awareness is the emergence of embarrassment at around 18 months of age. Already from 2 to 3 months, infants demonstrate behaviors that look like embarrassment (i.e., smile accompanied by gaze aversion) while, for example, encountering an unfamiliar person (Reddy, 2000). However, it is by 14 months that infants begin to manifest social embarrassment in a predictable and marked way, not only in the context of protracted attention on the self by others, but also in the context of a task or performance that can be evaluated by others.

By 18 months the young child begins to manifest explicitly that he can recognize himself in a mirror, trying, for example, to wipe a spot of rouge that has been surreptitiously put on his face and that he discovers in the mirror (Gallup, 1971; Lewis & Brooks-Gunn, 1979; Zazzo, 1981). Interestingly, aside from explicit self-recognition as in the rouge task, some infants by the second year also manifest embarrassment in front of their own specular image. This behavioral manifestation is very complex and even paradoxical, from the hiding of the face with arms and hands, gaze aversion, or sudden acting out in an apparent attempt to distract from what is revealed in the mirror (Fontaine, 1992). The emergence of these behaviors is linked to the development of co-awareness, in particular the awareness of others' view on the self. With embarrassment, children indicate that what they perceive in the mirror is not only an image that refers to themselves (the identified and conceptual "Me" according to William James), but also what others can see of the self (in other words, the "public and potentially evaluated Me").

The development of self-awareness opens the door to the development of self-presentation based on the very complex and often highly irrational process of representing how others perceive and evaluate our selves. This process certainly contributes to the development each individual constructs according to his or her circumstances of a sense of moral conduct (i.e., sense of what behavior is socially more or less acceptable) and of a sense of affiliation (i.e., sense of being more or less accepted by others).

It is also on the basis of this process that children learn to collaborate with others and are able to engage in a didactic (i.e., explicitly instructional) relationship, either as teacher or student, all of which rests on co-awareness. More importantly, it is on the basis of this process that children begin their career as compulsive seducers, exploring and exploiting for better or for worse the affective resources of their social environment, endlessly foraging for intimacy, proximity, and group affiliation.

## Conclusion: The Biological Roots of Co-Awareness

In this chapter, I attempted to show that individual awareness is a myth that needs to be replaced by the reality of co-awareness, an awareness that is dialogical and shared with others. Instead of an individualistic phenomenon, I proposed that awareness is first and foremost a social construction that is negotiated with others, not a rational (Cartesian) and individual phenomenon as it has been too often assumed by developmental psychologists and other cognitive scientists. We have seen that the construction of co-awareness is a long process that starts very early on in development, at least by 2 months with the emergence of the social smile.

An inescapable fact that any psychological theory should be built on is the fact that individuals live and develop *for* and *through* others. They do not develop in isolation as compartmentalized minds. This fact dictates the primary drive of individuals to attach and identify themselves to others, to maintain maximal physical proximity and psychological intimacy with others. Intimate fusion with others is the primary force that drives the mind, whether human or not (e.g., Dunbar, 1997). It appears that cultural and social learning, as observed in humans, great apes, and other mammals, always seems to boil down to the same basic need for conformity: the primary and urgent need to be *affiliated*, to belong and fuse with the life of others, from the mother to siblings, and eventually the larger group of conspecifics.

Primatologist Frans DeWaal (2001) recently proposed that in animals, including humans, the psychological development of the individual rests on a basic phenomenon combining attachment and learning by identification with others (what he calls "bonding and identification-based observational learning," or "BOIL"). According to DeWaal, this learning mechanism rests on the primary desire of the individual to conform to others. We might add that, conversely, what drives this mechanism is the fundamental fear of separation and isolation that is the mother of all anxieties.

Early on, in both ontogeny and phylogeny, behaviors seem to be dictated by the fear and the avoidance at all costs of social alienation (i.e., indifference and hostility of others, hence social isolation). Separation, rejection, abandonment, and estrangement from others form the supreme psychological threat to all individuals at all ages, and it seems across most mammalian species. The internalizing of this ultimate psychological threat as determinant of animal behavior is in all probability anchored in biological evolution, linked to the necessities of survival and the product of millions of years of natural selection (see, for example, the biological theory of infants' and children's attachment proposed by Bowlby). The supreme threat of separation and the primary urge for affiliation are probably well ingrained in the biological machinery from the outset, having a different expression as a function of age and of the sociocultural idiosyncrasies of each individual's environment.

I have tried to show here that from at least the second month of life, nurtured by caretakers' compulsive empathy toward them, infants' psychological development is shaped around the innate drive to promote *fusion and intimacy with others* via active seduction as the antidote to separation. It is in this primordial context that human and possibly other animals' awareness develops. This awareness is first social and shared, anchored in the need for fusion, affiliation, and sharing with others.

We should never overlook the fact that intelligence and reason are primarily working toward the quest and maintenance of intimacy which, paradoxically, more often than not, manifests itself in irrational ways, including uncontrollable passions, jealousy, and acts of seduction. It is this quest that unifies us as individuals and gives sense to our lives. What vary greatly and need to be further investigated are the levels of its expression across ages, cultures, and animal species.

## REFERENCES

Agnetta, B., & Rochat, P. (2003). Intentional stance in imitative games in 9-, 14-, and 18-month-olds. *Infancy*, submitted.

Anisfeld, M. (1991). Neonatal imitation. *Developmental Review*, 11, 60–97.

Bahrick, L. E., & Watson, J. S. (1985). Detection of intermodal proprioceptive-visual contingency as a potential basis of self-perception in infancy. *Developmental Psychology*, 21, 963–73.

Bakhtin, M. M. (1981). *The dialogic imagination*. Austin: University of Texas Press.

Baldwin, J. M. (1925). *Mental development of the child and the race: Methods and processes.* London: Macmillan. (Original work published 1884.)

Bates, E., Benigni, L., Bretherton, I., Camaioni, L., & Volterra, V. (1979). *The emergence of symbols: Cognition and communication in infancy.* New York: Academic Press.

Bertenthal, B. I., & Rose, J. L. (1995). Two modes of perceiving the self. In P. Rochat (Ed.), *The self in infancy: Theory and research* (pp. 303–26). Amsterdam: North Holland/Elsevier.

Bruner, J. S. (1983). *Child's talk: Learning to use language.* New York: W. W. Norton.

Butterworth, G. E. (1995). The self as an object of consciousness in infancy. In P. Rochat (Ed.), *The self in infancy: Theory and research* (pp. 35–52). Amsterdam: North Holland/Elsevier.

Campos, J. J., Anderson, D. I., Barbu-Roth, M. A., Hubbard, E. M., Hertenstein, M. J., & Witherington, D. (2000). Travel broadens the mind. *Infancy*, 1, 149–219.

Campos, J. J., & Stenberg, C. (1981). Perception, appraisal, and emotion: The onset of social referencing. In M. Lamb & L. Sherrod (Eds.), *Infant social cognition: Empirical and theoretical considerations* (pp. 274–313). Hillsdale, NJ: Erlbaum.

Cenami-Spada, E., Aurelli, P., Verbeek, P., & DeWaal, F. (1995). The self as a reference point: Can animals do without it? In P. Rochat (Ed.), *The self in infancy: Theory and research* (pp. 193–220). Amsterdam: North Holland/Elsevier.

Cole, M. (1985). The zone of proximal development: Where culture and cognition create each other. In J. V. Wertsch (Ed.), *Culture, communication, and cognition: Vygotskian perspectives* (pp. 146–61). Cambridge: Cambridge University Press.

DeCasper, A. J., & Fifer, W. P. (1980). Of human bonding: Newborns prefer their mothers' voices. *Science*, 208, 1174–6.

DeCasper, A. J., LeCanuet, J.-P., Busnell, M.-C., Granier-Deferre, C., et al. (1994). Fetal reactions to recurrent maternal speech. *Infant Behavior and Development*, 17 (2), 159–64.

DeVries, P. I. P., Visser, G. H. A., & Prechtl, H. F. R. (1984). Fetal motility in the first half of pregnancy. In H. F. R. Prechtl (Ed.), *Continuity of neural functions from prenatal to postnatal life* (pp. 46–64). Oxford: Blackwell.

DeWaal, F. (1996). *Good natured: The origins of right and wrong in humans and other animals.* Cambridge, MA: Harvard University Press.

DeWaal, F. (2001). *The ape and the sushi master.* New York: Basic Books.

Dunbar, R. I. M. (1997). *Grooming, gossip and the evolution of language.* London: Faber & Faber.

Fernyhough, C. (1996). The dialogic mind: A dialogic approach to the higher mental functions. *New Ideas in Psychology*, 14, 47–62.

Field, T., Healy, B., Goldstein, S., & Perry, S. (1988). Infants of depressed mothers show "depressed" behavior even with nondepressed adults. *Child Development*, 59, 1569–79.

Field, T., Woodson, R., Greenberg, R., & Cohen, D. (1982). Discrimination and imitation of facial expressions by neonates. *Science*, 218, 179–81.

Fontaine, A.-M. (1992). *L'enfant et son image.* Paris: Nathan.

Freud, S. (1962). *Three essays on the theory of sexuality*. New York: W. W. Norton. (Original work published 1905.)

Fridlund, A. J. (1994). *Human facial expression*. San Diego, CA: Academic Press.

Frye, D. (1991). The origins of intention in infancy. In D. M. C. Frye (Ed.), *Children's theories of mind: Mental states and social understanding* (pp. 15–38). Hillsdale, NJ: Erlbaum.

Gallup, G. G. (1971). It's done with mirrors: Chimps and self-concept. *Psychology Today*, 4 (10), 58–61.

Gergely, G., & Watson, J. S. (1996). The social biofeedback theory of parental affect-mirroring: The development of emotional self-awareness and self-control in infancy. *International Journal of Psycho-Analysis*, 77 (6), 1181–1212.

Gergely, G., & Watson, J. S. (1999). Early socio-emotional development: Contingency perception and the social-biofeedback model. In P. Rochat (Ed.), *Early social cognition: Understanding others in the first months of life* (pp. 101–36). Mahwah, NJ: Erlbaum.

Goubet, N., Leblond, C., Poss, S., & Rochat, P. (2001, April). Emerging collaborative stance by 9- to 18-month-old infants. Poster presented at the Biennial Meeting of the Society for Research in Child Development, Minneapolis, MN.

Haith, M. M., Bergman, T., & Moore, M. J. (1977). Eye contact and face scanning in early infancy. *Science*, 198, 853–5.

Hopkins, B., & Prechtl, H. F. R. (1984). A qualitative approach to the development of movements during early infancy. In H. F. R. Prechtl (Ed.), *Continuity of neural functions from prenatal to postnatal life* (pp. 179–97). Oxford: Blackwell.

James, W. (1890). *The principles of psychology*. New York: Henry Holt.

Jouen, F., & Gapenne, O. (1995). Interactions between the vestibular and visual systems in the neonate. In P. Rochat (Ed.), *The self in infancy: Theory and research* (pp. 277–302). Amsterdam: North Holland/Elsevier.

Levy, R. I. (1973). *Tahitians*. Chicago: University of Chicago Press.

Lewis, M., & Brooks-Gunn, J. (1979). *Social cognition and the acquisition of self*. New York: Plenum.

Mahler, M. S., Pine, F., & Bergman, A. (1975). *The psychological birth of the human infant: Symbiosis and individuation*. New York: Basic Books.

Marlier, L., Schaal, B., & Soussignan, R. (1998). Neonatal responsiveness to the odor of amniotic and lacteal fluids: A test of perinatal chemosensory continuity. *Child Development*, 69 (3), 611–23.

Maurer, D., & Salapatek, P. (1976). Developmental changes in the scanning of faces by young infants. *Child Development*, 47 (2), 523–7.

Meltzoff, A. N. (1990). Foundations for developing a concept of self: The role of imitation in relating self to other and the value of social mirroring, social modeling, and self-practice in infancy. In D. B. M. Cicchetti (Ed.), *The self in transition: Infancy to childhood* (pp. 139–64). Chicago: University of Chicago Press.

Meltzoff, A. N., & Moore, M. K. (1977). Imitation of facial and manual gestures by human neonates. *Science*, 198, 75–8.

Meltzoff, A. N., & Moore, M. K. (1992). Early imitation within a functional framework: The importance of person identity, movement, and development. *Infant Behavior and Development*, 15 (4), 479–505.

Morton, J., & Johnson, M. H. (1991). CONSPEC and CONLERN: A two-process theory of infant face recognition. *Psychological Review*, 98 (2), 164–81.

Neisser, U. (1991). Two perceptually given aspects of the self and their development. *Developmental Review*, 11 (3), 197–209.

Neisser, U. (1995). Criteria for an ecological self. In P. Rochat (Ed.), *The self in infancy: Theory and research* (pp. 17–34). Amsterdam: North Holland/Elsevier.

Piaget, J. (1936). *La naissance de l'intelligence*. Neuchâtel: Delachaux & Niestlé.

Piaget, J. (1954). *The construction of reality in the child* (Trans. M. Cook). New York: Basic Books.

Pinker, S. (1994). *The language instinct*. New York: William Morrow.

Prechtl, H. F. R. (Ed.). (1984). *Continuity of neural functions: From prenatal to postnatal life*. Oxford: Blackwell.

Preston, S. D., & DeWaal, F. B. (2002). Empathy: Its ultimate and proximate bases. *Behavioral and Brain Sciences*, 25, 1–72.

Reddy, V. (2000). Coyness in early infancy. *Developmental Science*, 3 (2), 186–92.

Rizzolati, G., Fadiga, L., Gallese, V., & Fogassi, L. (1996). Premotor cortex and the recognition of motor actions. *Cognitive Brain Research*, 3, 131–41.

Rochat, P. (1989). Object manipulation and exploration in 2- to 5-month-old infants. *Developmental Psychology*, 25 (6), 871–84.

Rochat, P. (1997). Early development of the ecological self. In C. Z.-G. P. Dent-Read (Ed.), *Evolving explanations of development: Ecological approaches to organism-environment systems* (pp. 91–121). Washington, DC: American Psychological Association.

Rochat, P. (1998). Self-perception and action in infancy. *Experimental Brain Research*, 123, 102–9.

Rochat, P. (2001a). *The infant's world*. Cambridge, MA: Harvard University Press.

Rochat, P. (2001b). The dialogical nature of cognition. *Monograph of the Society for Research in Child Development*, 6 (2, Serial No. 265), commentary pp. 133–43.

Rochat, P., & Goubet, N. (2000). Connaissance implicite du corps au début de la vie. *Enfance*, 3, 275–85.

Rochat, P., Goubet, N., & Senders, S. J. (1999). To reach or not to reach? Perception of body effectivities by young infants. *Infant and Child Development*, 8, 129–48.

Rochat, P., & Hespos, S. J. (1997). Differential rooting response by neonates: Evidence for an early sense of self. *Early Development and Parenting*, 6 (3–4), 105–12.

Rochat, P., Neisser, U., & Marian, V. (1998). Are young infants sensitive to interpersonal contingency? *Infant Behavior and Development*, 21 (2), 355–66.

Rochat, P., Querido, J. G., & Striano, T. (1999). Emerging sensitivity to the timing and structure of protoconversation in early infancy. *Developmental Psychology*, 35 (4), 950–7.

Rochat, P., & Striano, T. (1999a). Social-cognitive development in the first year. In P. Rochat (Ed.), *Early social cognition: Understanding others in the first months of life* (pp. 3–34). Mahwah, NJ: Erlbaum.

Rochat, P., & Striano, T. (1999b). Emerging self-exploration by 2-month-old infants. *Developmental Science*, 2, 206–18.

Rochat, P., Striano, T., & Blatt, L. (2002). Differential effects of happy, neutral, and sad still-faces on 2-, 4-, and 6-month-old infants. *Infant and Child Development*, 11, 289–303.

Ruff, H. A., & Rothbart, M. K. (1996). *Attention in early development: Themes and variations*. New York: Oxford University Press.

Spitz, R. A. (1965). *The first year of life: A psychoanalytic study of normal and deviant development of object relations*. New York: Basic Books.

Stern, D. (1985). *The interpersonal world of the infant*. New York: Basic Books.

Striano, T., & Rochat, P. (1999). Developmental link between dyadic and triadic social competence in infancy. *British Journal of Developmental Psychology*, 17 (4), 551–62.

Striano, T., Tomasello, M., & Rochat, P. (2001). Social and object support for early symbolic play. *Developmental Science*, 4 (4), 442–55.

Toda, S., & Fogel, A. (1993). Infant response to the still-face situation at 3 and 6 months. *Developmental Psychology*, 29, 532–8.

Tomasello, M. (1995). Joint attention as social cognition. In C. D. P. J. Moore (Ed.), *Joint attention: Its origins and role in development* (pp. 103–30). Hillsdale, NJ: Erlbaum.

Tomasello, M. (1999). *The cultural origins of human cognition*. Cambridge, MA: Harvard University Press.

Tomasello, M., & Farrar, M. J. (1986). Joint attention and early language. *Child Development*, 57 (6), 1454–63.

Tomasello, M., Striano, T., & Rochat, P. (1999). Do young children use objects as symbols? *British Journal of Developmental Psychology*, 17 (4), 563–84.

Tronick, E. Z., Als, H., Adamson, L., Wise, S., & Brazelton, T. B. (1978). The infant's response to entrapment between contradictory message in face-to-face interaction. *Journal of the American Academy of Child Psychiatry*, 17, 1–13.

Vygotsky, L. S. (1962). *Thought and language*. Cambridge, MA: MIT Press.

Vygotsky, L. S. (1978). *Mind in society: The development of higher psychological processes* (Ed. M. Cole). Cambridge, MA: Harvard University Press.

Wallon, H. (1970). *De l'acte à la pensée: Essai de psychologie comparée*. Paris: Collection Champs Flammarion. (Original work published 1942.)

Watson, J. (1995). Self-orientation in early infancy: The general role of contingency and the specific case of reaching to the mouth. In P. Rochat (Ed.), *The self in infancy: Theory and research* (pp. 375–94). Amsterdam: North Holland/Elsevier.

Wertsch, J. V. (1991). *Voices of the mind.* Cambridge, MA: Harvard University Press.

Wolff, P. (1987). *The development of behavioral states and the expression of emotions in early infancy.* Chicago: University of Chicago Press.

Zazzo, R. (1981). Miroir, images, espaces. In P. Mounoud & A. Vinter (Eds.), *La reconnaissance de son image chez l'enfant et l'animal* (pp. 77–110). Neuchâtel: Delachaux & Niestlé.

# 11
# Processes of Development in Early Communication

*David Messer*

## Introduction

Communication is usually regarded as a crucial process in the development of infant capacities. At birth there are only rudimentary acts of communication, such as crying, whereas by the third year children have the sophistication and competence to use language. This chapter will consider two major topics: joint attention and language acquisition. Rather than providing a detailed review of the process of communicative development, the purpose of this chapter is to present arguments about the need to look beyond the form of communicative behavior to try to understand the important aspects of knowledge and representation which allow infants to be involved in communicative processes.

## Origins and Development: Procedures and Assumptions

Communication is usually regarded as involving the transmission of information. The communication of information can be considered to occur without the intention to affect others, as when a newborn baby cries. However, this chapter will concentrate on communicative behavior that appears to involve some form of

Many thanks to Suzanne Zeedyk and Gavin Bremner for their comments on an earlier version of this chapter.

specific intentionality on the infant's part, as this seems to be associated with and give rise to important human capacities.

One of the main arguments put forward in this chapter is that when considering development, it is useful to distinguish between *procedures* and *assumptions*. I will use the term "procedure" to refer to either behaviors directed toward some specific objective that we can observe (e.g., an infant pointing at an object) or forms of information processing of stimuli that can be inferred from observation and testing (e.g., an infant following an adult's point). Consequently, there is usually little in the way of disagreement among investigators about whether a procedure is present or absent. In contrast, "assumptions" involve knowledge or perspectives about the world, and the presence of assumptions has to be inferred from the organization of behavior and/ or information processing (e.g., infants may assume that people are different from objects). As a result, procedures are influenced by the assumptions that infants have about their world. It should be apparent that there is likely to be much more debate amongst investigators about the presence and nature of assumptions.

Thus, pointing at an object or monitoring the gaze of another person can be thought of as procedures. Such procedures are largely automatic and do not usually involve conscious control beyond deciding whether to point, or whether to continue to monitor the gaze of the person. As children develop, procedures usually become more skilled, efficient, and effective (see Bruner, 1977). Procedures might also occur in parallel, such as when infants smile and wave their arms in excitement at greeting someone. Infants have a number of primitive procedures to help them manage social interaction, for example smiling, vocalizing, expressing pleasure, turning away, and crying.

It is worth commenting that much of the recent research on communication during infancy has concentrated on procedures associated with the processing of information rather than on the communicative acts of infants. Part of the reason for this is that there are relatively few conventional gestures, apart from pointing, to study (but see Bruner, 1975; Lock, 1980), and that the coding of less conventional movements is extremely difficult. It could be objected that the monitoring of gaze of another person or working out what is the referent of a word are aspects of information processing. I agree that this is the case. However, these aspects of information processing are in a sense complementary to producing an act of communication such as pointing; communication involves both producing communicative acts and decoding the communicative acts of others. In both cases, infants can become more skilled, effective, and efficient as they become older and more experienced. For example, Hollich, Hirsh-Pasek, and Golinkoff (2000) have shown the way that infants between 12 and 18 months greatly expand their ability to make a link between a word and an object. Older infants are much better at identifying relevant objects because they are much better at understanding the format of social interaction and the perspective of other people. These infants are able to divorce themselves from the attractiveness of objects to become able to relate to objects in which an adult is interested. Nor does it seem that this is the result of a major cognitive reorganization; much more likely is that it is a gradual change in efficiency and effectiveness.

As already mentioned, the term assumptions will be used to refer to the knowledge or perspectives that guide procedures. In these terms, infants' understanding of object permanence can be regarded as an assumption about their world, and investigators studying cognitive development have been particularly good at identifying such assumptions. However, I will argue that investigators interested in social and communicative development have paid less attention to assumptions and, as a result, we still have a partly fragmented picture of the organizational processes that are responsible for behavior. Furthermore, although I will be discussing procedures and assumptions about the communication of information, the perspective also could be applied to socioemotional aspects of communication. In addition, it is worth stressing that assumptions can most clearly be identified from evidence that various behaviors across different situations show evidence of the same principles being employed. Such assumptions in infancy will be implicit in nature, but like object permanence they involve processes which result in infants displaying a coherent strategy in relation to a range of entities in a range of situations. In other words, to be psychologically interesting, the assumption usually needs to be present in more than one type of behavior or setting. As will be discussed later, there is the suggestion that the changes in communicative abilities at around 9 to 10 months are a result of new ways of processing information, possibly because of an understanding of means-end relations and/or intentionality. In relation to the terms that I am using, the procedures of regularly looking at one's partner at crucial junctures during social interaction might reflect new infant assumptions. A task analysis approach can help to identify assumptions that underlie behaviors. However, it should be admitted that such an analysis is unlikely to be definitive and will depend on the perspectives and interests of the investigators.

It could be that the development of procedures and assumptions occurs at different points on a continuum. For example, the ability of infants to follow points behind themselves involves the simple extension of procedures to a new problem, or it may involve a new realization that objects located outside their field of vision may be referred to by others. My argument is that for this new assumption to be psychologically interesting, one would need to establish that infants make attempts in a number of different situations to locate referents of communication that are not present in their visual field. Thus, the term procedure will be applied to developments that occur in limited circumstances and involve a change in behavior which does not generalize to other contexts. The term is designed to capture developments that occur at a behavioral level and do not reflect new general ways of thinking, as these would involve a change in both procedures and assumptions.

Interesting complications occur when we try to consider the development of procedures and assumptions. My argument is that incremental changes often occur in procedures as they become more efficient and effective. The learning processes by which this occurs are briefly discussed later in the chapter. However, I also argue that procedures can change because infants develop new assumptions about their world, and these new assumptions provide the basis for a more sophisticated organization of behavior. This is not to claim that there is a simple, direct path from new assumptions to new procedures. More likely there is a process akin to assimilation and accommodation whereby there are reciprocal, if not simultaneous, bidirectional influences in the generation of behavior, the acquisition of new information, and the change in organizational principles. For the moment I would like to emphasize that changes in behavior can involve relatively low-level "procedural" processes that result in greater effectiveness, or they can involve higher-level "assumptions" that involve more major changes in thinking or knowledge.

This chapter first considers, in some detail, findings about joint attention. The ability to engage in joint attention is often regarded as providing the essential stepping stone to language. Two aspects of joint attention will be considered: following the gaze of a partner and pointing. These sections will involve a review of the emergence and development of these behaviors, which at the end of the first year appear to mark a change in communication, with infants taking a much more active role in the process. This makes the topic particularly appropriate to use as a test of whether the idea of procedures and assumptions can add a useful perspective to our understanding of these processes. The second topic involves a much briefer discussion of theories about language acquisition, and here it is argued that these theories can be distinguished by the emphasis given to the role of procedures and assumptions in their explanations.

## Joint Attention

In considering joint attention, I will review research findings about infant abilities to follow adult gazes and points. I will try to show how ideas about procedures and assumptions can help us understand these developmental processes.

### *Gaze*

The ability to follow the gaze of another person is a vital component of the coordination of social interaction. The work of Collis (Collis, 1977; Collis & Schaffer, 1975) suggested that mothers will spend much of their time following the direction of infant gaze and talking about the object at which the infant is looking. Because of this, young children often experience social interaction that is organized around their activities and interests.

Establishing when infants can follow adult gaze is not as simple as might be thought because the criteria for success have been assessed in various situations and ways. Scaife and Bruner (1975; see also table 11.1), in one of the first investigations of this issue, reported that infants between 2 and 14 months of age were capable of turning their line of gaze to follow that of an adult. In this situation, the experimenter sat opposite the infant, engaged in eye contact, and then moved head and eyes 90 degrees to hidden targets on the left or right. This general procedure has been used in most of the subsequent investigations, although the positioning and presence of targets have been varied (one general criticism of this methodology is that the interaction is unusual and probably maximizes infants' chances of success). Scaife and Bruner reported that 30 percent of 2-month-old infants followed the general direction of adult gaze in at least one of two trials, and the figure at 11–14 months was 100 percent. Thus, it would appear that the ability to follow another's gaze occurs surprisingly soon after birth, especially surprising when account is taken of the limitations of infant visual perception during the first few months of life.

**Table 11.1** Summary of methods used in investigations concerning infants' ability to follow adult gaze

| *Researcher* | *Target visible to infant* | *Target position(s) in degrees* | *Who directs attention* | *Length of adult look (sec)* | *Criterion for a hit (degrees)* | *Criterion for a hit (time)* |
|---|---|---|---|---|---|---|
| Scaife & Bruner (1975) | No | 90 | Experimenter | | Same side | |
| Butterworth & Cochran (1980) | Yes | 25, 40, 70, 125, 150 | Mother | 6 | Not given | First eye movement in 6 sec |
| Butterworth & Jarrett (1991) | Yes | 30, 60, 90, 120, 150 (4 targets) | Mother | 6 | +/−30 | |
| Morissette, Ricard, & Decarie (1995) | Yes | 20, 20 | Mother | 5 | Not given | 5 sec |
| Corkum & Moore (1995) | No | 31, 61 | Experimenter | 7 | To side with target or opposite side | First look in horizontal plane |
| Corkum & Moore (1998) | Yes | 90 | Experimenter | 7 | Same as above | As above |
| Carpenter, Nagell, & Tomasello (1998) | Yes | approx. 40, 80 | Experimenter | Not given; could be repeated | Not given | Not given; could be variable |
| Deak, Flom, & Pick (2000) | Yes | approx. 40, 60, 75, 130, 150 | Parent | 15 (could be multiple) | Camera above head<br>Head +/−25 | All looks within 15 sec |
| Butterworth & Itakura (2000) | Yes | 10, 35, 41, 53 59, 65 | Experimental; usually mother | 6 | Not given | Not given |

Scaife and Bruner's findings were extended by Butterworth and his colleagues in a series of ingenious investigations (Butterworth & Cochran, 1980; Butterworth & Grover, 1988; Butterworth & Jarrett, 1991). Infant responses were coded in terms of gazes to: the target; the appropriate side of the room, but not at the target; the opposite side of the room to the target; or no response (looks at the mother or down at the ground). The statistical analyses involved comparing the frequency of looks at the target with looks at other positions; infant looks at the mother, down or up, were excluded from the analysis. Given the unpredictability of infant responses and the difficulties they might have in attending to a maternal gaze, this provides a reasonable basis for statistical analysis.

The findings revealed that when 6-month-olds responded, they reliably turned to look in the same general direction as their mother but were not able to precisely locate a target object. Furthermore, at this age, when there were two objects in the infants' visual field, infants tended to fixate on the first object they encountered even if this was not the target. At 12 months, the ability to accurately identify the target in these circumstances was variable. Butterworth and Grover (1988) report that 12-month-old infants reliably looked at the target and could identify a target when it was the second object on their gaze path, but could not locate targets situated behind them and, as a consequence, outside their visual field. Similarly, Butterworth and Jarrett (1991) report a near significant effect of following adult gaze to a second object on the gaze path. Eighteen-month-olds were found to be significantly more accurate at following adult gazes to the target than to the distractor. At this age, infants also were able to follow maternal looks to a target behind the infant's head if there were no distractors present, but were unable to do so reliably when another object was present.

The findings were interpreted by Butterworth and his colleagues as showing a three-stage progression in the ability to follow another's gaze (and pointing). Before 12 months, it was suggested that infants operate in an "ecological" manner and follow the general direction of maternal gazes, but this does not involve a sharing of attention in the sense of understanding that the other is attending to the same target (Butterworth & Jarrett, 1991). At around 12 months it was claimed that geometric principles start to be used to identify the location of the target, but there is no "need to postulate knowledge of other minds, or 'mindreading'" (Butterworth & Jarrett, 1991, p. 70). The third stage that develops at about 18 months involves an ability to understand that reference is being made to targets outside infants' visual field. Progress between stages is supposed to occur because infants learn better ways to discover interesting events. Using the terminology I am advancing, the understanding of geometric principles seems to involve new assumptions, including a new understanding of the relation between adult pointing and a target. This interpretation is strengthened by findings suggesting that infants' ability to follow adult gaze involves more than a simple progression from their previous abilities and by similar procedures being used when following adults' pointing (see later). It is less clear whether the ability to identify objects outside the visual field represents a general cognitive advance in the understanding of the world or a procedural extension that is limited to the context of gaze and pointing. Further research is needed to clarify whether this ability occurs in relation to other problems.

More recently, Butterworth and Itakura (2000) have investigated the ability of infants to follow adult gaze (and pointing). In this experiment the targets and distractors were dolls whose legs and arms were activated when the infant first looked at the target or the distractor. The findings revealed that infants aged between 6 and 17 months were able to reliably follow adult gazes to a target rather than to a distractor object only when the target was positioned almost directly in front of them (the target being 10 degrees from midline and as a consequence always the first object on their gaze path). Thus, infants up to 17 months did not reliably follow adult gazes to targets which were at an angle to the infant and second on their gaze path.

However, the ages at which infants are able to follow various types of adult gaze have become a matter of debate. Deak, Flom, and Pick (2000) carried out a complex investigation and suggest that Butterworth et al. may have underestimated the infants' ability to follow adult gaze. The initial analysis of Deak et al. concerned the total number of "hits" or looks at the target. This revealed there were no main effects due to whether the targets were in front of or behind the infants. However, only about a third of gazes were to the target, so such responses were not particularly reliable. Further analyses involved selected comparisons, which revealed that even 12-month-olds were able to locate targets in their visual field which were the second object on their visual path. Deak et al. also carried out an analysis to identify whether infants could locate targets behind their head. This involved subtracting the average number of looks at the three distractor objects from the number of looks at the target. Scores above zero indicate the infant was looking at the target more often than at the distractor objects. The 12-month-olds had significantly higher scores than zero. The authors partially attribute their findings to the greater attractiveness of the objects they used as targets, although another potentially important difference could be the length of time in which a look at the target could be considered to be a "hit" (15 sec as opposed to the more usual 5–6 sec allowed for a following response).

A study by D'Entremont, Hains, and Muir (1997) also suggests that infants below 6 months may be able to follow adult gaze. An unusual set-up was employed where there were two puppets with large eyes suspended and slowly moving either side of the experimenter's head, all contained within a 60 cm square aperture. The first look of 73 percent of infants aged between 3 to 6 months followed the experimenter's headturn to the target, and this was significantly higher than to the nontarget object, with there being few looks at the experimenter. This is a much earlier identification of following than most other studies, with a much smaller distance between adult and target than is usual. The investigators partially attribute this to the experimenter continuing to talk to the infant while turning his head.

Other studies have provided a more conservative analysis of infant capacities. Morissette, Ricard, and Decarie (1995) compared the likelihood of infants following a maternal gaze with the likelihood of gazes to other positions (including at the mother or simply down at the floor). Stricter criteria for success allowed the investigators to identify the age at which infants start to follow maternal gazes reliably, and the analysis did not make allowances for occasions when infants are not motivated to follow or do not attend to maternal gazes. Analysis revealed that 6- and 9-month-old infants usually looked at the mother rather than at the target or other objects. At 12 months, infants looked significantly more to the same side of the room as the target, but did not reliably identify the target. By 15 months, infants were significantly more likely to look at a target object than elsewhere (both 20- and 70-degree responses were combined in this analysis), but only at 18 months were looks significantly more likely to be at 70-degree targets than elsewhere in the room.

Further studies with similar methods of analysis have drawn similar conclusions. Corkum and Moore (1995) compared looks to the same side of the room as the target with looks to the opposite side of the room. According to this analysis, the ability to follow the general direction of adult gazes emerges at 10–12 months. In another study, Corkum and Moore (1995, 1998) also found that it was not until 10–11 months that infants reliably looked in the same general direction as the adult. Similarly, Carpenter, Nagell, and Tomasello (1998) report that it is not until 13 months that infants are successful in following a total of two adult gazes to one of four objects in a room. Thus, the majority of studies suggest 10- to 12-month-old infants are not particularly good at locating the target of an adult gaze.

The findings that have been considered so far have involved situations where both the adult's head and eyes are directed to the target object. A number of studies have investigated the effectiveness of these two cues in isolation. Lempers (1979) investigated this issue in 9- and 12-month-olds, Butterworth and Jarrett (1991, Exp. 2) in 18-month-olds, and Corkum and Moore (1995) in 6- to 19-month-olds. Generally, the findings reveal that combined head and eye movements are the most effective cue, with eye movement alone being the least effective cue. In addition, comparisons made by Deak et al. suggest that infants are more successful in following head movements when they involve greater changes in the orientation of the adult's head. Another finding was that infants located more correct targets when the stimuli were interesting and varied than when they were identical.

Taking all these findings together suggests that there are procedural changes in the ability to follow gazes and that there might be changes in the assumptions underlying such developments. Prior to about 9 months of age, infants tend to look at the mother when she attracts their attention (Corkum & Moore, 1995, 1998; Morissette et al., 1995). If infants look around the room in these circumstances, they tend to look in the same direction as the mother but are not particularly accurate in locating the target (Butterworth & Jarrett, 1991). This suggests that young infants have only rudimentary procedures for following the interest of others, and that their assumptions involve only a primitive understanding of significance of other people's gaze direction.

Somewhere between 9 and 15 months, infants are able to disengage from the mother and look significantly more in the same general direction as her (Corkum & Moore, 1995; Deak et al., 2000; Morissette et al., 1995). When one considers only infant looks at objects that are potential targets, then analyses indicate that 12-month-old infants reliably follow adult gazes (Butterworth & Cochran, 1980; Butterworth & Grover, 1988; Deak et al., 2000). But when looking at the target object is compared with looks at other locations (including the mother), Morissette et al. found that it was only at 15 months that infants were reliably successful. Whatever the precise age of the accomplishment of this ability, it would seem that infants have developed more effective procedures to locate target objects, possibly by using geometric principles. Equally importantly, this seems to involve new assumptions in which the communicative significance of another's gaze is much better appreciated, an issue that will be returned to later in relation to adult pointing.

In the case of target objects that are not visible to the infant, there are inconsistencies in the age at which they are reported to be able to follow gazes (Butterworth & Jarrett, 1991; Deak et al., 2000). It is not entirely clear why there is this discrepancy, but several differences in methodology could be responsible, and these are likely to be especially important for abilities that still need to undergo further development. As has already been discussed, it is unclear whether this development represents a new assumption or merely a procedural development.

In relation to these findings, it is useful to make two comments. The first is that investigations of a single dimension of behavior, such as following adult gazes, are unlikely to identify new assumptions because, by definition, these need to be identified from behaviors that occur in other circumstances. However, studies of a single dimension can identify potential assumptions that can be followed up in other investigations. The second point to make is that there is a need to move away from focusing on whether or not a behavior occurs at a particular age. Instead, it is important to recognize that success depends on the precise nature of the task and the support that is available. It also is worth stressing that development does not necessarily involve a capacity being absent or present, but probably involves a more gradual emergence through the acquisition of the components of an ability.

## *Infant comprehension of pointing*

The ability of infants to follow points has been investigated in a range of studies, some of which have already been described in relation to infants' ability to follow adult gaze, with the investigations using the same methods to study both gaze and pointing. When their infants are 9 months and below, mothers do not seem to regard pointing as a particularly effective gesture. Mothers report that they do not point to objects at a distance, and, when pointing, were observed to supplement the gesture with finger clicking and even resort to turning the infant's head (Murphy & Messer, 1977). However, around 9 months, several studies have revealed that infants are able to follow points where the pointing finger and target object are in the same visual field, either because of proximity (Lempers, 1979) or because of the geometric arrangement of hand and target (Murphy & Messer, 1977).

The latter investigation found that 9-month-old infants were able to reliably follow points to a position only where the pointing finger and target were in the same visual field. However, 14-month-old infants could follow points to most of the targets that were in front of them, and Murphy and Messer suggested that this involved some understanding of geometric principles. Butterworth and Grover (1988) make a similar suggestion regarding early performance, namely, that before 12 months infants respond to adult pointing by looking at the pointing finger and then at its close surroundings. Morissette et al. (1995; see above) also report that 6- and 12-month-old infants look at the pointing hand rather than follow the direction of the point. Their analysis revealed that 12-month-old infants were significantly more likely to follow points to a 20-degree target rather than to look elsewhere. However, it was not until 15 months that infants made significantly more responses to the correct 70-degree targets than to other positions. More recently, an investigation by Butterworth and Itakura (2000) revealed that infants aged between 6 and 17 months reliably followed points when the target was positioned 10 degrees from their midline and, as a consequence, was the first object on their gaze path. Infants aged 10–13 months were also able to reliably follow points to some other locations (10, 41, and 53 degrees); these targets were positioned at angles nearest to the infant. Infants aged 14–17 months were able to follow points to almost all locations (10 to 59 degrees).

As with gaze, there is a difference in the age identified at which infants can follow points to locations outside their visual field. Butterworth and Grover (1988) report that at 12 months the directional indication of the finger can be used to identify distant objects, but targets located behind the infant cannot be identified (1988, reported in Butterworth, 1991). Butterworth and Grover (1988) also report that 15-month-old infants are able to ignore the first object encountered to directly identify a second target object. However, Deak et al. (2000; see above), as in their study of gaze, claim that at 12 months infants can follow points to locations behind their own head. Thus, in general terms, the findings about adult pointing are similar to those about gaze, except that the task is slightly less difficult (Butterworth & Itakura, 2000; Deak et al., 2000).

These findings about pointing echo and in many respects support the inferences made about infants' abilities to follow another's gaze. Around 9 to 12 months, infants appear to be able to follow simple points, and this seems to be partly the opportunistic location of targets when they are in the same visual field as the hand that is pointing. It is surprising that the primitive ability to follow another's gaze seems to be present before the ability to follow pointing (e.g., findings from Scaife & Bruner, 1975; although it should be acknowledged that there is an absence of studies concerning the ability to follow points before 9 months). This might be because although pointing is a clearer and easier gesture to follow, infants at first do not appreciate the significance of the gesture, while they have some appreciation of the significance of eye direction (e.g., Baron-Cohen, 1995).

Taken together, the findings about the ability to follow adult gazes and points suggest that between 9 and 12 months, infants have procedures which enable them to engage in joint attention. However, the findings also suggest that the assumptions underlying this ability are limited and infant responses are largely opportunistic rather than the result of a higher-level strategy. Furthermore, with both pointing and gaze there are suggestions that an understanding of geometric principles emerges sometime between 12 and 14 months, reinforcing the idea that there are new assumptions which enable infants to accomplish these information-processing tasks.

## *Production of pointing*

The investigations of infants' ability to follow adults' gaze and points have largely focused on describing increasing levels of competence. In contrast, studies of the production of pointing have been more concerned with the origins of this behavior, and the assumptions that might underlie and guide the behavior. Much of the research has examined whether pointing develops from reaching, or whether it is a demonstrative act with origins largely independent of reaching.

It is generally acknowledged that infants have motoric procedures to point before they use the gesture as referential communication. Infants in the first 2–6 months of life are able to extend the index finger, but there is little in the way of evidence that such acts have a referential function, though it has been suggested that this behavior may have a more general communicative function (Fogel & Hannan, 1985; Trevarthen, 1979). Thus, it is of relevance that Masataka (1995) showed that the use of "index-finger extensions" at 4 months was associated with producing syllabic, speech-like vocalizations during social interaction, and that both these behaviors had a higher rate of occurrence when mothers responded contingently rather than noncontingently to their actions. The age of referential pointing is reported much later at 340 days by Butterworth and Morissette (1996) using parental questionnaires, whilst Derochers, Morissette, and Ricard (1995) found that 50 percent of their 12-month-old infants pointed at objects.

Several observations of the way pointing is first employed suggest that initially infants do not fully understand its functional significance. Bates, Camaioni, and Volterra (1975) recorded that early pointing occurred when a child was alone. Murphy and Messer (1977) described pointing at 14 months as not being very well directed, and that on occasions a hand would be left pointing at an object while the infant's attention was distracted. One infant even pointed with both arms. Similarly, Franco and Butterworth (1996) observed that in 10-month-old infants, points were sometimes directed at the mother during occasions when interesting events occurred.

Lock, Young, Service, and Chandler (1990) report that during natural interaction, 80 percent of maternal responses to pointing treated the gesture as being referential. They also found that infant pointing usually involved a body posture of "sitting back," whereas reaching involved the body being angled toward the object. Butterworth, Franco, and their colleagues, in an extensive series of studies, have drawn attention to the different uses of pointing and reaching. Franco and Butterworth (1996) investigated the functional use of pointing by putting infants in situations where different types of response were appropriate. The three conditions were: (1) referential – two dolls were activated to move their arms and legs at a distance from the mother and infant; (2) instrumental – two toys were demonstrated and placed on a table just out of reach of the infants; and (3) mixed – a radio-controlled car was moved near to the baby.

Ten-month-old infants only pointed and did not reach in the referential condition, whereas they both pointed and reached in the instrumental condition, suggesting that even at this early age infants have some understanding of the functional value of pointing and reaching. This conclusion was largely confirmed by a more extensive study of infants who were 12, 14, 16, and 18 months old. Thus, infants seemed to use pointing in situations where they might want to draw attention to an object, and where they wanted to obtain an object. However, reaching was mostly used in situations where infants might be able to obtain an object. Franco and Butterworth use this evidence to suggest that reaching and demonstrative pointing have different core functions and originate from different contexts of communication.

Butterworth and Franco's analysis of the infants' looks at the mother while they were pointing and reaching has provided useful information about the purpose of these gestures. At 12 months nearly half of the points were accompanied by looks at the mother, and these increased with infant age. This looking tended to occur immediately after pointing at 10 and 12 months, whereas at 14 months it tended to occur during pointing, and by 16 months tended to occur before the point. At 16 months infants often looked at the partner before a point, initiated the point, and then checked the reaction of the partner. Franco and Butterworth argued that looking at the partner before pointing suggests infants have an awareness that the partner should be looking at them before they initiate a point. Interestingly, the organization of infant looking at the mother was different for infant reaching. At 12 months looking toward the mother occurred almost equally before, during, and after the reach, but by 14 months occurred mostly during the reach. In addition, there were more multiple looks at the mother when infants were pointing rather than reaching, and these multiple looks increased in frequency with age. These are complicated patterns of behavior, but they appear to show that infants are interested in the reactions of the mother, and that there is a different organization of behavior for pointing and reaching.

Using a similar methodology, Butterworth, Franco, McKenzie, Graupner, and Todd (2002) found that target characteristics influenced the incidence of pointing and that the position of the target influenced which hand was used to point. In another study, Franco and Gagliano (2001) manipulated whether or not adults could see interesting visual targets that were presented to toddlers (aged 18–23 months, 24–29 months, and 30–36 months). The findings revealed that when adults could not see the target, even the youngest children produced more points, more points with visual checking, and more vocalizations with points. This was interpreted as showing an understanding of a link between seeing and knowing.

## *Summary: Gaze and pointing*

The findings indicate that as infants become older, they develop more advanced procedures to locate the target of adult gaze and pointing. An important question is whether and what assumptions underlie these dimensions. I will focus on two dimensions. First, the development of better and more accurate procedures for locating target objects is consistent with Butterworth's suggestion that there is a change from "ecological" responses prior to about 9 months to the use of some form of geometric principles and then to an ability to identify targets outside the visual field. The fact that similar changes occur in the ability to respond both to pointing and gaze supports the claim that these developments involve general changes in the assumptions underlying infant behavior. However, more conclusive evidence of changes in assumptions would involve data about comparable procedures involving different behaviors (e.g., the ability to search for referents outside the visual field when they are identified by, for example, speech).

Another dimension of these behaviors concerns a topic that is the subject of much current debate, the assumptions about other people. The early and unreliable procedures that infants have to follow adult gazes, and their apparent inability to follow points, suggest that these procedures involve very primitive assumptions about the nature of communication and the communicative purposes of adult actions. However, around 12 months there are new procedures that appear to be based on more sophisticated assumptions about the communicative process. Infants are less likely to simply look at the adult in response to an adult gaze or point. Infants start to point and they often look at the adult, presumably to check for interest or a response. All these changes suggest infants' communicative behavior involves a more advanced understanding of the purpose of communication and the communicative abilities of adults.

## *Mechanisms of change*

The studies of gaze and pointing have revealed that behaviors become efficient and effective. The mechanisms for the development of procedures are likely to correspond to traditional notions about learning, and the following section considers several mechanisms that could explain the increasing effectiveness of procedures. Following this is a consideration of the processes that might result in more advanced assumptions about the social world.

### PROCEDURES

Developmental psychology has a long tradition of supposing that children learn because of the consequences of their behavior.

This general idea has been applied to infants' ability to follow another's gaze or pointing. Butterworth and Jarrett (1991) suggested that the ability to follow adults' gaze and pointing is the result of secondary circular reactions where infants repeat behaviors that bring about interesting results. An experiment by Corkum and Moore (1995, 1998) successfully conditioned 8-month-old infants to follow adult gaze at the target object by contingently rotating and illuminating the target. Learning did not occur when adult gazes were to the opposite side of the room to the target. This suggests that infants have difficulties in learning associations which violate their assumptions about adult behavior. A general criticism of this type of explanation has been given by Tomasello (1995), who expressed concern that these accounts largely ignore the wider processes of communication and, as a result, do not take account of the fact that social interaction between adults and infants involves much more than the identification of interesting events.

Another tradition has been to explain early development in terms of a joint history of experience during social interaction (Bruner, 1975, 1977; Kaye, 1982). Bruner has emphasized the way that extensively practiced routines such as give-and-take can allow infants to develop new communicative accomplishments. Such approaches sometimes use ideas of scaffolding, where social interaction is structured by adults to support infant behavior. Of particular relevance is the work of Zukow-Goldring (1997), who has described the way that social interaction with sensitive caregiving can educate infant attention to the salient and culturally appropriate aspects of the environment. Her view about social ecological realism involves infants perceiving and acting in a unitary system of relations with the environment. Adults assist infant understanding by reducing ambiguity through using audio and visual marking of activities. In particular, nonlinguistic assistance is given on occasions when infants do not appear to understand communication. In this way, children come to understand the significance of maternal attempts at communication.

Another possibility is that new behaviors, such as pointing, develop out of existing abilities that are put to new uses. Vygotsky (1962) is credited with supposing that pointing is a stage in the transition from reaching for an object to using language to enlist another's help to obtain an object. For Vygotsky (1966), acts of reaching are transformed by the reaction of adults, and "only afterwards . . . does the child himself begin to treat this movement as a pointing gesture" (p. 43). However, it is not entirely clear from Vygotsky's account how reaching is changed into a conventional gesture of pointing with the index finger. Lock (1980), in his discussion of behaviors such as lifting of arms to be picked up, suggests that adults will react to selected movements and in this way infants come to understand the significance of their own acts. Consequently, new procedures may develop out of existing behaviors and, crucially, at some point these new procedures take on a new function because they become associated with new assumptions. However, the evidence is not particularly strong that pointing develops out of reaching (see Franco & Butterworth, 1996). It should be noted, too, that Werner and Kaplan (1963) provide the opposite perspective, that communicative pointing is functionally and developmentally different from reaching.

Bates et al. (1975) also suggest that new procedures can emerge by putting together different behaviors. For example, they write about a child who "passes through a peculiar transition period that looks very much like a rough effort to put two previous schemes together . . . she would first orient towards an interesting object or event, extending her arm and forefinger in the characteristic pointing gesture while uttering the breathy sound 'ha.' Then she would swing around, point at the adult with the same gesture, and return to look at the object and point toward it once again . . . this series of steps . . . puts together . . . the components that eventually form the smoother deictic act" (p. 217). Such a description suggests both the development of new procedures and new assumptions occurring in tandem.

The work of Meltzoff (e.g., Meltzoff & Moore, 1992) has drawn attention to the remarkable imitative abilities of infants. However, imitation can only assist development if there are assumptions to support the effective use of behaviors acquired in this way. Thus, imitation of adults' points could enable infants to acquire a new gesture, but unless infants also develop an understanding of the purpose of pointing, then the procedure is of little value to them. Although there is no evidence that pointing is first acquired through imitation, this possibility should be considered, especially as early communicative pointing does not seem to be fully functional (see above).

Thus, there are several mechanisms that could account for the emergence and development of procedures involving joint attention. Many of the suggestions are derived from more general accounts of developmental processes and there is little in the way of empirical evaluation of the different possibilities. An added complication is that different types of explanation are not mutually exclusive and that procedures may develop through different experiences in different children.

## ASSUMPTIONS

This section discusses some of the mechanisms that could result in the development of more advanced assumptions and concentrates on two themes that have been identified in the literature, communicative understanding and intentions. The section starts with a consideration of biological accounts and then moves on to cognitive-social accounts.

One important theme running through developmental psychology is that general changes in behavior can be explained in terms of genetic and biological processes. Most developmental psychologists accept that our biological make-up plays an important part in determining the nature of behavior and thinking. One set of arguments about this process is that there are inbuilt assumptions present at birth or soon after which provide a starting point for a range of understandings, including those concerned with communication and the properties of people. Trevarthen (1979), in his discussion of intersubjectivity, suggests that from an early age infants have the capacity to engage in communicative acts and respond to the communication of others. Similarly, Meltzoff and Gopnik (1993) claim that very young infants identify adults as "like me" and suppose that there is a very early understanding of the communicative capacities of others. Also the work of Hobson (1993) suggests that infants can directly read the emotions and feelings of others. Thus, in all these claims there seems to be a notion that infants have inbuilt assumptions which enable them to engage in communication in its broadest sense.

There also are claims about the biologically mediated maturation of specific capacities involved in joint attention. Baron-Cohen, Baldwin, and Crowson (1997) have written that "this whole system, again, appears to have a strong innate component, in that the timing of development of joint attention seems to be universal. . . . This is suggestive evidence for a maturational/ genetic account paralleling other universal developmental milestones such as walking" (p. 49). More detailed discussion is given in Baron-Cohen (1995) about an innate eye-direction detector (EDD), which identifies the direction of one's own and other organisms' gaze and is present from about 4 months. This system produces notations about whether both self and other are looking at one another, whether the other is looking at a third entity, and whether the self is looking at a third entity. A significant later development at between 9 and 12 months is the shared attention module (SAM), which allows infants to achieve a new level of understanding because they are able to detect whether they and the other person are looking at the same thing. Thus, the maturation of neurophysiological structures, according to this account, enables infants to have a fuller understanding of the perspective of others.

Biological developments often are placed within a modular cognitive system, and in this way the claim about genetically influenced maturation concerns a limited range of cognitive processes. However, it is surprisingly difficult to provide convincing evidence that there is a causal connection between biological and psychological changes that go beyond evidence of association. As a result, genetic and biological claims about development are difficult to validate. Nor is it always accepted that development is largely a result of the maturation of inbuilt structures. Recently, emphasis has been given to the way that psychological structures *emerge* as a result of the interaction of nature and nurture (Plunkett, Karmiloff-Smith, Bates, Elman, & Johnson, 1997).

Cognitive perspectives about the assumptions involved in the development of communicative intentions and the separation of self from others have drawn on Piagetian theory. Bates et al. (1975) proposed that at first infants engage in prelocutionary acts that can have an effect on the listener, but the effects are not anticipated by infants (e.g., crying in response to hunger). They suggest that around 10 months, infants begin to understand that their own actions are not the source of all events and begin to analyze and then make use of people to help achieve goals. This general capacity to produce and understand intentional acts is linked to Piaget's sensorimotor stage 5, when new means are used to achieve familiar ends (see Zeedyk, 1996, for a discussion of intentionality). Bates et al. also draw attention to the related development of the use of proto-imperatives, where adults are used to obtain objects, and protodeclaratives, where objects are used to obtain adult attention. Bates et al. claim that pointing is first used as a proto-imperative with no account being taken of adult attention, and then used as a protodeclarative with infant looks at adults being used to check on their attention.

More recently, the interest in children's understanding of others has renewed discussions about the assumptions needed to engage in joint attention. Tomasello (1995) has proposed that prior to 9 months, simultaneous visual orientation occurs. This involves an infant and adult looking at the same location, but not necessarily attending to the same aspect of the object or event.

He supposes that between 9 and 14 months, infants more frequently engage in joint attention and this involves both individuals attending to the same aspect of the environment (be it the color, shape, or movement of an object) and understanding that the other is attending to the same thing. Joint visual attention develops due to an emergent understanding of others as intentional agents. Such a change is signaled by the presence of gaze alternation between the target and the person, by other related behaviors such as social referencing, imitation, and by the whole nature of the interactive process.

For Tomasello, the key piece of the developmental jigsaw is infants being able to act intentionally when they differentiate between means and ends in their own activities. He goes on to suggest "that it is in their own intentional behavior that infants first understand intentionality," and this together with their experience of interactions with others provides "the impetus for new levels in the understanding of others" (p. 122). Tomasello believes a range of experiences enables infants to develop this understanding. These include caregivers' imitation of infant behaviors and reciprocity, where the behaviors of others complement those of the infant (e.g., the infant coos and the adult laughs).

Franco (1997) has built on these ideas. She believes that instrumental pointing to obtain a desired object does not necessarily entail understandings about other people. In contrast, she suggests that declarative pointing which draws another's attention to a topic involves the act of communicating "here is something interesting" (Franco & Butterworth, 1996). Franco suggests that this development opens the way for interpersonal understanding and involves an expectation that referential acts will alter the addressee's current behavior or experience. This in turn is seen as a precursor to a development in communication about internal experiences. Franco also argues that looking at the adult while pointing suggests that infants do not assume that the addressee is sharing the same event, and implies that infants are able to recognize that the addressee can share the same event.

Another idea is that new assumptions emerge when similarities are detected across different cognitive structures. Karmiloff-Smith (1992), in her representational redescription model of cognitive development, suggests that initially cognitive functioning involves implicit representations, which are isolated and not integrated with one another. This is followed by a level (E1) in which abstracted, compressed representations are formed. These representations can then be influenced by and influence other E1 representations. In terms of following a person's gaze, her model suggests that there are independent advances in different domains, and that following success and mastery, intra- and interdomain connections are made which can involve common assumptions. Tomasello (2000), in his discussion of language acquisition (see below), identifies a process somewhat similar to that of Karmiloff-Smith. He suggests that children will initially learn particular phrases by imitation, but such learning cannot support the production of novel utterances. He believes there is a period of using imitated and other similar phrases, and during this time common principles across these phrases are identified by a process of structural mapping that involves the detection of similarities in linguistic form and communicative function. These mappings are then used to construct higher-order relationships. Thus, in both these cases it is being suggested that new and more general assumptions develop because commonalities are detected and general principles are abstracted from what had been treated as separate procedures.

It is apparent that a range of proposals has been made which could bring about the development of new assumptions. Sometimes these are at different levels of explanation and, as a consequence, are not mutually exclusive, for example biologically based maturation could enable new cognitive processes to take place. It also seems to be the case that many of these explanations have, for the most part, not been evaluated, and as a result it is very difficult to choose between competing proposals.

Hopefully, it also is apparent from these discussions that different mechanisms of change are involved in the development of procedures and assumptions. Procedures are likely to be a product of behavioral change and involve processes of learning through reinforcement, imitation, and social experiences. In contrast, assumptions involve changes in the way that infants view their world and can involve processes such as the maturation of additional capacities and the extension of new principles to a range of new circumstances. However, I am not arguing that the development of procedures cannot result in the development of assumptions, rather that the development of procedures tends to take place in relation to a set of limited behaviors and circumstances, and that the emergence of new assumptions occurs when infants are able to extend and apply existing procedures to new circumstances. An example of such a mechanism is given by the representational redescription model of Karmiloff-Smith, which supposes that new thought processes occur when children achieve behavioral success with a task and then are able to abstract common principles from their successful experiences. Thus, the development of procedures and assumptions may not occur in parallel with there being, for example, the possibility of the development of more efficient and effective behavior without major changes in thinking.

These proposals about procedures and assumptions raise two important challenges for research. The first is to be able to select the most relevant assumptions to investigate. This process is not as easy as might first appear. For example, in the case of gaze and pointing, it would appear that at a general level this is likely to involve an understanding of the communicative abilities of others. However, any operationalization of this concept is likely to reveal that there are different levels and forms of understanding, so that it is unclear precisely which of the many assumptions about communication are critical to the development of gaze and pointing. Looking at the overall profile of development before and after the emergence of the target behaviors could give important clues as to the critical assumptions. The second challenge is to collect information to test for the presence of an assumption in a prospective rather than post-hoc manner. The tradition of describing behavior has been a valuable source of information in developmental psychology, but there is a need to go beyond this to test what assumptions give rise to the behaviors.

## Origins of Language

Current and past discussions about language acquisition have been concerned with nature and nurture. In the terms used in this chapter, I will argue that the debate can be seen as about whether language emerges out of the procedures developed in social interaction or whether language emerges because of genetically specified assumptions.

### *Language acquisition device (LAD) and parameter setting: Innate assumptions without procedures*

One of the most important accounts of language acquisition is that innate capacities are largely responsible for young children being able to produce the morphology and syntax of the language they hear around them, and it is suggested that these innate capacities are specific to language itself. Few would now dispute that human infants, unlike other species, inherit abilities allowing them to acquire language. The dispute is about how specific are these inherited capacities, and the role played by the environmental input.

Advocates of parameter setting suggest that children have innate templates which correspond to the morphosyntax of all human languages. The problem for the child is to match the template they have with the speech they hear (recently, critics of parameter setting have highlighted difficulties with this process; Theakstone, Lieven, Pine, & Rowland, 2001; Tomasello, 2000). When matches are made the parameter is set, thereby enabling children to master this dimension of language, and the setting of a parameter may have consequences for other related dimensions of language use. For example, English is regarded as a right-branching language as extra elements can be added to the right of a verb phrase (e.g., *Ben saw John who thought that . . .* ), whereas Japanese is regarded as a left-branching language. Experimental work (Lust, 1977; Lust & Wakayama, 1979) has been used to suggest that 2- to 3-year-old children set the parameter appropriately according to the language they hear about them.

Parameter setting appears to involve a claim that children have innately specified assumptions about the form of language, and these assumptions allow the surprisingly fast acquisition of a very complex system. The role of procedures is considered to be relatively minor; children overcome performance limitations and rapidly become efficient and effective in producing the relevant dimension of language. Furthermore, many advocates of parameter setting have argued against any significant role for procedures that would aid the development of language, such as simplifications of speech input and the role of learning through feedback about ungrammatical forms of speech (see Messer, 1994).

Thus, the parameter-setting account is chiefly directed to explaining children's ability to use morphosyntax. It takes for granted children's acquisition of vocabulary prior to language acquisition. Similarly, children are acknowledged to have communicative intentions, though these are not seen as particularly relevant to the cognitively more complex process of identifying the morphosyntactic structure of a language. Thus, although there has been discussion of the component skills needed for communication and language, advocates of the parameter-setting approach tend to believe that the crucial component for the acquisition of language is a set of innately specified assumptions that are present in the minds of all children.

## *Connectionist modeling: Procedures without assumptions*

An alternative way of explaining language acquisition has been put forward by those using connectionist models. Here there is not a denial of the role of genetic predispositions, but these are regarded as involving general capacities for information processing (Plunkett et al., 1997). In connectionist models, the presence of grammatical rules is a result of the whole functioning of the network, and they are not located or explicitly specified in the model (Rumelhart & McClelland, 1986). Rather, the grammatical rules are a product of many individual learning experiences which alter the associations between input and output. Thus, development according to connectionist models can be regarded as involving a change in procedures, but not in assumptions. It might even be said that if language (or behavior) is rule-like, then this is the fortuitous by-product of the processing of information.

Critics of this approach point to the fact that most connectionist modeling involves some type of feedback about errors, and most evidence suggests that children are not provided with such information. Furthermore, in terms of a task analysis of the problem space, connectionist models, somewhat like parameter setting, have concentrated on the acquisition of grammatical forms. It is unclear (at least to me) how connectionist modeling in its general form can account for some of the other components of language use, the understanding of other people, the motivation to communicate, and so on. Thus, connectionist models may have difficulties accounting for aspects of functioning that do not involve learning from associations and involve more general assumptions about communication.

## *Constructivists: The development of assumptions from procedures*

Several researchers have suggested that children initially produce speech in limited grammatical formats and these productions correspond to the speech that they have heard. Tomasello (1992, 2000) has presented data that suggest that when children learn a new word (e.g., verb or noun), they are very conservative in using this new word in an utterance. As a result, even though they may produce various grammatical structures for other nouns in their speech, they do not necessarily apply this knowledge to a newly acquired noun. Tomasello argues that such evidence presents major problems for parameter-setting accounts, which suppose that children should have general linguistic assumptions derived from the setting of parameters that will enable words from a particular grammatical class to be used in a range of different grammatical formats. Similar ideas to those of Tomasello have been proposed by Pine, Lieven, Theakstone, and colleagues (Pine & Lieven, 1993, 1997; Theakstone et al., 2001), who have discussed the way that the early use of determiners appears to have a rote-learned quality. A related idea is that children's utterances have a "slot-and-frame" format, with there being limited scope for insertion of nouns within the frames.

Thus, according to these accounts, initially speech develops in a procedural fashion with assumptions about general grammatical structures developing from the detection of similarities between words that have similar linguistic roles. Tomasello (2000) speculates that this may occur by use of analogy, in a process of what he terms structure mapping, which involves children identifying grammatical assumptions from a range of exemplars, and a process of structure combining, where existing structures are combined to give new forms of speech.

## Discussion

I have argued that it is useful to consider infant behavior and thinking in terms of procedures and assumptions. Such a focus directs our attention to both the actions that we can observe and the cognition underlying these actions. Furthermore, this division challenges us to think more carefully about the relation between behavior and thought.

After considering ideas about procedures and assumptions, it is appropriate to evaluate alternative views about the relation between infant behavior and thinking. As has already been discussed, connectionist models of development suppose that cognitive systems need not contain assumptions or symbolic rules that underlie the production of behavior. Instead, associations between input and output give rise to behaviors that can have the appearance of being rule-based, as in the case of the production of the past-tense form of English verbs (*play/played*; Plunkett et al., 1997). Consequently, this perspective does not identify a separate level of cognitive functioning at which assumptions are present. However, it is interesting that some of the tests of learning by connectionist systems involve assessing whether the trained connectionist system can respond appropriately to novel stimuli, in other words, whether the system involves the generalization of learning to new exemplars.

The main argument against the connectionist perspective is that infants' engagement in social activities appears to involve more than simple mechanical associations between input and output. Representations can be symbolic and involve affect, something that is not usually possible in pure connectionist networks (e.g., the representation of a parent seems to involve more than a set of input and output connections). Furthermore, the identification of assumptions that involve different domains (e.g., following adult gaze, social referencing, the development of communicative intentions, etc.) presents a challenge to connectionism as modeling is usually domain-specific. In terms of some of the material reviewed in this chapter, a crucial issue is whether the changes between 9 and 12 months involve more than a change in procedures. Certainly, there are many other related changes at this age that go beyond, but also are related to, joint attention. These include changes in attachment relations (van IJzendoorn & Schuengel, 1999) and social referencing (e.g., Walden & Ogden, 1988). Particularly relevant is an innovative study by Baldwin, Baird, Saylor, and Clark (2001), which revealed that by the age of 10–11 months, infants when viewing video recordings distinguish between adult behaviors according to whether or not an intentional act has been completed. A challenge for connectionism is to develop models that enable these general changes across different behaviors to be modeled.

A different argument that might be made is that the separation of procedures and assumptions becomes meaningless because they are so closely interrelated. For example, Piaget's ideas about accommodation and assimilation and the need for equilibration can be interpreted as suggesting that there is a continuous development of cognitive structures. However, what I have tried to argue in this chapter is that psychologically interesting relations between behavior and thinking involve assumptions that guide a range of behaviors and are not tied to specific procedures. Piaget's views about stage-like development also concern the way that new levels of cognitive functioning can influence a range of behaviors, but his concern was with a much more general level of cognitive functioning.

In the final analysis, the relation between procedures and assumptions is an empirical question. However, it should be admitted that it is surprisingly difficult using present methodologies to establish that assumptions guide a range of behaviors.

One obvious question to ask is whether, in terms of onset ages, there are correlations between procedures that are supposed to have common assumptions. Positive findings would suggest that there *could* be a common assumption underlying a diversity of behavior, but as correlations do not establish causality this would not be a definitive answer. Even with this caveat, there is only limited evidence available from existing studies. In the case of joint attention, Morissette et al. (1995) examined whether the ability to follow adults pointing or adult gaze emerged first. Their data indicated that there was not a clear order of progression. It was found that a high proportion of infants developed both skills in the same session, and there was a positive correlation found between the age of onset for gaze and pointing (0.51). In contrast, Derochers et al. (1995) found no significant relation between the onset age for the production and comprehension of pointing. My own feeling is that there is a lot of slippage when attempting to identify age of onset of any behavior, as this will depend on the methods of assessment, the type of support that is available, and whether other capacities limit the production of target behaviors. After all, developmental psychology is littered with examples of claims being made about the onset of a capacity, only for subsequent investigators to show that the capacity is present at an earlier age. It may be more important to investigate the relation between different ages of onset rather than to try to establish which of several related behaviors develops first.

Another technique to try to identify whether a particular assumption is present would be to investigate individual differences. If children who are advanced in their use of one behavior (e.g., following the gaze of another) acquire a second behavior (e.g., pointing) more quickly than children who have less advanced abilities in the first behavior, then this would suggest a generalization of the knowledge from the first behavior to the second. This type of evidence would support the idea of a common underlying developmental factor leading to both behaviors. In essence, the issue is one of detecting whether there is cognitive readiness for changes in a related domain. Training or intervention studies could be used to take further this method of investigation to examine whether assisting the development of a related behavior facilitates emergence of a target behavior.

A further source of evidence is the examination of children who have different patterns of development. A salient example is children with autism, who are known to have communicative impairments. If there are assumptions that guide a range of behaviors, then one would expect to see these behaviors absent or delayed relative to other behaviors. The limited evidence from children with autism is consistent with the idea that they have general problems with joint attention and reference (e.g., Mundy, 1995; Mundy & Sigman, 1989). Another example is children with Williams syndrome. These children appear to have general problems with triadic interaction involving objects, such as pointing, yet relate well to people during dyadic interaction (Laing, Butterworth et al., 2002). In both these cases, there is evidence of deficits involving a range of procedures which could share common assumptions.

To summarize, the purpose of this chapter has been to argue that we should pay greater attention to the way that development involves changes in both behavior and thinking. This is not a new idea and has been discussed in a number of forms. However, I hope that this chapter will renew and draw attention to the topic, and that my attempt to make a distinction between procedures and assumptions gives rise to new concerns about the relation between behavior and thinking. Much of developmental psychology consists of descriptions of what changes between certain ages. There is much less information about why behavior and thinking change between age points. Developmental psychologists have identified a number of processes that could assist behavioral change, but do not always evaluate the different possibilities. What seems to be even less well understood is the way that thinking develops, the way that new assumptions emerge, and what makes new forms of thinking possible. If we borrow from cognitive psychology, then it could be argued that what is needed are more detailed formal descriptions or models of the processes that occur at the two developmental points, followed by an analysis of what changes and why it changes. However, it should be admitted that such descriptions are much more difficult to achieve when considering social and communicative behavior, because it is much more difficult to separate out the critical components of these processes. The subject of social cognition was the topic of a book jointly edited by George (Butterworth & Light, 1981) and one which still deserves very serious consideration. It is a subject which, I suspect, will continue to challenge developmental psychologists for many years.

## REFERENCES

Baldwin, D. A., Baird, J. A., Saylor, M. M., & Clark, M. A. (2001). Infants parse dynamic action. *Child Development*, 72, 708–17.

Baldwin, D. A., & Moses, L. J. (1996). The ontogeny of social interaction gathering. *Child Development*, 67, 1915–39.

Baron-Cohen, S. (1989). Perceptual role taking and protodeclarative pointing in autism. *British Journal of Developmental Psychology*, 7, 113–27.

Baron-Cohen, S. (1995). *Mindblindness*. Cambridge, MA: MIT Press.

Baron-Cohen, S., Baldwin, D. A., & Crowson, M. (1997). Do children with autism use the speaker's direction of gaze strategy to crack the code of language? *Child Development*, 68, 48–57.

Baron-Cohen, S., Ring, H. A., Bullmore, E. T., Wheelwright, S., Ashwin, C., & Williams, S. C. R. (2000). The amygdala theory of autism. *Neuroscience and Behavioral Reviews*, 24, 355–64.

Bates, E., Benigni, L., Bretherton, I., Camaioni, L., & Volterra, V. (1979). *The emergence of symbols: Cognition and communication in infancy*. New York: Academic Press.

Bates, E., Camaioni, L., & Volterra, V. (1975). The acquisition of performatives prior to speech. *Merrill-Palmer Quarterly*, 21, 205–26.

Bruner, J. S. (1975). The ontogenesis of speech acts. *Journal of Child Language*, 2, 1–19.

Bruner, J. S. (1977). Early social interaction and language acquisition. In H. R. Schaffer (Ed.), *Studies in mother–infant interaction* (pp. 271–90). New York: Academic Press.

Butterworth, G. E. (1991). The ontogeny and phylogeny of joint visual attention. In A. Whiten (Ed.), *Natural theories of mind* (pp. 223–32). Oxford: Blackwell.

Butterworth, G. E., & Cochran, E. (1980). Towards a mechanism of joint visual attention in human infancy. *International Journal of Behavioral Development*, 3, 253–72.

Butterworth, G. E., Franco, F., McKenzie, B., Graupner, L., & Todd, B. (2002). Dynamic aspects of visual event perception and the procedure of pointing by human infants. *British Journal of Developmental Psychology*, 20, 1–24.

Butterworth, G. E., & Grover, L. (1988). The origins of referential communication in human infancy. In L. Weiskrantz (Ed.), *Thought without language* (pp. 5–25). Oxford: Oxford University Press.

Butterworth, G. E., & Itakura, S. (2000). How the head, eyes and hands serve definite reference. *British Journal of Developmental Psychology*, 18, 25–50.

Butterworth, G. E., & Jarrett, N. (1991). What minds have in common is space: Spatial mechanisms serving joint visual attention in infancy. *British Journal of Developmental Psychology*, 9, 55–72.

Butterworth, G. E., & Light, P. (Eds.). (1981). *Social cognition*. Brighton: Harvester.

Butterworth, G. E., & Morissette, P. (1996). Onset of pointing and the acquisition of language in infancy. *Journal of Reproductive and Infant Psychology*, 14, 219–31.

Camaioni, L., Caseli, M. C., Longobardi, E., & Volterra, V. (1991). A parent report instrument for early language assessment. *First Language*, 11, 345–60.

Carpenter, M., Nagell, K., & Tomasello, M. (1998). Social cognition, joint attention, and communicative competence from 9 to 15 months of age. *Monographs of the Society for Research in Child Development*, 63 (Serial No. 4).

Collis, G. M. (1977). Visual co-orientation and maternal speech. In H. R. Schaffer (Ed.), *Studies in mother–infant interaction* (pp. 325–54). New York: Academic Press.

Collis, G. M., & Schaffer, H. R. (1975). Synchronization of visual attention in mother–infant pairs. *Journal of Child Psychology and Psychiatry*, 16, 315–20.

Corkum, V., & Moore, C. (1995). The origins of joint visual attention. In C. Moore & P. Dunham (Eds.), *Joint attention: Its origins and role in development* (pp. 61–83). Hillsdale, NJ: Erlbaum.

Corkum, V., & Moore, C. (1998). The origins of joint visual attention in infants. *Developmental Psychology*, 14, 28–38.

Deak, G., Flom, R. A., & Pick, A. D. (2000). Effect of gesture and target on 12- and 18-month-olds' joint visual attention to objects in front of or behind them. *Developmental Psychology*, 36, 511–23.

D'Entremont, B., Hains, S. M. J., & Muir, D. W. (1997). A demonstration of gaze following in 3- to 6-month-olds. *Infant Behavior and Development*, 20, 569–72.

Derochers, S., Morissette, P., & Ricard, M. (1995). Two perspectives on pointing in infancy. In C. Moore & P. Dunham (Eds.), *Joint attention: Its origins and role in development* (pp. 85–101). Hillsdale, NJ: Erlbaum.

Fogel, A., & Hannan, T. E. (1985). Manual expressions of 2- to 3-month-old human infants during social interaction. *Child Development*, 56, 1271–9.

Folven, R. J., Bonvillian, J. D., & Orlansky, M. D. (1984/5). Communicative gestures and early sign language. *First Language*, 5, 129–44.

Franco, F. (1997). The development of meaning in infancy: Early communication and social understanding. In S. Hala (Ed.), *The development of social cognition* (pp. 95–160). Hove: Psychology Press.

Franco, F., & Butterworth, G. E. (1996). Pointing and social awareness: Declaring and requesting in the second year. *Journal of Child Language*, 23, 307–36.

Franco, F., & Gagliano, A. (2001). Toddler's pointing when joint attention is obstructed. *First Language*, 21, 289–321.

German, T., & Leslie, A. (2000). Attending to and learning about mental states. In P. Mitchell & K. Riggs (Eds.), *Assessing the mind* (pp. 229–52). Hove: Psychology Press.

Hobson, R. P. (1993). *Autism and the development of mind*. Hove: Erlbaum.

Hollich, G. J., Hirsh-Pasek, K., & Golinkoff, R. (2000). Breaking through the language barrier: An emergentist coalition model for the origins of word learning. *Monographs of the Society for Research in Child Development*, 65.

Karmiloff-Smith, A. (1992). *Beyond modularity*. Cambridge, MA: MIT Press.

Kaye, K. (1982). *The mental and social life of babies*. Chicago: University of Chicago Press.

Lempers, J. D. (1979). Young children's production and comprehension of non-verbal deictic behavior. *Journal of Genetic Psychology*, 135, 93–102.

Laing, E., Butterworth, G., Ansari, D., Gsödl, M., Longhi, E., Panagiotaki, G., Paterson, S., & Karmiloff-Smith, A. (2002). Atypical development of language and social communication in toddlers with Williams syndrome. *Developmental Science*, 5, 233–46.

Leslie, A., & Roth, D. (1994). What autism teaches us about metarepresentation. In S. Baron-Cohen, H. Tagler-Flusberg, & D. J. Cohen (Eds.), *Understanding other minds: Perspectives from autism* (pp. 83–111). Oxford: Oxford University Press.

Lock, A. (1980). *The guided reinvention of language*. New York: Academic Press.

Lock, A., Young, A., Service, V., & Chandler, P. (1990). The origins of infant pointing gestures. In V. Volterra & C. J. Erting (Eds.), *From gesture to language in hearing and deaf children* (pp. 42–55). Berlin: Springer.

Lust, B. (1977). Conjunction reduction in child language. *Journal of Child Language*, 4, 257–87.

Lust, B., & Wakayama, T. K. (1979). The structure of coordination in children's first-language acquisition of Japanese. In F. Eckman & A. Hastings (Eds.), *Studies in first- and second-language acquisition*. Rowley, MA: Newbury House Press.

Markus, J., Mundy, P., Morales, M., Delgado, C., & Yale, M. (2000). Individual differences in infant skills as predictors of child–caregiver joint attention and language. *Social Development*, 9, 302–15.

Masataka, N. (1995). The relation between index-finger extension and the acoustic quality of cooing in three-month-old infants. *Journal of Child Language*, 22, 247–57.

Meltzoff, A., & Gopnik, A. (1993). The role of imitation in understanding persons and developing a theory of mind. In S. Baron-Cohen, H. Tagler-Flusberg, & D. Cohen (Eds.), *Understanding other minds: Perspective from autism* (pp. 335–66). Oxford: Oxford University Press.

Meltzoff, A., & Moore, M. K. (1992). Early imitation within a functional framework: The importance of person identity, movement, and development. *Infant Behavior and Development*, 15, 479–505.

Messer, D. J. (1994). *The development of communication*. Chichester: Wiley.

Messer, D. J. (1999). Communication, bonding, attachment and separation. In D. J. Messer & F. Jones (Eds.), *Psychology and social care* (pp. 222–39). London: Jessica Kingsley.

Morissette, P., Ricard, M., & Decarie, T. (1995). Joint visual attention and pointing in infancy: A longitudinal study of comprehension. *British Journal of Developmental Psychology*, 13, 163–77.

Mundy, P. (1995). Joint attention, a social-emotional approach in children with autism. *Development and Psychopathology*, 7, 63–82.

Mundy, P., & Sigman, M. (1989). Specifying the nature of social impairment autism. In G. Dawson (Ed.), *Autism: New perspectives on diagnosis, nature, and treatment* (pp. 3–21). New York: Guilford Press.

Murphy, C. M., & Messer, D. J. (1977). Mothers, infants and pointing: A study of a gesture. In H. R. Schaffer (Ed.), *Studies in mother–infant interaction* (pp. 325–54). New York: Academic Press.

Pine, J., & Lieven, E. (1993). Reanalysing the rote-learned phrases: Individual differences in the transition to multi-word speech. *Journal of Child Language*, 20, 551–71.

Pine, J., & Lieven, E. (1997). Lexically-based learning and early grammatical development. *Journal of Child Language*, 24, 187–219.

Plunkett, K., Karmiloff-Smith, A., Bates, E., Elman, J. L., & Johnson, M. (1997). Connectionism and developmental psychology. *Journal of Child Psychology and Psychiatry*, 38, 53–80.

Rumelhart, D. E., & McClelland, J. L. (1986). On learning the past tense of English verbs. In J. L. McClelland, D. E. Rumelhart, and the Parallel Distributed Processing Research Group, *Exploration in the Micro Structure of Cognition* (pp. 216–71). Cambridge, MA: MIT Press.

Scaife, M., & Bruner, J. S. (1975). The capacity for joint attention in the infant. *Nature*, 253, 265–6.

Theakstone, A., Lieven, E. V. M., Pine, J., & Rowland, C. (2001). The role of performance limitations in the acquisition of verb-argument structure: An alternative account. *Journal of Child Language*, 28, 127–52.

Tomasello, M. (1992). *First verbs: A case study of early grammatical development*. Cambridge: Cambridge University Press.

Tomasello, M. (1995). Joint attention as social cognition. In C. Moore & P. Dunham (Eds.), *Joint attention: Its origins and role in development* (pp. 103–58). Hillsdale, NJ: Erlbaum.

Tomasello, M. (2000). Do young children have adult syntactic competence? *Cognition*, 74, 209–53.

Trevarthen, C. (1979). Communication and cooperation in early infancy: A description of primary intersubjectivity. In M. Bullowa (Ed.), *Before speech: The beginnings of interpersonal communication* (pp. 321–47). Cambridge: Cambridge University Press.

van IJzendoorn, M. J., & Schuengel, C. (1999). The development of attachment relationships: Infancy and beyond. In D. Messer & W. S. Millar (Eds.), *Exploring developmental psychology* (pp. 82–104). London: Arnold.

Vygostky, L. (1962). *Thought and language*. Cambridge, MA: MIT Press.

Vygotsky, L. (1966). Development of the higher mental functions. In A. Leontiev, A. Luria, & A. Smirnov (Eds.), *Psychological research in the USSR* (Vol. 1, pp. 11–46). Moscow: Progress Publishers.

Walden, T. A., & Ogden, T. A. (1988). The development of social referencing. *Child Development*, 59, 1230–40.

Werner, H., & Kaplan, B. (1963). *Symbol formation: An organismic-developmental approach to language and the expression of thought*. New York: Wiley.

Zeedyk, M. S. (1996). Developmental accounts of intentionality. *Developmental Review*, 16, 416–61.

Zukow-Goldring, P. (1997). Sensitive caregiving fosters the comprehension of speech: When gestures speak louder than words. *Early Development and Parenting*, 6, 1–17.

# 12
# Joint Visual Attention in Infancy

*George Butterworth*

## Introduction: Defining Joint Visual Attention

It is relatively easy to understand what is entailed in joint visual attention by defining it operationally as "looking where someone else is looking." Such a definition has the advantage that it is straightforward to establish whether and when babies can locate objects on the basis of a change in the direction of gaze of their partner. Put slightly more subtly, joint visual attention (henceforth JVA) may be defined as following the direction of attention of another person to the object of their attention (Emery, Lorincz, Perret, Oram, & Baker, 1997). As Bruner (1995) points out, however, there is much more to JVA than the mere coincidence of separate lines of gaze. Joint attention in infancy forms a bedrock for shared social realities, a precondition for the acquisition and use of language, and, in its deepest sense, for the formation and maintenance of culture: it also depends on sharing the focus, context, and presuppositions about objects that guide attention. For attention to be joint, separate individuals may have common knowledge of the focus of each other's attention and the focus of attention of one partner may be regulated by that of the other person. In some cases, the orienting behavior of one partner may have the effect of redirecting the focal attention of the other partner, to bring into the foreground what was previously in the background of awareness (Campbell, 2000). Joint attention

Reprinted from G. E. Butterworth, "Joint visual attention in infancy." In G. Bremner & A. Fogel (Eds.), *Blackwell handbook of infant development* (pp. 213–40). Oxford: Blackwell.

emerges when both participants engage focally with the same object.

Adamson and MacArthur (1995) list the constituent components for episodes of joint attention in infancy as: the developing infant, the caregiver, objects explicitly present in the immediate vicinity, and the symbolic elements implicitly present within culturally conventional codes of speech. The order in which these various components of joint attention first emerge in development has been the subject of some controversy, not least because the very idea that infants can share points of view with adults was not accepted in traditional theories that presupposed infant egocentrism (e.g., Piaget, 1954). Clearly, one would not wish to ascribe a capacity for shared attention to the infant if sharing depends solely on the adult monitoring the focus of the infant's gaze. Any sharing in such a circumstance would be entirely one-sided and not mutual.

The beginning of a more fully articulated definition of JVA rests on the idea that shared attention depends on deixis: a word derived from the Greek *deiknunai* meaning "to show" (Collins Softback English dictionary, 1991). In deictic gaze and in deictic gestures, such as pointing, there is reciprocity between the participants based on the complementarity of their separate perspectives. One member in the interaction takes the change of gaze, or the direction of the pointing hand, as a signal which "shows" the location of something of mutual interest. Showing, however, admits of various degrees of precision, ranging from drawing attention to whole scenes to individuating a particular object or part of an object. Different cues for joint attention vary in their effectiveness both at different times in development between species and in their precision of reference. The precision with which a referent is singled out in episodes of JVA is important because it relates to the question of ambiguity of reference, that is, how we can know precisely what someone is referring to.

The deictic definition of joint attention, which includes mutuality as a defining condition, may be teased apart even further. The earliest form of reciprocity may refer to shared experiences which do not actually involve inanimate objects as third parties. Infant and adult are mutually attentive in face-to-face interaction and each is the object of the other's attention. Trevarthen (1979) described such basic mutuality as "primary intersubjectivity," which he defines as a capacity for perceiving others as intentional agents with feelings. Primary intersubjectivity is especially evident in the emotional attunement of mother and her 3-month infant in dyadic interaction. The infant looks attentively at the mother's face, reacts with smiles, makes lip and tongue movements resembling speech, and gestures with the hands in a finely attuned, rhythmic, and reciprocal turn-taking (see also Trevarthen, 1993). Mutual gaze and gaze avoidance play an important part in regulating these early interactions, which are especially evident in the first 3 months, before babies become engrossed with handling physical objects.

Triangular interpersonal relations, as for example between mother, father, and the 3-month infant, are of particular interest. Fivaz-Depeursinge and Corboz-Warnery (1999) described such triangular sharing of attention in 3-month-olds. While the baby is interacting actively with one parent, she may nevertheless orient frequently to the other parent, not only looking but also smiling, transferring affect from one parent to the other as if intent on maintaining the experience of three people together. The authors suggest that such "social triangulation" may be a developmental precursor of the triadic referential relations which incorporate inanimate objects and which are typically observed later in the first year. Stern (1999) has described the experience of feelings in realtime by young infants as being modulated by "vitality contours." Vitality contours are a reflection of the manner in which actions are carried out; they are captured by such terms as surging, fading away, fleeting, explosive, or tentative that describe the dynamic flow of action and interaction. Of particular relevance to triangular relations is the way in which vitality contours give rise to attunement of affect, in which the parents amodally match the vitality contour of the baby's action, as a message indicating that they have shared the emotional experience (e.g., of joy or sorrow). Later in development, vitality contours carry information in the context of social referencing, as the baby seeks reassurance about how to act and feel with strange, perhaps frightening objects (Campos, Barrett, Lamb, Hill, Goldsmith & Stenberg, 1983).

Incorporating an external referent is evidence for a developmental change toward communication around a topic – what Trevarthen (1979) calls "secondary intersubjectivity" – and this marks an important progression in the infant's capacity for JVA. However, we should not forget that this progression builds upon earlier aspects of mutuality, shared attention and shared emotions.

The scope of contemporary studies of JVA has in recent years been extended to take into account comparative evidence from monkeys and apes (Itakura, 1996; Povinelli & Eddy, 1996a,b,c). The way in which jointly shared attention maps into language

**Table 12.1** Phases in the development of joint attention during human infancy

| *Developmental phase* | *Age of onset* |
|---|---|
| Shared attentiveness (primary intersubjectivity) | From birth |
| Interpersonal engagement Triangular relations | 6–8 weeks |
| Fragile triadic JVA | 3–4 months |
| Object involvement | 5–6 months |
| Robust triadic JVA (secondary intersubjectivity) | 9–15 months |
| Canonical pointing | 11 months |
| Emergence of symbols | 18 months |

*Source*: Adapted from Adamson & MacArthur (1995)

acquisition in toddlers has also been studied (Baldwin, 1993; Bloom, 2000). Links with developmental psychopathology have also been suggested, such that deficits in JVA may be among the primary causes of childhood autism (Baron-Cohen, Leslie, & Frith, 1985).

Table 12.1 helps to bring some order to the contemporary evidence in this complex field. It is a modified version of a table by Adamson and MacArthur (1995), which describes phases in the development of joint attention. Put very simply, Adamson and MacArthur (1995) suggest that, in the first 9 months, it is mainly mothers who adjust their gaze to the interests of the infant rather than vice versa. From 9 months onward the infant initiates more and the dyadic interaction becomes capable of incorporating "third-party" objects, with each participant contributing to the sharing of attention. The phases before and after 9 months have been respectively characterized as "supported" and "coordinated" JVA (Bakeman & Adamson, 1984). From about 13 months the conventional codes of the culture, including language, begin to emerge within episodes of joint engagement. This broad framework offers a useful timetable for the emergence of robust forms of JVA and for its potential links with language. However, recent research suggests that coordinated JVA, in which the baby follows the adult's change of gaze, can be observed long before the 9-month watershed if the testing conditions are right. Adamson and MacArthur's taxonomy needs to be modified to allow a capacity for "fragile" JVA at least as early as 3 months and an early capacity for triangular relations. Issues about the origins of JVA are important because they help to determine whether the capacity is acquired through social interaction (e.g., Vygotsky, 1962) or operant conditioning (e.g., Corkum & Moore, 1995), or whether it is itself constitutive of social experience and social learning as Bruner (1995) maintains.

## The Phylogeny of Joint Visual Attention

Coordinated visual attention is widespread in the animal kingdom. It is not a specifically human behavior and has been observed among birds (Ristau, 1991), monkeys, and apes (Itakura & Tanaka, 1998). However, a variety of mechanisms might explain visual co-orientation in animals and it is not necessarily the case that complex cognitive abilities involving mental-state attribution are implicated. For example, it is sufficient for one monkey simply to be in the proximity of food to attract another monkey to that place, an effect known as local enhancement, without any more specifically localized visual signal serving as a cue. It is only recently that the gaze cues (defined as coupled head and eye movement) to which monkeys and apes respond have been systematically studied. Itakura and Tanaka (1998) found that two 21-year-old chimpanzees (*Pan troglodytes*) and a 5-year-old orangutan (*Pongo pygmaeus*) could, after training, find hidden food when given cues by a human who either tapped on the correct container, gazed and pointed at the container, gazed with head movement close up to or further away from the correct container, or signaled with eye movements alone. The primates' performance was accurate and comparable to that of children aged 2.5 years. Capuchin monkeys can also be trained to use gaze cues but they failed, even with extensive training over 120 trials, to make use of eye movements alone to find hidden food (Itakura & Anderson, 1996). These results suggest that physical proximity to an object may be a sufficient signal for many species and that head movements, but not necessarily eye movements, serve as cues for attention among primates.

Tomasello and Call (1997), in a review of gaze following in nonhuman primates, note that most studies confound bodily orientation with gaze direction. This has also been true for most studies of human infant gaze following, an issue which will be considered later. Very few studies control for the different components of the signal, with the notable exception of Povinelli and

Eddy (1996a) with 7-year-old chimpanzees. In one condition, the human experimenter moved eyes and head, while in another only eye movements served as the cue. Chimpanzees looked to where the human was looking at above baseline levels in both conditions. Furthermore, chimpanzees would follow gaze into the visual space behind them, something achieved by human infants at about 18 months (Butterworth & Jarrett, 1991). If the experimenter's line of gaze was impeded by an opaque barrier, they attended to the barrier, as if they knew that it blocked the line of sight. This comparative study suggests that chimpanzees share or even exceed some of the capacities for JVA in babies. However, these experiments need not imply that chimpanzees (or babies) understand seeing as a mentalistic construct. In fact, Povinelli and Eddy (1996b) went on to show that chimpanzees mainly use forward-facing head orientation as a cue for attention, without any mentalistic understanding of seeing. Chimpanzees failed to identify the knowledgeable member of a pair of experimenters, when one had eyes open and one had eyes closed during food baiting of the rewarded location, so long as both persons faced forward. Similarly, when one of the forward-facing humans had a bandage over the eyes, or even when one of a forward-facing pair of experimenters wore a bucket over the head, chimpanzees failed to take into account that that individual could not have seen where the reward had been hidden. This argues rather strongly against mental-state attribution as the basis for JVA in higher primates and for body posture and facial orientation as the important signals on which shared attention is based.

Tomasello, Call, and Hare (1998) showed that individuals in five primate species (chimpanzees, sooty mangabeys, rhesus macaques, stump-tail macaques, and pigtail macaques) would follow the gaze of conspecifics to locate food on over 80 percent of occasions within 1 second of when the change of gaze occurred. They suggest that gaze following is common both in monkeys and apes. Perret and colleagues have discussed a possible neurophysiological base for JVA in monkeys (Lorincz, Baker, & Perret, 1999). They suggest that cells in the superior temporal sulcus of macaque monkeys may code attention direction. Some cells code for whether the monkey is being looked at or not, while other cells code for attention to locations in extrapersonal space. For the latter populations of cells, different types of posture information are coded in a hierarchical, coordinated fashion. For example, if a particular cell codes for gazing to the right, the same cell will respond even if the eyes are not visible but there is a right-facing profile. Even if the head happens to be occluded the same cell will respond to a right-facing body profile. Priority is given to certain cues: in some cells, eye direction takes priority in combining cues, whereas in other cells there is no priority. In macaques, visual cues from head posture proved to be more important than those from body posture. A change in eye direction with constant head direction increased the probability of following eye direction in static displays, even though macaques will normally follow changes in head direction in preference to changes in eye direction. Thus, at the neurophysiological level (if not always at the behavioral level), macaques use orientation of trunk and eyes to identify the locus of visual attention of other macaques.

In summary, visual co-orientation is readily observed in nature with examples documented in birds, monkeys, and apes. There is evidence that higher primates are similar to human infants in actually monitoring gaze (i.e., head and eye movements) for joint attention. To the extent that JVA occurs, cues for spatial orientation from head, eyes, and trunk are implicated, perhaps in a hierarchical fashion. Joint visual attention need not imply that an organism understands seeing as a mental state since the bodily orientation of the conspecific carries sufficient information for JVA to occur. Thus, joint attention in its most elementary form may be considered as a form of selective orienting based on postural cues of the social partner which serve as signals for potentially interesting objects in the environment.

## The Emergence of Joint Attention

The major theoretical impact of Scaife and Bruner's (1975) pioneering study was on received theories of infant egocentrism (Butterworth, 1987). Scaife and Bruner (1975) showed that infants as young as 2 months followed a change in the orientation of gaze of an adult. Their observation was initially met with some skepticism since JVA in infancy is not possible in traditional theories, such as Piaget's (1952, 1954); and Collis (1977) was unable to replicate the results with such young babies. In Scaife and Bruner's (1975) original study, babies followed the adult's direction of gaze, to left or right, into an empty visual field and the absence of objects may have made the effect particularly fragile. Many subsequent studies, which have incorporated objects, have placed the onset of JVA very much later, usually after 9 months (Carpenter, Nagell, & Tomasello, 1998; Corkum & Moore, 1995; Moore & Corkum, 1994; Morissette, Ricard, & Gouin-Decarie, 1995).

One reason why the age of emergence of JVA has been so much later in replication studies than in Scaife and Bruner's original observation is that conservative diagnostic criteria have often been adopted. The spatial conditions of testing may have placed great demands on babies' ability to integrate the change in the adult's focus of attention with the target. In Carpenter et al.'s (1998) study babies had to accurately localize targets placed at approximately 45 or 80 degrees to the right or left of the midline. Babies were not credited with JVA unless they could accurately localize all the targets (Carpenter et al., 1998, figure 1). Similarly, Corkum and Moore (1995) applied a stringent criterion that infants should show spontaneous gaze following and also produce five consecutive correct responses in order to be credited with the capacity of JVA. Morissette et al. (1995) also used large spatial separations of the targets and stringent scoring criteria which showed JVA to be coincident with comprehension of pointing at 12–15 months. Stringent performance criteria and demanding spatial conditions will certainly show when a *robust* ability for JVA is available (see table 12.1), but these criteria do not allow for early-appearing JVA.

Other studies, using less stringent criteria for JVA, have consistently claimed that joint visual attention can be observed at least as early as 3 months, as Scaife and Bruner (1975) claimed. For example, Butterworth and Cochran (1980) and Butterworth and Jarrett (1991) showed JVA in a simple, uncluttered laboratory environment in 6-month-old babies. More recently, D'Entremont, Hains, and Muir (1998) showed JVA in 4-month-old babies using targets that were placed each side of the baby's midline and in the periphery of vision. There was no requirement to single out a particular target among many potential targets and joint attention was inferred from the fact that the response terminated at the target located on the appropriate side. Thus, in the D'Entremont et al. study, the infant could succeed by simply encoding the direction of the adult's gaze (left or right), following which the specific referent would single itself out as it came into the periphery of vision. This interpretation is consistent with the finding of Hood, Willen, and Driver (1998) that babies of 4 months would look in a particular direction when cued by the orientation of the eyes on a face presented as a computer display.

In adults, the eye movements in computer displays take precedence in allocating attention, even when their direction does not predict the location of a subsequent event, a phenomenon which has been described as "reflexive social orienting" (Friesen & Kingstone, 1998, p. 494). Furthermore, adults are significantly faster in responding to a display comprising head and eyes when both are oriented in the same direction than when eyes and head are oriented in opposite directions (Langton, 2000). This suggests that, for adults, a directional decision may be based on the orientation of both the head and eyes, or possibly that incongruous signals, where eyes face one way and head the other, confound interpersonal and extrapersonal attention mechanisms (see discussion below of Butterworth & Itakura, 2000).

Clearly, the recent data from babies suggest that some components of JVA must already be in place by 4 months, albeit in fragile form, based on monitoring head orientation, eye movements, or both. Controlled comparisons at different ages are needed to establish what is changing with development of JVA. Butterworth and Cochran (1980) and Butterworth and Jarrett (1991) carried out such studies with participants as young as 6 months, in a homogeneous laboratory environment where the walls were screened by curtains to form a neutral background. Identical targets were systematically, symmetrically located, relatively close to the experimenter and infant (minimum and maximum distances in the infant's visual field were approximately 1 m at 60 degrees from the midline and 2.60 m at 30 degrees from the midline). Adults and infant were seated *en face,* at the same height as the targets. The adult changed her focus of attention to one of the targets by reorienting head, eyes, and trunk, holding her posture for approximately 5 seconds. The aim was to establish the spatial conditions under which 6-month-old babies could "follow into" a change in the adult's direction of gaze. Babies at 6 months showed significantly more responses to targets on the correct side and were clearly capable of triadic attention (Butterworth & Jarrett, 1991). Further studies showed that babies of this age could accurately locate the correct target either if it was stationary and first along the baby's scan path into the periphery of vision, or if both targets were simultaneously in motion and the correct target was the more peripheral of the two (Grover, 1988). That is, attention-worthy attributes of objects in the periphery of vision may assist the young baby to identify a common focus for joint attention.

There appear to be important developments in the extent of the visual field that a baby will scan in looking for an object. Butterworth and Cochran (1980) used the adult orientation procedure with an empty visual field. Babies at 12 months searched through about 40 degrees from their own midline following an adult orientation and then gave up. If the adult gazed at a target located in the space behind the baby, the infant at 12 months still turned only through 40 degrees and then gave up. This implies that, at 12 months, the infant takes the adult's gaze to refer to a potential object that is somewhere within a shared visual space. If the baby's own change in the focus of attention fails to locate an object (because the shared visual field is empty), the process of shifting attention terminates (see also Caron, Krakowski, Liu, & Brooks, 1996). However, Butterworth and Jarrett (1991) showed that by 18 months babies did search behind them when the visual field in front was empty, which suggests that they are now aware of a surrounding space. Therefore, once the competing evidence is carefully analyzed, it is clear that triadic JVA is possible, under appropriate conditions, before the 9–12-month watershed (Butterworth & Grover, 1988, 1989; Butterworth & Jarrett, 1991). With development, new abilities to attend to targets at greater and greater angular distances from the baby progressively supplement a basic "ecological" mechanism.

Butterworth and Jarrett (1991) suggested that three successive mechanisms of joint visual attention can be discerned in the age range between 6 and 18 months. At 6 months, babies look to the correct side of the room, as if to see what the adult is looking at, but they cannot tell which of the two identical targets on the same side of the room is correct, unless it happens to move or in some way be the more salient. Joint visual attention depends on the differentiated structure of the natural environment so that what initially attracts the adult's attention and leads her to turn (thus providing the baby with information about *spatial direction* through the change in her postural orientation) is also likely to capture the attention of the infant (thus providing information about *spatial location* through the object's intrinsic properties). This ecological mechanism enables a "meeting of minds" in the self-same object.

Between 12 and 18 months the infant begins to localize the target correctly, even when it is further into the periphery than an identical distractor target (Butterworth & Jarrett, 1991). This new mechanism was called "geometric" because it appeared to require extrapolation of a vector between the mother's head orientation and the referent of her gaze. Butterworth and Itakura (2000) investigated the hypothesis that babies become capable of "geometric" vector extrapolation, but it emerged that neither babies, children, nor adults used such a precise mechanism to locate the referent of another's gaze. Instead, it turned out that the onset of robust JVA is marked by a progressive increase in the ability to localize targets that are further into the periphery than a distractor target – thus, at this age, the attention-capturing properties of objects themselves become less important. However, JVA continues to be limited by the boundaries of the babies' visual space until 18 months of age when babies become capable of searching the space behind them.

Why does robust JVA take so long to develop? Among the most important constraints on joint attention in early infancy is the capacity to integrate actions and events across gaps in space and time. Millar and Schaffer (1972, 1973) showed that babies of 6 months readily learned to bang on a canister for contingent light reinforcement, which occurred at the same place where they were banging (i.e., under conditions of complete contiguity between stimulus and response). They also learned such a response when the location of the light reinforcement did not occur in the same location as the response, providing that there was a spatial cue within their visual field to draw attention to the light. However, when there was no visible cue to the reinforcement light, babies failed to learn the response. Millar and Schaffer conclude that, before 9 months, dividing attention between an action and its consequences presents major difficulties for the infant because attention must be coordinated between separate foci. Evidence is widespread that a rapid stage-like change occurs between 9 and 12 months in the ability to bridge such gaps. This change may be linked with maturation of frontal lobe functions, which allow infants to make rapid progress in solving delayed-response tasks (Diamond, 1991).

However, frontal lobe maturation may not be the whole story because, as was said earlier, babies of 3–4 months engage in triangular relations with adults across spatial separations which are much greater than those which they fail to encompass in triadic JVA (Fivaz-Depeursinge & Corboz-Warnery, 1999). It seems possible that the underlying change is from direct triangulation within social relationships, observed at least as early as 3–4 months, to referential triangulation (i.e., triadic JVA), in which the preexisting ability for social triangulation is now used to single out (refer to) inanimate objects. Careful experiments are needed to establish exactly how such a transition might occur, since factors such as the size, visibility, animacy, and distance of the people and objects involved in triangular vs. triadic relations have not so far been systematically controlled.

In summary, the ability to integrate information across spatiotemporal gaps may be one of the basic underlying processes that allows the transition to robust JVA. The increasing distance of targets that are accessible with age may simply reflect changes in the ability to integrate attention to events at differently spaced foci.

Other cognitive changes may contribute, however, particularly the ability to search for hidden objects on the basis of minimal cues. Robust JVA may mark a transition from communication primarily within directly perceived, effectively based human relationships to referential communication incorporating objects.

## Pointing and Joint Visual Attention

The characteristics of the signal that indicate a change in direction of gaze (change in head orientation with eye movements or eye movements alone) influence the incidence and accuracy of infant responses. It is relatively difficult to find evidence for eye movements alone being effective in joint attention in large-scale spaces before about 18 months (Butterworth & Jarrett, 1991; Corkum & Moore, 1995). Studies of older children and adults also suggest that eyes alone are not a good cue to gaze direction. Contrary to what one might have expected, Butterworth and Itakura (2000) found that adult observers were more accurate in locating a target when the experimenter was wearing sunglasses than when the eyes were visible; and children aged 4.5 years were more accurate in locating the target when the experimenter had his eyes closed rather than open. Findings such as these suggest that the eyes are not necessarily the primary source of information for singling out the object in triadic JVA. However, there is another cue that does appear to be uniquely important in determining the object of JVA – pointing.

The second major phase shown in table 12.1, which we have characterized as robust JVA, is marked by the onset of pointing. Index finger pointing is a means of making definite reference that is intimately linked to gesture and speech. Here we will examine evidence for its species-specificity to humans and will offer some evidence for the universality of the gesture. First, it is necessary to describe the typical posture of the hand in pointing to avoid confusion with other indicative gestures. In pointing, the index finger and arm are extended in the direction of the interesting object, while the remaining fingers are curled under the hand, with the thumb held down and to the side. The orientation of the hand, either palm downward or rotated so the palm is vertical with respect to the body midline, may also be significant in further differentiating subtypes of indexical pointing. Pointing is a deictic gesture which is used to reorient the attention of another person so that an object becomes the shared focus for attention. Rolfe (1996) offers three criteria for deictic pointing: (1)

it is dialogic in that it requires an audience and is for someone else's benefit; (2) the gesture serves to single something out which the addressee comprehends to be the referent; (3) the direction of what is being pointed at is seen as away from the pointing hand. These three characteristics constitute the contextual and cognitive requirements for the comprehension and production of pointing. We will begin by considering some comparative studies to evaluate the claim that pointing is species-specific to humans.

## *Comparative evidence on the species-specificity of pointing*

The precise definition of the pointing gesture is rather important in evaluating comparative evidence. For example, the pointer dog, according to Hewes (1981), has been associated with humans in hunting for at least two and a half thousand years. The dog aligns its whole body with the target, from tip of nose to extended tail, sometimes with a front paw raised, in a manner partly analogous to human deictic behavior. The orientation of the dog indicates the general direction of fallen wildfowl, which assists the hunter to locate the prey. However, it is not the case that the dog engages in a dialogue with the hunter and, furthermore, whole-body orienting differs in other important ways from indexical pointing. For example, the dog does not see itself orienting toward the prey, whereas sight of the hand and the object in the visual field may be integral to the production and comprehension of pointing in humans.

Chimpanzees (*Pan troglodytes*) and orangutans (*Pongo pygmaeus*) are capable of signaling with manual indicative gestures, in which the arm, open hand, and extended fingers are oriented in the direction of an interesting sight. The behavior is usually made by captive, trained chimpanzees to their human trainers and it is rarely seen between conspecifics. Higher primates generally give no prominence to the index finger in making indicative gestures (Blaschke & Ettlinger, 1987; Call & Tomasello, 1994; Menzel, 1974). Hewes (1981) describes an observational study of a pair of captive bonobos (*Pan paniscus*) in which only 21 indicative gestures were observed in 600 hours of filming. These were made by the male and served to indicate to the female that she should move to another part of the enclosure. The question is whether such open-handed, indicative gestures in chimpanzees should be considered equivalent to human pointing. Some authors have argued that they are equivalent and that the *function* of indicating is more important than the *form* of the gesture (Krause & Fouts, 1997). One factor that may limit index finger pointing in apes is the anatomy of the hand. An intriguing observation by Povinelli and Davis (1994) points to subtle differences in the anatomy of the human and chimpanzee hand: they noted that the resting posture of the index finger in anesthetized humans is slightly proud of the remaining fingers, whereas in chimpanzees all the fingers remain aligned when at rest.

However, this need not mean that indexical pointing is impossible for chimpanzees. It has recently been shown that chimpanzees (*Pan troglodytes*) can signal with an index finger (Leavens, Hopkins, & Bard, 1996). The clearest evidence came from a chimpanzee named Clint, aged 14 years, who extended the index finger through the cage mesh (with left and right hand) apparently as a request to the experimenter for food which had fallen on the ground. Index finger extension was less frequent (38 instances) than whole-hand indicative gestures (102 instances). Indicative gestures were used by Clint as an imperative for food items (i.e., give me that food) and it is possible that his index finger extensions may have been learned as a particular consequence of social contact with humans, since he was never observed to use index finger pointing with conspecifics. Nevertheless, some of his index finger extensions were accompanied by checking where the experimenter was looking – suggesting that the gesture required an audience – and he only made the gesture when the experimenter was facing him. Leavens and Hopkins (1998), in a study of 115 chimpanzees aged from 3 to 56 years, found that 47 animals made whole-hand indicative gestures and 6 animals used indexical points with arm extended to single out the location of food. Of 78 chimpanzees who made gestures of any kind, 35 percent of the gestures were accompanied by vocalization, a figure rather lower than usually found with babies. High levels of gaze alternation (checking) were observed, however (80 percent of animals showed checking from 8 years), which is typical of humans too.

Krause (1998) has reported human-like indexical pointing, with arm extension, in a 21-year-old captive chimpanzee who was trained to indicate to a naive experimenter which of four possible places contained a hidden object. These conditions required greater precision than is usually demanded of chimpanzees in such tasks, which may have influenced selection of the gesture. However, it is possible that the gesture was learned from human caretakers, since the chimpanzee was sign language-trained. Furthermore, it was made with scant regard to hand orientation, so that pointing was sometimes observed with the upside-down hand (M. A. Krause, personal communication, 1998). G. E. Butterworth (personal observation, 1998) found that 19 out of 20 examples of pointing in 10 babies occurred with the palm downward, and one with the palm sideways. That is, upside-down pointing never occurred, which suggests that Krause's chimpanzee may have been trained to point by molding the begging gesture.

As has already been noted, feral chimpanzees have not been observed to point indexically and, indeed, whole-body orienting may be sufficiently communicative for the chimpanzee's purposes in the wild (Menzel, 1974). Povinelli, Bering, and Giambrone (2000) note that neither of the two long-term studies of chimpanzees in the wild which extend over 40 years have ever reported pointing in chimpanzees. Furthermore, even if pointing in chimpanzees is morphologically similar to that in humans (and there is very little evidence for this), this would not necessarily imply that pointing is understood in the same way by chimpanzees and humans. Povinelli, Reaux, Bierschwale, Allain, and Simon (1997) showed that, whereas 2-year-old children had no difficulty finding hidden objects on the basis of a manual pointing cue (i.e., independent of gaze or distance cues), adolescent chimpanzees responded in terms of the distance between the pointing hand and the target, choosing whichever target happened to be the nearer to the hand. This suggests they do not comprehend the pointing gesture as referential. When the experimenter pointed across the body to a distant box, but his body was actually closer to the incorrect box, chimpanzees reliably chose the incorrect box. In contrast, a study by Lee, Eskritt, Symons, and Muir (1998) showed that 3-year-old children consistently responded to the pointing cue when they saw a videotaped event in which an actor pointed toward one object but looked at another. Furthermore, Couillard and Woodward (1999) showed that 3- to 4.5-year-old children could easily ignore a misleading cue about the location of a reward if it was a simple marker placed at the incorrect location of two. However, they were unable to ignore a misleading point, which suggests that the communicative functions of pointing tend to preclude its being interpreted as a deceptive cue until quite late into childhood.

The contrast in prevalence and comprehension of pointing in humans as compared with chimpanzees is graphically illustrated in a study of congenitally deaf infants by Goldin-Meadow and Feldman (1977). They found that 51 percent of as many as 5,000 gestures produced by toddlers aged 17 to 47 months were indexical points at things, people, or places (cited in Hewes, 1981).

Franco and Butterworth (1996) also found that pointing comprised more than 55 percent of the gestures of babies aged 14 months, whereas other indicative gestures involving the whole hand, or extended arm and closed fist, or isolated index finger extension, accounted for only 18 percent of gestures in total. Furthermore, whole-hand indicative gestures and index finger pointing were uncorrelated in development, with indicative gestures remaining at a low constant level between 12 and 18 months, whereas pointing increased exponentially. A similar low correlation between pointing and other indicative gestures was found by Lock, Young, Service, and Chandler (1990). All this evidence suggests that open-hand indicative gestures and pointing are unrelated and therefore may serve different purposes in communication. For babies indexical pointing is the preferred means of sharing attention, whereas for chimpanzees production of indexical behavior is at best very rare and may, in any case, serve primarily as a request (protoimperative) rather than to share attention (protodeclarative).

The recent upsurge of research on pointing in chimpanzees suggests that it is not possible to maintain an absolute divide between humans and other higher primate species with respect to open-handed indicative gestures. Thus, some aspects of the capacity for sharing attention by indicating may be shared with other primates. This makes explaining indexical pointing all the more interesting since, unlike the case for JVA, there are many strong contrasts between humans and chimpanzees. These include the incidence of the gesture, its precise form, and the preference for pointing in babies over other means of indicating. In particular, canonical index finger pointing in humans is done for conspecifics, whereas it has never been observed to occur between chimpanzees, and it is declarative (it serves to redirect attention toward an object), whereas in chimpanzees almost all examples are imperative (it usually serves as a request). On the evidence to date, by these broader deictic criteria, declarative indexical pointing is probably species-specific to humans, unlike gaze cues, which widely serve joint visual attention in nature.

## Pointing Comprehension in Humans

We will first discuss pointing comprehension, which begins around 11 months, before going on to factors involved in pointing production. Many studies agree that the comprehension of pointing slightly precedes its production, but this may simply reflect relative lack of knowledge about the precursors (Franco & Butterworth, 1996; Leung & Rheingold, 1981; Messer, 1994). There is evidence that the spatial conditions of testing influence whether infants comprehend pointing or not. An early study by Lempers (1976) found that babies of 9 months comprehend pointing to nearby targets and by 12 months they comprehend pointing to more distant targets. Morissette et al. (1995) in a longitudinal study also found that comprehension of manual pointing to relatively distant targets begins at about 12 months. The most frequent error of babies was to look at the pointing hand rather than at the designated target. Murphy and Messer (1977) found that pointing comprehension was earlier (9 months) for targets on the same side of the room as the pointing hand than when the point was into the contralateral half of the infant's visual space, across the body midline of the adult seated *en face* (12 months). Butterworth and Grover (1989) showed that pointing was understood by 12 months in that pointing produced headturning in the direction indicated by the pointing hand. By contrast, infants at 6 or 9 months were as likely to fixate the pointing hand as the designated target. Morissette et al. (1995) and Carpenter et al. (1998) found that pointing comprehension occurred earlier for nearby than for more distant targets and the angle subtended by the targets, relative to the baby, influenced the probability of pointing comprehension. Others have also found similar effects (Lempers, 1976; Murphy & Messer, 1977). Carpenter et al. (1998) noted that babies comprehended pointing to targets to their right two months before targets to their left, a phenomenon also reported by Butterworth and Itakura in a symmetrical environment (2000). These observations on asymmetries favoring the right side of space in JVA are very recent and they require further validation. In the Butterworth and Itakura (2000) study, the asymmetry in babies' attention was only apparent for gaze plus pointing which took attention further into the right visual periphery than the left. The asymmetry was not apparent for gaze cues alone, which took attention a lesser distance equally into the left or right periphery. Asymmetries in attention allocation to the right visual field, possibly mediated by left-hemisphere brain functions, could be very important in linking the pointing gesture in development with species-typical brain mechanisms for speech.

Detailed longitudinal studies are needed to establish exactly how babies begin to understand pointing. Mothers go to a great deal of trouble, with exaggerated hand movements, to lead the young infant's gaze from the hand onto the target (Murphy &

Messer, 1977). Grover (1988) showed that the infant's latency to fixate the correct target significantly decreased between 9 and 12 months, which suggests that the gesture rapidly acquired the status of a signal. Babies at 12 months were significantly more likely to respond to a change of gaze plus point than to gaze alone, and they fixated a target further into the periphery of vision for pointing than for gaze alone. When the salience of the targets was experimentally manipulated by setting them into motion, the infant's response to pointing increased to ceiling level. Target motion was sufficient to eliminate hand fixation in 9-month infants, although babies then went on to fixate only the first target along their scan path from the adult's hand. By 15 months, however, babies did alight on the second, more peripheral target, in a sequence of fixations. Thus, infants are not merely fixating the first object they encounter when they fully comprehend pointing. However, when babies first begin to understand pointing, the attention-worthy object may first "pluck" the child's attention from the pointing hand.

Butterworth and Itakura (2000) tested infants at 6 months, 12 months, and 15 months for the accuracy with which they could locate one of two identical targets at angular separations ranging from 25 degrees to 55 degrees. Mother and baby sat *en face* and one target was always at 10 degrees to the left of the baby's midline (the first target along their scan path from the mother), and the second was at a more peripheral leftward position. The mother either looked at the target (with head and eye movements) or looked and pointed at the target. For all three age groups there was little evidence that babies could accurately select the more peripheral of the pair just on the basis of head and eye movements. However, from 12 months, manual pointing had a significant effect on the accuracy of the response to the more peripheral target and, by 15 months, there was a clear advantage to pointing in localizing the more peripheral target at all angular distances. Infants' success following the pointing cue, despite the narrow angular separation between the 10- and 25-degree targets, suggested that they might be solving the problem by extrapolating a linear vector along the pointing arm to intersect with the object.

In further experiments with 4.5-year-old children and adults, Butterworth and Itakura (2000) tested the vector extrapolation hypothesis by presenting targets three at a time on each side of the visual field. The angular separations between targets varied from 4 to 45 degrees for adults and it was held constant at 10 degrees for children, again at 2.7 m (as for the babies). The task required the participant, who sat next to the experimenter, simply to state the color of the target that was being singled out by a pointing gesture or by combinations of head and eye movements. Children were accurate following pointing but they were not accurate for head and eye movements. Pointing allowed accuracy only to the periphery of each visual hemifield and children were inaccurate to the intermediate targets. Adults were generally as accurate following head and eye movements as following pointing to the targets at separations of 15 degrees or greater (i.e., about 70 cm separation between target centers). However, they were inaccurate for the intermediate target positions at separations of 15 degrees or less. That is, the pointing gesture successfully drew attention to the peripheral boundaries of vision both for children and adults, but precise linear vector extrapolation was not used to follow pointing since there is no reason why a linear vector should be less accurate for intermediate than peripheral positions.

Butterworth and Itakura (2000) explain the effect on accuracy of manual pointing to peripheral target locations in terms of the movement of the "lever" formed by the arm. For any given spatial separation between a pair of targets, the horizontal excursion of a long lever, like the arm, will be greater than that of a shorter lever, like the head and nose, or very short levers, like the eyes. Each component of the orienting system may serve to specify different regions of space. The eyes are most effective just each side of the midline and they serve as a particularly useful cue as to whether one is being looked at. Head orientation takes attention further away from the midline and pointing takes attention to the periphery of vision. Thus, one part of the body, the arm and pointing hand may have become specialized for referemial communication in humans because it is particularly useful in taking attention to the extreme periphery of vision (Butterworth, 1997). The results of the Butterworth and Itakura study show that, even for adults, following pointing is not a completely precise method of achieving JVA. The process of achieving JVA does not operate by extrapolation of linear vectors and, in a cluttered environment, accuracy also requires attention-worthy cues from the object to help single it out.

The conclusion from these studies is that babies, children, and adults are partially dependent on target qualities to identify the specific referent of the gaze or pointing signal. That is, JVA is a two-part process, one part being specified by change in gaze or postural orientation which define the broad zones of visual space likely to be of mutual interest, and the other part depending on the object to single itself out in a crowded environment. Thus, what attracts the adult's attention and leads her to turn eventually also captures the infant's attention and enables a meeting of minds at the location of the object. Head and eye movements, which are perceived as referential actions from early in development, come to be supplemented by the pointing gesture, which carries attention further into the periphery once the infant can integrate experience across the greater distances involved.

## The Production of Pointing

A number of studies now agree on the emergence of canonical pointing (as defined by the precise hand posture above) at an average age of 11 months, although babies as young as 8.5 months have been observed to point (Butterworth & Morissette, 1996; Schaffer, 1984). Approximately 33 percent of parents of 8-month-old babies in the United States report that their babies already point (Fenson, Dale, Resnick, Bates, Thal, & Pethick, 1994). Carpenter et al. (1998), in a longitudinal study of 24 babies, also in the United States, found that pointing to nearby objects occurred at 11 months, two months before more distal pointing. Butterworth and Morissette (1996), in a similar longitudinal study of 27 babies in England, also found the average age for pointing onset to be in the eleventh month (11.2 months for females and 11.7 months for males). Ohama (1984), in a longitudinal study in Japan, reported that five out of nine of her sample pointed by 11 months and eight out of nine by 13 months. By 12 months pointing comprises more than 60 percent of all gestures made by the infant (Lock et al., 1990). Pointing typically emerges suddenly (Lock et al., 1990), as if after a stage transition. Pointing is accompanied by checking with the adult (3.4 percent of points at 12 months, according to Lock et al., and about 20 percent at 18 months in Franco & Butterworth, 1996). Pointing is also accompanied by vocalization (50 percent of pointing gestures, according to Lock et al., 1990, 76 percent in Franco & Butterworth, 1996, 87 percent in Leung & Rheingold, 1981 – all at 12 months). L. Fenson (personal communication, 1997) found an accelerated pointing onset for female babies until 12 months, when the number of males who are said to point catches up. Sex differences in pointing onset could have important implications for understanding female advantage in aspects of language acquisition, further strengthening the link between JVA and communication development.

It was once widely believed that pointing emerges by the differentiation of index finger extension from a more primitive open-handed "waving" posture, after the seventh month (e.g., Leung & Rheingold, 1981; Murphy & Messer, 1977). Although the canonical form of pointing emerges toward the end of the first year, there is evidence that antecedents of pointing, in particular the independent extension of the index finger, can be observed much earlier than was traditionally believed. Isolated extension of the index finger, with the other fingers curled inwards in the pointing posture, has been observed in the 3-month-old baby, in close association with "speech-like" sounds, when the infant is engaged in social interaction (Fogel & Hannan, 1985; Hannan 1987; Masataka, 1995). In a longitudinal single-case study, Hannan and Fogel (1987) observed pointing movements, predominantly of the right hand, from 18 days. "Pointing" was accompanied by movements of the eyes and mouth which occurred as a cluster of orienting behaviors. The pointing movements occurred when the babies were engaged in social interaction and they continued until the age of 6 months (Fogel, 1981). These microanalytic studies of babies reveal that "embryonic" forms of the pointing gesture are already in the repertoire even though mothers are not typically aware that their babies are pointing. Thus, the typical pointing posture of the hand does not emerge from a less differentiated form but shows the typical hand shape from soon after birth.

There are isolated reports that babies can sometimes be observed making pointing movements for themselves before they engage in pointing for others. Tran-Duc Thao (1984) described such behavior as reinforcing for oneself the "sense certainty" of the object, and Lempert and Kinsbourne (1985) relate it to involuntary orienting movements, or expressions of interest, which are perhaps similar to the transitional phenomena observed by Franco and Butterworth (1996). These authors found that at 10 months babies sometimes point at an object, then turn to the mother as if to check with her, whereupon they point at the mother. This phenomenon was also noted by Masur (1983) when the mother was holding the object. It is as if visual checking and manual pointing are coming together in a new coordinated structure comprising pointing and checking, which is not yet appropriately sequentially organized across the spatial gap. Checking has been taken as strong evidence of communicative intent since the audience is being "interrogated" for comprehension. Lempert and Kinsbourne (1985) also suggest that such "dual directional signaling" is evidence for communicative intent. However, this does not mean that pointing that is not accompanied by checking is necessarily egocentric. An alternative hypothesis is that pointing is an aspect of a communication production system, whereas checking is a complementary aspect of the system seeking confirmation of comprehension. This requires further research. In general, the evidence on the antecedents of pointing takes the form of the gesture into very early human development, again suggesting it is of biological origin.

The social conditions necessary for pointing in babies were investigated by Franco and Butterworth (1990), who tested babies alone or when with adults who actively pointed or remained still. Pointing occurred only under conditions where a social partner was available for communication and babies did not point when alone with attractive objects. When reunited with the mother this often released a flood of pointing to the targets. Furthermore, pointing by the baby did not require that the adult also point, nor was the rate of infant pointing a function of the adult rate. That is, infant pointing implies an audience, even if the partner is another baby, and it is not a function of the adult also pointing (Franco, Perruchino, & Butterworth, 1992).

Butterworth, Franco, McKenzie, Graupner, and Todd (1998) carried out a series of experiments designed to test the "spotlight" metaphor of focal attention in pointing. Remotely controlled targets, comprising six doll figures that could move their arms and legs, were set in motion both focally and at different positions in the periphery from 50 degrees left to 50 degrees right of the midline. Each trial began with the baby fixating at the midline and then the dolls were set in motion, either singly or in combinations of pairs. When targets were activated singly, all positions were equally likely to elicit pointing, despite large differences in the distance from the initial fixation point, which suggests that stimulus factors eliciting pointing may operate in parallel and do not favor the initial focal position. When targets were activated in pairs, babies were more likely to point at the target on the right side of visual space than to the target on the left, which suggests that the conflict is resolved by attending preferentially to the right side of visual space. The primary effect of target position was to determine which hand does the pointing, with the right hand chosen most often. In subsequent experiments the dolls were modified so that sound was added to their repertoire. Babies could hear a voice saying "hello baby" on trials in which sound was combined with doll movement, and this was compared with trials in which babies heard sound alone (without movement) or movement (without sound). The bimodal condition proved to elicit significantly more pointing overall, and females produced significantly more right-handed pointing than males. Under unimodal visual conditions, the hand chosen tended to be ipsilateral to the side of target movement. In bimodal conditions, the right hand was favored among females even for targets to the left of the body midline (babies were aged 13.6 months). In another study, which involved a toy clown moving across the visual field, latency of pointing was shown to be a function of event complexity. Pointing to a simple translation of motion was significantly faster than if the clown moved or vanished during translation. Complex events of this nature actually tend to suppress pointing. Pointing was again mainly right-handed, despite the translation of the clown across the field of vision in both directions.

Thus, once pointing develops in babies, it meets Rolfe's (1996) criteria for deictic reference: it requires an audience, refers away from the hand, and has a dialogic character. Although pointing may terminate in focal attention, targets at widely spaced positions relative to the observer are equally likely to elicit the gesture. The right hand and the right side of visual space are privileged in eliciting pointing, but it occurs with either hand. When events differing in complexity are used to elicit pointing, there is a tendency for more complex event structures to suppress the gesture, as if the capacity for attention allocation is in danger of being exceeded.

## Pointing and Prehension

Traditional views of the origins of pointing are of two types, which stress either that pointing develops out of prehension (e.g., Vygotsky, 1988) or that it is a communicative gesture from the outset. Within the latter type of theory it is often assumed that pointing is initially performed for the self and becomes ritualized through social interaction until it serves purposes of social communication (e.g., Werner & Kaplan, 1963). Vygotsky believed that pointing derives from unsuccessful grasping movements, which are interpreted by the mother as a request. In coming to her infant's aid, the mother converts the movement into a gesture for others and it acquires an imperative character. No explanation for the specific hand posture is offered except that it is considered somehow transitional with grasping.

Franco and Butterworth (1996) tested both these types of theory in a study which compared the incidence of pointing and reaching gestures in 10- to 14-month-old babies in declarative and imperative communicative contexts. Babies had the opportunity to point at or make grasping gestures to interesting objects that were both in and out of reach. From the onset pointing was never confused with reaching gestures. It occurred primarily to distal targets (2.7 m away) and was accompanied by vocalization and checking with the partner. Both these accompanying behaviors increased exponentially with age. Reaching gestures were not strongly correlated with checking and they remained at a low level. These findings run against the view of the origins of pointing as theorized by Vygotsky (1988), since pointing was not tied in any way to failed grasping and there was no evidence that the imperative use of the gesture had primacy. Carpenter et al. (1998) in their longitudinal study also found no evidence that the imperative use of pointing emerges before the declarative. That is, on the detailed empirical evidence to date, the pointing gesture in humans initially serves a protodeclarative purpose (i.e., look at that) rather than a protoimperative purpose (i.e., give me that).

In a reinterpretation of the literature on early communicative development, Camaioni (1993) has argued that imperative and declarative pointing gestures may differ in their cognitive complexity. The former implies an understanding of others as "agents of action," whereas the latter implies an understanding of others as "agents of contemplation." Exercising a causal effect on the world through physical contact with a person is said to be intellectually less demanding than understanding that interactions can be causally influenced by distal means. Rather than the declarative function of pointing being derived from the imperative function, she suggests that they may be independent. This distinction may partly explain the use of indicative gestures in chimpanzees, where almost all the evidence shows they are used imperatively and not declaratively.

That is not to say that pointing has nothing at all to do with prehension in humans. A clue to the reasons for the morphology of the human pointing gesture comes from the specific adaptations of the hand. The human hand is highly flexible, with a very great capability for precision based on the fully opposable index finger and thumb – a factor considered to be one of the key features differentiating humans from other primates. Based on rather minimal evidence from two 2-year-old chimpanzees clutching a grape, Napier (1960) argued that only humans are capable of the pincer grip. The relative size and position of finger and thumb (the opposability index) sets limits on the extent to which the base of the thumb can be abducted against the tip of the index finger. He gave values for the opposability index of 0.65 for humans and 0.43 for chimpanzees, a difference due mainly to the relatively short thumb of the chimpanzee, which is positioned low down the wrist.

Two studies have recently reported that the pincer grip is in fact in the repertoire of the chimpanzee. In one experiment, 80 captive chimpanzees (*Pan troglodytes*) aged from 1 to 25 years were observed picking up raisins measuring 1.0 to 1.5 cm from the cage floor. A human-like pattern of pincer grip was observed at 2 years, which reached a peak of 10 percent of all responses at 6 years (Tonooka & Matsuzawa, 1995). The same study showed that males were more likely than females to use the pincer grip once they were over 10 years old. A second study of 13 captive chimpanzees (*Pan troglodytes*) aged from 2 to 5 years showed that precision grips involving the thumb and index finger at or below the first distal joint occurred on 25 percent of trials (Jones-Engel & Bard, 1996). The human-like pincer grip with thumb pad to finger pad abduction occurred on 2 percent of trials.

These studies suggest that chimpanzees are capable of a degree of precision but they do not establish how precision grips develop. In human infants the pincer grip and imprecise opposition of the index finger and thumb above the first distal joint (the inferior forefinger grip typically adopted by chimpanzees) can already be observed at 8 months. The pincer grip is systematically selected by 15 months to grip cubes of 0.5 cm. Power grips, where the object is held between flexed fingers and palm, without thumb opposition, are rarely used by human infants older than 15 months with objects of these sizes (Butterworth, Verweij, & Hopkins, 1997). To obtain more detailed comparative evidence, Butterworth and Itakura (1998) studied 11 captive chimpanzees (*Pan troglodytes*) aged from 4 to 20 years who were video-recorded grasping cubes of apple measuring 0.5, 1.0, and 2.0 cm. This study confirmed that chimpanzees do have precision grips in their repertoire, at least from the age of 2 years, where the object is held between thumb tip and at or below the first joint of the index finger. Precision grips increase in frequency slowly, until chimpanzees are adult, and they are not systematically selected on the basis of object size at any age. Chimpanzees also use a species-typical precision grip, from about 8 years, in which they hold a small object between the index and middle fingers (the so-called "cigarette" grip). Power grips are commonly selected in chimpanzees to the age of 8 years, even when grasping small objects. This new developmental evidence shows that chimpanzees, by comparison with human infants, lack strongly systematic selection of precise grips for small objects. Their relative lack of precision extends across the age range from 2 years to full adulthood. Although a human-like pincer grip is in their repertoire, generally the whole index finger is selected and the exact position of opposition of the thumb is relatively uninfluenced by object size.

Once again, the contrast with human infants is revealing since the chimpanzee makes a developmental transition from predominance of power to precision grips very much later than is observed in babies. In human infants, there is a transition (between 8 and 15 months) when power grips which do not involve the thumb are eliminated and the pincer grip is systematically selected by object size (Butterworth et al., 1997). In human infants, the pincer grip develops earlier in females than in males (Butterworth et al., 1997). Thus, just as for pointing and indicative gestures, the repertoire of precise grips in chimpanzees overlaps that of humans, but the rapid rate of development in humans, especially females, ensures that precision grips and pointing will be used consistently even in infancy. By contrast, precise grips are infrequent, not consistently selected, and more typical of adult male chimpanzees.

The theory to be proposed here is that the pincer grip and pointing are co-evolved but are different aspects of hand function that are specialized respectively for precise instrumental action and for precise communication (see Butterworth, 1997, 1998). The characteristic hand posture observed in human pointing may be related to the pincer grip, but as its "antithesis." Darwin (1904) first proposed the principle of antithesis to explain how animal communication often exploits visual signals to convey information. For example, an animal may signal readiness to attack by making "intention movements" which are preparatory to fighting. After a fight, the subdued posture of the defeated dog signals submission because the muscles are activated in the opposite configuration, or antithesis, to those involved in aggression (Marler, 1959).

In the case of pointing, the opposition of the tip of the index finger and thumb in the pincer grip is postulated to have pointing as its postural antithesis. This also involves a change in the focus of visual attention. In precise manual activities with tools, focal attention is on the hand, the tool, and the object in the service of precise control of manipulation. In pointing, by contrast, attention is outer-directed and serves rather precisely to reorient the attention of another person so that an object at some distance can become a focus for shared experience. On this theory, the emergence of pointing should be related to the development of other precise uses of the hand, and this indeed is what Butterworth and Morissette (1996) established. The pincer grip was invariably in the infant's repertoire and it was systematically selected by infants approximately one month before pointing onset, females earlier than males. Exploration of objects with the tip of the index finger (tipping) has also been linked to the onset of pointing (Shinn, 1900). Butterworth et al. (1997) showed that "tipping" and the pincer grip are closely related in development, with the incidence of tipping declining as the pincer grip becomes established.

In summary, the theory that pointing is the antithesis of the pincer grip links precise, instrumental, manual action, pointing onset, and species-specific aspects of hand anatomy and function to the underlying processes governing focused attention. On this argument, precise tool use and precise manual communication through the pointing gesture are co-evolved human abilities. Not only do we share some aspects of hand function with other primates, but also there are human species-typical aspects of hand function that harness the human capacity for precision both in tool use and social communication. Both the pincer grip and the pointing gesture require focal attention, but each is a specialized adaptation: respectively for precise instrumental action for the self in near space and for precise communication for others in more distal space (see Butterworth, 1997, 1998).

## Pointing and the Transition to Language

A variety of studies have linked preverbal referential communication with language acquisition. Baldwin (1995) points out that the baby, by monitoring the adult's attentional focus, should be able to link the adult's utterances with the correct referent and thus avoid mapping errors in speech acquisition. Baldwin (1991, 1993) tested the theory by labeling one object when 18-month-old babies were focusing on a different object. Babies turned to check the adult's referent and thus avoided mapping errors in speech comprehension. It seems very likely that it is the identity of experience of the object in JVA which authorizes the sound stream to be treated as an aspect of the jointly attended object. In speech production there is evidence that the amount of pointing at 12 months predicts speech production rates at 24 months (Camaioni, Castelli, Longobardi, & Volterra, 1991). Links between pointing onset and comprehension of object names have also been established, with infants understanding their first object name in the same week as they point (Harris, Barlow-Brown, & Chasin, 1995). Carpenter et al.'s (1998) study showed that maternal language following into the infant's focus of attention is the most important predictor of the infant's subsequent speech comprehension and production. For maternal following in to be effective, the JVA system must already be operating reciprocally between mother and baby. The duration of joint engagement around 14 months was particularly important for predicting subsequent speech production, which may link up with research by Butterworth and Morissette (1996), who found that changes in lateralization at this age, favoring right-handedness particularly among females, may contribute to rapid acquisition of speech.

Butterworth and Morissette (1996) studied the relation between age of pointing onset and the subsequent comprehension and production of speech and gestures. A longitudinal study was carried out linking pointing, handedness, and onset of the pincer grip to early verbal and gestural communication as measured by the MacArthur infant language inventory (Fenson et al., 1994). The earlier the onset of pointing, the greater was the number of different gestures produced and the greater the number of animal sounds comprehended at 14.4 months. That is, age of pointing onset appears to be related both to a gesture and an auditory-vocal developmental pathway. The relative balance of use between left and right hands in unimanual tasks predicted MacArthur speech production and comprehension scores at 14.4 months. Girls showed more right-handed pointing than boys. The amount of right-handed pointing, and the relative balance of pincer grips between the left and right hands (a measure of lateralized fine motor control), predicted speech comprehension and production at 14.4 months. Bimanual use of the hands, terminating in right-handed object retrieval, was significantly correlated with MacArthur speech production at 14.4 months. At this age boys had relatively few words in production (about three), whereas girls had on average 12 words. There is evidence from the MacArthur norms that by 16 months the sex difference in rate of speech production is marked. At that age females have 95 words in production, males 25 words, a difference which begins to even out by 20 months (Fenson et al., 1994).

Thus, earlier onset of pointing, earlier and more frequent right-handed pointing, and more rapid development of speech in girls may suggest that there is a link between pointing, cerebral lateralization, gender, and the development of language.

## Pointing, Theory of Mind, and Childhood Autism

In recent years the capacity for JVA has been linked to the acquisition of a theory of mind and to developmental psychopathology, particularly in the case of childhood autism. JVA has been proposed as a precursor for the later-developing ability to attribute to others mentalistic concepts, such as desires and beliefs. Baron-Cohen and Swettenham (1996), following a modular theory of brain organization, have suggested that humans are normally born with a shared attention module (SAM). According to Baron-Cohen and Swettenham (1996), SAM could develop in either of two ways: it either metamorphoses to become a theory of mind module (TOMM) or it activates an innate TOMM, much as a key opens a lock. The special purpose of SAM is to produce triadic representations from dyadic interactions such as may be expressed as "I see Mummy sees the cup is on the table." This theory needs to be modified to take into account the recent evidence on triangular and triadic relations in early infancy. Even so, Baron-Cohen, Cox, Baird, Swettenham, Drew, & Charman (1994) found that deficits in joint attention and pointing were diagnostic of autism. They screened 16,000 children aged 18 months in the south of England with a checklist that included declarative pointing, gaze monitoring, and pretend play. Ten out of the 12 children who failed this test were subsequently diagnosed as autistic, which suggests that pointing and JVA deficits may indeed be diagnostic indicators for autism.

The question is whether failures in JVA and the development of pointing are necessary and sufficient for autism. Boucher (1996) suggests that a single critical deficit in a shared attention module may not be a sufficient explanation for autism, since the *DSM-III* criteria by which it is diagnosed include variants, such as children with Asperger's syndrome, who do not show theory of mind deficits. Hobson (1991) has also been critical of a purely attentional approach to autism, emphasizing instead the importance of emotional relatedness and the attendant social-affective deficits typical of the disorder. Taking these criticisms into account suggests that there may indeed be an attentional deficit particularly evident in failures of declarative pointing, but other factors need to be considered.

Manual pointing is not observed in the congenitally blind, yet these individuals are not normally autistic (Fraiberg, 1977; Hewes, 1981). Pointing is present in the congenitally deaf, which suggests that auditory experience is not necessary for its development. Autistic children, in contrast, have particular problems with language and symbolic processes (Feldman, Goldin-Meadow, & Gleitman, 1978). The evidence already reviewed suggests that the age of pointing in typically developing babies predicts speech onset and that pointing has precursors in systems for monitoring gaze and the orientation of body posture. This may mean that the developmental link between JVA deficits and autism might be through deficits in orienting responses. We may think of the signals provided by a change in gaze, eye movements, or in the orientation of the trunk as the external manifestation of attention processes which reposition the body for optimal perception. Deficits in production of such signals may be accompanied by parallel problems in reading the same signals in the bodily reorientation of others. That brainstem-mediated deficits in orienting may be characteristic of autism is shown by recent research implicating damage to the motor cranial nerve nuclei, occurring between days 20 and 24 of gestation, at a time when the brainstem is being formed (Rodier, Ingram, Tisdale, Nelson, & Romano, 1996; Stromland, Nordin, Miller, Akerstrom, & Gillberg, 1994). This primary deficit may have developmental consequences for the subsequent growth of the limbic system (and emotion regulation) and for the cerebellum (and postural control).

If autism is fundamentally a social-affective disorder, then links with JVA may arise through an inability to share affective experiences in triadic relations. Mundy, Kasari, and Sigman (1992) found that normal babies display significantly more positive affect when establishing joint attention through pointing, or making eye contact, than when pointing or eye contact merely served as requests for an object. Positive affect accompanied joint attention for between 56 percent and 70 percent, whereas the range for requests was from 18 percent to 36 percent. Thus, sharing experience, the hallmark of JVA, is normally accompanied by sharing positive affect and autistic children may have deficiencies in both these areas. Further research on the affective aspects of JVA may be useful in reconciling the cognitive approach to autism typified by Baron-Cohen and Swettenham's (1996) model with Hobson's (1991) socio-affective theory. In such a reconciliation joint visual attention may serve as the common denominator between cognitive and emotional approaches to the origins of language and the mind.

## Conclusion

Joint visual attention in infants has been extensively studied over the last 25 years. This chapter has shown that gaze and whole-body orientation serve widely as signals in the animal kingdom. Comparisons with primates show that species differences emerge strongly only when manual pointing is separated out from the complex of bodily orienting movements that serve as signals for JVA. Even though chimpanzees can produce gestures that are morphologically similar to those of humans, they do not appear to interpret pointing as referential and actually seem to prefer gaze and trunk cues as signals rather than the pointing hand. Pointing in humans is intimately connected with species-typical handedness, with the precision grip, and with the acquisition of language. It is one of a set of indicative gestures, some of which overlap with those of the higher primates, but on the evidence to date, only humans use the pointing gesture declaratively to share attention with conspecifics. Pointing serves to refer as precisely as possible to objects in the periphery of vision for joint attention, cases for which eye and head movements do not provide accurate information about location. The relative precision of pointing may arise because it makes use of the same anatomical adaptations and attention mechanisms that serve precise tool use. Pointing serves not only to individuate an object but also to authorize the link between the object and speech from the baby's perspective. Finally, deficits in JVA and in pointing may be diagnostic of other problems in social relatedness which are especially apparent in autism. However, mechanisms for joint visual attention need to be linked with those responsible for emotional sharing and for postural reorienting to more fully explain developmental psychopathology.

## REFERENCES

Adamson, L., & MacArthur, D. (1995). Joint attention, affect and culture. In C. Moore & P. Dunham (Eds.), *Joint attention: Its origins and role in development* (pp. 189–204). Hillsdale, NJ: Erlbaum.

Bakeman, R., & Adamson, L. (1984). Coordinating attention to people and objects in mother–infant and peer–infant interaction. *Child Development*, 55, 1278–89.

Baldwin, D. (1991). Infants' contribution to the achievement of joint reference. *Child Development*, 62, 875–90.

Baldwin, D. (1993). Early referential understanding: Infants' ability to recognise referential acts for what they are. *Developmental Psychology*, 29, 832–43.

Baldwin, D. A. (1995). Understanding the link between joint attention and language. In C. Moore & P. J. Dunham (Eds.), *Joint attention: Its origins and role in development* (pp. 131–58). Hillsdale, NJ: Erlbaum.

Baron-Cohen, S., Cox, A., Baird, G., Swettenham, J., Drew, A., & Charman, T. (1994). Psychological markers in the detection of autism in infancy, in a large population. Unpublished manuscript, cited in Baron-Cohen & Swettenham (1996).

Baron-Cohen, S., Leslie, A., & Frith, U. (1985). Does the autistic child have a theory of mind? *Cognition*, 21, 37–46.

Baron-Cohen, S., & Swettenham, J. (1996). The relationship between SAMM and TOMM: Two hypotheses. In P. Carruthers & P. K. Smith (Eds.), *Theories of theories of mind* (pp. 158–68). Cambridge: Cambridge University Press.

Blaschke, M., & Ettlinger, G. (1987). Pointing as an act of social communication by monkeys. *Animal Behaviour*, 35, 1520–5.

Bloom, P. (2000). *How children learn the meanings of words*. Cambridge, MA: MIT Press.

Boucher, J. (1996). What could possibly explain autism? In P. Carruthers & P. K. Smith (Eds.), *Theories of theories of mind* (pp. 223–41). Cambridge: Cambridge University Press.

Bruner, J. S. (1995). From joint attention to the meeting of minds. In C. Moore & P. Dunham (Eds.), *Joint attention: Its origins and role in development* (pp. 1–14). Hillsdale, NJ: Erlbaum.

Butterworth, G. E. (1987). Some benefits of egocentrism. In J. S. Bruner & H. Weinreich-Haste (Eds.), *Making sense of the world: The child's construction of reality* (pp. 62–80). London: Methuen.

Butterworth, G. E. (1991). The ontogeny and phylogeny of joint visual attention. In A. Whiten (Ed.), *Natural theories of mind* (pp. 223–32). Oxford: Blackwell.

Butterworth, G. E. (1997). Starting point. *Natural History*, 106 (4), 14–16.

Butterworth, G. E. (1998). What is special about pointing? In F. Simion & G. E. Butterworth (Eds.), *The development of sensory motor and cognitive capacities in early infancy: From perception to cognition* (pp. 171–87). Hove: Psychology Press.

Butterworth, G. E., & Cochran, E. (1980). Towards a mechanism of joint visual attention in human infancy. *International Journal of Behavioural Development*, 3, 253–72.

Butterworth, G. E., Franco, F., McKenzie, B., Graupner, L., & Todd, B. (1998). Dynamic aspects of event perception and the production of pointing by human infants. Unpublished manuscript, University of Sussex.

Butterworth, G. E., & Grover, L. (1988). The origins of referential communication in human infancy. In L. Weiskrantz (Ed.), *Thought without language* (pp. 5–25). Oxford: Oxford University Press.

Butterworth, G. E., & Grover, L. (1989). Joint visual attention, manual pointing and preverbal communication in human infancy. In M. Jeannerod (Ed.), *Attention and performance XII* (pp. 605–24). Hillsdale, NJ: Erlbaum.

Butterworth, G. E., & Itakura, S. (1998). Development of precision grips in chimpanzees. *Developmental Science*, 1, 39–43.

Butterworth, G. E., & Itakura, S. (2000). How the head, eyes and hands serve definite reference. *British Journal of Developmental Psychology*, 18, 25–50.

Butterworth, G. E., & Jarrett, N. L. M. (1991). What minds have in common is space: Spatial mechanisms for perspective taking in infancy. *British Journal of Developmental Psychology*, 9, 55–72.

Butterworth, G. E., & Morissette, P. (1996). Onset of pointing and the acquisition of language in infancy. *Journal of Reproductive and Infant Psychology*, 14, 219–31.

Butterworth, G. E., Verweij, E., & Hopkins, B. (1997). The development of prehension in infants. Halverson revisited. *British Journal of Developmental Psychology*, 15, 223–36.

Call, J., & Tomasello, M. (1994). The production and comprehension of referential pointing by orangutans (*Pongo pygmeaus*). *Journal of Comparative Psychology*, 108, 307–17.

Camaioni, L. (1993). The development of intentional communication: A re-analysis. In J. Nadel & L. Camaioni (Eds.), *New perspectives in early communicative development* (pp. 82–96). London: Routledge.

Camaioni, L., Castelli, M. C., Longobardi, E., & Volterra, V. (1991). A parent report instrument for early language assessment. *First Language*, 11, 345–60.

Campbell, J. (2000). Two conceptions of joint attention. In N. Eilan, C. Hoerl, T. McCormack, & J. Roessler (Eds.), *Joint attention: Communication and other minds*. Oxford: Oxford University Press.

Campos, J. J., Barrett, K. C., Lamb, M. E., Hill, H., Goldsmith, H., & Stenberg, C. (1983). Socioemotional development. In P. Mussen (Ed.), *Handbook of child psychology* (Vol. 2, pp. 783–917). New York: Wiley.

Caron, A., Krakowski, O., Liu, A., & Brooks, R. (1996, April). Infant joint attention: Cued orienting or implicit theory of mind? Paper presented at the International Conference on Infant Studies, Providence, RI.

Carpenter, M., Nagell, K., & Tomasello, M. (1998). Social cognition, joint attention and communicative competence from 9 to 15 months of age. *Monographs of the Society for Research in Child Development*.

Collis, G. (1977). Visual co-orientation and maternal speech. In H. R. Schaffer (Ed.), *Studies in mother–infant interaction* (pp. 325–54). New York: Academic Press.

Corkum, V., & Moore, C. (1995). The origins of joint visual attention. In C. Moore & P. Dunham (Eds.), *Joint attention: Its origins and role in development* (pp. 61–83). Hillsdale, NJ: Erlbaum.

Couillard, N. L., & Woodward, A. L. (1999). Children's comprehension of deceptive points. *British Journal of Developmental Psychology*, 17, 515–22.

Darwin, C. (1904). *The expression of the emotions in men and animals*. London: John Murray.

D'Entremont, B., Hains, S. M. J., & Muir, D. W. (1998). A demonstration of gaze following in 3 to 6 month olds. *Infant Behavior and Development*, 20, 569–72.

Diamond, A. (1991). Frontal lobe involvement in cognitive changes during the first year of life. In K. R. Gibson & A. C. Petersen (Eds.), *Brain maturation and cognitive development: Comparative and cross-cultural perspectives* (pp. 127–80). New York: Aldine de Gruyter.

Emery, N. J., Lorincz, E. N., Perret, D. I., Oram, M. W., & Baker, C. I. (1997). Gaze following and joint attention in rhesus monkeys (*Macaca mulatta*). *Journal of Comparative Psychology*, 111, 1–8.

Feldman, M., Goldin-Meadow, S., & Gleitman, L. (1978). Beyond Herodotus: The creation of language by linguistically deprived deaf children. In A. Lock (Ed.), *Action, gesture and symbol: The emergence of language* (pp. 351–414). London: Academic Press.

Fenson, L., Dale, P. S., Resnick, J. S., Bates, E., Thal, D., & Pethick, S. J. (1994). Variability in early communicative development. *Monographs of the Society for Research in Child Development*, 59 (5).

Fivaz-Depeursinge, E., & Corboz-Warnery, A. (1999). *The primary triangle*. New York: Basic Books.

Fogel, A. (1981). The ontogeny of gestural communication: The first six months. In R. E. Stark (Ed.), *Language behaviour in infancy and early childhood* (pp. 17–44). Amsterdam: Elsevier.

Fogel, A., & Hannan, T. E. (1985). Manual actions of nine- to fifteen-week-old human infants during face to face interaction with their mothers. *Child Development*, 56, 1271–9.

Fraiberg, S. (1977). *Insights from the blind*. New York: Basic Books.

Franco, F., & Butterworth, G. E. (1990, August). Effects of social variables on the production of infant pointing. Poster presented at the 4th European Conference on Developmental Psychology, University of Stirling, Scotland.

Franco, F., & Butterworth, G. E. (1996). Pointing and social awareness: Declaring and requesting in the second year of life. *Journal of Child Language*, 307–36.

Franco, F., Perruchino, P., & Butterworth, G. (1992, September). Pointing for an age mate in 1 to 2 year olds. Paper presented at the 6th European Conference on Developmental Psychology, Seville, Spain.

Friesen, C. K., & Kingstone, A. (1998). The eyes have it: Reflexive orienting is triggered by non-predictive gaze. *Psychonomic Bulletin and Review*, 53, 490–5.

Goldin-Meadow, S., & Feldman, H. (1977). The development of language-like communication without a language model. *Science*, 197, 401–3.

Grover, L. (1988). Comprehension of the pointing gesture in human infants. Unpublished PhD thesis, University of Southampton, England.

Hannan, T. E. (1987). A cross-sequential assessment of the occurrence of pointing in 3 to 12 month old human infants. *Infant Behavior and Development*, 10, 11–22.

Hannan, T. E., & Fogel, A. (1987). A case study assessment of pointing during the first three months of life. *Perceptual and Motor Skills*, 65, 187–94.

Harris, M., Barlow-Brown, F., & Chasin, J. (1995). Early referential understanding: Pointing and the comprehension of object names. *First Language*, 15, 19–34.

Hewes, G. W. (1981). Pointing and language. In T. Myers, J. Laver, & J. Anderson (Eds.), *The cognitive representation of speech* (pp. 263–9). Amsterdam: North-Holland.

Hobson, P. (1991). Against the theory of theory of mind. *British Journal of Developmental Psychology*, 9, 33–51.

Hood, B., Willen, J. D., & Driver, J. (1998). Adult's eyes trigger shifts of visual attention in human infants. *Psychological Science*, 9, 131–4.

Itakura, S. (1996). An exploratory study of gaze-monitoring in nonhuman primates. *Japanese Psychological Research*, 38, 174–80.

Itakura, S., & Anderson, J. R. (1996). Learning to use experimenter-given cues during an object choice task by a capuchin monkey. *Current Psychology of Cognition*, 15, 103–12.

Itakura, S., & Tanaka, M. (1998). Use of experimenter-given cues during object-choice tasks by chimpanzees (*Pan troglodytes*), an orangutan (*Pongo pygmaeus*) and human infants (*Homo sapiens*). *Journal of Comparative Psychology*, 112, 119–26.

Jones-Engel, L. E., & Bard, K. A. (1996). Precision grips in young chimpanzees. *American Journal of Primatology*, 39, 1–15.

Krause, M. A. (1998, April). Comparative perspectives on joint attention in children and apes: Development, functions and the effects of rearing history. Paper presented at the 11th Biennial Conference on Infant Studies, Atlanta, GA.

Krause, M. A., & Fouts, R. S. (1997). Chimpanzee (*Pan troglodytes*) pointing: Hand shapes, accuracy and the role of eye gaze. *Journal of Comparative Psychology*, 111, 330–6.

Langton, S. R. H. (2000). The mutual influence of gaze and head orientation in the analysis of social attention direction. *Quarterly Journal of Experimental Psychology*, 53A, 825–45.

Leavens, D. A., & Hopkins, W. D. (1998). Intentional communication by chimpanzees: A cross-sectional study of the use of referential gestures. *Developmental Psychology*, 34, 813–22.

Leavens, D. A., Hopkins, W. D., & Bard, K. A. (1996). Indexical and referential pointing in chimpanzees (*Pan troglodytes*). *Journal of Comparative Psychology*, 110, 346–53.

Lee, K., Eskritt, M., Symons, L. A., & Muir, D. (1998). Children's use of triadic eye gaze information for "mind reading." *Developmental Psychology*, 34, 525–39.

Lempers, J. D. (1976). Production of pointing, comprehension of pointing and understanding of looking behavior in young children. Unpublished doctoral dissertation, University of Minnesota.

Lempert, H., & Kinsbourne, M. (1985). Possible origin of speech in selective orienting. *Psychological Bulletin*, 97, 62–73.

Leung, E. H. L., & Rheingold, H. L. (1981). Development of pointing as a social gesture. *Developmental Psychology*, 17, 215–20.

Lock, A., Young, A., Service, V., & Chandler, P. (1990). Some observations on the origins of the pointing gesture. In V. Volterra & C. J. Erting (Eds.), *From gesture to language in hearing and deaf children* (pp. 42–55). Berlin: Springer.

Lorincz, E. N., Baker, C. I., & Perret, D. I. (1999). Visual cues for attention following in rhesus monkeys. *Cahiers de Psychologie Cognitive.*

Marler, P. (1959). Developments in the study of animal communication. In P. R. Bell (Ed.), *Darwin's biological work.* Cambridge: Cambridge University Press.

Masataka, N. (1995). The relation between index-finger extension and the acoustic quality of cooing in three-month-old infants. *Journal of Child Language*, 22, 247–57.

Masur, E. F. (1983). Gestural development, dual directional signalling, and the transition to words. *Journal of Psycholinguistic Research*, 12, 93–109.

Menzel, E. W., Jr. (1974). A group of young chimpanzees in a one-acre field. In A. Schrier & F. Stollnitz (Eds.), *Behaviour of non-human primates: Modern research trends*. San Diego, CA: Academic Press.

Messer, D. J. (1994). *The development of communication: From social interaction to language.* Chichester: Wiley.

Millar, W. S., & Schaffer, H. R. (1972). The influence of spatially displaced visual feedback on infant operant conditioning. *Journal of Experimental Child Psychology*, 14, 442–52.

Millar, W. S., & Schaffer, H. R. (1973). Visual manipulative response strategies in infant operant conditioning with spatially displaced feedback. *British Journal of Psychology*, 64, 545–52.

Moore, C., & Corkum, V. (1994). Social understanding at the end of the first year of life. *Developmental Review*, 14, 349–72.

Morissette, P., Ricard, M., & Gouin-Decarie, T. (1995). Joint visual attention and pointing in infancy: A longitudinal study of comprehension. *British Journal of Developmental Psychology*, 13, 163–77.

Mundy, P., Kasari, C., & Sigman, M. (1992). Non-verbal communication, affective sharing and intersubjectivity. *Infant Behavior and Development*, 15, 377–81.

Murphy, C. M. (1978). Pointing in the context of shared activity. *Child Development*, 49, 371–80.

Murphy, C. M., & Messer, D. J. (1977). Mothers, infants and pointing: A study of gesture. In H. R. Schaffer (Ed.), *Studies of mother–infant interaction* (pp. 325–54). London: Academic Press.

Napier, J. (1960). Studies of the hands of living primates. *Proceedings of the Zoological Society of London*, 134, 647–57.

Ohama, K. (1984). Development of pointing behavior in infants and mother's responsive behavior: Longitudinal study of infants from 9 to 30 months. In M. Ogino, K. Ohama, K. Saito, S. Takei, & T. Tatsuno (Eds.), *The development of verbal behavior VI.* Bulletin of the Faculty of Education, University of Tokyo.

Piaget, J. (1952). *The origins of intelligence in children*. New York: W. W. Norton.

Piaget, J. (1954). *The construction of reality in the child*. New York: Basic Books.

Povinelli, D., Bering, J. M., & Giambrone, S. (2000). Chimpanzee pointing: Another error of the argument by analogy. In S. Kita (Ed.), *Pointing: Where language, culture and cognition meet*. Cambridge: Cambridge University Press.

Povinelli, D. J., & Davis, D. R. (1994). Differences between chimpanzees (*Pan troglodytes*) and humans (*Homo sapiens*) in the resting state of the index finger. *Journal of Comparative Psychology*, 108, 134–9.

Povinelli, D. J., & Eddy, T. J. (1996a). Factors influencing young chimpanzees' (*Pan troglodytes'*) recognition of attention. *Journal of Comparative Psychology*, 110, 336–45.

Povinelli, D. J., & Eddy, T. J. (1996b). What young chimpanzees know about seeing. *Monographs of the Society for Research in Child Development*, 61, 247.

Povinelli, D. J., & Eddy, T. J. (1996c). Chimpanzees: Joint visual attention. *Psychological Science*, 7, 129–35.

Povinelli, D. J., Reaux, J. E., Bierschwale, D. T., Allain, A. D., & Simon, B. B. (1997). Exploitation of pointing as a visual gesture in young children but not adolescent chimpanzees. *Cognitive Development*, 12, 423–61.

Ristau, C. (1991). Attention, purposes and deception in birds. In A. Whiten (Ed.), *Natural theories of mind* (pp. 209–33). Oxford: Blackwell.

Rodier, P. M., Ingram, J. L., Tisdale, B., Nelson, S., & Romano, J. (1996). Embryological origin for autism: Developmental anomalies of the cranial nerve motor nuclei. *Journal of Comparative Neurology*, 370, 247–61.

Rolfe, L. (1996). Theoretical stages in the prehistory of grammar. In A. Lock & C. R. Peters (Eds.), *Handbook of human symbolic evolution* (pp. 776–92). Oxford: Oxford University Press.

Scaife, M., & Bruner, J. S. (1975). The capacity for joint attention in the infant. *Nature*, 253, 265–6.

Schaffer, H. R. (1984). *The child's entry into a social world*. New York: Academic Press.

Shinn, M. (1900). *The biography of a baby*. Boston: Houghton-Mifflin.

Stern, D. (1999). Vitality contours: The temporal contour of feelings as a basic unit for constructing the infant's social experience. In P. Rochat (Ed.), *Early social cognition: Understanding others in the first months of life* (pp. 67–80). Hillsdale, NJ: Erlbaum.

Stromland, K., Nordin, V., Miller, M., Akerstrom, B., & Gillberg, C. (1994). Autism in thalidomide embryopathy: A population study. *Developmental Medicine and Child Neurology*, 36, 351–6.

Tomasello, M., & Call, J. (1997). *Primate cognition*. Oxford: Oxford University Press.

Tomasello, M., Call, J., & Hare, B. (1998). Five primate species follow the visual gaze of conspecifics. *Animal Behaviour*, 55, 1063–69.

Tonooka, R., & Matsuzawa, T. (1995). Hand preferences of captive chimpanzees (*Pan troglodytes*) in simple reaching for food. *International Journal of Primatology*, 16, 17–23.

Tran-Duc Thao (1984). *Investigations into the origins of language and consciousness* (Trans. D. J. Herman & R. L. Armstrong). Dordrecht: Reidel.

Trevarthen, C. (1979). Communication and cooperation in early infancy: A description of primary intersubjectivity. In M. Bullowa (Ed.), *Before speech: The beginning of human communication* (pp. 321–47). Cambridge: Cambridge University Press.

Trevarthen, C. (1993). The functions of emotions in early infant communication and development. In J. Nadel & L. Camioni (Eds.), *New perspectives in early communicative development* (pp. 48–81). London: Routledge.

Vygotsky, L. S. (1962). *Thought and language*. New York: Wiley.

Vygotsky, L. S. (1988). Development of the higher mental functions. In K. Richardson & S. Sheldon (Eds.), *Cognitive development to adolescence* (pp. 61–80). Hove: Erlbaum.

Werner, H., & Kaplan, B. (1963). *Symbol formation: An organismic-developmental approach to language and the expression of thought*. New York: Wiley.

# Afterword: Tribute to George Butterworth

*Peter E. Bryant*

In 1971 George Butterworth came to Oxford as a doctoral student and began the work on infant development that was to form the center of his research from then on. I was his supervisor while he was at Oxford, and I soon realized that I had taken on a quite remarkable person. It seemed to me then, and it still seems to me, that the most striking feature of his approach to research, and the secret of his resounding success, was his enthusiasm for theoretical ideas. He had a passionate interest in other people's theories and ideas, particularly in Darwin's, Gibson's, and Piaget's, and his aim was always to produce a workable theory of his own about the social and intellectual world of very young children.

This excitement in theory drove his empirical research throughout his working life and it gave his many and varied experiments their impressive coherence. It also made him a most unusual graduate student. During his time at Oxford, I became familiar with his greeting: "I've really got it now." "It" in this context was always the right grand hypothesis about infant's spatial and social understanding, and "it" changed from week to week, for George was not one to get stuck in a theoretical groove and was always searching for another way, a new way, of solving the problems that excited him so much.

His starting point was a very powerful idea indeed: it was Piaget's theory about infants' egocentrism. From what George told me then, I know that the notion interested him mostly because of its wide implications. It was, he recognized, a statement about perceptual, cognitive, and social development, about the understanding of space and about the child's ability to communicate, about having a point of view and distinguishing that from other people's points of view. It was also the springboard for George's research on all these diverse matters.

In his own research on egocentrism, he began with the cognitive end of things, and his first discovery was sensational. He started with a tidying-up operation. One of Piaget's main pieces of evidence for his theory of egocentrism is the stage 4 error: Piaget found that infants of less than roughly a year in age persistently search at place A for a toy that they have just seen hidden at place B. This mistake had always been catalogued as something to do with infants' understanding of object permanence and therefore with their knowledge about hidden objects. George was concerned about this link with hiding and disappearance, because, as he rightly pointed out at the time, no one had ever checked that the error only happened with hidden objects. So he set up an experiment (Butterworth, 1977) in which he repeated the classic AB experiment in the usual way, first hiding an object in one container and then hiding it in another, but also added conditions in which he went through the same sequence except that he kept the object visible throughout. In these new conditions, the object was still quite visible when he put it in the first container, and it remained just as visible when he put it in the second one.

This visibility had no effect. The babies persisted in reaching into container A after seeing the object placed in container B as much when the object was visibly present in A and visibly absent in B as when it was hidden in both places. This surprising result, he immediately saw, led to a major reconceptualization of the AB effect. It certainly cast doubts on Piaget's suggestion that babies keep on reaching to A because they think that it stopped existing when it disappeared and that their responding to A somehow reconstitutes the object and makes it appear again. This is a plausible story about babies and hidden objects, but not about babies and objects that stay constantly in view.

So what is left? The result shifted his attention to space (Butterworth, 1976). Whatever else the error is, it is definitely and primarily a spatial one. George's demonstration that babies make the mistake even in the face of blatant spatial evidence that the object is not where they are searching for it makes it clear that there is something very unusual about their use of spatial information. I don't know whether it was at that point or earlier that George's obsession with space began, but from then on space was at the center of all the research that he did.

This was a brilliant start and George followed it quite soon by turning his attention to space and communication. In Oxford at the time, Mike Scaife and Jerry Bruner (1975) did a small but highly influential study of infants' and mothers' looking patterns which made it clear that these are often well coordinated. George, of course, knew about the Scaife/Bruner study as it was being done and was excited by its results. He recognized the importance of the study and wanted to push it further. In particular, he wanted to work out its implications for the idea of egocentrism.

Together with some excellent colleagues and over a long period of time, he set up a series of simple, elegant, and remarkably successful studies (Butterworth, 1998a,b, 2001; Butterworth & Cochran, 1980; Butterworth, Franco, McKenzie, Graupner, & Todd, 2002; Butterworth & Jarrett, 1991; Butterworth & Morissette, 1996), all of them designed to answer the question whether young babies can follow the line of their mother's gaze, and whether they can work out what their mother is pointing at when she does so. I will not describe any of these studies in detail here, because they are justly famous already and have been described very clearly in various chapters in this book, but I do have two points to make about this work.

The first is that it will in future years serve as a lesson in how to pursue a topic both systematically and imaginatively. Starting with his demonstration that younger infants can work out some, but not all, of the locations that their mother is looking at, he then went on to investigate their ability to follow their mother's pointing, and the effect of different kinds of perceptual set-up, and the performance of special groups of children, such as those with Williams syndrome, in his ingenious tasks (Laing, Butterworth, Ansari, Gsödl, & Longhi, 2002). He applied this growing body of work not just to theories about how children's ability to extrapolate lines in space develops, but also to their understanding of communication, the beginnings of language acquisition, and to children's ideas about other people's knowledge and intentions (Butterworth & Grover, 1988; Butterworth & Morissette, 1996). Given the importance and the great success of this work, his publications on it were not all that numerous, but they set a wonderful example for people just beginning on research of how to do a consecutive series of powerful and valuable experiments.

My second point is that, at the time that we learned of the Scaife/Bruner results, I myself suggested another line of research to George. It seemed to me that we needed to know not just whether children can extrapolate single lines in space, but also whether they can work out the intersection of two extrapolated lines. This seemed to me the acid test for the understanding of Euclidean space and one that had considerable implications for children's ability to do geometry. George's response to this suggestion was sympathetic, but not positive. He could see the value of this line of research (which did eventually come to something; Somerville & Bryant, 1985), but he did not want to do it himself. All these years later, I can see that this was because the question that I raised had few ramifications beyond space itself and geometry. He wanted a theoretically richer line of research than that, one that led to theories about social development and about language and communication, and of course he found it.

George worked on many other topics, but all were theoretically related to the ones that I have already mentioned. These were the development of sensorimotor coordination (Butterworth & Hicks, 1977, Butterworth & Hopkins, 1988; Butterworth, Verweij & Hopkins, 1997; Lew & Butterworth, 1995, 1997) and cross-modal (visual-auditory) perception (Butterworth & Castillo, 1976), infants' categories (Rakison & Butterworth, 1998), children's representation of depth in drawings (Ingram & Butterworth, 1989), and, still unpublished, the conception held by young schoolchildren of the world. The nature of his experimental work varied enormously across these different lines of research, from playing sounds to neonates to asking 7-year-olds to draw pictures of the earth, but the theoretical links between all the different parts of his work remained strong. The only other example that occurs to me of a psychologist whose empirical work varied a great deal, but whose theories brought all the strands together, is Piaget. I suspect that George learned the lesson from his detailed study of the great man's work.

It is not surprising that someone as energetic and well organized, and as enthusiastic about developmental psychology, as George was, should become heavily involved in organizations and conferences. George's efforts in helping to set up and to run organizations like the International Society for the Study of Behavioral Development (ISSBD) and later the European Society were stupendous. One of his last main appearances was as the cheerful and omnipresent President of the European Society for Developmental Psychology at its large and highly successful conference in Spetses in Greece. In retrospect, it is easy to think of that meeting as setting a seal on his extraordinary career. He was rightly, and optimistically, in charge.

What about the prospect for his work and his ideas, now that George has gone? We are fortunate that he worked with excellent, and still very active, people. I am sure that Margaret Harris,

Brian Hopkins, and Fabia Franco, for example, will successfully develop the ideas and the techniques that they worked on with him in the past. If George had lived longer, it seems likely to me that he would have spent a great deal of time on linking his work to the growing body of research on neurocognitive development. Again, other people will probably make the connection with the developing brain that George almost certainly aimed to make himself.

Another useful way to push George's work forward, in my opinion, would be to turn to longitudinal research. For reasons which I don't remember ever having discussed with him, he appears to have preferred the cross-sectional method, and yet many of his ideas, I believe, do need longitudinal research as well. The rather intricate differences between age groups that he and his colleagues found in their joint attention tasks certainly need charting longitudinally. Longitudinal studies could tell us how suddenly these developmental changes happen in individual children, whether the changes are ever reversed, and even whether the course and speed of the developmental changes can be influenced by the child's circumstances and experiences.

Longitudinal work is also a valuable – some would say essential – tool in pursuing causal hypotheses of the sort that George produced in abundance (Hopkins & Butterworth, 1990). In general, predictive studies, in which the predictors are measures of infant behavior and the outcome measures are the same children's behavior several years down the line, have had some spectacular successes. The method could work with George's theory too. If you think, as he thought, that children's experiences in communicating about space play a crucial, causal role in their learning about communication in general, it would certainly help if you could support your hypothesis with longitudinal, predictive data. The extent of the individual children's success in the joint attention tasks should be a good predictor of their ability to communicate and to understand the nature of communication at a later age. Surely we, George Butterworth's successors, should work out how to use this method to pursue his superb ideas.

It is actually a tribute to his work that it is so easy and also so necessary for us to pursue his ideas ourselves. We shall miss this friend of ours who had such a lively mind and such an engaging disposition, but we will be grateful for having known him and his beautiful ideas.

## REFERENCES

Butterworth, G. E. (1976). Object identity in infancy: The interaction of spatial location codes in determining search errors. *Child Development*, 46, 866–70.

Butterworth, G. E. (1977). Object disappearance and error in Piaget's stage IV task. *Journal of Experimental Child Psychology*, 23, 391–501.

Butterworth, G. E. (1998a). What is special about pointing? In F. Simion & G. Butterworth (Eds.), *The development of sensory, motor and cognitive capacities in early infancy: From perception to cognition* (pp. 171–90). Hove: Psychology Press.

Butterworth, G. E. (1998b). A developmental-ecological perspective on Strawson's "the self." *Journal of Consciousness Studies*, 5, 132–40.

Butterworth, G. E. (2001). Joint visual attention in infancy. In G. Bremner & A. Fogel (Eds.), *Blackwell handbook of infant development* (pp. 213–40). Oxford: Blackwell. Reprinted as chapter 12 in this volume.

Butterworth, G. E., & Castillo, M. (1976). Coordination of auditory and visual space in newborn human infants. *Perception*, 5, 155–60.

Butterworth, G. E., & Cochran, E. (1980). Towards a mechanism of joint visual attention in human infancy. *International Journal of Behavioural Development*, 3, 253–72.

Butterworth, G. E., Franco, F., McKenzie, B., Graupner, L., & Todd, B. (2002). Dynamic aspects of visual event perception and the production of pointing by human infants. *British Journal of Developmental Psychology*, 20, 1–24.

Butterworth, G. E., & Grover, L. (1988). The origins of referential communication in human infancy. In L. Weiskrantz (Ed.), *Thought without language* (pp. 5–24). Oxford: Oxford University Press.

Butterworth, G. E., & Hicks, L. (1977). Visual proprioception and postural stability in infancy: A developmental study. *Perception*, 6, 255–62.

Butterworth, G. E., & Hopkins, B. (1988). Hand–mouth coordination in the newborn baby. *British Journal of Developmental Psychology*, 6, 303–14.

Butterworth, G. E., & Jarrett, N. (1991). What minds have in common is space: Spatial mechanisms serving joint visual attention in infancy. *British Journal of Developmental Psychology*, 9, 55–72.

Butterworth, G. E., & Morissette, P. (1996). Onset of pointing and the acquisition of language in infancy. *British Journal of Developmental Psychology*, 14, 219–31.

Butterworth, G. E., Verweij, V., & Hopkins, B. (1997). The development of prehension in infants: Halverson revisited. *British Journal of Developmental Psychology*, 15, 223–6.

Hopkins, B., & Butterworth, G. E. (1990). Concepts of causality in explanations of development. In G. Butterworth & P. Bryant (Eds.), *Causes of development: Interdisciplinary perspectives* (pp. 3–32). Hove: Erlbaum.

Ingram, N., & Butterworth, G. E. (1989). The young child's representation of depth in drawing. *Journal of Experimental Child Psychology*, 47, 356–69.

Laing, E., Butterworth, G. E., Ansari, D., Gsödl, M., & Longhi, E. (2002). Atypical development of language and social communication in toddlers with Williams syndrome. *Developmental Science*, 5, 233–46.

Lew, A. R., & Butterworth, G. E. (1995). The effects of hunger on hand–mouth coordination in newborn infants. *Developmental Psychology*, 31, 456–63.

Lew, A. R., & Butterworth, G. E. (1997). The development of hand–mouth co-ordination in 2- to 5-month-old infants. *Infant Behavior and Development*, 20, 56–69.

Rakison, D. H., & Butterworth, G. E. (1998). Infants' attention to object structure and its early categorisation. *Developmental Psychology*, 34, 1310–25.

Scaife, M., & Bruner, J. S. (1975). The capacity for joint visual attention in the infant. *Nature*, 253, 265.

Somerville, S., & Bryant, P. E. (1985). Young children's use of spatial coordinates. *Child Development*, 56, 604–13.

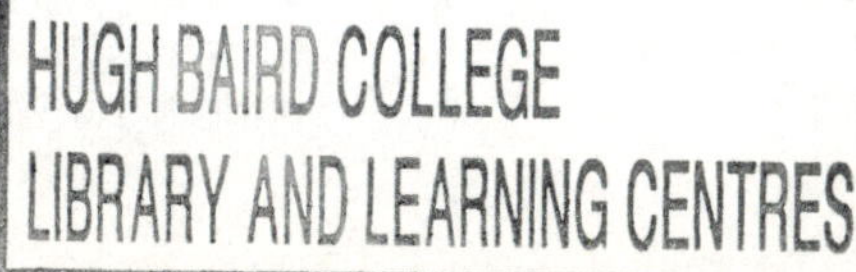

# Author Index

# Subject Index